WORLD COMMUNISM

WORLD COMMUNISM

A History of The Communist International

By F. BORKENAU

New Introduction by Raymond Aron

Ann Arbor Paperbacks
for the Study of Communism and Marxism

THE UNIVERSITY OF MICHIGAN PRESS

Fourth printing 1978
First edition as an Ann Arbor Paperback 1962
New Introduction copyright © by The University of Michigan 1962
ISBN 0-472-06067-8
Published in the United States of America by
The University of Michigan Press and simultaneously
in Rexdale, Canada, by John Wiley & Sons Canada, Limited
Manufactured in the United States of America

CONTENTS

NEW INTRODUCTION
by RAYMOND ARON

Of all history books, the most vulnerable to the test of time are those treating events whose significance is still unclear and whose consequences are not yet realized. Franz Borkenau's book was written on the eve of the war in 1939, when everyone was speculating on the possibilities of an entente between the Soviet Union and the Western democracies against Hitler and the Third Reich. It is not surprising, therefore, that its conclusions should be marked by circumstances in which the author contemplated the history of the Communist International in order to throw light on coming events. The phrase (p. 428): "It would be in the interest of Russia itself to dissolve the Comintern and to prove, by scrupulous abstention from interference abroad, that it can be treated on an equal footing with those democratic powers whose ideals it professes to share," cannot be understood outside the context of 1939. Borkenau—as we know from his later writings—never had any illusions concerning the ambitions of Stalin. The dissolution of the Comintern, which came about—on paper—in 1943, did not mislead him concerning the objectives of Soviet strategy.

What is striking, on the contrary, when we reread this work today, is not so much the difference between the historical perspective of 1939 and that of the present time, but rather the soundness of the book's content and the relevance of its analyses. The account that the book gives us of the defeats of the Comintern is all the more interesting to reread since we risk forgetting what happened between

3

1917 and 1939, obsessed as we are by its latter phase, the phase of its victories between 1945 and 1949, and by the present events of the cold war.

Borkenau's account has lost nothing of its timeliness because it is based upon a precise understanding of the nature of the Bolshevik party, of the 1917 revolution, of the proletarian movement in Western Europe, and of the psychology of the Bolshevik leaders. Notice this statement at the conclusion of chapter III, on the nature of the Soviet state: "The state he created was neither democratic nor Soviet, but simply a state of a totalitarian bureaucracy . . . Why, after all, should a totalitarian bureaucracy link its fate finally and definitely to any one single class" (p. 56). There is nothing to add to or take away from these propositions, which were by no means commonly accepted twenty years ago—are not accepted even today, but should be.

Likewise, the elucidation of the fundamental incompatibility between Bolshevik organization, techniques, and tactics and the tradition and realities of the proletarian movement in the West is no less valid, no less instructive, in 1961 than in 1939. Because they wished to impose their pattern on the workers' parties of Europe, the Bolsheviks in power brought about the schism between socialists and communists, weakened the proletariat and the leftist parties, and rendered inevitable their successive defeats in Hungary, Germany, and elsewhere.

Franz Borkenau's interpretation is that of neither the Stalinists nor the Trotskyites. Although he, too, had in his youth passed through communism, he readily understood the absurdity of turning to the concept of "treason" to explain the conduct of socialists in 1914 or of Stalin in the thirties. The socialists of France and Germany, despite Lenin's imprecations, were not being "traitors" in 1914, they were expressing the feelings of their forces in serving their native land rather than in obeying revolutionary marching orders. Stalin in power was not a traitor to Leninism or Bolshevism, as Trotsky tirelessly repeated in exile. The dictatorship of the party and not of the proletariat dates from 1917 and "the armed prophet" was never willing to recognize that the totalitarian and bureaucratic state grew directly out of the logic of power itself and not out of one man's perversion.

In this sense the history that Franz Borkenau recounts for us is, in large measure, that of a permanent cleavage between the actors' intentions and reality, between what men wished to do and what they accomplished in fact. In Western Europe the situation was never revolutionary, even while, in apparent conformity with Marxist premises, the capitalist productive machine was paralyzed and workers by the million were unemployed. The communist parties consequently tried vainly to exploit opportunities that did not exist.

The situation was not the same in Asia, and Borkenau, like many other observers (Lenin being one of the first and the most illustrious among them), was not unaware of the revolutionary potential of the peasantry in underdeveloped countries, colonized or semicolonized by the West: "In the West the Comintern had invented revolutionary situations where there were none. In China the Russian bureaucracy, the legitimate child of the Russian revolution, had wasted the one big revolutionary chance it had ever had" (p. 318).

We know today—twenty years later—that the opportunity was not lost, that the Chinese Communist party, crushed in the cities, found again, in Kiangsi first, and then, after the great march to the northeast, on the Mongolian frontier, a popular base among the peasants. Mao Tse-tung and Li Li-sian, who had their quarrels in 1931, are both still alive and the former is the undisputed master of Red China. What appeared in 1939 a fatal error is now, to our view, nothing but a setback—a short-term error, perhaps, but not a decisive mistake. No more than a penchant for dialectics would suffice to bring to light the rationality that events conceal more than they disclose.

The 1917 revolution, the dictatorship of the party, the founding of a totalitarian and bureaucratic State in the name of a doctrine of Western origin, carried with them, from the inception, a fundamental contradiction: the Bolsheviks claimed to bring the only historically valid answer to the crisis in capitalistic industrial society, whereas, in fact, their action and their accomplishments were at the very most adapted to the needs of a society which was industrialized slightly or not at all, in a sphere of civilization only half, or even not at all, Western. Starting from this initial contradiction, the Bolsheviks had the choice between two courses: either to avow the *particular* character of their enterprise and renounce more or less overtly their universal mission of revolution, or to compel progressively the socialist parties to recognize the exemplary value of the party and the Bolshevik revolution, and to transform the workers' movements of the entire world first into an instrument submissive to soviet-Russian politics, and then into agents of a structure modeled on the Russian-soviet one.

Writing in 1939, when he was astounded by the bloody liquidation of the Bolshevik leaders of the Left, Borkenau suggested the first position as the most consistent with Stalinist logic—socialism in a single country—as well as the one most in line with the interests of Russia and the struggle against Fascism. In 1961 the choice of the second alternative is evident, whether the choice has been dictated by men or by circumstances. The Communist party is in power in the Forbidden City of Peking. In Eastern Europe communist parties rule.

But another dialectical reversal has supervened. In China, wrote Borkenau, a revolutionary situation existed and Stalin let his opportunity escape. In Europe, on the contrary, he could not seize an opportunity that existed only in his imagination. Today, we are tempted to say that the revolution in China, although it was, in large measure, inspired by the 1917 revolution, was authentically Chinese. It was the Red Chinese army that won the civil war against the troops of Chiang Kai-shek. Mao Tse-tung affects a certain doctrinal originality in regard to Marxism-Leninism-Stalinism, and he is manifestly not under orders from Moscow. On the other hand, it was the *Russian* Red Army which put the Rumanian, Polish, Bulgarian, and Czech communist parties into power. The less these parties express the genuine will of their peoples, the more docile they are to orders from Moscow, the more they imitate Big Brother. The Comintern was condemned to failure between 1917 and 1939, as long as it counted on the worker movements to follow the example of the Russian Bolshevik party. But *any* self-styled communist party can construct a bureaucratic, totalitarian state, as long as the Russian army is present. Thus is explained the paradox that the more closely the popular democratic regimes tend to resemble the Soviet Union the more they are foreign to the aspirations of their people and to their national traditions. The Chinese regime is more Chinese than the Rumanian regime is Rumanian, because the first was inspired by Russian experience whereas the second was imposed by the Red Army.

The dialectic does not stop there. The discrepancy between the regimes of eastern Europe and the sentiments of their peoples exploded in 1956, in the Hungarian and Polish revolutions, one tragically repressed in blood, the other tolerated at first, but, little by little, snuffed out. As for the Chinese regime, it declares itself autonomous, however faithful it may be to Marxist-Leninist doctrine and to the socialist bloc. In 1939 Borkenau expected and hoped for a true dissolution of the Comintern. In 1961 it would be senseless to cultivate illusions about the imminent disintegration of the Soviet bloc, but it would be scarcely less foolish to ignore the inconsistencies—antagonistic or not, it matters little—which are created by the Bolsheviks' claim, maintained now for almost a half-century, to give *universal* significance to a *particular* revolution and doctrine.

PREFACE

A few years ago there would have been little point in writing a history of the Communist International. As recently as 1933 there was not a single country outside Russia where the communists counted as a political force. But since 1934 the Communist International has evolved a new policy, has claimed to defend democracy, has sought alliances of the closest kind with the democratic parties of various countries, and has, during this latest period, increased very considerably in strength. To-day it is again important to know the Communist International. This conclusion was forced on me with particular strength when, during my field-study of the political and social problems of the Spanish civil war, I realized how important a force the Communist International had once more become.

The one correct approach to an understanding of the Comintern seems to me to be an historical account of it. Communism is not one of those stable forces which are to-day what they were decades ago. It has repeatedly changed its whole policy, all its leading staffs, has risen high and fallen deep; and these evolutions are not yet at an end. Only a study of its history gives a chance to find the law which stands behind these apparently unconnected changes. And a history of the Communist International is the more necessary because the communists themselves, owing to the rapid and violent changes of their policies, do not like to recall, during one phase, what they have done in earlier phases. Yet only the whole of their history can give a correct idea of what they are. It is a history little known to the public at large, but least of all to the members of the communist parties themselves, who are never

9

taught much about what preceded the present version of communist politics. While much has been written about the Russian revolution, little attention has generally been paid to the details of the history of the Communist International. This history is full of interest.

The Communist International, being an important political force, arouses violent political passions, among both its adherents and its adversaries. The following study attempts an unbiased approach to its history and activity through historical and sociological analysis. The question arises immediately: Is an unbiased study of a contemporary movement such as international communism possible? The communists would not hesitate one moment to deny it. And, in the case of the author of this book, they may have a particularly strong case. I was myself a member of the German Communist Party from 1921 till 1929; during the later part of this period I worked directly, though only in a scientific capacity, for the machinery of the Comintern. I had to study the international labour movement and to report periodically about it. During the last months of my membership I was in the immediate service of the Western-European bureau of the Comintern, on whose behalf I visited various communist parties. At that moment I had already doubted for some time the correctness of communist policy. Closer contact with its machinery made me decide to break with it. This study, however, is not a book of disclosures. My own experiences, limited as they were, may have sharpened my perception of certain aspects of Comintern life and politics; but the following study is exclusively based upon printed materials. The communists, nevertheless, will certainly ask: How can a man who has worked in the Communist International, and broken with it, be unbiased and impartial?

The answer to this seems to me a relatively simple one. As every student of politics, I have my own political opinions, which naturally will have influenced my judgement. I should be deluding myself to deny it. But the fact that complete impartiality is impossible in matters which concern us all very directly and immediately does not imply that no impartiality whatsoever is possible. It is the latter which the communists would like to maintain, pretending that there is no objective science whatsoever, but only class-science. With this point of view I am inclined strongly to disagree. There is a sphere of thought where impartiality is impossible and another one where it is perfectly possible.

The history of the Comintern is not yet achieved. It exists, it acts. A final judgement on it, as on all historical phenomena, will only be possible when it belongs entirely to the past. Human history is a chain where every link influences the next. Therefore, human history continuing to proceed, there is no period which can be studied without any reference to the present and, in consequence, with complete impartiality. The further, however, history recedes into the past, the fewer are the controversies about it (except the controversies of mere fact); the nearer it comes to the present day, the more controversial it becomes. In this sense, the history of the Comintern must be one of the most controversial subjects. Some believe that the Communist International will save the world; others, that it is the shape of the devil in our present time; some, and among them the author of this book, that it is neither the one nor the other, but simply a failure. Only the future can finally decide the issue. In the meantime the three views just mentioned will inevitably colour the interpretations given by various students to the past history of the Communist International.

But this concerns *interpretations*; it does not concern *facts*. Having myself passed through the school of dialectics during my communist membership, I am well aware that sometimes the facts the historian relates cannot be completely stripped of an element of subjective interpretation. Between fact and interpretation there is no absolute dividing line. Yet facts are one thing and interpretations another. The general strike in Britain in 1926 ended with a defeat of the trade unions. Nobody will dispute this *fact*. It ended in defeat because the forces of the workers were too weak, or because the strike was badly prepared, or because it was betrayed by its leaders, or because the workers broke away. These are interpretations, and no two people of different political opinions will agree about them. To stick to the facts only, without any attempt at interpretation, is the method, not of the historian and the sociologist, but of the mere chronicler. To write a mere chronicle of international communism would be preposterous. But even within the wider scope of an historical account the elements of an honest chronicle must not be absent. They represent the element of unbiased impartiality obtainable by everybody who is sincerely willing to keep to the truth. Not to stick to the requirements of an honest chronicle is equivalent to an attempt to forge history. I cannot help feeling that the so-called Marxist attempts to explain away the duty of honesty in historical research—because everything is supposed to be determined by class interests—are an attack upon scientific research as such and a menace to the moral values upon which scientific research is based. As for my interpretations, I must wait to see how much conviction they carry with others. As for the facts, I hope to have established them with as much accuracy as is obtainable in a subject about which we are still lacking the evidence of the archives.

I have already noted that the basic interpretative assumption of this study is that the Comintern as a whole is a failure. This implies that I do not share in the views of any of the official or oppositional communist tendencies. But as the debate around Leon Trotsky rages, at present, with particular violence, it is perhaps necessary to say a word about my point of view concerning this controversy. The subject in itself is much less important than is sometimes believed, and little space will therefore be devoted to it in the following account.

The basic assumptions of Trotsky are the same as those of the communist parties. Trotsky accuses the communist parties of having departed from these assumptions in fact, while still keeping to them in words. One of the main tasks of the following study will be to prove, on the contrary, that while there is naturally evolution and transformation in international communism as in everything else, the later developments are the logical result of the basic assumptions of Lenin and of the early history of the Russian revolutionary régime and the Communist International. Leon Trotsky dislikes the present Russian régime, with its ruthless persecutions, and the policy of the Communist International; about this, there is no need to argue. But he himself has laid the foundations of what has arisen in Russia to-day, and even to-day he continues to advocate all those principles of dictatorship from which he, himself, is first to suffer. He would like to see the dictatorship in an eternal state of revolutionary purity, but this would be beyond the scope of human possibilities. In one word, to the reality of the Russian régime and of the Communist International Trotsky opposes a Utopian ideal which never existed, least of all while he was one of the rulers of Russia. Trotsky finds the present Russian régime intolerable. So will all those who believe in democracy and the values which go with it. We who believe in them have a right to complain about Russia and its methods; those who do not believe in them, who defend the principles of dictatorship, have no right to complain.

As to the facts of communist history, it is perhaps more difficult to group them than is the case with most historical accounts. There is the constant interaction of Russian affairs and affairs abroad. The scene of the history of the Comintern is the whole world. And it has been impossible to confine myself closely to the affairs of the Comintern only. The general background of the politics of many countries had to be evoked continually, and a number of introductory chapters, without which the history of the Comintern would remain unintelligible, sketch the revolutionary movements out of which the Communist International arose. As it stands, the present book is a history of the revolutionary movements of the post-war period, seen as a setting for Comintern history. But the enormous scope of such a study made a very strict selection of facts necessary, and whatever I regarded as minor events I had to suppress very rigidly, in order not to dissolve the main outline of events into a series of unrelated accounts of details. Differences of opinion may arise about what is primary and what is secondary in Comintern history. I am convinced, however, that, whatever may be the value of my general conclusions, the introduction of new facts into the debate would not alter the issue. Ampler details would only emphasize the outlines here given. I do not expect anything but complete rejection of my views from communist quarters. But should this rejection be based on a charge of inadequacy of my factual account, then I am quite willing to discuss the new facts which may be brought forward.

CHAPTER I

INTRODUCTION

The working classes have entered the scene of modern history as a revolutionary vanguard. It was during the great French Revolution that Europe, for the first time, became aware of their political existence; and already, at this first appearance, the proletariat seemed to be a force liable to overthrow the whole structure of the existing social order, all existing hierarchies, all existing values, and to set in their stead either anarchy or a civilization entirely of their own. The French Revolution, in itself, was not an affair of the proletariat. It is generally recognized to-day that it was essentially a fight between the moneyed and the landed interest, between the bourgeoisie and the feudal class, between liberalism and monarchical absolutism. But the French bourgeoisie itself was tied to the *ancien régime* by many links. When the hours of heroic decisions came, when the king conspired with Austria and Prussia against the revolution, when war from without and rebellion from within threatened the very existence of France, the bourgeoisie failed the revolutionary cause. Then a more advanced party, the 'Jacobins', backed by the destitute workers of the Paris *faubourgs*, took power into its hands, established a régime of terrorism against all enemies of the revolution, enforced a democratic equality of suffering and sacrifice, and saved the country. The proletariat, in the end, obtained nothing for itself; but it gave victory to the revolution.

The example of the French Revolution made a tremendous impression. It led to the belief that in every coming upheaval the proletariat would again be the most advanced section of the revolutionaries. Karl Marx, the founder of the theory of the revolutionary labour movement, was fed from childhood with these traditions and never rid himself of them during all his life. And this view was undoubtedly justified as far as revolutionary crises similar to that of France were concerned. Wherever a feudal class and an *ancien régime* came to grips with the rising forces of modern industry and of the industrial bourgeoisie, the working classes sided with the latter against the former; and where the bourgeoisie shrank from the cruel implications of the fight, the proletariat took the lead. This was the case in Germany in 1848, in Russia in 1917, in China in 1926, in Spain in 1936. But such is not a complete description of the role of the proletariat in a 'bourgeois' revolution. It is true that the proletariat in these revolutions was the most advanced section. But it is equally true that it moved only at the call of the bourgeoisie. The French Revolution was not started by the proletariat; it arose out of the conflict between the king and the rich tax-payers about financial matters. Once the crisis had opened, the proletariat played its role as long as the revolutionary crisis lasted. When in 1794 the French bourgeoisie, having obtained its aims, overthrew the revolutionary dictator Robespierre, the proletariat withdrew from the revolutionary scene and receded into the background almost as suddenly as it had entered the proscenium two years before. And what applies to the French Revolution can be said, *a fortiori*, of later revolutions. The German proletariat in 1848 was less active than the Paris proletariat in 1793, because revolution as a whole was weaker in Germany. The proletariat acted always as the most advanced wing of the bourgeoisie, not as an independent force of its own.

The best example for this is provided by English Chartism, a movement which deeply impressed Karl Marx and Friedrich Engels during the time when they first formed their revolutionary views. To them Chartism appeared as a clear expression of the revolutionary will of the proletariat. In fact, Chartism was mostly the reflex of the reform era among the lower classes. Before the Reform Act of 1832, which gave the bourgeoisie the vote, no separate working-class movement of any importance had existed; the lower classes expected to be included among the voters. Only when this hope failed them did the classes which had been excluded from the suffrage unite in a claim for its extension, for a new democratic 'Charter'. But Chartism was not an exclusively proletarian movement. It grouped together all those sections which had been denied the vote; it did not launch any specifically proletarian claims, either for social legislation, for shorter hours or for higher wages; it limited itself entirely to democratic claims and was deeply convinced that general suffrage was a remedy for everything. The one really proletarian feature of the movement concerned means, not ends. A general strike was attempted, but it was a strike with an exclusively democratic programme. Chartism was most surprising in its end. It broke down in 1846 and not even the Continental revolutions of 1848 gave it new life. The year 1846 is a big date in English history. It is the year of the abolition of the Corn Laws, of the final victory of the liberal economic principles of the bourgeoisie; it is the year which marks the end of the reform era. As in France at the end of the eighteenth century, so now in England the proletariat receded into the background as soon as the bourgeoisie had definitely conquered power. It had acted as the servant of the moneyed interest, though as a somewhat excited and unreliable servant.

But the 'fifties of the nineteenth century marked a new development, marked the emergence of a movement which was truly proletarian. From that time dates the rise of the British trade unions. They were pledged to constitutional means and they strove for gradual improvement of the lot of the workers. At first they despised politics altogether, trusting entirely in the organized action of their members, without state interference. Later, with the increasing importance of social legislation, they realized the importance of parliament and finally formed a political party of their own. But the gradualist, reformist, constitutional outlook remained. And the aims were always more or less limited to matters directly concerning labour. To this day the Labour Party has not found a way to oppose a programme of its own to that of other parties in matters of national policy not directly concerning the peculiar interests of the workers.

At first the example of the British trade unions seemed to be an exception in the world of labour. At that time, during the 'fifties, Karl Marx had already laid down the basic elements of his theory, which was to become of such tremendous importance for the history of the labour movement. Here is not the place to discuss this theory. We must be content to mention, from time to time, what is important in our context. Marx was convinced that the very progress of industry, the introduction of machinery, the growth in size and number of the factories and of the proletariat, would increase the class antagonism between the workers and their employers, would unite the proletariat in an ever-growing revolutionary self-consciousness. The evolution of the English trade unions ran directly counter to these views. It was perhaps due to the torpor which grasped the labour movement after the defeat of 1848. But the torpor passed and the reformism of the English unions remained. Or it was a phenomenon limited to the highest strata of the working classes, to highly skilled labour which could obtain, by means of a powerful organization, a share of the profits of the bourgeoisie. Yet the organization of the 'workers' aristocracy' was followed, in the 'eighties, by the emergence of the unions of the unskilled workers. These unions could indeed obtain less through their own power. Therefore they relied more upon social legislation and carried the labour movement along the path of parliamentary action and the formation of a labour party. But the gradualist, reformist, constitutional character of the movement remained; the proletariat had no revolutionary ideas whatsoever, and its standard of living increased substantially.

Then Marx and Engels found another explanation of a fact so thoroughly in contrast with their revolutionary hope. The reformism of the English unions was due to specific national conditions, to the existence of a big and profitable empire. The workers shared in the colonial profits and therefore were interested in the permanence of this empire and the domination of the British bourgeoisie. Lenin, mixing moral with economic issues, later formulated the same idea by saying that the bourgeoisie, notably the English bourgeoisie, had 'bribed' a section of the proletariat into 'betraying' the interests of the class.

Marx and Engels had expressed this theory in the 'seventies and 'eighties. It was contradicted by the developments of these same years. After 1870 the English methods spread to the

Continent. A powerful labour movement evolved in almost every Continental country, and the trade unions, with their peaceful means and the improvement of the worker's lot following their work, were invariably the backbone of the new movement. True, the Continental movement did not follow entirely English lines. In England no political issue of major importance divided for a long time the workers from the rest of the nation. On the Continent the labour movement was subjected to political persecution. Bismarck, notably, made himself the agent of the employers with his law against the socialist organizations. At the same time issues which, in Britain, had been settled during the reform era, remained alive on the Continent. Parliamentary government was not established in Germany before 1918, was hotly contested in France till the beginning of the twentieth century, and never really obtained in Austria and Italy. Though the revolutionary era had passed away, a certain tension continued to exist. In Germany notably most 'bourgeois' parties opposed the régime, and the socialist movement did the same, but expressed its ideas more forcibly. All this gave the Continental labour movement a misleading revolutionary flavour.

In Britain and in the United States revolution had never been a practical issue inside the labour movement. But on the Continent the situation was different. On the one hand the unions and the parliamentary parties carried out large-scale activities on an entirely peaceful basis. On the other hand the orators of the parties used strong language against the political régime. Here was a manifest contradiction. A right wing, whose chief spokesman was the Frenchman Jean Jaurès, urged the movement to make words agree with facts. While fighting for democracy, the movement ought to drop the idea of a proletarian revolution. It was manifest, the right wing asserted, that the workers could improve their lot within the framework of the existing society, that this society was gradually changing its character, that state interference was extending, and that a gradual transition from 'capitalism' to 'socialism' was under way. The right wing urged collaboration with other parties of the left in order to further this transformation.

The left wing, in opposing these ideas, based itself upon the work of Karl Marx. In the early days before the bourgeoisie had fully established itself on the Continent, Marx had already pronounced its 'Mene-Tekel'. With specious economic arguments which we cannot here repeat he attempted to prove that the existing 'capitalist' society, based upon private property and *laisser faire*, was bound to perish from inherent contradictions which would exert an increasingly disastrous influence. He prophesied that capitalism would founder in a series of ever-increasing economic crises, which would ruin the whole texture of society. The end would be the upheaval of the proletariat, which, having grown together with industry, was not interested in private property in the means of production, and would organize a collectivist society instead of the existing individualist one. In the meantime the task of the socialists was to organize the workers and to train them, in skirmishes, for the decisive battles.

In the rejection of every compromise with other parties, the left wing of Continental socialism based itself upon these views. Looking backward, however, we can see that they were tainted with a double fallacy. Socialist intellectuals of the left put forward Marxist views in order to oppose the peaceful tactics of the trade unions. But they themselves did not oppose these tactics in earnest. Not a single worker would have followed them had they tried to do so. The whole contention was about the interpretation and the scope to be given to these tactics. The right wing tended to regard them as the Alpha and Omega of working-class policy. The left wing regarded them as an intermediate stage which, in the future, would give way to a new era of revolution. There was considerable support for this view among the masses, who hated the autocratic régime and did not distinguish between a revolution against autocracy and one against democracy. Not even in their wildest dreams would the left-wingers have regarded a political revolution against democracy as possible; yet it was precisely this idea which was later to become the root and core of bolshevism. Thus an essentially peaceful movement, with vague democratic aspirations, continued to indulge in grandiose revolutionary verbiage. A bitter awakening was inevitable.

This leads to the second fallacy implied in the situation. The theoreticians were not altogether wrong in their expectations regarding the future. The nineteenth century had been one of peaceful evolution; the twentieth soon announced itself as one of revolutionary change. The big convulsion in Russia in 1905 opened a series of political upheavals which is yet far from its end. Neither did the enormous economic crises which Marx had predicted fail to come. But he had misinterpreted the future in one respect, the role of the proletariat. He had predicted that an ever-widening gulf would divide proletariat and bourgeoisie. In fact the sixty years after the revolution of 1848 had done everything to fill that gulf. The proletariat had risen with modern industrial society as a whole. It must inevitably suffer, if this society was jeopardized in its existence. The hopes placed in revolutionary action by the proletariat were deceived by the event.

There was one exception. In Russia a long revolutionary movement culminated in the victory of the Bolsheviks, a party which regarded itself as the standard-bearer of proletarian revolution. The contrast between the success of proletarian revolution—or what appeared as such—in Russia and its failure in the West was enormous and it impressed deeply the revolutionaries in the East and West. The Bolsheviks had inspired themselves with the ideas of revolutionary Marxism which they had learned from the German socialists. But that which the German socialists had failed to carry out, the Russians had put into practice. It was a paradoxical situation. By their success the Bolsheviks uprooted one of the basic ideas of Marx. Marx had believed proletarian revolution to be the result of a very high stage of industrial development. Revolution came in an industrially backward country. If the ideals of the socialist revolutionaries were to be put into effect, the Russian example must be followed. Out of the violent contrast between the failure of the Western labour movement to become revolutionary, and the spectacular success of revolution in Russia, sprang the Communist International. It has its roots in two different soils: on the one hand there is the Russian revolutionary movement, which we must now consider more closely; on the other hand, there is the labour movement of the West, with its queer mixture of revolutionary theory and peaceful practice, whose study would make a book in itself. We have given here its merest outlines, in order to indicate the background against which Bolshevism arose.

CHAPTER II

THE RUSSIAN REVOLUTIONARY MOVEMENT

There are not many contrasts in history so sharply outlined as that between the Western and the Russian labour movements: the former mainly unaggressive in spite of a revolutionary creed; the latter revolutionary, even where it pretends only to strive for reforms; the former, practical, matter-of-fact, uninspired, in spite of a pretence that it heralds a new epoch in the progress of humanity; the latter, enthusiastic as the *millénaires* and the Fifth Monarchy men, in spite of a paradoxical 'materialistic' faith; the one thoroughly 'bourgeois' in mind and sentiment, though aiming officially at the destruction of the bourgeoisie; the other really and totally anti-bourgeois, though aiming, officially, through two decades, at nothing but the achievement of a 'bourgeois revolution'. In these strange contrasts, which tinge with an ironical element the history of both, the difference between an old and a young civilization is revealed.

The Russian labour movement, like the Russian revolutionary movement in general, owes its origin to the impact of the West upon a half-barbaric country. Russia, in common with every nascent civilization, speaks in the tongues of the older civilization, under which shadow she was born, that is to say, she speaks in the scientific and philosophical language of the West. But this is mainly due to the fact that Russian civilization has not yet developed so far as to be able to stand upon its own feet; the concepts which it uses are as unfit for native conditions as the concepts of Greek philosophy were unsuited to express the real feelings of the Christians of the second century: Russia, and the thing called 'labour movement' in Russia, borrowed much from the West, only in order to transform it into something entirely different. And, as every old civilization in its straits, the West to-day looks upon the achievements of the nascent Russian rival half with horror, half with envy of her youthful and barbarous strength.

The labour movement in the West, even more than the revolutionary conflicts of the bourgeoisie, turned and still turns around material interests, around wages, working hours, social legislation and the best organization of economic life in general. It would be a mistake to assume that the labour movement is exclusively determined by these material aims. In our modern West there prevails the worship of two chief gods or idols besides Mammon: the state and the nation. The devotion to these is no less strong among the working people than among other classes. But precisely because all classes join in this cult of the state and nation, it is not a distinctive feature of the labour movement, and therefore remains mostly in the background, only to emerge in hours of decisive importance for the nation as a whole.

But in the Russian labour movement, and for that matter in Russian revolutionism as a whole, the position is just the opposite. Material interests are there, undoubtedly, as everywhere in human society, and play their part; they are even emphasized, beyond their real weight, by the materialistic philosophy which the Russian revolutionaries, for reasons soon to be explained, have borrowed from the West. But at the core of the movement there is something entirely different, something which can only be adequately described as religious. The whole Russian revolutionary movement, whether 'bourgeois' or 'proletarian', whether 'liberal' or 'socialist', has one element in common: the existence of organizations of 'professional revolutionaries', formed of young men of all classes who break every connection with their social background and live in hiding, in a close community resembling that of the early Christians, for the sole purpose of revolutionary work; men as ready for self-sacrifice and martyrdom, as contemptuous of the good things of the world, as devoted to the work to which they have vowed their lives, as those early Christians themselves. If morals determine religion rather than dogmas, devotion rather than abstract faith, then these movements, in spite of their materialistic creed, are among the strongest religious forces of our time. This is not meant as an expression of unqualified admiration. For it is a religion of a special kind. Throughout the history of Russian revolutionism, from very early times, goes a streak of moral indifference in the service of the cause which balances, which indeed is, the devotion of everything *to* the cause; a conviction that, in the service of revolution, everything, absolutely everything, is permitted: not only to kill one's adversaries and to 'expropriate', by means of robbery, the individual property of individual bourgeois, but equally to mislead one's own followers, to start movements based on actual forgery, to kill innocent people in order to create an indissoluble link between the accomplices. Be it remembered that one of the earlier Russian revolutionaries, Nechaev, proclaimed these principles openly with the utmost candour and logical rigidity.

Nechaev represents fairly well the Russian 'professional revolutionary' type, of which he is one of the earliest representatives. He worked in the 'sixties and died in the 'eighties of the nineteenth century. His readiness for self-sacrifice went almost beyond belief. After having been chained to the wall of a humid jail for many years, he managed to get into contact with revolutionary groups in the outside world, especially with the strongest, the Narodnaya Volya ('Will of the people') Party. They offered to free him. But he, realizing that this would keep the main forces of the organization busy for many months, refused the offer and advised his friends to let him rot in jail and concentrate upon a single aim: the assassination of the Tsar. This was the same Nechaev who, when forming the first revolutionary groups, had pretended to his followers that he was the head of an all-Russian secret society of many thousands, which was absolutely non-existent; he had done so in order to impress and win them. Later, he made them kill one of their own comrades, under the consciously false pretence that the man was going to turn informer; he did so for the unique purpose of knitting them together in a common crime. He escaped to Switzerland, while his comrades were caught and tried. Hunted even there, he left, but not before he had attempted to steal private correspondence, not of enemies of the revolutionary movement, but of the arch-revolutionary

Bakunin himself; caught in the attempt and questioned by his friends, he bluntly admitted that it was his system to compromise his friends, in order to keep them in complete obedience.

The case of Nechaev issued in a big public scandal, and Russian revolutionaries ever since have officially rejected any connection with his ideas. In fact, however, Nechaev, to whose mentality Western concepts of moral obligation were utterly foreign, but the ideas of certain fanatical Islamic sects very close, is in more than one sense the spiritual father of the Russian revolutionary movement as a whole. The filiation between him and Lenin is almost direct. It has already been mentioned that while in prison he kept in constant contact with the strongest of the revolutionary groups, Narodnaya Volya, which, not much later, assassinated Tsar Alexander II. Narodnaya Volya, with A. Shelyabov and Sonya Perovskaya at its head, has been admired by all subsequent Russian revolutionaries for the strength and wide ramification of its organization, for its iron revolutionary will, and for the unlimited heroism of its members. Yet Shelyabov himself—undoubtedly the greatest of the Russian revolutionaries before Lenin—wanted to free Nechaev in order to make him the leader of his organization. This amounted to a formal endorsement of Nechaev's principles by the biggest and most important revolutionary group. And the link between Lenin and Narodnaya Volya was an unusually close one. The leaders of Narodnaya Volya were caught and hanged after the assassination of the Tsar, but a young man called Alexander I. Ulyanov, inspired by boundless admiration of their methods and achievements, tried to continue their work, was caught during preparations for the assassination of Tsar Alexander III, and hanged. This young man happened to be the elder brother of Vladimir Ilyich Ulyanov, who in later life called himself Lenin. In his own career Lenin always professed the greatest admiration for Narodnaya Volya, for its heroism and for its methods of organization. Nor is there a single word against Nechaev in his writings.

The clue to Lenin's personality, both private and public, is undoubtedly the fearful shock the seventeen-year-old boy experienced when his brother was hanged. Nadeshda Konstantinovna Krupskaya, Lenin's widow, relates a family tradition which, whether exactly true or not, illustrates very well the essential situation. The young Lenin is said to have paced up and down his room, the day of the execution of his brother, saying again and again: 'No, it is not this way, not this way, which one must follow.' The obvious implication, in the light of Lenin's later policy, is that Lenin agreed with the aim of his brother, the aim of all the revolutionaries, the overthrow of Tsardom and '*the* revolution'. But he disapproved of the method of individual terrorism, not, of course on moral grounds—he has expressed his moral indifference in the matter repeatedly—but on grounds of political expediency. Later in life, in one of the first of his pamphlets, Lenin extolled Narodnaya Volya as the model which the revolutionary Marxist must strive to imitate. Only, where Narodnaya Volya had spent all its strength in a vain attempt to disorganize the Tsarist régime by repeated assassinations, the Marxist must strive to lead the masses to the revolutionary attack.

The organization of professional revolutionaries, strictly selected, bound to absolute obedience towards the superiors of the organization, ready for any sacrifice, severed from every link with the outside world, classless in the most emphatic sense of the term, knowing neither satisfaction nor moral obligation outside the good of their organization, is a specific creation of the Russian soil, indigenous long before any labour movement existed there at all. Lenin transferred this organization, with its peculiar methods of selection and work, its peculiar religious enthusiasm and its equally peculiar indifference to ordinary moral standards, into the Russian labour movement. Having conquered Russia with his organization of professional revolutionaries, he attempted to transfer the same methods to the West. The history of this attempt is the history of the Communist International. The whole conception was foreign to even the most revolutionary socialists of the West. Insoluble conflicts inevitably ensued between those who followed Russian revolutionism in its practical, religious, and moral aspects and those who lived by the concepts of the West. They create part of the interest of the story we are going to tell. The history of the Communist International is, largely, an instance of a clash of cultures.

As we said, the concept of a close, select organization of

professional revolutionaries is not due to Lenin. He only transferred this concept into the nascent labour movement. But
what was the revolutionaries' aim before there was a labour
movement? It is very difficult to say. There is no lack of definite statements, of ideals, both borrowed from the West and
evolved in intentional antagonism to the ideals of the West.
But the scene is extremely shifting. Starting with the peculiarly
European ideals of liberalism and parliamentary democracy,
the movement soon turns towards socialism; then it evolves an
ideology of its own, emphasizing the specific creative power of
the Russian peasant; then turns back to the ideals of the
European labour movement. Tactics are as shifting as ideals.
From an initial stage of military insurrection they evolve
through the formation of small propagandist circles; continue
with propaganda among the peasant masses; shift back to the
work within narrow groups, but this time with the aim of
assassinating the Tsar; twist to the support of the nascent
spontaneous revolt of the new Russian proletariat, and finally
issue into leadership of a revolution of the people as a whole.

There is something peculiarly Russian, quite un-Western in
these shifting aims and methods. It would be only natural that
there should arise, first a liberal party of the bourgeoisie; then
a democratic party of the lower middle classes; then a revolutionary movement of the peasant serfs and of the urban proletariat. But this was not what actually happened. From about
1820 till 1903 all these variations of tactics and opinion went
on, not within different classes of society, but within the same
narrow circle of revolutionaries, always backed by one and the
same social group: the intelligentsia. The fact shows how little
Western formulae are applicable to Russian reality. In the
West liberalism, democracy, socialism corresponded to material, economic realities, to the interests and beliefs of certain
classes. In Russia these classes scarcely existed. There had been
revolutionary groups, risings, assassinations, for half a century,
with liberal programmes, before the first factory worked by
free labour was established, before the first bourgeois industrial
capitalist had made his appearance in Russian society. What
corresponded to Marxist interpretation in the West, did not
correspond to it in Russia. In the West, as Marx had pointed
out, the great political trends of modern life, such as liberalism,

democracy, and socialism, corresponded to real classes; in Russia they were ideals in a void. Marxism, too, in Russia, was at first an ideal of the intelligentsia, and not the expression of any real labour movement; just as liberalism was mainly an ideal and not the expression of real claims of a real bourgeoisie. A somewhat heretical communist—Lominadse, Stalin's brother-in-law, who has since committed suicide for his heresies—once said that in China there are 'only shadows of classes'. The description, though thoroughly un-Marxist, is excellent, and would fit Tsarist Russia nearly as well.

But if all these creeds were only ideals, what was the reality behind that one constant fact in the shifting of convictions, the organization of professional revolutionaries? It was, obviously, the revolutionary intelligentsia, whose views the professional revolutionaries expressed, whose most self-sacrificing members they selected. It would be odd to call the revolutionary intelligentsia a 'class', but it certainly was a well-defined and important social group. What were its reasons for being revolutionary? The answer is simple enough, if one does not cling to the vain attempts of this intelligentsia to give expression to its aims in the language of the West. Unable to express their real aims adequately, for the simple reason that these aims themselves were anything but well defined, they attempted to put on the costume of Western parties. But whether they spoke of the necessity of political liberty, of the plight of the peasant or of the socialist future of society, it was always their own plight which really moved them. And their plight was not primarily due to material need: it was spiritual.

The boundary which divided the intelligentsia from other classes in Russia was itself determined not by material but by spiritual facts. There was little in common, economically, between the discontented aristocrats who gave Russia such revolutionary thinkers as Bakunin, Kropotkin, and Tolstoy, and the well-to-do engineers such as Krassin and Krishanovski, teachers, sons of priests, etc. What bound them together was one thing and one thing only: they were the groups which had fallen under the spell of European civilization. The very existence of an intelligentsia in Russia, and its revolutionary moods, are the result of the impact of the West upon Russian civilization. This impact was felt, very strongly, after the first profound break with ancient Russian tradition under Peter the Great.

We should never forget, during the course of our investigation, that this old Russian tradition itself did not derive directly from the primitive customs of the Slavs alone, but had been deeply influenced by Byzantium. But Russia never became a country with a fully developed Byzantine civilization. It was a borderland of this civilization, never fully amalgamated; yet one finds in Russian history, and again in the history of the Communist International, many features which are specifically 'Byzantine'. The habits and beliefs which had emerged out of the contact of the primitive Slavs with Byzantium remained very deep rooted among the common people. They were broken among the upper classes. Those upper classes were launched upon a career of imitation of Europe, in a social milieu which did not provide any of the primary requirements for such a transplantation. In the end the people, while remaining deeply Slavonic and Byzantine, were deprived of that inspiration from above which subsists where the higher and the lower classes have their basic convictions and aims in common. The higher classes were severed from their native people without being able really to become Westerners. This break between the people and the ruling stratum was at the root of the Russian tragedy, as most Russian thinkers knew only too well.

A comparison will make the point somewhat clearer. A sharp severance of the ruling strata from the people is not a specific mark of the Russian situation. On the contrary, it goes, as a rule, with all deep social crises. It is, for instance, the plight of contemporary Spain just as much as that of Russia. But in Spain it is far from the whole of the upper class, and not even all the intellectuals, who have been dislodged from the soil of native tradition through the impact of the West. On the contrary, the group cut adrift is so small as to be almost negligible. And the deep cleavage between the higher and lower classes in Spain is in no way due to their belonging to different civilizations. On the contrary, the spiritual inheritance of the Spanish aristocrat and of the Spanish land-labourer is very much the same. This makes the clash perhaps even more disastrous, but it deprives it of the spiritual implications which it contained in Russia. Out of the conflict of two totally different civilizations on Russian soil a third and new one seems to be emerging, while the West gazes upon the tremendous drama half in horror and half in admiration.

For a century after Peter the Great it was the Russian upper classes who stared admiringly at Western civilization; they could imitate its paraphernalia, but its core was inaccessible to them. They felt, by comparison, that their own life was barbarous, undignified; they found the air of Russia suffocating. But they could not help it. The civilization of the West stood in front of them like a rock. It still had its well-established traditions, religion, and hierarchy. It could only be accepted or rejected *en bloc*. And, in spite of all vain dreams, it was impossible to transfer it *en bloc* to the Russian soil.

Old civilizations are impermeable to nascent young ones so long as the old civilization stands in its integrity. The Russian upper stratum got real access to the West only when the West had become critical, sceptical, and destructive. The French Revolution was the breach through which, after a century of vain admiration, Russia gained real access to the civilization of the West. In order to become civilized in the Western sense Russia needed to abolish the autocracy of the Tsar, the tyranny of a corrupt bureaucracy, the brutishness of serfdom. And yet the Russian upper classes, which had lost their roots in their native soil, looked helplessly to Paris for a model. Adaptation to the West implied revolution in Russia, and yet the Russian upper classes which looked for a lead to the West had to wait for a revolution in the West in order to learn what to do in their own country. As a stable civilization the West had only acted upon Russia as a disintegrating factor. It became constructively important only through its own revolution.

'Revolution', from those days onwards—or more correctly, after the later Napoleonic wars, which brought many Russians into direct contact with France—became the watchword of the whole of the Europeanized upper classes. The people was wholly indifferent. And there developed the strange spectacle of a revolution without and against the people. In Russia the central problem of the revolutionaries was from the beginning and remained to the end one which, in the West, would have sounded almost absurd; how can the revolutionaries, the ostensible champions of the people, get into contact with the people? For seven decades, the revolutionary movement failed to do this. And the second problem facing the movement was hardly less paradoxical. What was the revolution to aim at? The destructive aspect of the programme was easily defined, and all revolutionaries were more or less agreed on that much: overthrow the Tsar, destroy the corrupt bureaucracy, free the peasants. Those were ideas evoked directly by the clash between Western models and Russian conditions. But what to put in the place of the destroyed? Ideas about that were of the very vaguest. When any positive assertion was made, however logical it was, practice invariably proved that it was not meant seriously.

The first important military revolt in 1826, organized by officers who had served in France, showed clearly enough that the rebels had entered on insurrection without being at all clear in their own minds what they would do if their *coup d'état* should succeed. After the failure of this rising of the Decabrists —called after the month of December, in which it took place— there followed more than two decades of discussion in small circles—about the aims of revolution. Those young people were in no doubt that revolution was necessary—they only doubted why. And they hammered their heads against the problem whether the individual, in the society to come, should be allowed or prohibited existence as an independent unit. Dostoevski has told the story.

The history of Russia is sharply punctuated by shocks that derived their force from the West. The first—or perhaps not even quite the first—of these shocks was produced by the reforms of Peter the Great, which uprooted the aristocracy. The second was produced by contact with the French Revolution, and it brought the Russian revolutionary movement into being. The third was dealt by the country's defeat in the Crimean War. This forced the Government to take one more important step along the trail blazed by Peter the Great; in order to assimilate Russia to the West and to fit her better for economic, and so for military, competition—Tsar Alexander II freed the serfs. Since Westernization was the battle-cry of the revolutionaries, this step lay directly in the line indicated by the revolutionary movement, and for a time a sort of armistice ensued between the Tsar and the revolutionaries. But not for long. The liberation of the serfs was counteracted by a most iniquitous division of the land between the lords and the peasants. During this period of reform the question of Polish autonomy came inevitably to the front; half-hearted attempts at a new régime in Poland resulted in a big Polish rising which was cruelly crushed. The liberation of the serfs had been welcomed by the revolutionaries as a first instalment of the grant of full civil and political liberties. But the Tsar was much too closely associated with the bureaucracy and with the landlords —who wanted reform on Western lines but did not want to bear its economic burden—to go any further in this direction. Frightened by the extremism of the movement which it had let loose, the government turned back in sharp reaction. This meant the opening of an era of violent struggle between the Tsar and the revolutionaries.

The main events of this struggle are quickly told. The revolutionaries hoped that the peasants would share their disappointment, and, uprooted from their traditional life through the Act of Liberation but discontented with its effects, would be ready to rise. They changed their tactics accordingly. Previously they had relied upon discontented elements in the army, and had failed. Then for decades they had had nothing to rely upon. Now for the first time a mass force, the strongest in Russia, the peasantry, seemed to provide a basis for their activities. For the first time appeared the feature which was later to become decisive in Bolshevism: the revolutionary intelligentsia attempted to rely, for the performance of its plans, upon the spontaneous impulses of another class; they tried to lead and to wheedle this other class along the path which corresponded with their own aims. It was a position fundamentally different from any in the West. The labour and peasant parties of the West express the real aims of those two classes, and the intellectuals which they count in their ranks are essentially technicians advising on the political fight or carrying it out according to orders received from the big class organizations. The dominating role of the trade unions in all the strongest labour parties of the West reflects this position. In Russia the masses, with their vacillating impulses towards revolt, were always a tool in the hands of the revolutionaries if they allowed themselves to be led by them. Often enough they failed to respond, and remained in their traditional apathy. This happened in the 'sixties, in spite of the shock of the liberation of the serfs. The revolutionaries, with a generous impulse, attempted to 'go among the people', to dress as peasants and start a big propaganda campaign in the villages. The peasants were quick to discover the intellectuals behind their peasant masquerade, and failed absolutely to respond. The revolutionaries then considered how the peasants could be forced along the road which they refused to travel. A forged manifesto of the Tsar was issued, urging the peasants to rise in his name and overthrow the landlords; again there was no response. The only thing that happened was that the revolutionaries, not yet trained in the business of underground propaganda, were arrested in their hundreds.

From this moment onwards the revolutionary camp began to divide into those who saw no salvation but in continued efforts to come closer to the masses, and those who turned resolutely away from the masses and embarked on an attempt to disorganize the government by repeated assassinations. The latter group, the Narodnaya Volya already mentioned, was destroyed after the assassination of Tsar Alexander II. Its main achievement was the creation of that type of 'professional revolutionary organization', with iron discipline, absolute centralization, and strict selection of members, working in all classes of society, which was to become the model for Lenin. It must be insisted, however, that this type of organization, though brought into being for the first time by Narodnaya Volya, had been tried repeatedly before. It had been in the minds of almost all the revolutionaries. Not because discipline, selection, and a narrow group are especially necessary for assassinations. Bakunin, the father of the more modern school of Russian revolutionaries, had already preached this centralized clandestine organization of selected revolutionaries, but not under Tsardom in Russia; he had attempted to create it in the West, among the members of the First International led by Karl Marx. His argument was: a mass movement is inevitably shifting, uncertain and half-bourgeois. Only a clandestine group of selected, disciplined revolutionaries can guarantee revolutionary purity. If Shelyabov, the leader of Narodnaya

Volya, is, in more than one sense, the spiritual father of Bolshevism, Bakunin must be counted one of the chief precursors of the Communist International. The communists, naturally, do not admit this, as it would clash with their Marxist creed.

But of course Shelyabov is a precursor of Bolshevism only in so far as the forms and methods of organization are concerned. His tactics of assassination are directly opposed to those of the Bolsheviks, who always rejected 'individual terrorism' and believed in the mass movement. In this respect they stood much nearer to the other section of the big revolutionary movement, the section which was willing to rely upon the peasant. It is this latter section which is usually called 'Narodniki', the party of the people.

It is easy to give a schematic survey of the evolution of the Russian revolutionary movement—which is sometimes so puzzling to the Westerner—by taking account of the fact that, at the core, there are always small groups of the revolutionary intelligentsia, and that the line of division is, chiefly, not aims but tactics. Very roughly those groups, according to their tactical differences, can be grouped as follows:

I. No mass movement:

(1) Narodnaya Volya: chief means, assassinations; extinguished after the death of Alexander II in 1881.

II. Trying to establish contact with the masses:

(2) For an alliance of the intelligentsia with the peasantry: Narodniki of various shades, very strong during the 'seventies and early 'eighties, gradually fading during the 'nineties.

(3) For an alliance between the intelligentsia and the industrial workers: Marxist social-democrats, later Bolsheviks, since the early 'nineties.

(4) For an alliance of intelligentsia, peasants, and workers: 'Socialist revolutionaries', since the beginning of the twentieth century.

This schematic survey brings to light what is probably the decisive fact in the history of the whole Russian revolutionary movement: its change of character with the appearance of the working class. The terroristic experiment had thoroughly failed, and ended in the destruction of Narodnaya Volya. There was simply no way out except an alliance with the masses. But the peasant, despite all efforts, did not respond. When, however, in the late 'eighties, modern industry began to grow in Russia, the workers appeared upon the stage. And they *did* respond to the appeals of the revolutionary intelligentsia. The peasant, in spite of the shock of the liberation, had remained an apathetic traditionalist. The worker, completely uprooted from his traditional milieu, shaken by the convulsions of the trade cycle and burdened with the sufferings of the industrial revolution, was permeable to the idea of a violent revolution. He was never allowed to care simply for his immediate interests. The intelligentsia always remained the officers' corps of the labour movement in Russia. But now, after eight decades of failure and unavailing efforts, the revolutionary intelligentsia felt firm ground under their feet, the officers had found their men. This is the root of the enormous prestige of Marxism in Russia. Where every other hope had failed, industrial development, by providing the revolutionaries with an army, seemed to show the way of salvation. Here starts the history of Bolshevism.

But before entering upon it we must, for a moment, leave problems of tactics and revert to the problem of the ultimate aims of the revolutionaries. We have already discussed that peculiar feature of the movement, that '*the* revolution' was an undisputed goal, whereas its meaning was as vague as it could possibly be. These aims, or rather the official declarations concerning aims, shifted with the appearance and disappearance of prospective allies. In the late 'sixties the revolutionaries had, for the first time, tried to establish close contacts with the peasants. It was for them the first contact with Russian reality as such. And it became apparent immediately that the slogans of the West, liberalism, democracy, and industrial socialism, had little meaning on Russian soil. In its inspiration the revolutionary movement was essentially 'Western'. But under the pressure of contact with Russian reality it immediately performed a complete *volte-face*. Realizing that the conditions which had bred revolution in the West were absent, the Narodniki began to find and soon to praise the seeds of a specifically Russian revolution which their native soil contained. The Russian Marxists have thrown scorn over these ideas, which nevertheless corresponded fairly well with reality. Russia, the Narodniki contended, need not pass through capitalism before reaching socialism. The Russian village contained already all the elements of socialism: it had its 'Mir', the peasant community, which regarded the land as common property and at intervals redistributed it according to the needs of the individual households. This 'communist' village organization need only be liberated from the oppression of the Tsar, the bureaucracy, and the landlord to become a fully communist society. Russia, they contended, was nearer to communism than the West.

It was an essentially conservative ideal, not unlike the ideals of the official conservatives, the 'Slavophils', whose chief mouthpiece was Dostoevski; they extolled the intrinsic qualities of the Russian peasant, loathed the upper classes as un-Russian and Westernized, hated St. Petersburg just as the Narodniki did; they differed from the Narodniki mainly on the questions of violence and atheism. It is fairly obvious that the ideal of the Narodniki, in so far as it was not conservative, was Utopian. It proved to be Utopian, in the first place, to hope for revolution based on the peasant alone. The revolutionary intelligentsia was not a sufficient stimulus; this stimulus was provided by the workers. It proved Utopian to try to keep Russia free from the stain of industrialism; industrialism increased. In this matter the Narodniki had underestimated the strength and importance of the Western element in Russian history. On the other hand, they had overestimated, in certain respects, the capacity of Russian society for change. The idea of abolishing bureaucracy proved Utopian; instead of the old bureaucracy, which was, in fact, overthrown, there emerged under the régime of the Bolsheviks a new one, much more powerful than the 'Chinovniks' of the times of the Tsar. It was a Utopian ideal to abolish Tsardom and establish a federation of free peasant communities. The hereditary dynasty of the Romanovs was overthrown, but in its stead emerged a non-hereditary dynasty of 'adoptive emperors'. The one really revolutionary item in this strange conservative-revolutionary programme which proved to be practicable was the overthrow of the landlords.

But the conservative elements of the Narodniki programme proved to be much more realistic. In spite of all the scorn poured upon them by the Marxists, it must be admitted that the Narodniki, and not the Marxists, had foreseen the essentials of the impending revolution. The chief point of contention between the two was this: must Russia before revolution pass through a period of fully and highly developed capitalism or not? The answer of the Narodniki as against the Marxists was in the negative, and their view was borne out by the facts. The revolution 'jumped over' the capitalist phase. The second point of contention was, whether the revolution would be essentially a peasant revolution or not; the answer of the Narodniki proved correct: it was essentially a peasants' and soldiers' revolution, the soldiers themselves being mostly peasants. They had only overlooked the fact that the labour movement would be the tiny spark which set the big powder-barrel of the peasantry afire. The third question was this: Could the 'Mir', the semi-communist peasant community, survive and provide the basis for the new Russian society? The Marxists hotly denied it. But the 'Mir' has survived, in modernized forms, as 'kolkhoz'.

But if the Narodniki and their heirs, the 'socialist-revolutionaries', were right on so many points, why then were they defeated? The answer is simply that on the fields of history the prize does not go to the man who holds the soundest theory about racing but to the man who runs best. The Marxists had neglected many essentials of the Russian scene, which the Narodniki saw clearly. But the Narodniki had overlooked one element, a minor one in the long run, but in the short run decisive: they had overlooked the fact that the whole Russian revolutionary movement, including their own section of it, derived from the influence of the West. This influence of the West, in Russian history, was, and is, no more than a spark to light the powder, no more than a small lever to move enormous weights. But there is no fire without a spark, no moving of a load without a lever. This lever, European influence, mainly operating through the labour movement, the Narodniki in their profound enmity to the West failed to acknowledge in its true function. They were right in essentials. And it is perhaps not rash to prophesy that the future of Russia, in the long run, belongs to Dostoevski and to the Narodniki; it is certain that it does not belong to Marx. But for the decisive short run of time it was not the Narodniki who were right; it was Lenin. He had got hold of the lever. He moved the load.

CHAPTER III

BOLSHEVISM

After the reforms of Peter the Great, after the contact with France during the Napoleonic wars, after the Crimean defeat and the liberation of the serfs, the emergence of a modern industry in the 'eighties and 'nineties of the nineteenth century finally brought about the overthrow of old Russia. Tsarism was wholly unable to cope with these new forces, and the old order entered on a phase of visible disintegration. Tsarism tottered, and two authentically Western forces, the bourgeoisie and the proletariat, appeared upon the Russian scene, the ready heirs of the falling *ancien régime*.

This was good news for the professional revolutionaries. The revolutionary intelligentsia, after the double failure of propaganda among the peasants in the 'seventies and of revolutionary terrorism in the 'eighties, was in a state of despondency, until, in 1896, a big strike of the Petersburg textile workers showed that here was a new force, able and willing to fight. Here, after almost a century of vain attempts, was found the ally who would bring the revolutionaries success. The whole intelligentsia founded their hopes on the workers; and, the revolutionary working-class movement of the West being Marxist, the intelligentsia turned Marxist also for a few years. It was during these years that Lenin started his political career.

But the alliance with the working class imposed sacrifices. If they were to win, the proletariat must be strong. It could be strong only if industry grew unchecked. Therefore the Marxists must favour a capitalist régime and a liberal-democratic 'bourgeois' revolution. It implied a complete renunciation of the old dreams of the Narodniki that Russia could avoid

39

the era of capitalism. A considerable section of the Narodniki refused to accept the alternative, and they formed the party of the 'socialist revolutionaries', which recognized the importance of the proletariat, but refused to accept the necessity of a bourgeois era; they fought for a direct socialist revolution of the whole people and combined mass propaganda with revolutionary terrorism.

The programme of the socialist-revolutionaries contained one firmly held conviction: No bourgeois revolution was possible in Russia; growth of industry did not necessarily mean growth of a national bourgeoisie. The small national bourgeoisie felt weak before the Tsar, and it felt still weaker before the people. It was neither able to overthrow Tsarism with its own forces, nor willing to let the people do it. A first large revolutionary attempt, in 1905, failed mainly because, at an early stage, the liberal bourgeoisie made their peace with the Tsar. The second attempt, in 1917, went obviously astray after having achieved nothing but the overthrow of the dynasty; one knows that, in the end, not the bourgeoisie but soldiers, peasants, and workers brought the revolution of 1917 to victory.

When, at the end of the 'nineties, Marxism won over a large part of the revolutionary intelligentsia and a social-democratic party was founded, it saw itself at once faced with a problem. To rely on the workers' movement was sound enough. But what would be the character of the coming revolution and what the task of the Social-democratic Party in it? Should it conquer power? Or help the bourgeoisie to grasp power? One wing of the movement, the Mensheviks—the word signifies 'minority wing' and is taken from the result of an important vote at the second congress of the Social-democratic Party— decided for the latter alternative. A bourgeois revolution must be a revolution of the bourgeoisie. The workers must primarily care for their immediate interests, and secondly help the bourgeoisie to establish a liberal democracy. The Mensheviks were partisans of a working-class movement of the Western type. They sincerely believed that such a movement, while fighting mainly for the direct interests of the workers, could at the same time support the bourgeoisie in its fight for democracy. But the trouble was that the bourgeoisie neither wanted nor was able seriously to fight for democracy. With the level of the bourgeois-democratic movement considerably lower than it had been either in the English or the French revolutions the line of conduct proposed by the Mensheviks must inevitably lead to passive acceptance of the inertia of the liberal bourgeoisie. The Mensheviks advocated a democratic government of liberals, to be supported by the labour movement. But at the same time the liberals tried to bring about a coalition with the moderate conservatives under the Tsar. It was an impossible and contradictory position.

From these paradoxical circumstances Leon Trotsky, then a young man completely isolated within the party, attempted to draw all possible inferences. The problem of the Russian revolution, he contended, was insoluble as long as a revolution was attempted on Russian soil only. Tsarism was deeply shaken and bound to fall, but the bourgeoisie was too weak to overthrow it; therefore the leadership in the anti-Tsarist revolution must fall into the hands of the proletariat. Then what would the proletariat do once it had taken power into its hands? It would be confronted, again, with an insoluble problem: Russia, with four-fifths of its population still agricultural, was not ripe for socialism, but the proletariat, once it had taken power into its hands, would not be willing simply to establish a liberal democracy and then recede peacefully into the background. It would attempt to use power in its own interests, to expropriate the private owners of industry and of the larger estates, and would thus be driven into conflicts with all those classes the support of which it could not obtain. The situation would be more favourable to the Russian proletariat if it could succeed in extending the conflict beyond the borders of Russia. The Russian revolution would be the prelude to a proletarian revolution in other countries, mainly in Germany with its higher industrial development; in Germany, the proletariat was strong enough to hold political power, once grasped, and the German proletariat would come to the rescue of its Russian class-brothers. This is the conception commonly known as the famous 'theory of permanent revolution'. As its exponent Trotsky must be regarded as one of the chief precursors of the Communist International.

Between the two sides, the Mensheviks and Trotsky, stood

Lenin. As against Trotsky, he held the belief that the Russian revolution could be brought to a successful end within the borders of Russia. If the revolution must proceed until it had reached the stage of dictatorship of the proletariat, then indeed such a dictatorship could only hold out with the help of the proletariat of one or several Western nations. But Lenin denied, during the early years of his career, this necessity. He agreed with the Mensheviks that the impending revolution would be a bourgeois-democratic revolution, a revolution which would lead to the establishment of a capitalist republic. But he disagreed with the Mensheviks' theory that the bourgeoisie would carry through such a revolution in Russia. It could therefore be carried on to final victory only by an alliance of the proletariat and the peasantry in a 'democratic dictatorship'. Lenin believed that the proletariat would impose upon itself the necessary self-restrictions, provided adequate leadership was available. This leadership he meant to provide himself.

To-day it is obvious that Lenin's idea of a 'democratic dictatorship of the proletariat and the peasantry' has not come true. A bourgeois revolution supposes a strong and self-confident bourgeoisie, and such a bourgeoisie was not lacking only in Russia. It is absent in all those countries where modern industrial progress is mainly due not to efforts at home but to pressure from the big industrial countries of the West. In this respect the plight of Russia is the plight of China, of Spain, of South America. In all those countries the impact of Western capitalism has shattered the *ancien régime* without creating modern classes which could take the lead in reconstruction, and they are therefore compelled to choose either interminable and futile convulsions or the establishment of some sort of dictatorship to execute the task in which the bourgeoisie fails, namely, to modernize the country. Whether the dictator calls himself Lenin or Ataturk or Chiang Kai-shek matters less than may sometimes appear; it is not decisive whether originally he starts from a dogma of proletarian revolution, of national or of religious revival. The fact of a modernizing dictatorship is decisive.

It is here that Lenin showed real genius. Theoretically, his point of view was less consistent than both that of the Mensheviks and that of Trotsky. But neither the Mensheviks nor

Trotsky had a practical way out. The Mensheviks attempted to imitate the Western labour movement, with its mass organizations, its slow and indecisive actions, its freedom of opinion and discussion, its limitation to the immediate interests of the workers; a structure totally unsuitable for the gigantic task of modernizing Russia. Trotsky, who knew more about dictatorships and their necessities, was and remained all his life an isolated individual. Lenin alone found the solution of the practical problem; whatever his *ideas* may contain of contradictions and inconsistencies, he founded the *organization* able to dictate, his party, the Bolshevik Party. The word 'bolsheviki' simply signifies 'majoritarians'—of the Social-democratic Party—in contrast to the 'minoritarians', the 'mensheviks'.

This idea of an organization of professional revolutionaries, with iron discipline, absolute centralization, and unity of policy, matured in Lenin's head before the issue about the future of the Russian revolution had become clear. He found the idea, ready made, in the traditions of the Russian revolutionary movement, in the history of Narodnaya Volya. The idea had been widespread among Russian Marxists of all shades. The central organ of the Social-democratic Party, *Iskra*, of which Lenin was an editor, had for years carried on a campaign in favour of such an organization. The second congress of the Social-democratic Party met in 1903, first in Brussels and then in London, precisely to carry out the task of bringing such an organization into being. But when the discussion of the statute to give the young party clarified all the implications, the spirits divided. Lenin stood for a very narrow party, a party which should consist only of professional revolutionaries. These revolutionaries would not be accepted into the inner organization—which, in Lenin's view, was identical with the party—simply by their own will, but would be selected by the party from volunteers; they would be directed in all their doings by the central committee.

More important even than the conception itself is the reason given for it by Lenin. He saw this type of a narrow inner party of professional revolutionaries not only in the light of a technical necessity for the fight against the Tsarist police. Here, almost all Marxists agreed and this was the common conviction upon which the campaign of *Iskra* had been based. Lenin urged a narrowing of the accessibility of the party beyond what, in the opinion of all the other leaders, was technically necessary. He regarded these self-imposed restrictions as a guarantee against 'opportunism'. The Mensheviks suggested that the doors of the party be opened to all workers as widely as was compatible with the technical necessities of the fight against Tsarism. To this Lenin objected with the argument that the ordinary worker, by the experiences of his daily life, develops, not a full revolutionary class-consciousness, but only the 'consciousness of a trade-unionist'. Only those who have theoretically assimilated Marxism and devoted all their life to the revolutionary fight are reliable revolutionaries.

This is the basic concept of the Bolshevik Party which Lenin tried to extend, after the revolution of 1917, all over the world. At the time when Lenin first voiced this view he was far from clear himself about all the consequences, and the fight against opportunism was only one among several arguments in favour of a 'narrow' party. In the course of time, however, it became clear that here lay the root of the matter. No less than a wholesale rejection of the basic contention of Marxism was implied. Marx believed that the proletariat, by the natural course of industrial progress and the increase of destitution and exploitation which he supposed went with it, became more revolutionary every day. Otherwise he could not have expected a proletarian revolution. This Lenin emphatically denied. The proletariat by itself never becomes revolutionary, he contended. Lenin's revolution is essentially not a proletarian revolution, it is '*the* revolution' of the intelligentsia, of the professional revolutionaries, but with the proletariat as their chief ally. Allies, however, are exchangeable. The course of the Russian dictatorship has proved that instead of the proletariat other groups could step in. It is important to note that Lenin had reached this view by instinctively clinging to the old anti-Western tradition of Russian revolutionism. What he feared was the evolution he saw in the West: big unions and labour parties caring little for revolution and busy with practical everyday issues only. Instinctively he shrank from this unpleasant reality. But intellectually he believed in that principle for the West which he wanted to avert at home. He had an apparently absolute confidence in the revolutionary spirit of the German socialists, and in these very debates about organization proposed them as a model for the Russians. Intuitively, the religious *élan* of the revolutionary intelligentsia had seen the way to dispose of historical materialism; intellectually, the same intelligentsia drew from the wealth of theory in the West. Instinctively, the enthusiasm of revolutionary ascetics who had consecrated their lives to the holy task found a way to use the workers as tools of their revolutionary impulse; intellectually, they justified it, in the most incoherent way, with the contention that only the professional revolutionaries of the intelligentsia could fight the fight of the proletariat. In fact, the proletariat was not admitted. The most outstanding personalities of the revolution of 1917 were Lenin, Trotsky, Sinoviev, Kameniev, Sverdlov, Smilga, Bukharin, Dzershinski, Stalin; there is not a single working man among them. A state of things inconceivable in the West.

This distinction was more correctly appreciated in the West than by Lenin himself. Until 1914 Lenin believed it his task simply to defend the ideas of revolutionary Marxism in Russia. His inconsistency was exposed by the acknowledged leader of the extreme left wing of Western socialism, by Rosa Luxemburg. This remarkable woman, a native of Warsaw, herself came from the East, but had found a second home in Germany and strongly shared the 'Western' conception of the labour movement held by the Mensheviks. In an article which appeared in 1904 in *Neue Zeit*, the theoretical review of the German Marxists, she protests against Lenin's idea of an organization of professional revolutionaries *linked* with the working classes. 'In fact,' she says, 'the Social-democratic Party is not *linked* with the organizations of the working class, it is itself the movement of the working class.' She goes on to demonstrate the bureaucratic tendencies inherent in Lenin's conception, speaking prophetically of the inevitable strangling of individual initiative in such an organization, and pointing out clearly that bureaucracy can just as easily work against as for revolution. In a footnote she adds a shrewd observation: the Webbs too, she says, favour bureaucratic as against democratic organization within the British trade unions. She was the first to discover between the views of the Bolsheviks and of the Webbs an analogy which was to evolve into very

45

active sympathy as soon as Bolshevism had ceased to be revolutionary. At the time when Rosa Luxemburg wrote, in 1904, the observation seemed rather beside the point. But she goes on to conclude, against Lenin, against the Webbs, and, in general, against labour bureaucracy: 'The one personality which can now lead [the working-class movement] is the mass-ego of the proletariat itself, which insists with all its force on committing its own mistakes and learning historical dialectics through its own experience. And finally let us speak openly within our own circle: mistakes committed by a really revolutionary working-class movement are historically infinitely more fertile and valuable than the infallibility of the very best "central committee".' The only trouble was that this 'really revolutionary working-class movement' in which she believed did not exist. It was this deep truth which Lenin had found out, intuitively. And the problem which became more urgent every day was this: without a revolutionary movement not only the socialist revolution would never come, but not even the overthrow of Tsarism. There was no revolutionary bourgeoisie in Russia. There had never been, in any country, a proletariat revolutionary on its own account. Lenin rightly scented that it would be no different in Russia. He discovered the solution of the problem: a revolution *made* by the masses, but *led* by professional revolutionaries. This presupposed, of course, that the masses would allow themselves to be led. The masses in the West would not, but in Russia they were full of a religious readiness to believe and to follow, and the existence of groups of professional revolutionaries provided the leadership.

Who was this young man who, at the age of thirty-three, had defied all the basic concepts of the pundits of orthodox Marxism and got away with it? We must devote a few words to him, as man, as leader, and as thinker. Little is to be said about the first. In contrast with most of the professional revolutionaries, he was an essentially normal, well-balanced personality. The fearful shock of his youth, the execution of the brother who had attempted to assassinate the Tsar, had matured him before his time, and deprived him of that *joie de vivre* which ordinarily goes with youth, but it had not deflected him. He was orderly, and hated the long and useless discussions so characteristic of the average young Russian. He preferred to spend his leisure time in recreations such as skating and hunting. Otherwise he was completely identified with his work. He was a loyal, affectionate, and faithful husband; his wife was the general secretary of the party. He never had a friend who was not at the same time a close political associate. This is perhaps the secret of his immense success as a leader of men: they did not count for him outside politics, and his treatment of other human beings was never influenced by any purely personal impulse. His life was his work: he followed the path of his resolve slowly, without impetuosity, but with iron determination. He soon acquired the conviction that he alone could lead along this path; that all the others were lacking, not so much in insight as in determination and steadiness of purpose. His methodical ways and singleness of purpose were the only really un-Russian things about this greatest of Russians.

The peculiar character of his greatness has unfortunately been obliterated by the uncritical worship the communists offer him as their god. Theologians always found it difficult to define God by any but negative attributes; the figure of a living man with a very peculiar approach to things, his strong and his weak points, disappears behind a Byzantine ikon, a Byzantine mausoleum, and a Byzantine hair-splitting inter-pretation of his texts. Worst of all, his followers claim infalli-bility for his utterances. Yet greatness cannot be understood without the foil of shortcomings which it has overcome.

The main outlines of Lenin's political personality are trans-parent at the very moment when, by splitting the Social-democratic Party over the problem of organization and forming his own 'bolshevik' group, he enters the historical stage, in 1903. All his activities are as if stretched between two extremes: Russia and his political instinct on the one hand, the West and his theoretical convictions on the other. In matters of Russian practice he was the most independent and the most clear-sighted of men. He has often been accused of oppor-tunism, and rightly so, in so far as he utterly disregarded the main items of his own Marxist creed when expediency demanded. But this mastery of practical Russian politics is strangely contrasted with his dependence on the views and opinions of second-rate theoreticians as often as matters of general Marxist principle were concerned.

47

In this, he was an incarnation of the Russian revolutionary movement. Two things were clear to him: he must achieve the victory for his organization of professional revolutionaries, and he must bring it about by '*the* revolution', the old aim of the revolutionary intelligentsia. Tsarism, landlordism, and the bureaucracy must be overthrown. But when it came to positive creation ideas become vague, shifting, changing. It is a strange thing that in a revolution the last thing settled should be its aim; that means should be constant, but aims be variable according to circumstances. Yet this was the case with the whole Russian revolutionary movement, whose highest expression is Bolshevism. In a Western country it would be unthinkable for a party first to aim at a democratic revolution, only to destroy, a few years later, democracy itself and to carry out what had been shortly before rejected, namely a socialist revolution. Yet such is the precise history of Bolshevism between 1903 and 1917.

Thus, to repeat, the aim, however defined—and definitions of the aim change repeatedly—remains in reality vaguely '*the* revolution'. But precisely because it is so vague, abstract formulae acquire an enormous importance. In his concrete actions Lenin did not care in the least for the established theories; he remoulded for the purpose what had been the accepted teachings of international Marxism, and in doing so did not shrink from overthrowing one day what he had established the day before. It would be easy to give many instances, but this is not a history of the Russian revolution. Contrasted with this vagueness of ultimate aims and with this pragmatism of practical views stands a religious belief in certain basic items of 'Marxism'. The deeper the revolutionary upheaval, the more uncertain the way ahead, the greater the desire for a fixed point at which to make a stand. It is this fixed belief in formulae such as 'historical materialism', 'dictatorship of the proletariat', and many others which gave Lenin the necessary certainty and steadfastness in his shifting practical actions. The strangeness and the interest of the personality lie encompassed in this queer contrast between ruthless practical opportunism and religious belief in the formulae of Marxist atheism and materialism.

The weakest and, at the same time, the most revealing

expression of this attitude is decidedly the big volume Lenin published about problems of philosophy, under the title *Materialism and Empirio-criticism*. Here Lenin attacks, with only the slightest knowledge and no understanding at all, the bulk of modern critical and sceptical thought as expressed by Henri Poincaré, Ernst Mach, Bertrand Russell, and all the others who have achieved the task of demonstrating the limitations of modern natural science. The work, as every other line written by Lenin, has been admired by his followers, but has, rightly, received no consideration outside the ranks of Bolshevism. Siegfried Marck, a German Marxist socialist, has expressed his regret at seeing the great politician 'walk, in matters of philosophy, on the roads of a narrow philistinism'. If we mention this work at all, it is because no other work reveals so clearly the negative aspect of Lenin's personality, his limitations, his incapacity to deal with matters of abstract theory. No other work reveals so clearly his pragmatism, his desire to subordinate generalizations to narrow immediate practical aims. At bottom, he is not interested in natural science at all, which is hardly a reproach for a great statesman. If he dealt with it, nevertheless, it was because he saw the purity of his religious faith in danger. Criticism and scepticism, he contends, open the door to 'fideism'—a monster-word which he applies instead of religion. If we do not know that the world consists wholly of matter, that space and time are realities, how then can we deny the existence of God? Therefore a Marxist must be a philosophical materialist; otherwise he could never be safe from faith, and, thus insecure, would fall into the snares of Christianity. That which makes the work so important is Lenin's complete unawareness of the fact that he himself, with his absolute belief in materialism, is just as religious as those 'fideists', in other words those Christians, whom he fights, and much nearer, in psychology and method, to an Eastern ascetic than to the thorough religious indifference of a Poincaré or a Mach; he does not even suspect the paradox and defends materialism with the fury of an inquisitor.

This attitude extends into politics. Together with the religious reverence for materialism and Marxism went the adoration of the representatives of the true dispensation on earth. This admiration for the Western Marxists has played Lenin more than one trick, and it is the more remarkable because his reverence was spent on men who, without one single exception, were his inferiors in every respect. Two cases are particularly interesting. The one concerns G. V. Plekhanov, the man who had first introduced Marxism in its original form into Russia. Plekhanov had published a number of studies on philosophy which, though one-sided, are probably superior to Lenin's work; as a politician he was of no account. He ended as an extreme partisan of Menshevism, openly fighting Lenin. Nevertheless Lenin kept a particular admiration for this man during all his life; he had brought Marxism to Russia! But the case of Karl Kautsky, the official theoretical mouthpiece of German Marxism, is much more remarkable. Anyone who takes the trouble to collect the quotations concerning Kautsky in Lenin's pre-war writings will soon be convinced that Lenin regarded this man as no less than an oracle. Kautsky, it is true, was the delight of that German Marxist left wing which so miserably collapsed in 1914 and after. This was no reason for Lenin to admire him, yet he did. For Lenin believed as firmly in the German socialists as in Kautsky. The latter was a man timid and slow in politics, wooden and unoriginal in theory, true to the type of philistine who would appear a theoretician. A few mocking remarks about him survive in the correspondence of Marx and Engels. As to the German Socialist Party, which Kautsky represented, Lenin trusted it so firmly that when, in 1914, he learnt of their voting for the war credits he first believed it to be a forgery of the German Foreign Office. Thus, in Lenin's mind, implicit adherence to a sacrosanct faith implied reverence for the community of the believers and the chief prophets of the faith on earth. It is obvious that here the articles of the faith of the Russian Church have been reversed, but the religious attitude with all its paraphernalia remained.

Naïve religious beliefs are a strong and a constructive force in history, even when spent upon a negative faith of destruction of the old, without a clear conception of what to put in its place. This religious belief, this implicit acceptance of Marxism, not as a method of research but as a creed, responded to an urgent practical necessity. Without it, Lenin might have been a better student of social problems; but without this firm conviction he could not have been the man with an iron will and a single purpose, '*the* revolution'. Again, in this narrow dedication of everything to one single aim, the true religious fanaticism of an early civilization reveals itself, a mentality which, if realized in its true character, can only provoke among men of the West the wonder which the early Christians provoked among the Greeks. It is no less a tremendous practical force for all its intellectual limitations. An attitude such as Lenin's was felt by the Mensheviks to be the attitude of a narrow fanatic who did not understand the world; one of the Menshevik leaders, Potressov, in an article published in 1927, recalls the surprise he felt when he first listened to Lenin and saw so much intelligence and concentration of will deformed—as Potressov saw it—by so much rigidity and heresy-hunting. And in fact, an attitude such as Lenin's might have been the attitude of a narrow fanatic, bound to break his head against a pitiless world. Such an attitude must become entirely out of place in a Western milieu profoundly resistant to both the naïveté and the enthusiasm upon which it is founded. But, in Russia, this is not inevitable. The limitations of outlook and understanding made themselves felt most strongly in matters of abstract belief and in matters concerning the West, which, for Lenin, this truest of all Russians, remained a book with seven seals, as it did for Tolstoy and Dostoevski. On his native Russian soil his naïveté and fanaticism hampered Lenin as little as it had hampered Mohammed to be, at the same time, a visionary and the shrewdest politician. On the contrary, inconsistencies and adaptations which would have broken the resolution of any less deeply convinced man did not distress Lenin: he could take every liberty with the principles he confessed because something much deeper than intellectual formulae guaranteed him against becoming what he called a 'traitor', against losing sight of the ultimate aim, '*the* revolution'.

It is, unfortunately, impossible to write the history of a religion without writing the history of its dogma. This makes our subject more complex, but it is inevitable continually to have to confront reality with theory in a movement such as Bolshevism. We saw the first clash between the two emerge when Lenin, in 1903, split the Social-democratic Party and founded

Bolshevism. Without a moment's hesitation, he sacrificed the basic article of Marxism, the belief in the revolutionary capacities of the proletariat, to the practical necessity of forming a party of really reliable professional revolutionaries.

This first spectacular step was soon followed by another, which finally and definitely separated Bolshevism from the Marxism of Marx himself. One of the basic convictions of Marx was that the proletarian revolution could only come when the proletariat had become by far the strongest class of society; this it would become by the gradual destruction of all small owners, primarily the peasants, through competition. The peasant problem had considerably exerted the minds of the German socialists. The right wing in accordance with experience contended that the peasantry was not prepared either to disappear or to become revolutionary, and that, in consequence, the socialists, as practical politicians, must try to come to an alliance with this important social group on its own terms. To this Kautsky and the other advocates of orthodoxy opposed the teaching of pure Marxism: the party of the revolutionary proletariat cannot win over the small proprietors, least of all the peasants, before they are at the brink of destruction; but their ultimate destruction will come, by the inexorable laws of the superiority of large-scale agriculture over small-scale agriculture. Lenin, during his early years, and up to the end of the Russian revolution of 1905, had defended this view. But when, in 1907, he had returned to exile and started considering the teachings of the revolutionary years, he saw that the inadequacy of peasant support had been one of the chief reasons for the failure of the revolution. He decided that the peasant would be ready to co-operate only on his own terms, which were summed up in the redistribution of the land of the aristocracy and the Church. This, in the eyes of all orthodox Marxists, was an abomination. To parcel large estates into small ones? Go back from the more progressive form of large-scale agriculture to peasant ownership? Establish, instead of a revolutionary agricultural proletariat, a property-minded satisfied peasantry? Delay the success of socialism for an incalculable period, for the mere sake of immediate advantages in the course of a bourgeois revolution? And, in fact, when Lenin decided that the peasant must be granted the landlords' land, he turned his back on every chance of a socialist revolution, which brought him into conflict, not only with Trotsky but even with the Mensheviks. But he alone, practical genius as he was, saw instinctively, and in spite of the views of his heroes, of Marx, Kautsky, and the German socialists, that without 'The land to the peasant!' no revolution was possible in Russia, not even a bourgeois one. Later on, with that lack of discrimination between the West and Russia which he always showed, he tried to transfer the same policy to the West, where it proved to be a miserable failure.

The next important step was the extension of the schism from Russia to the world. This happened in 1914, when, all over the world, the socialists joined their respective governments in the defence of their countries. The study of Lenin's attitude in this crisis must be reserved for a later chapter. We note here only that he took revenge for his own illusions upon Karl Kautsky, upon whom, from 1914 till his death, Lenin poured more abuse than upon any other single adversary; which means much, in view of the unscrupulous forms of abuse which Lenin, as other fanatics, consistently used in his polemics. In fact Kautsky had been more reserved in his patriotism than most outstanding Western socialists, and his attitude was of very little practical account. But for Lenin he had been the prophet of the true faith and he never forgot his 'betrayal'. The chancellery of the Kaiser knew the German socialists and had little fear that they would refuse to help in fighting the war. Lenin, however, had believed words which, for him, had been articles of faith, and for others nothing but formulae easily abandoned at a decisive juncture. He saw a complete reversal of policy where, in reality, a policy followed from the beginning had only become a little more articulate in an hour of emergency.

From this day onwards Lenin waited for the revolution; not only the Russian but the international revolution, which should issue from the war. It came, in Russia, without the direct intervention of either himself or his party. But it produced the biggest shifting of policy he had ever effected, a change which made Bolshevism into what it is to-day. When, in March 1917, the Tsar was overthrown all parties united in the task of national defence. This meant that the landlords kept their land and the peasants' claims were deferred *ad kalendas Graecas*; it meant, therefore, that the old social régime would continue, and that there was a big chance of reversion to the autocracy of the Tsar after a time; it meant, finally, that Russia, involved in war, could not give the signal for an international revolution. There seemed to be no escape from this situation. All Russia, with the one exception of Lenin's own party, was pledged to the policy of national defence. His own Russian lieutenants, with Stalin and Kameniev at their head, had joined in it. Democratic elections would most certainly defeat his policy. Yet democracy had been the aim of the masses and had hitherto been the ideal of every Marxist. Lenin, at a stroke, decided that if this went on '*the* revolution' would be lost. And, with a stroke, on his return to Russia in April 1917 he reversed the whole policy of the party and his own previous theories.

The central point of his policy was to carry through the revolution, which could not be effected by means of democracy, by breaking democracy. There is no sign that he had ever dreamed of that before. Certainly it shocked all the established ideas of Marxism about the matter. To-day, when through Lenin's success we have acquired the habit of associating revolutionary Marxism with the 'Soviet' system, it is difficult to realize the depth of the democratic convictions of pre-war revolutionary Marxists. In 1871, after the Franco-German War, the Paris proletariat had risen and established a sort of independent republic, the Commune, which had fallen after a heroic struggle. It had been an entirely democratic régime, based upon general suffrage, a variety of parties, the liberty of the Press and of association, even of the adversaries of the Commune. This régime Marx had exalted as the truest form of a proletarian dictatorship, and Engels, commenting upon Marx's vindication of the Commune, had proclaimed that absolute democracy was the natural form of the dictatorship of the proletariat. This tradition, perhaps the deepest of all among Western Marxists, Lenin now attacked. And still another doctrinal difficulty was implied in the change of policy. It was impossible to conceive a bourgeois revolution otherwise than in the establishing of a democratic régime; and that the Russian revolution must be a bourgeois revolution Lenin had always maintained, against both Trotsky and the

socialist revolutionaries. If he was going to overthrow democracy, he must at the same time allow the workers to establish
their own rule.

In order to establish the dictatorship of the Bolshevik Party
a broader institution than the party itself was necessary. Such
an institution was provided by the Soviets. These representative bodies of the factories and—during the war—of the regi-
ments had first appeared in 1905, when they had been led by
Leon Trotsky. Lenin at that time had rejected the Soviets, a
fact never contested but carefully forgotten by the official
historians of the Bolshevik Party. Lenin was a 'narrow one'.
He saw in the Soviets, as in any other mass organization, the
danger that the masses, left to their own instincts, would
escape the control of the professional revolutionaries and fall
into opportunism. But he had thought better of it when, after
1905, he considered the reasons for the defeat of the Bolsheviks.
Now the Soviets were the one instrument to be opposed to
democracy. It was only natural that Leon Trotsky, their traditional leader and the old champion of a proletarian revolution,
should now come over to Lenin.

Lenin could not make the decisive step without finding a
theoretical justification for it in a text of Marx. Thus, during
the very days before the final rising he sat down and consulted
his holy books, just as Cromwell and his officers, before first
purging, and then dissolving, the Long Parliament, had consulted the Bible. But in the case of Lenin it was very difficult to
find scriptural evidence. He had to twist Marx's writings about
the dictatorship of the proletariat, which all insisted upon the
democratic form of this dictatorship, until they covered the
overthrow of democracy by the Soviets. The latter, Lenin
contended, being elected directly by the toilers themselves,
directly dependent upon them, combining legislative and
administrative activities, excluding all the exploiters and
suppressing them with the help of the armed workers, were
the one real democratic institution which, at the same time,
embodied the dictatorship of the proletariat. But history has a
taste for the ironical in moments of decision. The rising of the
Bolsheviks on the 7th November 1917 was the prelude to
tremendous achievements. Only the one achievement which
Lenin had regarded as essential, the Soviet régime, never came

into being. This was not, as Trotsky would to-day like to represent it, a result of the 'degeneration' of the dictatorship of Lenin, after Lenin's death. It was the direct result of Lenin and Trotsky's own doings. From the first day of the Bolshevik revolution the Soviets lost power to the dictatorship of the party. They lost all practical importance when all parties but the Bolsheviks themselves were driven underground and the Soviets, instead of expressing anybody's opinion, became mere administrators.

Here as in most other respects, the results stood in a supremely paradoxical relation to Lenin's expectations and theoretical assumptions. He had set out with the aim of creating a revolutionary working-class movement, and had achieved a party of professional revolutionaries, under his own personal orders, strictly differentiated from the real proletariat, ready to dominate the workers as well as every other class. He had intended to establish a revolutionary democracy, but when, in March 1917, democracy came it proved to be unrevolutionary. He then turned to the establishment of a 'Soviet democracy' and a 'proletarian dictatorship' which was to set out to build socialism. The state he created was neither democratic nor Soviet, but simply a state of a totalitarian bureaucracy. To discuss whether he achieved at least his aim of 1917, a régime primarily based upon the proletariat, is beyond the scope of this book; the present chapter aims only at outlining certain features which have become important for the international policy of Bolshevism. In matters of economic and social policy, the 'Soviet' Union has been just as shifting as in any other respect. It has attempted to destroy all classes; a few years later it has reinstated the peasant and the merchant in their rights; it has abolished these rights a second time, with the Five Year Plan, and then again shifted to new formulae. Why, after all, should a totalitarian bureaucracy link its fate finally and definitely to any one single class? But in the West, to which we now return, Bolshevism was confronted with the problems of real class movements of the workers.

CHAPTER IV

LABOUR IN THE WAR

The outbreak of the war led to the immediate dissolution of the Western version of revolutionary Marxism. And the breakdown was all the more significant of weakness because the war did not take the Marxists by surprise. The congresses of the 'Second International', which linked most of the labour organizations formed all over the world on a class basis, had for a couple of years discussed the imminence of war, the fight against the danger of war and the measures to be taken in case the war should come despite the opposition of labour. On this question, as on many another, the left held more international congresses than the right; in 1907, at the international congress at Stuttgart, a considerable majority had voted an amendment moved by Lenin and Rosa Luxemburg to the effect that socialists must regard a war as a big opportunity to prepare and carry through the overthrow of the bourgeoisie.

But almost the very moment war broke out, all these declarations were forgotten. They had been nothing but verbiage, like most of Western revolutionary Marxism; it was always easy to vote for a revolution. It was a different thing to carry it through. The shallowness of those declarations had been more or less realized in the chancelleries of Europe, and no government was very much concerned about the chances of revolutionary activities in the first days of the war. The socialists had lived in a realm of imagination, and were surprised to see that they themselves were different from what they had believed themselves to be.

The swift *volte-face* of socialism all over the world was determined by a variety of causes, some of them of an international, others of a purely national character. But the main cause was undoubtedly the wave of patriotism which swept through all the belligerent countries, and maintained its sway over the masses, till the end in the victorious countries, and almost till the end among the defeated. This wave of patriotic enthusiasm overrode at once the border-lines of party convictions, showing that political passions and interests in this our world are still most deeply aroused not by the international antagonism between class and class, but by the antagonism between nation and nation.

Looking back upon those days, old Karl Kautsky, in a voluminous study of *War and Socialism* which has recently appeared in German, insists upon the fact that this patriotic current was much stronger among the masses than among their leaders. Some of the latter have left moving accounts of the conflict of conscience which the outbreak of war brought to them, when it put before them the choice between the patriotic loyalties which, as they suddenly discovered, were not dead in their hearts, and their previous revolutionary convictions. In later days the communists never mentioned these events without speaking of the 'betrayal' of the Social-democratic and Labour Parties. It can be contended, reasonably, that both leaders and masses 'betrayed' the ideals of revolutionary socialism; the charge, however, that the leaders betrayed the masses is meaningless. The leaders did exactly what the masses wanted and, had they acted otherwise, would have found no mass support. Those few convinced revolutionary socialists who, from the first day onwards, tried to stem the tide, had a tale to tell of how they met, not only lack of understanding, but actual hatred among the masses on account of their anti-patriotic attempts. In the early months of the war those few remaining revolutionaries explained this to themselves as an effect of the surprise evoked by the outbreak of the war. But the masses had four years in which to reconsider the position, and there was no fundamental change. Enthusiasm naturally abated with the long duration of the war and all the sufferings it entailed, but a very considerable amount of patriotic loyalty—or, in the language of the revolutionaries, 'betrayal of socialism and revolution'—remained till the end; though to a lesser degree in the defeated than in the victorious countries. The revolutionary proletariat proved to be a myth.

There were other important arguments for a policy of national union in those days. Undoubtedly, serious attempts to thwart military operations would have brought the heavy hand of the state upon the labour organizations. And for that the latter were absolutely unprepared. They had never done anything except form and extend open mass organizations, and those were the only organizations adapted to forward the primary aim of the movement: the fight for the day-to-day interests of the workers. An underground organization would have been the right thing for preparing a revolution; but that would have meant abandonment of the old objective, the old achievements, and the old leadership. So there could be no question of that. Thus the Labour and Socialist Parties had only the choice between a policy of active support of the war or of passive, sulking abstention. It was only natural that the former prevailed at a moment when passivity of any sort very naturally held no attractions.

The loyalty to their organizations felt by both leaders and masses of the working class was a result of the enormous improvements those organizations had obtained for their adherents through decades of struggle. If these organizations were to be destroyed by the police, those gains would be seriously menaced. If the nation were defeated they would be completely lost. Both considerations argued in favour of a policy of national union, and men's interests joined with their deep-rooted instinctive loyalties to make that the only possible policy. Lenin, who hated it, was the first to point out that there was only one serious alternative: to wish and work for the defeat of one's own country. But this could only have been done had Marx's saying been true, that 'the workers have no fatherland'. And it could only be true where conditions were so intolerable as to make national defeat preferable to the continuation of the existing political régime. In some degree that was true of Russia, but nowhere else.

There were, moreover, individual national considerations in every single country. Belgium and France were clearly forced into a position of national defence. Whatever the responsibility of French finance for the tension which had led to war—it was

this 'imperialistic character of the war' which constituted the
chief argument of the out-and-out revolutionaries—a victory of
Germany over France would have meant the victory of autocracy over democracy. Similar arguments applied to England.
In Germany and Austria, on the other hand, it was the victory
of Tsarism which was feared by the labour movement. Only in
Russia did the socialists find it difficult to back up their
patriotism with arguments taken from the relatively progressive
character of their government compared with the government
of their enemies; but Russia was the ally of the Western democracies and this, by the patriotic section of Russian socialists,
was regarded as decisive.

The decision to help in the defence of the fatherland was not
incompatible with a sincere desire and earnest attempts to
make peace again at the first opportunity, even if further loss
of life might lead to better peace conditions for one's own side.
Even a big success was likely to cost too much to make the
spoils worth while to the working class; they were mainly
interested in the defence of home and country. Here ran a real,
not an idealist, line of division between the labour parties and
the extremists of war to the bitter end. This, during the latter
part of the war, made the French socialists join hands with
Briand against Clemenceau; the German socialists join hands
with Catholics and democrats against Ludendorff. But all that
mattered very little to those who, before the war, had been
revolutionary Marxists and had entirely dropped their old
convictions when they were converted to patriotism. For them
it was an axiom that any hope of mitigating national antagonisms within the capitalist system was useless. The revolutionary Marxists had been convinced that if there was no
socialist revolution the imperialist antagonisms would inevitably be fought out to the bitter end. Now those who refused to
believe that this was the hour of the socialist revolution were
inclined to think that the wailing for a speedy peace was bunk,
and that the business must be carried through. And the result
was that those who, before the war, had been regarded as
revolutionaries, were much more patriotic now, on the average,
than those who had been classified as the 'right' wing, as
reformists. Those reformists had never refused to be regarded
as patriots, but at the same time they *had* refused to be

'historical materialists'; they had humanitarian ideals, and the horrors of the war, which the Marxists were inclined to regard as a simple historical necessity, were an indescribable ordeal for them.

The old lines of division were not simply controverted; they broke down. People who had been in opposite camps suddenly found themselves in the same camp; people who had been in the same camp suddenly found an abyss between them. But the general trend was for the revolutionary Marxists to go to the right and become ultra-patriotic, while numbers of the 'reformists' remained pacifist. In England the small Marxist 'Social-democratic Federation' lined up for the war, although this produced a split; but Hyndman disregarded the split and held to his patriotic position. On the other hand those who, within the labour movement, stood nearest to liberalism, men like Philip Snowden and Ramsay Macdonald, stood up against the war. In France, Guesde, the official leader of French Marxism and a staunch fighter against 'reformism', joined the cabinet almost immediately after war was declared. Jaurès, however, a reformist who had never denied that he was a patriotic democratic Frenchman, was regarded as being so dangerous a person in time of war that he was murdered; the murderer remained untried during the war, which proved that Jaurès had been regarded as dangerous by many, and not only by one excited individual. In Russia there were few non-Marxists within the social-democratic movement, and arguments there followed a different line; but the main outlines of division were the same. Plekhanov, the founder and head of Russian Marxism, became a passionate 'social-patriot', as Lenin used to call him. The man who had been regarded as the chief brain of the moderate wing, Paul Axelrod, and his chief pupil, Julius Martov, both came out against the war. In Germany the antagonisms were somewhat less sharply outlined. Kautsky, the official head of Marxism, did not fully join the patriots; it must not be forgotten, in this context, that he himself was not a German but an Austrian. But most of the other leading Marxists, Lensch, Cunow, Haenisch, did so, and became violent champions of the extreme right of the party. On the other hand Eduard Bernstein, the head and founder of 'revisionism', the German version of anti-Marxism within the labour movement, very soon joined the adversaries of the war. In the Czechoslovak labour movement inside Austria Šmeral, the head of the left wing, became an eager defender of the Hapsburgs; Tusar and most of the other moderate socialists joined the national revolutionary movement which stood for separation from Austria. The division does not apply, however, to the German labour movement in Austria, to Italy, to the Balkans, and to the neutral countries, which we shall shortly consider.

The arguments in favour of peace as against war carried special weight in those countries which might conceivably have remained outside altogether. In the first place, this applied to England. Here, a certain section of liberal opinion contended that it would have been possible to remain neutral. This was the view which was accepted by Snowden and Macdonald and was the basis of the opposition of the majority of the I.L.P. to the war.

The argument carried more weight the later a country joined in the struggle. Japanese socialism was of no account; in Turkey, too, there did not exist a socialist party worth speaking of. But there was a serious labour movement in Bulgaria. This movement had split, at an incipient stage of its development, in 1903, on the same lines as the Russian. Later official communist sources are inclined to minimize, to a certain extent, the importance of this split, contending that the Bulgarian left only sided with Kautsky and not with Lenin. But as Lenin then himself sided with Kautsky, that does not matter. The Bulgarian left, in 1903, espoused just that idea of a narrow, pure organization of revolutionaries which was at the core of Lenin's policy. But in Bulgaria the split had effects different from those it had in Russia. The police régime in Bulgaria was not a mild one, yet political liberty was considerable, and the problems that make for 'bourgeois' revolution were non-existent, as the landlords had mostly been Turks, who were driven out at the time of the liberation, after 1879. Intellectually, Bulgaria and the Bulgarian labour movement was deeply influenced by Russia, but its practical problems were relatively nearer to those of the West. The Bulgarian left, whose members called themselves proudly 'the narrow ones' (Tesnyaki), was heavily defeated by the right wing, 'the broad-minded ones'. The latter won a splendid electoral success after the defeat of Bulgaria in the second Balkan War, in 1913. But this success proved to be unstable. In 1915, part of the socialist right took sides with the war party; the socialist left stood up against the war like one man. It was not isolated in this, but its views were shared by the Peasant Party and its chief, Stambuliiski, the leader of Bulgaria in later years. Anyway, the participation of the right-wing socialists in a war policy which was to prove so disastrous for Bulgaria was the starting-point of a swift rise of the forces of the anti-war faction of the Tesnyaki. Be it noted that in this as in other matters, close contacts, both personal and political, always existed between the Bulgarian left and the Bolsheviks. Blagoyev, the founder and leader of the Tesnyaki, had studied in Russia, and there, as a young man, participated in Narodnaya Volya first, and afterwards in the earliest Marxist circles. The contact was indeed of the closest.

The anti-war policy of the Bulgarian Tesnyaki was not determined by the fact that Bulgaria joined in the war at a relatively late stage; but this fact—the fact that quite obviously Bulgaria need not have joined, or, at least, need not have joined on the side of the Germans—brought the Tesnyaki a good deal of the mass support they had during the war. In Serbia it was a different matter. The weak Socialist Party of Serbia was deeply under the influence of both the Bulgarian and the Russian left. If there was one country in the world which had been violated, and was fighting for its existence, it was Serbia. Nevertheless, the two Serbian socialists in the Skupstshina, the Serbian chamber, voted at the outbreak of the war against the credits, being the only socialists outside England who did so in August 1914. But the result was very different from what it had been in Bulgaria. The Serbian socialists found no support among the masses, and when, in autumn 1915, their country fought its death struggle against the invaders, the Serbian socialists turned round and supported the government.

There was as yet hardly any working-class movement noticeable in Greece. The Roumanian movement too was weak. Both, at the outbreak of the war, began to oppose it as best they could. The Roumanian party was intellectually dominated by the powerful personality of Christian Rakowsky, who was a standard-bearer of Russian influence.

We have had to linger so long over these rather obscure Balkan movements because they played a considerable part in the foundation of the Communist International. It will have become apparent by now that they did not really belong to the sphere of thought and method of the Western labour movement. They were, partly at least, derivatives of the Russian revolutionary movement.

In Italy it was different again. Italy belonged emphatically to the West, though its labour movement always had many peculiar features and was, in fact, probably more revolutionary than any other Western movement with the exception of Spanish anarchism. Anyway, the Italians had just had an experience in the conduct of affairs in war-time through the Libyan campaign of 1911. On that occasion the party had split and a minority of pro-war socialists had been excluded. Moreover, in Italy there was a very big current among the 'bourgeois' parties against the war. Nevertheless the party split a second time, and Mussolini with a few followers left it in order to promote the movement for joining in the war. A French socialist who had been a left-winger, Marcel Cachin, was operative in bringing about the split; he went to Italy, as an agent of the French Government, and helped Mussolini to set up his new paper, the *Popolo d'Italia*. 'Habent sua fata libelli ... atque homines'; Marcel Cachin, in later years, became a leading French communist.

Apart from these minor divisions, the Italian Socialist Party went through the war unabashed. Together with parties of the 'bourgeois' left, it opposed it from beginning to end. Certainly its attitude was very moderate: 'Neither support nor sabotage the war' was the slogan. The big defeat of Caporetto in November 1917, which brought the country to the brink of ruin, somewhat shook this altogether philosophical attitude, and Filippo Turati, the leader of the right wing, made a speech in the Chamber promising the help of the socialists in a national emergency. But then the horizon brightened again, and the incident was forgotten. There were mass movements against the war, however, especially in 1918, and a number of people were killed in riots in Turin. But that was not a matter of party policy; it was mainly a spontaneous outbreak.

In the United States, finally, socialism had been very weak, but it grew considerably during the first years of the war. The Socialist Party, naturally, stood for peace, as long as there was peace; it continued to stand for peace when war had been declared. This produced a minor split, certain leaders following Wilson, the war-maker, as they had followed him when he stood for peace. But it was not an important split. The party fought the war with a considerable amount of vigour, which was only natural. More than half its membership was not of American but of eastern and southern European origin and shared in the radicalism of the socialist parties of their fatherland. Besides, in the Far West the influence of the syndicalist I.W.W., which had always been under strong anarchist influence, made itself felt. Eugene Debs, the leader of the Socialist Party, went to jail for his anti-war activities; after victory the country was swept by a fierce reaction against the 'Reds'.

If we combined in one broad picture all the varying shades and details of activity just described, we might say that in the countries which entered into the war immediately, socialism entirely renounced its distinctive policy. Outside England and Serbia not a single vote was cast in any parliament against the declaration of war. Even in Russia not only the Mensheviks but even the Bolsheviks—to Lenin's fury and despair—abstained from voting, instead of voting against, the war credits. Small minorities within the party, from the beginning onwards, worked for peace, but at first in an unobtrusive way. Socialist opposition was much stronger within those countries which entered the war at a later stage. Then it was not isolated, and in almost all those countries where there was time to make a considered choice 'bourgeois' parties joined hands with the socialists in opposing the war. Generally speaking, opposition was the stronger, the later any particular country came into the war.

But the war influenced the neutrals too, and that deeply. At the end there were only six neutral countries left in Europe, and they must be considered one by one. The deepest movement, though the one least noticed abroad, was engendered by the war in Spain. Spain, like all other neutrals, did very well commercially during the war, and its industry expanded rapidly. Deeply rooted in the Spanish soil was the tradition of arch-revolutionary anarcho-syndicalism, which cannot be analysed in detail here. It gained strength through the difficulties and the moral shock of the war and through the increase in numbers of the working class. At the same time the bourgeoisie made a great effort to overthrow the corrupt and tottering *ancien régime*. The year 1917 saw a very big general strike, aiming, in fact, at the proclamation of a republic. This failed, but it opened a revolutionary period which is not yet at an end.

In two other neutral countries anarcho-syndicalism of a somewhat different kind developed. In Holland anarchism, with its insistence upon individualism and the value of small groups, had always had a strong footing. In fact, the oldest labour organization in Holland, the N.A.S. (Nationale Arbeider-Secretariat—National Workers' Secretariat) had been anarcho-syndicalist. But during the last two decades before the war the so-called 'modern' trade unions, which were social-democratic in programme and methods, had made headway, and anarcho-syndicalism was on the decline. Together with the 'modern' unions the Socialist Party had gained strength, in spite of a minor split in 1907. This split, which deprived the Socialist Party of only a few hundred members, was nevertheless to have a certain importance for the early history of the Communist International. For the party expelled consisted mainly of Marxist intellectuals, who had fought a fierce fight against the 'opportunism' of the official party, and of whom some had a standing in international socialism. Among them were Anton Pannekoek, dogmatic Marxist but above all an astronomer of international fame; Hermann Gorter, incontestably the leading figure in contemporary Dutch poetry; and Henriette Roland-Holst, one of the founders of the International Women's Socialist Movement. Before the war, this group had had very little importance. But now the war brought with it three things that worked havoc within the socialist and 'modern' trade-union movement: it brought big orders for Dutch industry, which meant a very strong position for the workers and high wages; but it also brought food shortage, and it brought mobilization. This, of course, was far from being a peculiarly Dutch situation. Everywhere the war brought the workers heavy sufferings and at the same time made them even more indispensable than in peace-time; a very peculiar position, because usually periods of good business mean higher real wages for the workers and in consequence less desire to use violence, while periods of bad business bring to bear the heavy pressure of unemployment and thus diminish the workers' fighting power. The war gave rise to a number of circumstances through which the working class won a degree of fighting power which it usually only holds during periods of good business, together with sufferings which usually only accompany periods of heavy industrial depression. Under this double pressure the peaceful tradition of the 'modern' unions broke down, and the small group of Marxist intellectuals made an unprincipled alliance with the anarcho-syndicalists of the N.A.S., whose membership rapidly rose again to fifty thousand; a very considerable number in a country like Holland. The revolutionary movement led to serious riots, culminating in the assumption of power by the workers' organizations in Rotterdam at the time of the armistice. For a few days the town was virtually under the dictatorship of Troelstra, the official leader of the Socialist Party, who personally had strong revolutionary leanings, although his party held to the constitutional creed. But the other socialist leaders interceded, demobilization was rapidly effected, the food situation improved, and the revolutionary movement faded out without leaving much trace behind.

Norway, too, came under the sway of anarcho-syndicalism. The Norwegian labour movement had scarcely existed before 1905, the year when Norway won its national freedom from Sweden; up till then the nation as a whole was preoccupied with the struggle for liberty. After that date the movement grew rapidly. At the same time Norway started on the road of a very rapid industrial development, and took mighty strides along that road during the war. Like every labour movement in its infancy, the Norwegian movement tended towards radicalism. The earlier national strife, with the sharp-shooters' corps as its main instrument, was still in everybody's memory when the war broke out. The individualism of a sparsely populated country with a strong protestant tradition contributed to the furtherance of anarchism. Norwegian anarcho-syndicalism differed from the Dutch and the Spanish versions in two main features: it shunned violence—in which it was truly Scandinavian—and believed in general strikes as the one effective means to bring about social revolution; and it never tried to destroy the old party and the old unions but rather attempted, successfully, to permeate them. At the head of the anarcho-syndicalist movement which first permeated the youth organizations of the party, then the unions, and finally the party itself, stood a young house-painter, Martin Tranmael, a man of quite unusual gifts. Within the narrow compass of a country of two and a half million inhabitants, he was perhaps not inferior to Jean Jaurès in France. A man of extraordinary purity of mind and habits, a passionate teetotaller and moralist, he was, at the same time, a brilliant speaker, a supremely able journalist, and a great organizer. His popularity among the Norwegian workers knew—and until this day knows—no bounds. During the war Tranmael and his group, starting from Bergen, first conquered the movement, and then led a series of big strikes and mutinous movements of the reservists (who had been called to arms) which culminated in the formation of soldiers' councils; a revolution seemed approaching when the armistice, here as elsewhere, caused the tension to abate. The Norwegian movement was also to contribute strongly to international communism.

In Sweden as in Norway, there existed a fairly strong anarcho-syndicalist movement besides the Socialist Party. But here the developments were different from those in Spain, Holland, and Norway. Those three, before the war, had not been very industrial countries, and the sudden industrialization under quite abnormal circumstances brought a strong ferment of unrest with it. In Sweden, however, industry had been strongly developed before the war; the workers' organizations were both old and strong, and the majority of the working class stood undoubtedly behind the Socialist Party, its leader, Hjalmar Branting, and his reformist-socialist policy. Branting, like the socialists of most neutral countries, and especially those of the right wing, sympathized with the Allies against Germany, seeing in the war a fight between democracy and autocracy. But Branting leaned more heavily towards the Allies than other socialist leaders in other countries, so as to make Swedish socialism almost a power standing for war. This, together with the common plight of all neutrals during the war—food shortage and mobilization—produced a split within the party. The left wing, altogether something like one-fifth of the total, seceded under the leadership of Lindhagen, the Mayor of Stockholm, and Zeth Hoeglund, who had been leader of the Socialist Youth Movement. Hoeglund, who was a member of the Second Chamber, carried on a violent and successful agitation against war and mobilization; he kept in close touch with the Russian Bolshevik Bukharin, who was living in Stockholm at that time. From this co-operation there resulted a number of important contacts between the Bolsheviks and the Scandinavian labour movement. But nothing like the movement in Spain, Holland, and Norway ensued in Sweden.

Denmark, being mainly agricultural, was in a better position as to food, and since it also lacked sharp social contrasts it remained relatively quiet. Yet on one occasion there occurred a certain amount of friction within the Socialist Party there. This occasion was itself rather remarkable. In Belgium, France, and England socialists joined the cabinet during the war in order to strengthen national defence. In Denmark this happened, for the first time in the history of international socialism (apart from the very peculiar case of Millerand in France in 1899), in a country which was in no particular emergency. It was a radical break with deeply ingrained traditions; but in the turmoil of the war it passed off without much difficulty, and the opposers were won over to the majority point of view after a few years. In Denmark communism never took any appreciable root; not even when, in later years, an authentic Graf Moltke took over the leadership of the small Communist Party. As to joining the Cabinet, Branting in Sweden soon followed the model of Stauning in Denmark.

Much more complicated was the position in the last of the neutral countries, Switzerland, which was sharply divided between German and French sympathies. The party there was mostly in the hands of the radicals, under the leadership of Naine in French and Grimm in German Switzerland. Both stood out against the war and for a very extremist policy. The Swiss were most active of all socialist parties in their attempts, soon to be described, at re-organizing the Socialist International, during the war, against the war. At home the movement, after many riots—Switzerland was particularly badly off for food—culminated, just as in Holland, in a big general strike at the time of the armistice. But the issues were ill defined; French Switzerland, which was in a paroxysm of joy over French victory, refused to follow the leaders, and the strike movement broke down in the general relaxation brought about by the armistice itself.

The factors which produced a general trend towards extremism within the labour movement of the neutral countries naturally worked with even greater strength among the belligerents. But there existed forces within the belligerent countries to balance these trends by antagonistic ones. The extremists in neutral countries did not feel that they jeopardized the future of their respective fatherlands. On the contrary, they felt proud of helping them to keep out of the war. It was the opposite among the belligerents. Here extremism worked clearly for defeat, an admittedly immediate evil whose promotion was regarded by public opinion as the worst of crimes. The belligerents suffered more heavily in every respect than the neutrals, but on the other hand anyone among them who took up a defeatist attitude or simply an attitude of indifference towards the result of the war incurred a far heavier responsibility. Not one but both scales were therefore more heavily weighted, which made for acrimony when opposite views were debated, and tremendous rackings of conscience for the individuals who had to make and act upon decisions unhappy either way.

Generally speaking most labour organizations, under the pressure of those seemingly interminable sufferings of the war, gradually came round to an anti-war policy. That was least the case in Belgium, for very natural reasons. Belgium was occupied by the Germans, who did not allow any political movement. What anti-war work was done in Belgium did not appear as such, because inevitably it was at the same time anti-German work. The leaders of the party were in exile. Vandervelde, leader of the Belgian Workers' Party, had joined the Cabinet at the outbreak of the war. The leaders of the orthodox Marxist wing, de Brouckère and de Man, heartily joined in his policy. No other policy, in fact, was imaginable in Belgium. The whole working class was swept by one fierce hatred, of Germany, and this went so far that for one whole year after the war the Belgian Workers' Party refused to participate in the reconstitution of the Socialist International because they did not want to sit at the same table as the German representatives. It was also as a result of the war that the Communist International could never gain ground in Belgium.

Developments were much more complex in France. Real defeatism was naturally unthinkable, but the peace movement grew strong in the latter years of the war, especially when Clemenceau's 'jusqu'au-boutisme', while undoubtedly saving France from war-weariness, created the impression that peace could have been had, if the government had been willing to seek it. The opposition was naturally strongest within the *Confédération générale de travail*, the French T.U.C. As is well known, French labour has had a very peculiar development. Trade unions and political parties there—of which there have at times been many—were always sharply divided, and, in contrast to the position in other countries, the trade unions were regarded as more radical than the political socialist movement. They were small organizations, formed mainly from the best-paid categories of workers who had a tremendous sense of their own importance, and were very much under anarcho-syndicalist influence. Outstanding chiefs of the C.G.T., such as Merrhein and Dumoulins, declared against the war in 1917. Opposition to the war within the party was much weaker. At the beginning of the war both right and left wing joined in the defence of the fatherland, and only at the end of 1916 did a very few deputies begin voting against war credits. There was no consequent split within the party. But with the ascendancy of Clemenceau and the sharp break between left and right in the Chamber, the socialists naturally sided with the left, and in the summer of 1918, when the worst danger was over, the majority of the Socialist Parliamentary Club decided in favour of voting against war credits: a decision which even the pro-war minority loyally put into effect. Characteristically, however, no attempt was made to make political capital out of the big army mutinies which followed the terrible failure of the Nivelle offensive in 1917. It was one thing to speak and to agitate against the war; a very different thing to attempt to break the front.

It would have been natural for the English labour movement to be much fiercer than the French in its opposition to the war. England was in less immediate danger than France and nothing like the almost terrorist régime of Clemenceau existed on this side of the Channel. Yet opposition to the war was actually much milder in the English than in the French labour movement. The original group of opposers centred round Ramsay Macdonald did not increase very much throughout the war. On the other hand representative leaders of the Labour Party, such as Arthur Henderson and J. H. Thomas, joined the Lloyd-George Cabinet. The difference is mostly to be explained by the difference of structure and tradition of the French and the English labour movements. In France, from 1793 onwards, there existed a strong revolutionary tradition; it was a tradition in which the ideals of social revolution and national defence were mingled and therefore, in part at least, it worked for and not against national unity. But all the same it gave a foothold to those who, within the labour movement, cherished revolutionary ideals. Moreover, the French labour organizations, being very weak, did not very directly express the feelings of the masses. In England, on the other hand, no revolutionary tradition existed; the masses felt themselves directly responsible for the fate of their country as it was—to a degree unknown in any other country. It was English democracy which, on this occasion, stood the test of national coherence. The group of 'conscientious objectors' in England was small.

Characteristically, things went another way in Scotland, with its rather different political complexion. In Scotland the tradition of religious radicalism which has dominated the history of the Scotch since the sixteenth century persisted within the labour movement, which therefore to a considerable extent opposed the war from an early date. It was typical of Scotland that there an industrial and a moral movement mingled. The latter, conscientious objection, was mainly directed against the un-English but inevitable measure of conscription. It was non-revolutionary, and largely religious in its inspiration. The other movement consisted of the 'shop-stewards', who won considerable allegiance on the Clyde. The shop-stewards were not so thoroughly pacifist as the conscientious objectors, and even sometimes talked of revolution. But in practice they were occupied much less with revolution than with a thoroughgoing defence of hours and wages, without concern for the wishes of the Ministry of Munitions. Lenin and the Russians, and at one time even certain of the shop-stewards themselves, believed that they were Soviets. In reality the institution of shop-stewards, in itself, is quite a normal development of trade-unionism. In many countries the trade unions organize shop-stewards as a regular part of their activities, and in some they have become legal institutions. In Scotland they emerged because the workers felt that their interests were not sufficiently safeguarded by the unions, whose officials were closely in touch with the Ministry of Munitions. The Scottish Shop-stewards were essentially a trade-unionist institution, though an unofficial one, and their real activity and achievements followed industrial rather than political lines. Their ideas were often indistinguishable from those of the conscientious objectors. But on occasion it happened that a very small and advanced group, the 'Socialist Labour Party', won influence in the movement. This S.L.P. had been organized under the influence of Irish revolutionaries, and James Conolly, who fell in the Easter rebellion in Dublin, had for a time been one of its leaders. Accordingly it was strongly revolutionary, tinged with anarcho-syndicalism, anti-parliamentarian—and very small. Gallacher expressed its main ideas within the shop-steward's movement, which, after all, was no more than a minor incident.

It can be said that, after all, the Western democracies stood the terrible test of the war surprisingly well. What movements of opposition there were kept within the limits of mild protest. And even those were not very widespread. It was quite a different matter with the autocracies, all of which broke down under the stress. The story of Russia has been given already. Detailed description of it may readily be found in many works of the highest merit; it is not a part of the subject-matter of this book. We must turn now to Germany, Austria, and Bulgaria.

There were two reasons why political affairs in these countries followed a course profoundly different from the course of politics within the countries of the Allies. First, the Central Powers suffered infinitely more, mostly through famine. These sufferings, in the end, became humanly unendurable. But secondly, the peoples of the Central Powers did not feel responsible for the fate of their countries, because they had never been allowed to feel any political responsibility. Bulgaria was not, in the proper sense of the word, an autocratic country; but there the people had been forced into the war against their manifest will. In Austria, the political situation varied enormously from province to province; in Hungary, Galicia, Bosnia, Croatia, and Dalmatia the government was actually a tyranny in some ways worse than that of the Tsar. In the German and Czech districts it was a civilized régime, though very incalculable, and continually wavering between weakness and ruthlessness. In Hungary the Magyars, the dominant race, for a long time accepted everything in order to keep their domination. The national minorities, Roumanians, Slovaks, Ruthenians, and others, hated not only the war but Hungary as such. Bosnia, too, hated Austria and Hungary deeply and wanted to become Serb. In Galicia the Poles ruled, and they hoped to make it the birthplace of a greater Poland; consequently they were patriotic; the Ukrainian minority was, from the start, mainly pro-Russian, and was treated accordingly. The Croats, in spite of their plight, remained faithful to the Hapsburgs, because they hated the Italians more than the Magyars. The Italian minorities in the south, and most of all the Czechs in Bohemia and Moravia, were violently disaffected, though they had been treated less harshly than other races. The Germans were to be counted upon, for a certain time. And all this muddle of national problems made the Austrian labour movement a tangle of wires which only the expert can, with considerable time and trouble, hope to unravel. In Germany, however, things were simple enough. There all the grievances which before the war had tended to make the socialist take an attitude of principled negation against the state, were felt even more acutely during the war. While the country was facing the whole world in an unequal struggle, the ruling military clique fostered wild plans of expansion, and the *de facto* autocracy of the régime deprived all other classes of any opportunity to make the weight of their opinions felt in decisions which involved the fate of the nation for decades at least. In Germany, therefore, political antagonisms became more acute every day, not only because the war brought tremendous sufferings, but because at the same time it raised with particular urgency the problems of democratization which, in Germany, had already been much too long delayed.

Everywhere within the territory of the Central Powers the revolutionary forces grew during the war. It was not—as it is usually represented in socialist literature—a proletarian movement. The peasantry, the lower middle classes, the bourgeoisie of the oppressed races, were just as eager to overthrow the existing régime, in fact, were often more eager than the proletariat. The forms through which this revolutionary movement expressed itself were very different, according to tradition and political situation. In Bulgaria it took the shape of a movement for a peasants' dictatorship. In Austria-Hungary it mostly merged with the movements for national liberation. In Germany it naturally ran within the compass of the old-style revolutionary Marxism. But even in Germany, as later events were to show, the masses really did not aim at anything but getting the decision about peace and war into their own hands.

Germany was the one country in the world where the war led to a complete split of the socialist movement. The starting-point of this split was the voting on war credits. In other countries, such as England and France, after a certain time the patriotic socialist majorities had tolerated the voting of the pacifist socialist minorities against war credits, without making it a ground for complete rupture. In Germany, when the pacifist dissentients came into the open at the end of 1915, it led to a schism within the party. Here again the difference between the labour movements of democratic and of autocratic countries became apparent. The discipline of the German socialists was largely modelled on the discipline of the Prussian army and the Prussian administration. In the democracies an open vote of a minority within the party against a majority view was, in itself, nothing unusual, least of all in France. In Germany a 'breach of discipline' within the Socialist Party was regarded as almost as criminal as the mutiny of soldiers against their superior officers. This conception of discipline was probably primarily responsible for the split. The responsibility, however, must also be attributed to two other important elements. The one was a rather deeply ingrained tradition of 'principled' abstention in politics. To vote the credits was, for most German socialists, an act just as dreadful as to break party discipline. The minority did the first, but the majority did the latter. Voting credits had always been the most natural thing in the world in the British labour movement and had been practised even by the majority of the French socialists occasionally at least. But when, in the last years before the war, a few socialists in southern German diets followed suit by voting their provincial budgets, a tremendous scandal ensued within the party. 'To *this* régime no man and no penny' ran one of the chief party slogans before the war. 'This' régime was the autocratic régime. Now the majority had 'betrayed' the workers to 'this' régime. And there existed, besides the heart-burnings of the dogmatic party militants who wanted to continue with their old drill, very real differences between the position in England and France on the one hand and that in Germany on the other. In both England and France the labour movement during the war was represented by some of its members within the cabinet; in England 1918 saw an important extension of the suffrage. In Germany no participation of the socialists in the government was so much as mentioned until the last weeks of the war; and even a mild reform of the severely limited Prussian suffrage was delayed until the proclamation of the republic put the whole problem on a different footing. The German socialists had to swallow bigger things than those of England and France, in a régime clearly hostile to them, and without any adequate compensation. It was hardly possible for the adversaries of the war to let such a policy go unchallenged; and it was precisely the difficulty of defending their policy that drove the majority to stern measures.

Thus out of the difference of opinion on the question of voting war credits there arose, first a split of the Social-democratic Parliamentary Party, and later a split of the social-democratic organizations. By spring, 1917, the minority had definitely organized themselves into a party of their own, called the 'Independent Social-democratic Party' (U.S.P.). It took with it a very considerable number of the personnel of the old party, and in some important centres such as Berlin and Leipzig actually a majority of the membership seceded when the schism occurred. It was a split which had great importance in the subsequent history of the Communist International.

The split did not extend to the unions. The leaders of the new party stood, not for revolution, but simply for democracy and peace. This brought them enormous prestige during the following year, when the U.S.P. was the one party to fight against the continuation of the war which everybody wanted to see ended. But naturally, from the very beginning, those few individuals who did not want only peace but also revolution joined the U.S.P. They divided themselves into three groups.

The least-known of these groups, but by far the most important, were the 'Revolutionary Shop-stewards' ('Revolutionaere Obleute') in Berlin. This originally was simply the trade-union committee of the turners, a sub-committee of the local branch of the Amalgamated Engineers. This Berlin committee started by taking union affairs into their own hands, just as the Scotch Shop-stewards had done, because they thought the interests of the workers were not being sufficiently safeguarded by the paid union officials, who were collaborating with the military commands. At the head of the committee stood one Richard Mueller, a man much respected by his colleagues, who proved to be a consummate tactician so long as he acted on the scene, well known to him, of the Berlin metal industry; later, during the revolution, as president of the workers' and soldiers' council, he was far from filling his role so successfully. As time went on, this shop-steward committee began to tackle political affairs and to organize opposition to the war among the engineers, which meant neither more nor less than organizing the munitions industry to prepare revolution. In the later years of the war this secret committee actually reduced the official union to a state of helplessness in what was then the most important industry of the Reich. They extended their contacts, after the second year of the war, beyond Berlin over the whole Reich. These Revolutionary Shop-stewards organized their first important political strike on the occasion of the trial of Karl Liebknecht in August 1916.

Karl Liebknecht, together with Rosa Luxemburg, stood at the head of the second of the revolutionary groups, the Spartakusbund. The name was rather unfortunately chosen from the chief of the Roman slave rebellion, Spartacus, who died heroically in a hopeless fight. This group had from the beginning differed from the mere pacifists on almost every point. Rosa Luxemburg maintained from the first day of the war that the government must be fought at any price, with revolution as the aim. Around her there formed a small circle; her husband Leo Jogiches; an intimate friend of his named Karski; Clara Zetkin, the leader of the socialist women's movement, who had been married to a Russian—the whole group was deeply under the influence of the revolutionary movement of the East. Mass support there was none in the beginning and very little indeed to the end. Karl Liebknecht, a deputy to the Reichstag, soon joined them. He had never been a Marxist, and even after his death a volume of miscellaneous writings of his was published in which Marxism was strongly criticized. But he had been a very active anti-militarist and a convinced socialist. The horrors of the war shocked him to the heart. He alone defied the socialist majority and in December 1914, a year before the rest of the minority, started voting against war credits. Thereafter he made what use he could of his parliamentary seat to fight the government, winning great popularity through it when the sufferings of the war grew deeper and deeper. Rosa Luxemburg was arrested soon after the outbreak of the war. Karl Liebknecht was arrested when addressing a May demonstration in 1916, and sentenced to five years' forced labour; this made him the hero of the movement, without, however, bringing increased strength to the Spartakusbund. The latter, on the contrary, was definitely unpopular with the Revolutionary Shop-stewards, who alone commanded the direct confidence of a mass-movement. Richard Mueller and his men charged the Spartakusbund with spoiling every hope of successful action for the sake of bringing out ultra-revolutionary slogans too early. Till the end of the war, the Spartakusbund won no influence over the revolutionary mass movement.

We must anticipate here by stating that the Spartakusbund was at odds with Lenin and his group too. But Lenin had his own small group in Germany, which followed Karl Radek. Radek was a Pole who in Poland had struggled bitterly with Rosa Luxemburg, perhaps more for personal than political reasons. He wielded considerable influence in the not very important social democratic branch at Bremen, and employed it in the fight against Rosa Luxemburg. The Spartacists, for their part, made use of what mass influence they had, through the personality of Clara Zetkin, in the one provincial organization of Würtemberg.

In Austria the patriotic attitude of the great majority of the German and Hungarian socialists almost drove to despair a small and uninfluential circle of socialist intellectuals. In October 1916 one young man, Friedrich Adler, the son of Victor Adler, the leader of the party, could bear it no longer and assassinated Count Stuergkh, the Prime Minister. He was brought to trial after the Russian February revolution, which had made a considerable impression in Austria, and his defence met with an entirely unexpected wave of popular sympathy. It suddenly became apparent that, while the official leaders were still keeping faith with the monarchy, the masses, irrespective of class or other distinction, wanted one thing above all: peace at any price. As long as the Russian menace existed, the masses were held together by the natural fear of a more highly civilized country of the victory of an inferior civilization. But when Russian defeat became practically certain, this last line broke, and a flood of hatred swept over the dying empire.

So things stood when the Bolshevik revolution of 7th November 1917 changed everything.

CHAPTER V

BEFORE AND AFTER
THE RUSSIAN REVOLUTION

From the first days of the war onwards Lenin stood like a rock amid a whirlpool. For him there was no doubt that this war was the introduction to an international revolution, and that it was the duty of a revolutionary to organize for it. It took him a few weeks to realize that all his heroes, Kautsky and Plekhanov, the French and the German revolutionary socialists, had 'betrayed' this idea. But at that time he took its acceptance for granted, and without a moment's hesitation started to prepare for the new phase.

Others believed that the breakdown of the Second International was only temporary; after the war, everything would be all right again. For Lenin this was worse than actual betrayal. The first step, for him, was to realize that the Second International was dead and done with. A few months after the beginning of the war he openly launched the slogan of preparation for a third international. And, as usual, he had a clear practical idea about what to do next, and a bad theoretical reason for it.

To him, the situation presented itself as follows: the poison of opportunism had been allowed to grow unchecked within the socialist parties of the West. The majorities had been orthodox, but the opportunists had not been expelled. Then, at a moment of particular difficulty, they had been proved to be the really dominant force within international socialism. A new international would be nothing but a second edition of the old one, and still more defective, unless this primary condition of its downfall was first mended. This could only be done by creating safeguards which would effectively exclude opportunism; there must be ideological control from an orthodox centre over the whole party, and it must be subjected to rigid discipline.

Before the war Lenin had trusted the Western socialists, and in particular the Germans. He had been mistaken. He concluded that safeguards similar to those required in Russia must be introduced into the Western labour movement. He reacted against the catastrophe of Western revolutionary Marxism by attempting to introduce the principles of the Russian 'professional revolutionary' organization into the Western movement. This is the idea of the Communist International in a nutshell. It was conceived in Lenin's head in the first months after the outbreak of the war.

Let us very briefly recapitulate the things on which this type of organization depends: first, a relatively broad movement of people ready to live and to die for the revolution, and of sufficient ability to form such an organization; and, second, the readiness of the masses to be led by such a group, neglecting their immediate interests. If nothing else, the outbreak of the war and what happened then had proved conclusively that both these conditions were lacking in Europe. A single group in the whole world outside Russia had more or less lived up to Lenin's ideal: the German 'Spartacists', and their leaders were almost all of them Russians, Russian Poles, and people closely connected with Russia. Even with them Lenin was quarrelling. But Lenin was convinced that the crisis of the war would help to overcome all difficulties, once the right idea was launched.

For Lenin action was not everything. He must have a theory. Had he regarded the downfall of Western Marxism as a temporary incident no such theory would have been necessary; but as he regarded it as final, and wanted to embark upon an entirely new venture, a far-reaching justification must be found. Marx had taught that the labour movement was by nature revolutionary. Events had proved that it was not. How combine the facts with the faith?

It might conceivably have been done by returning to the argument which Lenin had proffered when he split Russian socialism: the workers, by themselves, only develop the 'mentality of trade-unionists'. It is not quite clear why Lenin did not do that. Whatever the reason, he now put forward another argument, which probably attracted him because it combined a good reason for the split with an equally good reason for opposing the war. The war, he insisted, was an 'imperialistic' war, which meant a war by which the bourgeoisie of the big powers aimed at securing monopolistic, colonial, and semi-colonial markets for their export trade and their capital export, and cheap raw materials. Therefore it must be opposed by all socialists. But this very imperialism, by providing colonial 'extra-profits' for the bourgeoisie, put it in a position to bribe the upper strata of the proletariat; these strata, so bribed, naturally behave as 'traitors'. It is the members of these strata who must be expelled from the movement. It is in order to keep them out that a strict, centralized control of the movement must be imposed. In other words, Lenin came back to the theory of the 'labour aristocracy'. Engels had used this theory in order to explain why the English workers failed to be revolutionary. Lenin now used it to explain why the workers of all big industrial countries were non-revolutionary.

The practical consequences of this theory were considerable. For the question was: which layers were 'bribed'? Only the most highly paid groups? Then it was difficult to explain why the whole of the movement had acted as 'traitors'. Or all the better-paid workers? Where, then, was the boundary line? In fact, Lenin's practical politics had, as usual, very little to do with his theories, so little indeed that it needs all the faith of the faithful not to see the glaring incongruities. In practice Lenin did not take the standard of living as the dividing line. It so happened that in Germany, in France, in Sweden, in Italy, and in a number of other countries, it was precisely the best-paid workers who flocked to the communists, and that for reasons which will become clear in the course of our account. But the theory of the workers' aristocracy nevertheless had its practical importance. First of all it gave another reason for the split than simply the emergency of war; it justified the split once and for all, so that it was never to be healed. It gave, moreover, a basis for a fight of unprecedented fierceness within the labour movement. Some of the workers themselves, it suggested, had been *bribed* and *therefore had betrayed* their fellows; this charge was the root of those typical communist slanders, methods of debate, and agitation which within the party had never been used before. The communist worker was induced to regard his immediate colleague with somewhat higher pay or a somewhat different political opinion as his worst enemy. But, most important of all, the border-line between the bribed aristocracy and the genuine working man was and remained undefined. This gave an opportunity to extend and narrow the concept according to various tactical considerations. At times the concept of the workers' aristocracy was narrowed down until it became coincident with the workers' bureaucracy, the paid personnel of the socialist parties and the trade unions. At other times it was extended so as to include every trade-unionist, even every man in employment. The history of the tactical changes of the Comintern might be written in terms of the changes the concept of the labour aristocracy has undergone.

But all that only began to matter at a later stage. At the beginning of the war Lenin's group was small indeed; and he had to fight in order to convince, not the partisans of the war, but its adversaries, of the soundness of his basic concepts.

The one thing which counted for Lenin at this juncture was the chance to make use of the war to bring about '*the* revolution'. He saw clearly enough that revolution had the best chance, not in the industrialized West, but in Russia, whose government was weakest. He was still far from entertaining about the revolution the ideas which he formulated in 1917. Against Trotsky and against the socialist revolutionaries he still maintained that it would be a bourgeois revolution, culminating in a 'democratic dictatorship of the proletariat and the peasantry'; but at the same time he now emphasized that, under the circumstances of the war, revolution in Russia must be a prelude to revolution in the West; and the revolution in the West could only be a proletarian, socialist revolution.

There were other very serious disputes with Trotsky, which occupied almost the whole of the period from 1914 till the end of 1916. During all the years since 1903 Trotsky, in spite of his ultra-revolutionary views, had been in constant alliance with the Mensheviks on that one decisive question: the problem of party organization. He had been one of the leaders of a bloc of groups which intended to force Lenin to give up his separate, centralized, exclusive, and select group of 'Bolsheviks'. Now, at the beginning of the war, this close alliance between Trotsky and the leading Mensheviks found a very natural outlet in collaboration in opposing the war. Trotsky and Martow, the leader of the Mensheviks, in fact formed one group at that period, and had their chief slogan in common; it was: 'Peace at any price.'

Lenin hated and despised the peace slogan. He deeply believed in the 'imperialist character' of the war, which meant, among many other things, that he believed that the ruling classes as a whole were pledged to expansion in every country; that therefore compromise was a utopian conception and the war would have to be fought out to the bitter end. Consequently he regarded the pacifist whining of certain left-wing socialists as an outrage, a political abdication almost as bad as that of the official 'social-patriots', just another sort of 'betrayal' of orthodox Marxism. Moreover, he not only did not believe in the possibility of a peace by conciliation; he did not think it was desirable. He wanted to turn the war into a revolution, and humanitarian considerations were of little account as against this desire.

There was more. It is impossible, he contended, to fight for revolution within a country at war unless one is prepared to accept defeat for that country; if you grant the necessity of national defence, you will not be able ruthlessly to smash the existing order. Moreover, defeat would definitely give the best opportunity for a revolution. It was the duty of a revolutionary to work for defeat; the peace slogan and practical work for peace clashed directly with this desire for defeat and revolution. To the slogan of Trotsky and Martov, 'Peace at any price', Lenin opposed this other slogan: 'Turn the imperialistic war into civil war.'

This was a thoroughly logical argument and Lenin was certainly right—with his usual uncanny clairvoyance in practical matters—in contending that revolution depended upon defeat. Nevertheless he remained almost completely alone in his tactical views during the first three years of the war, and this was not only due to lack of understanding on the part of his adversaries. It was due to an ambiguity both in his position and in theirs.

The majority of the 'pacifists' in the camp of international socialism certainly did not so much as think of a revolution. Kautsky, Bernstein, Ramsay Macdonald, in agitating for peace, wanted peace, not as a means to bring about social convulsions, but on the contrary as a means to avoid them. But the situation was such a peculiar one that even the most decided revolutionaries had to join in the peace agitation. For what the masses wanted was obviously not revolution; it was peace. They might be prepared to make a revolution if it was conducive to peace, but the aim of the mass movement would inevitably be peace and nothing else. This made it impossible to draw a line between mere pacifists and revolutionaries who used the fight for peace only as an access to revolution. But Lenin, more than ever, was intent upon drawing boundary-lines. He had been convinced that the lack of revolutionary orthodoxy had been the reason for the breakdown of the Second International, and he enunciated his formula, 'Transform imperialist war into civil war', as a shibboleth. Outside Russia he did not find a single partisan for this formula in any belligerent country. He got the assent of the Swedish and the Norwegian left—they had no war to transform into anything—of Radek's Polish group, and the left of the Latvian socialists. Even Rosa Luxemburg refused to follow his lead.

As soon as the Russian revolution made the whole proposition less abstract and more practical, the inadequacy of the boundary-line which, during the first years of the war, had divided the various opponents of the war, became obvious. Martov on the one hand and Trotsky and Rosa Luxemburg on the other parted company. Martov was against the taking of political power, the other two were for it. And as soon as this dividing-line had been clearly established—not over the matter of immediate peace or civil war, but over the problem of Soviet power or not—Lenin dropped the fight with Trotsky. He revised his position silently, as was his custom; with all his readiness to admit practical mistakes he never liked to confess a change of mind in matters of principle. But in fact the Bolshevik *coup d'état* was made with the threefold slogan, 'Peace, liberty, and bread', which, after all, was not even Trotsky's 'Peace at any price'.

But there was another matter of contention between Lenin

and even the most advanced section of the revolutionaries in the West, and that was of a much more lasting significance. Almost from the first day of the war Lenin insisted that the collapse of the Second International should be openly announced to the masses and that the banner of a new international should be raised. Again he was seconded by Radek with his following in Poland and his small group in Bremen, by Hoeglund and his group in Sweden, and by nobody else. Rosa Luxemburg and her circle consistently refused to launch the slogan of a new international. The difference was not one about the resuscitation of the Second International. During the war Rosa Luxemburg wrote and smuggled out of jail a pamphlet signed 'Junius' and entitled 'The Crisis of German Social-democracy', later generally known as the 'Junius pamphlet'. As an appendix it contained 'Theses for the Reconstruction of the International', which outlined principles for an international of a character entirely different from that of pre-war days. It should organize strict discipline in all international matters, and all its members must be pledged to oppose any future war. It would be absurd to attribute to Rosa Luxemburg the idea that such an international could be founded without a split with the out-and-out 'social-patriots'. She did not want to raise the matter at that time.

In what did this difference of opinion consist? It was again the all-important question of organization that was at the bottom of it, and the division of opinion roughly coincided with the contrast between Russia and the West. Lenin, living in the tradition of the Russian revolutionary movement, was not at all afraid to build the new international upon small groups of professional revolutionaries; he hoped and believed that as the sufferings of the war continued these revolutionaries would be able to win over large groups of the people without difficulty. Rosa Luxemburg was afraid of precisely these groups of professional revolutionaries. Her whole background was different, indeed absolutely antagonistic to that of Lenin. Radek, who in those years was Lenin's closest follower and almost the only one who was not a Great Russian, was hated by Luxemburg because of an ancient quarrel over Polish politics. The Bolsheviks as a whole she intensely disliked for their tactics of permeation and wire-pulling of the mass move-

ments; she believed in the spontaneous evolution of the proletariat towards revolutionary action. The premature formation
of a new international, in her opinion, could only sever the
small groups of revolutionaries from the masses. She wanted a
new international; but she wanted to form it only after powerful anti-war and revolutionary mass movements had grown up
in all the decisive industrial countries of Europe. Moreover,
she was thoroughly afraid of an international mainly led by
the Russian Bolsheviks, whom she distrusted. This fact was
amply revealed when her collaborator, Paul Levi, left the
German Communist Party in 1921 and published incomplete
manuscripts of hers, dating from the last months of her life,
which showed her in constant disagreement with the Bolsheviks. Oral evidence which I collected for several years from
many of her collaborators—including the late Ernst Meyer,
who led the Spartacus organization while Rosa Luxemburg
was in jail—entirely confirms Levi's statements, which are,
moreover, substantiated by every known political act of Rosa
Luxemburg until the very day of her death.

Here was a deep cleavage indeed. The two protagonists of
international revolutionary socialism agreed upon most funda-
mentals. But Lenin stood for an international which should
begin as a small body and be under the strictest control of his
party, which he had come to regard as the one safeguard of
practical and theoretical orthodoxy. Rosa Luxemburg stood
for an international which should be mainly based upon mass
parties in the West and which, while definitely excluding the
pre-war socialists and a good many of the wavering elements,
would still not be particularly busy with 'orthodoxy'. The two
concepts were never reconciled, and the division was aggra-
vated by a fight to the finish within the International. In this
matter, unlike so many others, Trotsky, who had originally
sided with Luxemburg against Lenin, went over to Lenin's
point of view during the first phase of the Russian revolution.
The general outline of their relation was thus once more confirmed; Lenin in 1917 tended to come over to Trotsky's view
on many points of policy; Trotsky submitted to Lenin on every
matter of organization, both national and international.

As far as Rosa Luxemburg is concerned, her disagreements
with Lenin did not stop at that point. Among the materials

published by Paul Levi in 1921, almost four years after Rosa
Luxemburg's death, the most important is an unfinished
manuscript about the Russian revolution which, while giving
high praise to Lenin for his unrelenting fight against the war
and his courage in taking power, attacks his policy after the
coup d'état on almost every point. Of her many criticisms we are
here concerned with only two items. The first is a violent
attack on Lenin's policy towards the peasants. In making the
peasants satisfied proprietors of the land, Rosa Luxemburg
contends, he transformed them from a revolutionary into a
counter-revolutionary force. It is the old argument of the
socialist left which Lenin had himself eagerly defended in his
early days and later on abandoned through his experience of
failure in 1905. Lenin was to meet this argument again and
again from various quarters. But much more serious and
incisive was Rosa Luxemburg's criticism of Lenin's concept of
'dictatorship'. In her heart of hearts Rosa Luxemburg, like
every Western socialist, be he never so revolutionary, was a
democrat. She objected, with unusually pointed arguments, to
the dissolution of the constituent assembly, which had had an
anti-Bolshevik majority. She advocated a combining of the
Soviet régime with parliamentary democracy. She condemned
the régime of oppression which the Bolsheviks had already
instituted against dissentients. Pointing to the slogan of
'Liberty' which the Bolsheviks had issued when fighting for
power, she dryly stated that 'liberty is always the liberty of the
man who thinks differently'. And she concluded that the
living stream of revolution would dry up, and with it all the
beneficial effect of the Bolshevist revolution would disappear,
unless such liberty were granted and the tendency to what we
to-day call the 'totalitarian state' were checked. It was the
same argument as that with which she opposed Lenin in 1904.
Only then Rosa Luxemburg had fought against the conception
of a bureaucratic dictatorship within the party; now she
fought against a bureaucratic dictatorship within the state.
German communists later on suggested that Rosa Luxemburg
would certainly have changed her views had she lived. The
fact, however, is that she did not change them as long as she
lived. And her reluctance to join an international dominated
by Lenin was based upon her profound distrust of a bureau-

cratic dictatorship, which she foresaw—if oral reports on the matter deserve credit—would be extended to the international. The issue of Lenin *v.* Rosa Luxemburg was one of centralized dictatorship of a small group over the rest—in state, party, and international—as against democracy. Certainly only Rosa Luxemburg's idea of revolution corresponded to what Marx had imagined the dictatorship of the proletariat would be; but the idea of a dictatorship based upon a class hypothetically revolutionary—the proletariat—was wholly incapable of realization in actual life. Luxemburg was a true disciple of Marx, but not a realist in this decisive matter. Lenin had to distort every line of Marx on the subject in order to prove himself still a Marxist; but he had reality on his side.

It is only natural, however, that, with such stout opposition from even the most revolutionary elements in the West, Lenin during the whole war made very little headway with his idea of a new international. In Germany, Radek's group in Bremen was for him, but insignificant; the Spartakusbund, while promoting a break between the pacifists and the patriots, preferred to remain within the fold of the U.S.P., the left-wing party which had issued in 1916 from the disruption of social-democracy and which drew together those masses who were against the war. In France Lenin had not a single follower before the October revolution; nobody there so much as thought of a split. In England a few small sects outside the Labour Party might have sided with Lenin, but contacts with London were broken off because Havelock Wilson and his union of seamen, furious at the Germans on account of the submarine war, prohibited all the left-wingers from travelling to the Continent. The left in Norway, while sometimes voting for Lenin, was actually organizing not for a split but for the capturing of the Labour Party as a whole, which it achieved in 1918. The Bulgarian Tesnyaki, who were so close to Lenin in most matters, together with Rakowski and the Roumanian socialists, followed the lead of Trotsky, who was not yet a friend of the idea of the third international. There remained Radek, Radek, and once more Radek, and in addition the Swedish left and the small and uninfluential group of the extremists in Holland. That was what Lenin was able to muster in the West before—and even after—the October revolution.

Very naturally, not much attention was paid to that small group in those conferences of anti-war socialists which met during the war. Before the entry of Italy into the war the Italian socialists had taken combined action with the Swiss Socialist Party to bring together all the elements which opposed the war. Even earlier, Roland-Holst in Holland and Clara Zetkin in Germany, the leaders of the International Socialist Women's Movement, had convoked a women's conference at Berne. It was only natural that women should be more pacifist than men. It was more remarkable that the International Socialist Youth Organization, under the leadership of Willi Münzenberg, also sided with the 'internationalists'. It was here that Lenin, without capturing the organization as such, won a considerable amount of personal influence.

Late in 1915 the 'Italo-Swiss Committee' succeeded in organizing an international conference in Zimmerwald, near Berne, which set up a permanent secretariat of the internationalists and issued a manifesto against the war. In 1916 the same groups met again, at Kienthal, also in the Canton of Berne, and decided that all internationalists had to pledge themselves to vote against war credits. Finally in 1917 the socialists of the Central Powers met the Russian socialists at Stockholm, in a vain attempt to bring about peace. The majority of the conference consisted of the official, 'social-patriot' parties; but there was a *Zimmerwald* minority which held a separate conference in addition to the official one, and decided, in September 1917, to organize a body which was intended to last beyond the war. This was not the international which Lenin wanted; on the contrary, the pacifism of Bernstein and Macdonald would have had a clear majority in this new international. Lenin felt anything but enthusiastic about it. One month later, however, the Bolshevik revolution made the whole idea obsolete. The *Zimmerwald* secretariat remained in the hands of Angelica Balabanoff, a Russian who had spent all her life in the Italian socialist movement and had been very close to Mussolini before he went over to the patriots. Now she became for a time a convinced Bolshevik, and kept the threads in her hands, with the help of Vorovski, the new Russian ambassador in Stockholm. But not much could be done in the way of direct international contacts.

If Lenin had failed, and still failed, to build up an international under his orders, the October revolution nevertheless gave enormous prestige to the Bolsheviks, who until then had been unknown to the Western proletariat even by name. They were the people who, alone in the world, had made an end with war. Now they were menaced by German bayonets. They appealed, from the forum of the Brest-Litovsk peace negotiations, for the help of the Western proletariat. And their request did not remain unanswered. The sufferings brought by the war were too great.

As a matter of fact, nothing stirred among the Allied Powers, but the masses of the Central Powers answered the call. All their grievances had been stirred by the Russian revolution. It was not at all a specifically proletarian movement. All over Austria, in particular, the peasants were in revolt, the peasant soldiers in their thousands deserting with the help of fellow peasants into the great forests and carrying on life there as brigands. But the proletariat was capable of more concerted action. When it became clear that the German General Staff would not give a decent peace to the Russians, the powder-barrel exploded.

It started at the factory of Manfred Weiss, in Csepel, near Budapest, by far the biggest munitions factory in Hungary. Later on, the Hungarian Soviet dictatorship came into power by a movement in the same factory. But then, on 14th January 1918, it was not yet a question of the dictatorship of the proletariat. It was simply a question of peace. And the way the movement started was typical. Hungarian social-democracy had, on the whole, been loyal to the Hapsburg monarchy and the Hungarian aristocratic régime, which was perhaps the most reactionary in Europe outside Tsarist Russia. If some intellectuals had certain misgivings about the wholesale support which the party gave to the war, the trade-union leaders at any rate were decided that they would oppose any revolutionary movement. The Hungarian labour movement was entirely based upon and almost coincident with the trade-union movement, and traditions of trade-union discipline were very strong among the Budapest engineers. Nevertheless, this time a small committee of revolutionary pacifists, composed exclusively of very young intellectuals with no experience and hardly any contact with the labour movement, got into touch with the men at Csepel, and without any difficulty pushed the official leaders aside. The strike broke out at the instigation of this committee. And after that anything might be expected.

The strike spread like wild-fire, first to other industrial centres in Hungary; by the 16th January it had reached the munition factories of Lower Austria; on the 17th all Vienna went on strike. A few days later Berlin munition workers followed suit, and then the engineers and many other branches of industry all over the Reich. Nowhere had the official leadership called the strike. In Vienna as in Hungary it was sponsored by a small group of extremely young intellectuals, who had set themselves the task of imitating the Russian Bolsheviks, and called themselves 'left-radicals'. In Berlin the strike had been prepared for some weeks and was led by the Revolutionary Shop-stewards, who, as has been described in a former chapter, were at any rate workers and trade-unionists. In Brunswick the Spartacists led the strike. But in most of the provincial towns of Germany the leaders were anonymous.

In spite of this, or rather for this very reason, it was in more than one sense the biggest revolutionary movement of properly proletarian origin which the modern world has ever seen. Though vaguely connected with the general peasant unrest, it relied upon its own forces. And, most remarkable of all, it was the one important international strike action of which history knows. The international co-ordination which the Comintern later so often tried to bring about was here produced automatically—within the borders of the Central Powers—out of the community of interests in all the countries concerned, and the common predominance of two main problems, bread and the Brest-Litovsk negotiations. The slogans everywhere demanded a peace with Russia without annexation or compensation, better rations, and full political democracy.

The movement shook the Central Powers to their very foundations. It is certainly untrue to say that the loss of the war was due to the activities of the revolutionaries, for the Central Powers were beaten in the field. But it accelerated their defeat and shaped the outlines of the coming revolution. It was due to, or its most immediate cause was, the Russian revolution.

And it remains a remarkable fact that the biggest effect which the Russian revolution ever had upon Europe was achieved before there was a Communist International.

In its immediate aims, however, the movement failed. There was a big array of forces against it. In Germany and Hungary the power of the military, yet intact, could not be overcome. Moreover, in those two countries the patriotic social-democratic leaders did everything to bring it to a speedy end; they still commanded the allegiance of a considerable section of the workers, and the fear of the military did the rest. But the movement, before it collapsed, had in many places gone so far as to lead to the formation of rudimentary Soviets.

The situation in Vienna and the surrounding industrial districts was a peculiar one. Here, the workers were confronted not with their co-nationals in arms, but with troops from Bosnia and Galicia, who did not speak their language. Moreover the secret committee of the Czech nationalists in Prague, in which the Czech socialists co-operated, kept Prague entirely quiet while Vienna was on the brink of revolution. Tušar in Prague took orders from Masaryk and Beneš, and they did not want to help a movement which was instigated by the Bolsheviks, and consequently directed just as much against the Allies as against the Hapsburgs. In the domination of the Czech national committee over the proletariat of Prague and the Czech territory (with the exception of Brünn) the proletarian revolutionaries met, for the first time, that self-confident and deep-rooted revolutionary nationalism which later on did so much to thwart their efforts. The official leadership of the Austrian party had always been against the strike. They went so far as to dissociate themselves from the extreme patriots among the German socialists, but they hated the idea of a revolutionary fight. Within the party, since the assassination of Count Stuergkh by Fritz Adler, a left wing had grown up, led by Otto Bauer, the later leader of Austrian social-democracy. While the official leadership defended the Austrian empire to the end this left wing foresaw the inevitability of its collapse and disintegration. But it is doubtful whether they wanted to go any further than non-resistance to the process of disintegration. They certainly did not want to put themselves at the head of the disintegrating forces.

Had the left, during those days, launched the slogan of Czech national independence it is doubtful whether the Czech national committee would have been able to keep back its masses. That would have meant, not a proletarian, but a national revolution. The war might have ended in January instead of November. Lenin would certainly have tried that road. But again, as in so many other cases, the tradition of orthodox Marxism, in the Western interpretation of the word, stood in the way. Marxism and nationalism seemed incompatible.

In the political field nationalism is the fact against which the Marxist theory breaks itself. Here is a force which has proved definitely stronger in the modern world than the class struggle which for orthodox Marxists makes the essence of history. The natural result was that the Marxists constantly tended to underestimate a force which did not easily fit into their ideas, and which at the same time was clearly contrasted with the ideals of the class-struggle. It became almost a mark of an orthodox Marxist to despise every nationalist feeling—a mistake which has done the labour movement enormous harm down to the days when Fascism won in central Europe. The more to the left the greater generally the mistake. Rosa Luxemburg had made it almost the core of her programme, both in Poland and in Germany, to disregard nationalism, and she violently attacked Lenin for the deep and constant attention he paid to the problem.

Lenin's practical genius here as always subordinated theory to the requirements of practice. He made no serious attempt to reconcile the existence and growth of nationalism with Marxism, but he gave it due attention in practice. He clearly saw that the world was full of national grievances, that these grievances were inflammable material to be used by the revolutionary, and that if he disregarded them they would become the greatest imaginable obstacle to the revolutionizing of the proletariat of all the oppressed nations. Much of the later policy of the Comintern is based on this insight.

Now the Austrian socialists had one thing in common with Lenin in this respect. Like Lenin, they did not try to overlook the problem. Nationalism among the subject races of Austria had not only shown no signs of subsiding in favour of the class struggle; on the contrary it had split the originally united socialist movement into linguistically separated independent parties. So the Austrian socialists sat down and studied the problem, and there is hardly any doubt that, as to theoretical views, they went a good deal deeper than Lenin. The work of their leader, Otto Bauer, on the 'problem of nationalities' was, incidentally, admired by Lenin. But Otto Bauer, though a splendid parliamentarian, a fine orator and writer, and an erudite scholar, was essentially a man of contemplation, who never in his life plucked up the courage to make a definite decision on either side, the right or the left. Otto Bauer deduced theoretically the inevitability of Austria's downfall, but he did not think he was under any obligation to bring it about. The lead in the process was taken, nine months later, by the Czech National Committee. What was perhaps the biggest political opportunity of any Western proletariat was thus lost; the leading role in the impending democratic revolution had been handed over to the bourgeoisie of the minorities before the revolution had so much as started.

In those January days the Austrian government hastened to increase the rations of the principal workers' groups; and democratic reforms were promised. Both the right and the left wings of the Austrian socialist movement then decided to call off the strike, and carried through their intention in the face of considerable resistance from the masses. In the following months similar strike movements occurred in Hungary, Austria, and Germany, but of minor extent. The final catastrophe, in November 1918, was not brought about by them. And its immediate prelude was not a proletarian rising but a peasant revolt in Bulgaria, in which the working class took no part.

In September 1918 the German armies in the West were in slow retreat before the Allies, putting up a staunch resistance. At that moment, unexpectedly, the Bulgarian front broke down. A big gap opened in the Balkans which Ludendorff had no more troops to fill; he asked for peace.

This event is worth closer study in our context, first on account of its historical importance—though the war would have been lost for Germany without it—because it was the most direct contribution of any revolutionary movement outside

Russia to the result of the war, and because the party of the Bulgarian left-wing socialists which was involved in it later on became one of the mainstays of the Communist International. In essence, as already stated, it was not a workers' but a peasants' rising. And there had been more than one symptom of the approaching storm. Early in the summer a change had taken place in high quarters and the pro-German Prime Minister Radoslavov had been replaced by the pro-Allied Malinov. Then, throughout the summer, deserters straggled home *en masse*, in order to till their derelict fields. The authorities tolerated it. And word went round among the soldiers that the fight must be ended by the 15th of September; they would fight no longer. The Peasant Party of Stambuliiski co-operated in these anti-war activities with the Tesnyaki, the socialist left. Then, on 15th September, General Franchet d'Espérey launched his offensive, and the Bulgarian soldiers left the trenches undefended and simply went home.

But on their way home, not far from Sofia, at Dubnitza, they were met by Stambuliiski, who incited them not simply to go home but to overthrow the government and create a republic. The situation, however, was complicated by one factor. Since 1913 by far the greater part of Macedonia was in the hands of the Serbs, much against the will of the population, and a huge number of Macedonian refugees had crowded into Sofia. They were prepared to fight to the end; thus the government in Sofia, unlike any other government in central Europe at the time, had at its disposal reliable troops. These select troops were sent down from Sofia to meet the rebels, and defeated them. Only after the success of the loyalists did Tsar Ferdinand abdicate and his son Boris ascend the Bulgarian throne.

What was the attitude of the Tesnyaki, the friends of Lenin, the revolutionary socialists, and future communists during this crisis? We had best let them speak in their own words, contained in an official statement of the Bulgarian Communist Party made two and a half years after the event in a Vienna periodical, *Kommunismus*, of 31st May 1921: 'Stambuliiski', runs this statement, 'had one more conversation with Blagoyev [the founder and leader of the Tesnyaki] and suggested that the latter, together with the Peasants' Party, should join in the rising. His [Stambuliiski's] first and last platform of negotiations was only the establishment of a bourgeois democratic republic. Never did Stambuliiski suggest any other condition for our common action. Naturally Blagoyev refused to give any sort of support. This whole rising [of Dubnitza] was ultimately reactionary. It was a rising of the peasants against the urban population and against King Ferdinand.' And further on: 'The "Bulgarian revolution" of September 1918 was not a fight of the proletariat and its party against the bourgeoisie, it was a fight within the bourgeoisie itself.' The party which, in 1921, made this statement and behaved as outlined in it, was much the nearest to the Russian Bolsheviks of all movements outside Russia. The inadequacy of any attempt to transform a movement of that character into something similar to the Bolsheviks is obvious when one looks back at it in the perspective of eighteen years of vain attempts.

To start with, the very statement of the facts contradicts the conclusions drawn from it by the party leadership. If Stambuliiski proposed a close alliance with the communists (we call them communists though they assumed that name only a few months later) the fact itself provides conclusive evidence that Stambuliiski wanted to form an alliance of the poor against the rich and not of the country against the towns. On the contrary, it was the refusal of the urban workers to co-operate which forced the Bulgarian Peasant Party to rely exclusively on the peasants' dislike for the town, and to follow the road which eventually, in 1923, led to Stambuliiski's own destruction. What is more important, the Bulgarian communists had proclaimed for many years that they were fighting for democracy as—to put it in Lenin's words—'the best approach to the dictatorship of the proletariat'. Now they had only to move in order to obtain it; a few battalions could not have subdued the united forces of the workers and peasants. At this moment of all others they discover that to do this is not worth while; that the fight is 'only' about the overthrow of monarchy and the creation of a 'bourgeois democratic republic'. Such problems might interest the bourgeois; let them fight them out between themselves; it is below the dignity of a real revolutionary to care for such trifles. Only one year later Lenin was to pour scorn and laughter upon that sort of thing; but the lesson was not learned. We shall see the Bulgarian party tread the same path no less than three times in its history.

At decisive moments such as these one sees, at a glance, what in ordinary times is hidden behind a screen of carefully worded formulae. The Bulgarian Tesnyaki did not choose the way of abstention out of physical cowardice; they have amply proved that by their later feats. On the other hand, they certainly did not remain at home because, while others fought for trifles, they were in a position to organize the rapidly approaching fight for the dictatorship of the proletariat. The simplest explanation of their inactivity is probably twofold: first, pre-war Marxist orthodoxy prohibited any alliance; he who concluded alliances was branded as an 'opportunist'. Stambuliiski was infinitely stronger than the communists were, and when one compares his actions with theirs one understands why. In a common fight he would be the leader, they would be only followers; and they were afraid to come down from their lofty dreams and recognize that, in real life, they were still a second-rate force. And this failure of leadership had happened within a party not of 'social-patriots', 'social-traitors', 'social-pacifists', to quote Lenin's pet terms of abuse, but within a group which took a leading part in the formation of the Communist International.

But while in Bulgaria a big chance was thrown away through the fault of the communists, a disaster which they could not possibly have forestalled befell their nascent organization from another quarter. The collapse of Bulgaria gave the signal for the collapse of Austria-Hungary; and this immediately let loose national revolutions all over central and south-eastern Europe. Nations which had lived partly within the Hapsburg empire and partly under the constant menace of its domination suddenly felt and became free, victorious, and powerful. In regions where the people were occupied with the process of organizing a new state the idea of a social revolution could not be even entertained. They were regions which, during these decisive months of transition, would otherwise have been an easy prey for the promoters of social upheaval. In January 1918 the big strike of the united proletariat of the Central Powers was broken, less by the Prussian and the Hapsburg administrations than by the Czech National Committee in

Prague. This process was repeated on a gigantic scale during the latter part of 1918 and the whole of 1919. While defeat drove some states towards social revolution, victory made others a reliable barrier against it. And victory meant infinitely more to the liberated nations of the east than to England and France. Here it only signified a narrow escape from disaster: there, the achievement of age-long hopes and dreams.

Of all those national and democratic revolutions which contributed to the forming of this barrier against Bolshevism that of Roumania, least noted at the time, was probably the most important. When Roumania entered the war on the side of the Allies, late in 1916, it was a country in which a very small group of 'Boyars' owned almost all the land, in which the peasants starved amidst the richest cornfields of Europe, and a bureaucracy corrupt as no other in Europe—with the possible exception of Turkey—had completely disorganized the machinery of the state. If any country in the world politically resembled Tsarist Russia it was Roumania, and similar effects were to be expected. But in Roumania, as against Russia, the ruling group, under pressure of defeat in the war, had the good sense and energy to carry out the necessary revolutionary reforms themselves. In the winter of 1917, after Bukharest had been taken by the Germans, a law was promulgated which represented a tolerable compromise between the peasant and the lord. The peasants got a considerable amount of land, though not all. The effects were sweeping: the Roumanian peasant, who had surrendered half the country to the Germans almost without resistance, defended the other half stubbornly and successfully. The Russian revolution came; then came Bolshevism. The Roumanian troops, on the southern sector of the Russian front, were interspersed with Russians; but while the Russians disintegrated, the Roumanians remained firm. Roumania signed a treaty of peace, but did not for a moment fall a victim to Bolshevism. No sign of revolution appeared in the country; and in the summer of 1919 the Roumanian peasant was ready to fight again and defeat the Hungarian Soviets.

The agrarian reform in Roumania was perhaps the strongest single obstacle that opposed the advance of Bolshevism towards the West. It was very far from solving all problems,

99

even for the peasantry, but for a decade took the sharp edge off them. Revolutionary trends among the proletariat remained, but the proletariat alone was nothing in Roumania, and revolutionism among its members was more of a convulsion than a clearly defined movement. A cruel and efficient political police dealt with that. Christian Rakowski had gone to Russia to join in the revolution. A communist party was formed, had to go underground almost immediately, and never gained any substantial influence. We shall have no occasion to come back to Roumania in this whole story. Let us only remember that Roumania was considerably extended by the peace treaty, that it won, among other regions, Transylvania, which had belonged to Hungary and where the Hungarian magnates had owned all the land; that the Roumanian government expropriated the Hungarian magnates much more ruthlessly than its own Boyars, in favour of the Roumanian peasantry.

The second big blow to Bolshevism was more directly connected with the break-up of the Prussian and Austro-Hungarian empires. Poland won its independence. This meant little practical change for those parts of the new state which had been under Austrian domination, because the Poles in Austria had been, together with the Germans and the Magyars, a privileged race. But it meant enormous relief for those parts of Poland which had been under Prussia and Russia. The agrarian problem in Poland was bad enough, but not nearly so bad as in Roumania. The Polish-speaking peasant had land, although he had much too little of it. The really acute tensions existed in the east of the new nation, where in eastern Galicia, the Ukrainians, farther north the White Russians, and in the region of Vilna the Lithuanians, were much stronger in numbers than the Poles; in all these eastern border regions the Poles constitute the land-owning aristocracy, whereas the minorities consist of peasants and are nearly landless. The tension is as acute as it was in Roumania before the agrarian reform, and is sharpened by national antagonisms. Most of the national minorities have their co-nationals on the other side of the Russian border, where they won, during the first year of the Bolshevik revolution, both land and recognition for their native tongues. Therefore these border regions of

Poland have been from the beginning and remain to this day the only regions in the world where Bolshevism, outside Russia, has maintained a continuous and deep-rooted influence over very large sections, possibly over the greater part, of the population. Be it noted, as a characteristic detail, that these are regions almost completely without industries and that the Bolshevik movement there is entirely a peasant movement. Later on we shall have to enlarge upon the non-proletarian character of those very battalions of international Bolshevism which have proved themselves the strongest.

The condition of the backward and illiterate peasantry of a few border regions was, however, only a minor problem in Poland. The Polish majority withstood Bolshevism because it would have meant the return of Russian domination. The Poles cared little whether the Russian bureaucrat was a servant of the Tsar or of Lenin; he wanted to be rid of both. And the Poles, who scented from experience how much the traditions of Tsarism persisted in Bolshevism, were not impressed by revolutionary slogans. As agrarian reform in Roumania slammed the door between Russia and the southeast and killed the Hungarian Soviets, so national unity in Poland slammed the door between Russia and Germany and brought defeat to the Russian offensive against Warsaw in August 1920.

This is the appropriate place to say a few words about the emergence of the Communist Party of Poland. The Polish labour movement under Tsarism had been sharply divided into two sections, the one led for a long time by Pilsudski, the other by Rosa Luxemburg and her friends. The former, the 'P.P.S.' (Polish Socialist Party) was primarily nationalist; it stood at the head of the movement for the liberation of Poland and was in consequence supported by a very strong body of intellectuals, besides having preponderating influence in the trade-union movement. Rosa Luxemburg's group called itself 'S.D.K.P.L.' (Social-democracy of the Kingdoms of Poland and Lithuania), a provocative self-description intended to convey that this group accepted the subjection of Poland to Russia, defied nationalism, and intended to co-operate with the Russian revolutionary movement. Lenin, as already mentioned, while heavily condemning the close alliance between the P.P.S. and the bourgeois nationalist parties, opposed Rosa Luxemburg's indifference to the national problem and insisted that Poland must be given a chance to secure her national liberty.

November 1918 solved the problem. Polish independence became a fact and Pilsudski and the P.P.S. contributed enormously to its achievement. This gave them immense authority among both the intelligentsia and the workers. The labour movement of Austrian Poland—Galicia—had always been completely under the sway of the P.P.S.; now that party had the allegiance of the great majority of the Russo-Polish workers too. This sweeping victory of the P.P.S. also reflected in the field of organization the completely non-revolutionary mood of the Polish proletariat at that juncture.

On the other hand, the achievement of Polish national unity and independence settled many problems, and gave the Marxist movement a new start. The *fait accompli* of national independence destroyed the chief stumbling block to co-operation between the Russian Bolsheviki and the Polish S.D.K.P.L. The latter was among the first parties to join the Communist International after its foundation. At the same time the achievement of Polish unity provoked a regrouping within the P.P.S. The indifference of Rosa Luxemburg to the national claims of Poland had placed a barrier between her organization and all those who wanted national liberty. Now that Poland was free it became apparent that a fairly numerous section within the P.P.S. objected to the close collaboration of the socialists with bourgeois parties in the new state and that this section stood for revolutionary politics. Even before joining the Communist International, the S.D.K.P.L. merged with this left wing of the P.P.S. and together they formed the Communist Party of Poland. It was as yet a skeleton organization. The Polish proletariat had been carried away, in enormous numbers, to Germany, and Polish industry was only slowly reconstituted. The traditions of the Polish movement, however, were partly revolutionary, and this gave the new party a chance. In the meantime the Ukrainian movement, which was striving for separation from Poland and to join the Soviet-Ukraine, set up an organization which was called 'The Communist Party of Western Ukraine' and in practice acted independently of the Polish party, with its headquarters at Warsaw.

Similar effects were produced by the national revolution of October–November 1918 in Greece and in the newly founded states of Czechoslovakia and Yugoslavia. In Greece the victory of Venizelos, the proclamation of the republic, the enormous extension of the national territory, and the war against Turkey —eagerly entered upon, at first, by the whole nation—made the growth of a revolutionary mass party impossible. For many years the Comintern had no serious section in Greece, and not before 1935 did it win influence in national politics.

In Yugoslavia events took a somewhat different course. The Serbian Socialist Party, which had proved to be very much to the left during the war and had been strongly under the influence of Lenin, of Rakowski, and of the Bulgarian Tesnyaki, quite naturally declared for communism. Those who, in the days of national emergency, had joined in national defence were excluded. And the first elections to the new parliament of the enormously extended state brought this young and feeble party startling success. In most of the newly acquired territories, in Croatia, Slavonia, Bosnia, and Macedonia, political life had been undeveloped before the advent of Serbian rule. Very soon all these parts developed serious resistance to the centralization from Belgrade; in Bosnia and Croatia this regionalist resistance against the predominance of the Serbs merged with the movement for agrarian reform. All these discontents, vague and various but acute, automatically united in the support of the one declared opposition party, the Serbian socialists, who now called themselves communists. To its own tremendous surprise the young party, which had been represented by two deputies in the Serbian Chamber at the outbreak of the war, found itself with fifty-four representatives in the new Chamber after the war. But the disproportion between its revolutionary words and parliamentary strength on the one hand, and its lack of real coherence on the other, was too great. The administration carried out a bold stroke and simply prohibited the new party. The bubble burst immediately; the party, which had been only just second to the 'radicals', the party of the government, disappeared at once, never to reappear. The discontent of the newly acquired provinces flowed into its natural channels, the regionalist peasant parties, of which the Croatian peasant party of Stepan Radič was the most important. The communists spent what little strength they had left in endless internal squabbles which ruined their underground activities completely. Repeated attempts to form an open party and let it participate in elections only disclosed the fact that the party as such had lost all influence, though a general vague sympathy for communism remained a constant element of mass movements in Yugoslavia. It never materialized into anything concrete. So the Yugoslav communists follow the Roumanian communists out of our story.

Communism in Czechoslovakia had an infinitely more complex and more important history, which will occupy us at a later stage, but in 1918 and 1919 it did not exist, not even in the embryonic stage of spontaneous revolutionary movements. The Czechs had gained enormously, both in pride and material advantage, through the formation of their state, and the proletariat profited at least as much as other classes; before, all the well-paid jobs tended to be given to Germans. The Germans, on their side, were intent on defending, by a union of all German parties, their national rights. The national motive proved to be stronger than the social one. And Czechoslovak troops fought with discipline, though without distinction, against the Hungarian Soviets in the spring of 1919.

But if the doors from Russia to the south-east and to central Europe were slammed by the gale that blew across Europe in October–November 1918, the door to the north had already been slammed, a few months before, by a single frightful catastrophe. Finland throughout the twentieth century had been torn by two opposing tendencies. The desperate efforts of a highly civilized people to defend its distinctive culture from destruction by Russian Tsarism drove them towards an alliance with Germany, the one power which could help them in that aim. The misery of the Finnish tenant-farmer who lived at the mercy of the Swedish-speaking landlord, drove the Finnish left, however, towards an alliance with the Russian revolutionary movement. In fact, the Finnish socialist movement had always been much more a movement of the small tenants than a proletarian movement; the Finnish proletariat was weak.

But the deep cultural cleavage between the Scandinavian civilization to her west—based on the most literate population in all Europe—and the semi-barbarous Slavonic neighbour to the east had forced the Finnish labour movement to tread a rather lonely path. The Russian revolution forced both the national and the social problems to a climax. The Russian democratic government of 1917 attempted to refuse Finland complete independence, but Lenin, as soon as he had come to power, granted it immediately. At the same time the big upheaval in Petrograd, only a few miles beyond the Finnish border, and the presence of numerous Russian troops in full revolution in the country itself, offered a strong attraction. The social-democratic party had roughly 50 per cent of the total poll at the last elections. A small minority within the party carried the day with a proposal to imitate the Bolsheviks, and proclaimed the dictatorship of the proletariat.

I must confess that I have found it impossible to retrace the real history of this rising. What material there is in Swedish and in the publications of the Communist International is worthless. The opponents of the Finnish dictatorship have published pamphlets telling the world that the Reds killed many people, which is certainly true but can hardly be regarded as an exhaustive study of the problem. The communists, through the mouth of the Finn Kuusinen—who later became an important leader of the Comintern—have told the world that the social-democrats betrayed the rising. That they would say in any case, and it is again not very revealing. It is impossible to see even the merest outlines of the Finnish tragedy without knowing Finnish. One thing, however, is certain. The Finnish dictatorship broke down, from a military point of view, even before the Germans arrived. In the north General Mannerheim with the help of the Swedish right organized an army, and proceeded southwards, fairly rapidly. The 'Reds' proved unable to resist. Then, early in April 1918, the Germans intervened, landing at Hangoe, in the rear of the Red front. The central command of the Reds sketched a sensible plan of evacuation of the whole Finnish proletariat to Russia—after all the Finns as a whole number only something over three million people. But their intentions were defeated by the indiscipline of the troops, who acted on a policy of *sauve qui peut*. Tens of thousands were captured and sent to concentration camps, where many of them died of hunger and exposure. It was the first instance of that white terror which avenged a few hundred victims of the propertied classes in the blood of tens of thousands of the poor. Most of the leaders escaped. In Russia they formed a communist party, accusing the moderate wing of the old Socialist Party of having lost the revolution by their hesitations. Their influence in Finland remained considerable for a number of years, and the communist underground organization kept control of most of the industrial unions, while the tenant vote went largely to the social-democrats. Finland as a whole, however, from that day onwards leaned heavily to the right.

Then, at the beginning of 1919, the last loophole was closed. The German volunteers in the Baltic provinces and the national armies organized with English and French help drove the Bolshevik troops out of Riga and Reval, which the Germans had occupied after the breakdown of the German Empire. In October 1919 Yudenitch advanced to the gates of Petrograd. The three Baltic republics were established. In Lithuania there was never a labour movement worth speaking of. In Latvia and Esthonia the movement split sharply between Bolsheviks and anti-Bolsheviks, the latter backed by the new nationalism of the freed populations. Here as in other states agrarian reform decided the issue. The Lithuanians ruthlessly expropriated the Polish landlords, the Latvians and Esthonians the Baltic barons of German origin and Tsarist allegiance. A more or less satisfied propertied peasantry formed the backbone of the new states, while industry, with the loss of the Russian market, rapidly declined. In Latvia and Esthonia the communists, driven underground, nevertheless for years continued to keep control of the trade unions. But their influence slowly faded out, partly through their own mistakes, and then the labour movement, isolated from the peasants which had supported it under Tsarism, was no longer a matter of primary concern.

This defeat of Bolshevism in the Baltic provinces happened just in the very days when the Communist International was coming to birth. Looking back upon that moment we are able to understand that the battle was already half lost before it started. Bolshevism, having practically no support in the West and having completely failed to establish itself in the south-east and the Russian border states, could only attack in central Europe, where material defeat and disintegration gave it a chance. But then the very fact of failure elsewhere made the attempt at social revolution in central Europe a very dubious affair, because revolution there would be jammed between political adversaries east and west; for Bolshevism to conquer in the countries just defeated, those countries would first have to win a new international war, which was a hopeless prospect. But that could not be seen so clearly at the time. Undoubtedly the foundation of the Communist International is intimately connected with the revolutions in central Europe, to which we must now turn. They fall naturally into three groups. Revolution in Hungary developed into a short Soviet dictatorship under the immediate influence of Russia; the Hungarian revolution deeply influenced events in Austria. These two from the first stand together. In Germany revolution, though generally influenced by Russian Bolshevism, did not follow the Russian lead; but here the revolution, in the end, led to the formation of a strong communist party upon which Moscow's gaze was concentrated for many years. Finally, in 1920, Italy, which had come out of the war almost as shattered as a defeated country, came to the brink of revolution. The German, Austrian, and Hungarian events are directly connected with the foundation of the Communist International. We shall have to consider them first, in two separate chapters. The Italian movement, while contributing little to the formation of the Comintern, deeply influenced its early development. We shall turn to it in a later section.

CHAPTER VI

THE HUNGARIAN DICTATORSHIP

Hungary, in the ostensible form of a modern parliamentary constitution, had remained a country as feudal as could be. By far the larger part of the land was owned by the magnates and a considerable part by the gentry; hardly anything remained, in most regions, for the peasant, who, as poor tenant or almost landless labourer, continued to live in serfdom. Magnates and gentry together, with a very few upstarts from the bourgeois intelligentsia, ruled the country. In true feudal manner it was deemed a defilement to earn one's living by work—except in the army and in the thoroughly feudal civil service—and in consequence the whole bourgeoisie, financial, commercial, and industrial, was Jewish; in Hungary the Jews have kept much more than elsewhere the stigma of an outcast race, deriving from the Middle Ages. Industry was exceedingly weak, commercial policy exclusively devised to protect the interests of the landlords, the administration was corrupt, the country extremely backward. A cleverly designed distribution of parliamentary seats, the barring of the lower classes from the vote, together with violence and corruption at the polls, preserved this régime politically intact. The national minorities, actually proved by official statistics to be the majority of the population, were deprived of all their rights, including that of being taught in their own language, and every attempt at resistance was cruelly crushed. More than half the population were illiterate.

At the same time the Hungarian ruling class was powerful. It had always shown in decisive moments that capacity for unity of action which is the peculiar quality of narrow, clannish aristocracies and which had been developed into a fine art by the last great leader of old Hungary, Count Stephan Tisza. In contrast with the Austrian part of the dual monarchy, which was clearly disintegrating, Hungary produced the effect of a well-united state, capable of consistent political action. Hungary, in fact, dominated Austrian politics.

There are obviously deep analogies between pre-war Hungary and pre-war Russia. The bourgeoisie in Hungary was even weaker than in Russia, because it belonged altogether to the foreign and ostracized Jewish race, if for no other reason. It could never hope gradually to climb into an influential position in the higher administration. It could never make its weight felt in the decisive questions of commercial policy. The bourgeoisie being of no account, the logical conclusion seemed to be that if, one day, international events brought about the downfall of the Hungarian aristocratic régime and a rebellion arose against the aristocracy, it would be a replica, on a smaller scale, of the Russian phenomenon. The proletariat, guided by an organization of professional revolutionaries, would push the weak bourgeoisie aside, draw the peasantry with it, and establish a dictatorship after the Russian pattern.

But no organization of professional revolutionaries arose. Why did Hungary develop nothing similar to Narodnaya Volya and still less anything like Lenin's party? The Russian intelligentsia was faced by cultural problems which their Hungarian class-brothers did not have to consider. The Russian intelligentsia came from the people, came under the influence of the West, and solved the conflict between its Byzantine-Slavonic background and its Western education by going back into the people, with a Westernized theory enlivened by the religious enthusiasm of a Byzantine pattern. Nothing similar happened in Hungary. There the intelligentsia, of which the vast majority was Jewish, did not belong to the people, could not draw from the strength of the people. As far as they were educated, they simply and unreservedly looked to the West for inspiration. Where Tolstoy, Dostoevski, and Lenin had come back from the West with a strange mixture of awe and antipathy, the leading intellectuals of Hungary simply participated in the life of Heidelberg and Paris.

Similar differences existed between the Russian and the Hungarian proletariat, and this was not due only to the lack of revolutionary leadership, though that was one determining factor. In fact, the Hungarian labour movement was one of the most 'reformist' in the world. While all political rights were denied to the Hungarian workers, social-democracy was loyal to the end of the war. And the workers were loyal to the party until almost the end of the war, and became loyal to it again after the breakdown of the dictatorship. This is largely to be explained by the privileged position of the Hungarian urban proletariat, not, of course, in comparison with the Western proletariat, but with its own peasantry. There hardly existed a trade-union organization outside Budapest and the mining districts, but there the unions were strong, especially the union of the engineers, and obtained wages which, while miserable by European, were high by Hungarian standards. Here the reality behind Lenin's theory of the 'workers' aristocracy' can be seen. It is ridiculous to contend that the Hungarian workers were 'bribed' by any extra-profits of the Hungarian bourgeoisie, which itself was weak, economically and politically. Neither were these wages so much as tolerable compared, not merely with the standard of London, but with the low standard of Vienna. But wealth is relative. In conditions of general misery very small advantages create a privileged class. And there is no group of the working class all over the world which, in course of time, has not obtained such advantages. This is only one aspect of the general rule that everywhere the proletariat has something to lose. But it feels most concerned about it, not where, within a generally high standard of living, it has achieved much, but where among general misery it has achieved something. The Hungarian workers, while defending with vigour and heroism their trade unions against repeated attacks by the régime, very soon started to accept, *de facto*, this same régime. In the end something like a practical compromise between the régime and the labour movement was evolved. The workers renounced their attempts to carry the movement beyond Budapest and the mining districts and kept away from revolutionary activity; the régime, in exchange, left the unions undisturbed. This compromise was embodied in a formal treaty, shortly after the defeat of the dictatorship; it had in fact existed before it. One of the chief results of this state of things was that no serious peasant movement ever came into existence. The landlord saw to it that the peasants did not organize themselves, and the régime saw to it that they were not organized by the workers.

Upon this régime, in 1918, came crushing defeat. The national minorities emancipated themselves, which meant that the feudal class automatically lost half their lands. In addition thousands and thousands of officers and civil servants found themselves without employment. Industry lost most of its raw materials and a good deal of its already narrow markets. Much unemployment ensued, as sharply felt among the intellectuals as among the workers. The unemployed captain and head of a department made a contribution to the revolutionary movement as valuable as that of the unemployed workman. The national territory was curtailed, first by the armistice and then by repeated subsequent decrees of the Allied Powers; and the humiliation was deeply felt among every class. There was only one thing which, so far, the country had been spared: famine. Being an agrarian and a very fertile region, Hungary during and immediately after the war suffered much less than Germany, Austria, or Turkey.

In the last days of October the old régime broke down without any real resistance. A 'national council' was formed out of all progressive groups. A few days later a republic was proclaimed. Count Michael Karolyi, a Whig magnate who, in the old days, had fought vigorously for complete independence from Vienna and the Hapsburgs, was proclaimed first premier and later president of the republic. But the one real, organized power upon which the government could rely was the Social-democratic Party. From the beginning of the revolution onwards, and more from month to month, the Social-democratic Party exerted a real dictatorship.

The new régime was faced with four main problems: to make peace; to carry through democratic elections; to democratize the administration; and, more decisive than any other, to carry through agrarian reform. In all these countries where the feudal manor with its dependent serfs still exists, *de facto* if not *de jure*, there is no room for democracy. Whether it is Russia or Spain, Hungary or Roumania, the first condition for a working democracy is a strong, land-owning, self-confident peasantry. Otherwise the choice lies only between 'Bolshevism' and feudal reaction. And even Russian Bolshevism could live only by giving the land to the peasants.

The Karolyi government did not achieve even one of its four principal tasks. It can hardly be held responsible for the failure to make peace; for from month to month the French military commander of the south-east front, General Franchet d'Esperey, put new demands, narrowing the territory of the young republic, and taking away from it districts which were undoubtedly purely Magyar in race. The Karolyi government, whose chief personalities had all been pledged to the ideals of Western democracy before the war, and had enthusiastically welcomed Wilson's programme at a time when to hold such opinions brought a man nearer to the gallows than to power, was discredited by these strokes; it was precisely the old military and administrative caste which, deeply wounded in their national pride, started to see the one remaining hope in Bolshevism, and a new war in alliance with Russia.

Again the responsibility for not carrying through the agrarian reform cannot be laid at the door of Count Karolyi and his personal friends; it must be charged to the account of both the social-democrats and their rising communist rivals. Agrarian reform in itself was very difficult. To carry it through with the old administration, which was under the control of the feudal caste itself, was out of the question. But as no other group had had political and administrative training, the elements for a rapid change of personnel were lacking. That, in itself, drove matters towards a revolutionary solution; the peasant masses would, probably, earlier or later, take things into their own hands. But again they had no organizations of their own. There was only one force which could help: the urban workers and their organizations. But they refused. Hungarian social-democracy in those days was not simply 'reformist'. It was going to take power and hold it. It had destroyed the old, clannish parties of the aristocracy; and by all available means it obstructed the formation of new ones, of a 'bourgeois' character. The new trade unions of the intellectuals, which tended towards a policy of liberal democracy, were forced, against their will, into the social-democratic

T.U.C. The organizing work of the incipient Peasant Party was obstructed. The electioneering campaigns of the democratic parties were stopped forcibly by social-democratic workers, with the approval of a considerable section of the party bureaucracy. Finally, the government had to drop the intention of carrying through the elections; a 'democratic' government was unable to convoke parliament!

Thus, while violence was rampant all over the country both the reform of the administration and the creation of a strong peasant party became impossible. Nothing was achieved. Worse, the labour movement worked actively against any progress towards a solution of the decisive agrarian problem. As in Germany before the war, it was regarded as a sign of opportunism to care for the peasant. As in a peasant country such as Bulgaria the orthodox Marxists a few months before had refused to collaborate with the peasants in a fight for the republic, so now in Hungary both social-democrats and communists repudiated the idea of parcelling the latifundia and giving the peasants the land. This, the pundits of official Marxism in both camps declared, was a reactionary measure, bound to decrease the output and to make the task of nationalization of the land more difficult. For the more extreme sections of the labour movement the Russian example counted for much, but they interpreted it in their own way. Lenin in Russia had set out to create socialism in a backward country. Why then should not they try to do the same in Hungary? But, at the same time, they looked down upon the boorishness of the Russians. If over there they had had no choice but to give the peasants the land—which, surely, would jeopardize all Lenin's further steps towards socialism—then they would show the world that in the West a proletarian dictatorship could and would go forward without and in spite of the peasant. Most of the social-democratic theoreticians and all the communists applauded this policy. Thus the lack of care of the trade-unionist worker for the peasant, whom in all countries he despises as backward and stupid, and the haughty contempt for this people of an intelligentsia severed from them, decided the fate of the Hungarian revolution from the start.

It was in these conditions that Bolshevism grew in Hungary, or, more precisely, in the industrial districts of Hungary.

There was general unrest and bitter suffering everywhere and no constructive effort anywhere. These two things made not so much for revolution and deep change as for a violent and terrible outbreak. Bolshevism was brought to Hungary and Austria by war prisoners sent back from Russia. Many of them had been released immediately after the peace of Brest-Litovsk, but the more politically minded had been kept and trained in Russia and sent home after the November revolution. None of these men had had any serious revolutionary or even political training before the war; none had held any position of confidence in the labour movement of their home-country. The elements for a serious revolutionary leadership in Hungary were lacking. The Russians had no choice; if they wanted to have small, disciplined groups of Bolshevist leaders in the West they had to introduce leaders of that type. No others were available. Naturally, these people had learnt Bolshevist agitation during the Russian revolution: they had learnt little else, as later events were to show.

This applies in the first place to Bela Kun, the leader of the Hungarian dictatorship. The background of this man is obscure. He had dabbled in journalism, both in bourgeois and social-democratic papers, but never achieved distinction. He had been secretary of a workers' sick fund at Kolosvar, in Transylvania, and had played a role in the labour movement of that town, a movement weak in numbers and spirit. He had drawn his inspiration from Russia. Lenin, who was such a splendid psychologist among his own Russians, was so much mistaken as to entrust to this man the task of carrying through revolution in Hungary. In Russia Kun had seen three things which were of primary importance for a Hungarian revolutionary: the agrarian revolution; Lenin's fierce fight against the 'reformists'; and the peace negotiations with the Germans at Brest-Litovsk. From these three experiences Kun seems to have drawn the surprising principles that one must not give the land to the peasants; that one must make war at any price; and that, at the decisive moment, a revolutionary must form an alliance with the reformists.

Kun's personality remained always somewhat in the shadow, because it was hidden behind his public activity. But the thing which appealed to Kun in this activity was less its political aspect than the chance it gave him to express himself in violent and hysterical agitation. Balance in this man there was none. It is on record that the leader of the dictatorship broke into tears repeatedly, not only on the day of the fall of the 'Soviets' but for instance—one among many cases—during a crisis at the party congress of June 1919. He was not physically courageous. When the dictatorship fell he negotiated with Vienna for a private train to escape, taking with him only his family and his nearest friends, forgetting, in the excitement of danger, to get safe conducts for many of his close associates. But he was cruel. During the dictatorship two Ukrainian officers, sent by Rakovski in order to keep contact between the Hungarian and the Ukrainian armies, thought Kun's policy not sufficiently revolutionary and entered into a military conspiracy against it. The case undoubtedly deserved a court-martial, and probably a court-martial behind closed doors. But Kun simply ordered the two conspirators against his life to be thrown into the Danube—not as a deterrent, but in secret; he was a frightened tyrant. Later on, in 1920, he was chief political commissar in the last campaign of the Russian civil war. A considerable section of the 'white' army of Baron Wrangel was captured in the Crimea; they were mostly officers. The civil war was obviously at an end. Nevertheless, hundreds —according to some reports thousands—were put to death. The device employed to do it quickly was to tie heavy stones around them and throw them into the sea—the scene has been described by Gladkov, a first-rank Soviet writer, in his *Cement*. And Kun was the political commissar under whose aegis the atrocity was committed! Lenin was notoriously beside himself, as he very rarely was, when he heard of the massacre. Nevertheless, in 1921 Kun, at a decisive juncture, was again sent to Germany, where we shall meet him again. There was no choice—the best Russians were needed at home and adequate personnel from the West was lacking. One should not think of Kun, however, as an inhuman monster. He was simply a weakling incensed by a sanguinary theory whose emotional paraphernalia were all he could grasp; and he was thrown hither and thither between fright, anger, and—incredible as it may sound —his good heart. Wilhelm Boehm, the commander of the Red army, loathed Kun; nevertheless, in his memoirs, where he accumulated evidence against Kun both as a man and as a politician, he reports half a dozen names of aristocrats whom Kun saved during the dictatorship, not out of political calculations, but because he could not bear the sight of human suffering when it came too close to him. (Kun was arrested a few months ago, on the charge of semi-Trotskyism. It is perhaps equally difficult to sympathize with the man who has so many things upon his conscience as to applaud his destruction on the charge of the one crime which he certainly never committed.)

The first step Kun took after coming home was to push aside the group which had led the big strike of January 1918. It was a group of honest and intelligent, if somewhat naïve, intellectuals. He objected to their qualms about the limits which were to be set to demagogy. He had no such doubts as they. Without hesitation he started discrediting both the government and the Social-democratic Party by putting claims so high as to make it absolutely impossible to grant them. This was the chief reason for his speedy success. It was also the reason for his failure. The cadres of the young organization were not nearly strong enough to control a wild crowd with excited appetites. The movement was brought to power on the strength of these exaggerated hopes, and when the dictatorship eventually brought hunger instead of plenty, it found itself alone. Lenin too had played a high game of demagogy. But he was able to fulfil at least two of his chief pledges: the end of international war and the granting of land to the peasants. Kun's success was based upon promises of wage increases, big indemnities for the retired soldiers, and the like, which could not be fulfilled.

In its early stages the communist movement in Hungary was not proletarian in character. Its mainstay was the soldiers in demobilization, of which at least a considerable part were peasants. Here was an enormous danger. The young republic had no armed force of its own. As in other matters, so in this, it was unable to take a decision. It had to rely in the end upon those soldiers who had remained with the colours, i.e. officers who wavered between Bolshevism and counter-revolution, troops from the occupied regions who could not go home and were a prey to every sort of demagogy, and young people without jobs. The workless, too, provided considerable reinforcement for the communist propaganda. At first the organized trade-unionists withstood the onslaught of the communist agitation; but with increasing difficulties, and with food getting short—a result of the occupation of large districts by the enemy and of the collapse of both industry and administration—the tension increased and the workers began to go over to the communists. The rapid growth of the new party naturally bred disagreement among the social-democrats. One wing wanted to compete with the communists in popularity, another one wanted to keep the masses back sharply; some were for military action against Kun and his following, others relied on conviction. Then, suddenly, one final blow brought down the whole structure of Hungarian democracy.

On March 20th Lieutenant-Colonel Vix, chief of the armistice commission at Budapest, informed the government that it must evacuate one more important section of the country—including Debreczen, Hungary's second town—and that the new line of demarcation ought to be regarded as the provisional political frontier. This was the end: the government had definitely failed with its confidence in Wilson. Acceptance was out of the question, but a policy of resistance could not be carried out, so it was thought, by Karolyi and his group. Acceptance was rejected on the grounds that the whole country would rise against it and that the storm must inevitably lead to counter-revolution. It was assumed that the social-democrats should take over and come to 'some sort of agreement' with the communists. Negotiations between socialists and communists were opened immediately.

They lasted for only half an hour, taking place in one of Budapest's chief prisons. Kun had been arrested a few weeks earlier. Now he and his staff were immediately released, and the negotiators came back with an agreement on only two points: the two parties would merge again, and together set up a Soviet government. But Karolyi was not informed of this. While in the town power was already taken over by socialists and communists together, the socialist ministers sat quietly with Karolyi at the last Cabinet meeting. He was kept in the belief that he would have a constitutional socialist government to succeed him. In the evening papers appeared a proclamation by which he handed over the government to the Soviets.

He had never written or signed this proclamation, which he first saw in print.

Later, when the dictatorship culminated in a frightful catastrophe, both socialists and communists naturally tried to disclaim responsibility for their pact. The chief point of contention was not the proclamation of the Soviet republic; it was altogether obvious that this was the condition which the communists had forced upon the socialists and without which their collaboration was not to be had. But both partners later on claimed that the other side had insisted upon the unification of the party. The socialists, afterwards, wanted to repudiate their responsibility for communist policy, while the communists, from the beginning, incurred the strong displeasure of Lenin for their merging with the socialists. The wireless correspondence between Lenin and Kun about the matter was published in number 2 of the *Communist International* during the dictatorship itself. Lenin urged Kun to organize an independent communist party, but Kun bluntly refused.

It is easy to see, however, that far from being forced into unity by the other, both sides wanted it. This is sufficiently proved by the very fact that the negotiations lasted only for half an hour, just time enough to formulate the pact; no serious discussions about its content can have taken place in so short a time. Moreover, the reason for this eagerness to merge is obvious. The choice lay between fighting and combining. The peaceful co-existence of two parties, with very different views, within the dictatorship was impossible. For the dictatorship, by definition, could not grant the right of free discussion. Fighting would have wrecked the Soviet experiment at the outset; there remained only co-operation. The socialists hoped that merging would put an end to the violent attacks brought against them, especially within the trade unions. The communists, on the contrary, hoped that merging would allow them to permeate the machinery of the mass movement with greater ease. But the truth was that neither had any choice. The socialists felt unable to take over the government with the communists attacking them in the flank. The communists were too weak to take power alone, with the socialists resisting them. They did not feel in a position, either, to refuse to participate. For everybody was convinced that after the note of Lieutenant-Colonel Vix the alternative to a militant Soviet régime was counter-revolution. The two parties must co-operate; and they could co-operate under a dictatorship only if they merged. At the time nobody doubted the course to take and nobody could doubt.

Yet it may be asked whether, after all, the Karolyi govern-ment could not have attempted to carry on. And, from the communist point of view, it may be asked whether it was not their job, at this juncture, to force the government to carry on. Rosa Luxemburg had envisaged for Germany precisely the situation which now arose in Hungary. It was altogether obvious that, in the frightful chaos which followed the war in the defeated countries, some government, finding itself in an impasse, might prefer to leave things to the revolutionaries. On the first platform of the Spartakusbund after the war Rosa Luxemburg, discussing this possibility, had said: 'The Sparta-kusbund will not accept power for the mere reason that all other parties failed.' And she went on to explain that only a safe majority within the working class could give the com-munists a chance not only to win power but also to hold it. Kun was lured by the phantom of an easy capture of power. He seized it, not after a big class struggle carried through to the end, but as the result of a crisis of wounded national pride. Even then there was a chance, provided the government kept its origin in mind and carefully put the national issue before the social. This would not indeed have been the sort of régime Kun had imagined. It is doubtful whether there can ever exist, in the West, a 'proletarian dictatorship' of the true type, in other words, whether, in the West, there will ever exist a safe majority for social revolution within the proletariat; all expe-riences of the last two decades seem to tell against it.

As it was, Kun set out on his adventure with a proletariat which wanted at best to give the dictatorship a chance, but was certainly not prepared to defend it whatever happened. The social-democratic leaders, with whom he had to co-operate, were by far his superiors in political tradition and perception, but lacked at the same time that iron decision which is the primary requirement of leadership in moments of big crisis. Some of the leaders were almost openly hostile. And then followed blunder after blunder.

THE HUNGARIAN DICTATORSHIP

While Kun refused to copy Lenin's agrarian policy, which even as it stood might have saved the dictatorship, he copied religiously an experiment which Lenin had never really welcomed but had been compelled to try: 'war-communism'. This consisted essentially of the abolition of all private property in the means of production, at one stroke. Matthias Rakosi, second Commissar of Commerce, published a decree, the second day of the new régime, closing all shops except grocers, tobacconists, and chemists and announcing the death penalty for any other commercial transaction made before an inventory had been taken. The decree was revoked a few days later. But private commerce had been frightened away and never returned; the more so as persecution continued. The new rulers seemed to think that it was an important task of socialism to nationalize children's sweetmeats and barbers' perfumes. And the very idea of dealing with private commerce by any means than the death penalty would have seemed to them the height of opportunism. It is true that while a certain amount of terrorism was going on in reality, many more threats were uttered than were ever put into effect.

As to the land question, with the exception of the estate of Count Karolyi, offered by himself for parcelling, not a single estate had been distributed before the communists came into power. The peasants were waiting. The new régime took hope away from them. A decree of socialization of the big estates was issued and they were put under state administration. But as adequate personnel was entirely lacking, the previous owners or their administrators saw themselves named state administrators on most of the large estates. Thus the Soviet régime kept the estates intact for their previous owners, under their own administration. And to make things worse it was openly canvassed in government quarters that, once the administrative difficulties with the big estates had been solved, peasant property would be nationalized too.

But the peasant had grievances more immediate than even the menace to his modest plot of land. Since the end of the war industrial output had been declining, partly through lack of raw materials, but even more through lack of discipline in the factories. The proclamation of the Soviet régime increased the drop in production and the People's Commissar for

Nationalization, Eugene Varga, complained bitterly that this drop was mainly due to the complete disintegration of spontaneous discipline. Under the double pressure of lack of supplies and lack of hands willing to work industry broke down. And Budapest suddenly found itself unable to offer the countryside anything for the food it must take away from the peasants.

At the same time inflation of a quite peculiar kind beset the unhappy country. The Austro-Hungarian monarchy had had only one central bank, at Vienna, which alone had the right to issue notes. During these months the 'successor states' were nationalizing their currencies; and Hungary had to do the same, in the turmoil of revolution. The government, which had neither taxes nor other sources of income to rely on, had to fill the gap with the help of the printing-press. Unhappily, the old notes of the Austro-Hungarian bank continued to circulate, while the Hungarian Soviets had no adequate printing-press and their 'white' money was sharply contrasted with the 'good old blue money' of the dual monarchy. Soon peasants, workers, and civil servants alike tried to refuse the worthless 'white' money and to enforce payment in 'blue' money, of which there was only a very limited quantity. The circulation of goods and money broke down. Budapest became acquainted with the only one of the four apocalyptic horsemen which it had not yet known: Famine.

In such a state the country had to go to war. It had to, because only war could keep the government popular. In the early hours it had been welcomed everywhere. There is good warrant for the story that at Szeged, the third town of Hungary, which fell into the occupied zone, the French commander gave leave to those of the inhabitants who were for the Reds to leave the town and cross the border; he had expected them to be a few hundred, but over ten thousand went. The Soviet government, in the first days, was simply regarded as a government of national defence in alliance with Soviet Russia. Unfortunately, precisely during the first weeks, the Russian Soviet troops, which in March had stood almost at the Polish border, had to retreat to Kiev, under the combined pressure of Denikin and Petljura. And no help was available from that side. It was clear that the Roumanians were going to occupy the territory attributed to them by the Vix note, and the Soviet republic would have to fight if it wanted to live.

During these anxious weeks General Smuts came to Budapest with the intention of negotiating. He offered a new demarcation line, almost identical with that existing before the Vix note, which would have been virtually annulled had his offer been accepted; his conditions were that the Soviet government must keept the conditions of the armistice—i.e. not mobilize—and abstain from propaganda abroad. He added that he would use his influence in order to provide Hungary with flour and fats, but that his conditions must be accepted immediately, *en bloc*. What was behind this offer?

Kun, with a mentality characteristic of people of his type, put a double interpretation on General Smuts's offer. First 'they' felt obviously weak at Paris and London; second they tried to make him fall into a trap. The offer must certainly be declined. With a logic which would have been well adapted to political methods regarded as normal in the East, Kun reasoned that if his adversaries offered a compromise, he could squeeze them into a better one. The 'big four' in Paris had really been somewhat frightened by the unexpected results of their uncompromising attitude. Even Clemenceau was disheartened and the British took the opportunity of gaining a point for the milder policy they advocated. A different man than Kun might have seen this opportunity to drive a wedge, by unreserved acceptance of Smuts's offer, between the British and the French, between Smuts and Franchet d'Esperey. If Smuts's offer took effect, it meant both a gain of time—invaluable at the moment of initial chaos—and a big gain of prestige. If the offer was not carried out honestly there still remained time to mobilize as the later mobilization within two days has proved. But Kun decided that war there must be. He gave a dilatory answer; so Smuts's offer fell to the ground. Where Lenin, one year before, in Brest-Litovsk, had made tremendous sacrifices in order to escape a disastrous war and gain time for the strengthening of his government, Kun intentionally drifted into war, in the belief that it could save him. It is true that no other course was open to him unless he dropped his policy of complete nationalization and satisfied the peasants. That he would not do; and therefore he had to rely upon nationalism.

He got the war he wanted. The Roumanians attacked, and the remainder of the Hungarian army broke like straw before them. Debreczen was lost and the Roumanians, in the last days of April, not much more than a month after the beginning of the dictatorship, approached Budapest. At that moment something unexpected happened. The workers of Budapest rose. They saw that the victory of the Roumanians meant the victory of counter-revolution. The old feudal parties had already started reorganizing and formed a 'White' government at Szeged. The victorious Roumanians would give them power. Thus the class instinct merged with hurt national pride into a splendid gesture of heroism. Perhaps half the Budapest proletariat volunteered for the front. As there was no time to create a military organization off-hand they were formed into factory companies and battalions. Many professional officers volunteered for the war of national defence. And not less than four regular army corps were set up at a stroke.

That started the counter-offensive. A leading trade-unionist, a convinced social-democrat, Wilhelm Boehm, was named chief commander, and a colonel of the old army, Aurel Stromfeld, a man of quite exceptional strategical gifts, became his chief of staff. (He later died as a member of the underground Communist Party in Hungary.) The Roumanians had delayed their advance unduly. In the middle of May they were attacked and after short fighting driven back over the Theiss. Here the offensive stopped, because another danger had appeared on the horizon. The Czechs, under French commanders, pushed forward through Slovakia to Budapest. They were attacked on the flank, beaten again and again, and almost all Slovakia reconquered. Amidst the misery brought over Hungary by the economic policy of the government, enormous rejoicing over the successful war filled the country. Boehm and Stromfeld had almost achieved what Kemal Pasha, two years later, completely achieved in Turkey.

But at this decisive moment the economic failure broke the backbone of the military advance. A terrific storm was brewing to the west of the Danube, in the regions near the Austrian border. The commander of the army corps operating in that sector, Colonel Craenenbrock, was a traitor to the Soviet cause and in understanding with the White government at Szeged.

But the outbreak was not his work, he only welcomed it and allowed it to proceed unchecked. Between 6th June and 8th June the railwaymen of the Western lines went on strike. The leader of their union, Dr. Eugene Landler, was the truest of the true, then commander of the 3rd army corps, soon commander-in-chief of the Red army, and afterwards a leading communist in exile. But he could do nothing. The railwaymen at Szombathely, who went first on strike, put a number of very reasonable and natural demands about rations and food, but primarily they claimed to be paid in blue instead of white money. The strike spread rapidly over the whole western net, and on the third day reached the Budapest Western Station. There was nothing for it but to give in to the railwaymen's demands, which, naturally, gave the signal for similar claims from other quarters.

West of the Danube the latifundia were less numerous and the peasant-holdings both larger in size and more important in numbers than in other parts of the country. Therefore the requisitions of cereals, carried out by detachments of the Red army, created even more resentment here than elsewhere. The railway strike in these districts was the signal for a peasant rising; and this, again, was the signal for a fierce outbreak of 'Red terrorism'.

In the first days of the Soviet republic a gang of demobilized sailors who called themselves 'Lenin-boys' had quartered themselves in one of the biggest hotels of Budapest, under the command of one Czerny. They professed profound contempt for the humanitarianism of the government, and accordingly carried out arrests, and occasionally executions, on their own account and decision. Most stories about the tortures they inflicted upon their prisoners were probably untrue, though Czerny, after having been a 'Red' terrorist, is said to have become a 'White' one. The government itself found itself repeatedly menaced by this gang. Finally they were led into a trap and disarmed. But now the necessity of cruel repression of counter-revolution was felt, and some of those who had served under Czerny were enrolled in the special detachments entrusted with this task. At the head of the punitive expedition to western Hungary went a certain Tibor Szamuely, who before the war had been a journalist. He had been occupied previously, with work of the secret police, which, it must be said to the honour of the men in charge, was not nearly so sanguinary as that of the awful Cheka in Russia; nevertheless, the leaders were later hanged by the Whites. As to Szamuely, he was not a sadist, or at least not simply a sadist. He had served and continued to serve the Soviet government in many and varied capacities, all of them dangerous enough, and fulfilled his tasks with unswerving devotion. But, profoundly believing in violence and in violence alone, he knew no doubts and no hesitation. He transformed his repression of the rising in the west into an orgy of blood. Landler saved his railwaymen. But the peasant villages were punished as such, not the individual peasants who had taken arms. Occasionally a patrol was ordered to shoot the first three peasants it would meet when entering a particular village; and there were plenty of hangings of hostages. The peasant rising was broken, but the power of the victorious offensive, which was to proceed by a flanking movement precisely from that region, was broken as well.

At this juncture the Allies interfered a second time. Clemenceau sent a note calling on the Soviets to evacuate the territory of Slovakia they had conquered and promising that, in exchange, the Roumanians would evacuate what Hungarian territory they still held. Kun felt unable to continue the war. In the meantime the pressure of the socialists had become very strong, and many socialists were for peace at any price. Faced with famine and disaster the masses turned back to them. The party congress in June brought the country near to a social-democratic rising and an attempt was made to out-vote all the communist leaders and to form a central committee consisting of social-democrats only. The rising was averted, at the last moment, because Johann Haubrich, the military commander of Budapest and a right-wing social-democrat, for reasons described by Boehm as 'inexplicable', refused to rise against Kun. The newly elected central committee was again composed of members both of the old social-democratic and of the old communist parties. But it was now obvious that it was difficult to continue the war against neighbours with very strong socialist opposition at home. Kun decided to accept Clemenceau's offer and Slovakia was evacuated. This step roused tremendous opposition among the nationalist elements which had hitherto backed the dictatorship and supplied it with the major part of its officers. W. Boehm, the chief commander, resigned in protest, though he was himself a social-democrat, and his chief of staff, A. Stromfeld, resigned with him. A few weeks later their dark views about the future proved to be true. Roumania did not evacuate the region occupied by its army, and the allies at Paris endorsed its action. The sacrifice of Slovakia had led to nothing. And the surrender of all the gains of the war estranged from the dictatorship the masses of the middle classes. It was the beginning of the end.

But the army was disintegrated by the action of other factors as well. While the officers were driven into the camp of the Whites by the conclusion of the armistice with the Czechs, the workers were driven away from the army by the economic administration at home. While they fought at the front their womenfolk went hungry at home, and this not merely on account of lack of food. It was largely a question of distribution. The complete nationalization of economic life—with the exception of the small farms—had led to an enormous increase of the bureaucracy. Already under the Karolyi government the personnel for a thorough administrative reform had been lacking. It was still less available for the enormously increased tasks incumbent upon it under the communist dictatorship. This automatically led to the employment of the old bureaucracy, almost *en masse*, for the non-political work, including the administration of ration-distribution. This old bureaucracy had been hated for its corruption and for its rude ways of dealing with all those who had no special claim on it. Now this same bureaucracy, which the workers hated, was invested with the power to give or not to give bread to their starving wives and children and that with the backing of the authority of an uncontrolled dictatorship! It was the complaints about the helplessness of the women against the 'bread-chit bureaucrats' which made the workers drift home from the army in their thousands and thus broke the front.

Some sort of freedom of political expression and discussion, of public control, might have brought relief. The Soviets, in theory, were supposed to afford such an instrument of control.

But in the 'Soviet' republic there were no Soviets. Or rather there was an institution called a 'Central Soviet', which had been elected not after a contest between various candidates, but upon one single list. In one district of Budapest a list of communist extremists had been smuggled in and won against the list of the united Socialist-communist Party. The vote was annulled and a second poll brought the desired result. This body was of no account and did not take part at all in the real decisions, which were arrived at in negotiations between the leading people; the 'Soviet' had only to register them. Thus the workers were helpless against the bureaucracy. It is interesting to note that Trotsky, to-day, complains bitterly about the lack of 'Soviet democracy' in Russia, but neither Trotsky nor Lenin ever criticized Bela Kun for the sort of 'Soviet' régime which he introduced in Hungary. Those who have been driven out of the Comintern in one of the numerous factional contests, have long desired the 'proletarian democracy' which existed in the good old times of Lenin, but historical evidence rather tends to show that, though some difference between then and now undoubtedly exists, it is, in fact, smaller than is generally assumed.

Since the beginning of June it was obvious that 'Soviet' Hungary could not hold out. Kun sought salvation in an extension of its territory through a revolution in Vienna. But there he found conditions much more unpromising for his work than they had been when the dictatorship was established in Budapest. Austria had a numerous proletariat, well organized and well controlled by social-democratic leadership. The prestige of this leadership had been increased by the success of the left wing, the pacifists, within the party during the last months of the war. At the head of this group stood Friedrich Adler, who in 1916 had assassinated Count Stuergkh, and Otto Bauer, who was then Foreign Secretary. Moreover, the peasants, though strongly republican after four years of war, were Catholic and hated every idea of social revolution. Austria, in contrast with Hungary, had solved its land-problem by a thorough abolition of all feudal forms of tenure as early as 1848. It was obvious, moreover, that both Czechoslovakia and Yugoslavia would take very serious measures and that a simple blockade would be enough to bring to bay within a fortnight a country which had experienced four years' starvation. And the visible failure of the Hungarian dictatorship did the rest. Tentatively, some of the Austrian socialist leaders asked Budapest whether it could feed Vienna for a couple of months; the request was refused and the leaders made up their minds.

The small group of 'left-radicals' which had stood for rapid revolutionary action during the last year of the war had formed themselves into the 'Communist Party of Austria' on 3rd November 1918. They were strengthened by war prisoners released from Russia. The premature step had been taken at the urgent advice of the Russian representative, who wanted to give a signal for the formation of communist parties in other countries. The 'left-radicals', though themselves a small group, had enjoyed considerable following among the munition workers because they had fought courageously for peace. But just now, when peace was made, a republic proclaimed, a workers' army formed by the socialists, and these very socialists were clearly the real rulers of the country, few workers could see the reason for a split. The small group was left alone by their vague following in the factories—and never recovered from this original mistake.

As in Hungary, the groups attracted by the new organization were not primarily factory workers but unemployed, war invalids, soldiers shunning demobilization, etc. But whereas in Hungary the small stratum of organized trade-unionists had finally been swept along by the wave of popular excitement, nothing similar took place in Austria. The workers stood firm by the Socialist Party, though the communists had an enormous amount of money at their disposal. The leaders of the Communist Party stood wavering, arguing, and grumbling. Then Kun decided that things must change. He sent an agent, one Dr. Ernst Bettelheim, to Vienna, in order to 'make' the revolution. There was no question of winning the majority, or even a considerable part, of the factory workers. The communists definitely set out to win power without the consent of the workers, in the hope of convincing them later on. Armed clashes between the communists and the police had happened before and ended inconclusively. But now Bettelheim set out for a big *Putsch*. This word, untranslatable, but very current in the political jargon of almost all Continental languages, means an attempt by a small group without adequate popular backing to seize political power, arms in hand. *Putsche* played a big role in the earlier part of Comintern history.

Bettelheim launched his *Putsch* on 15th June 1919. The armistice commission had ordered a reduction of the 'people's army', which sent the demobilized soldiers to join the ranks of the unemployed. The communists tried to incite the soldiers to a rising, but at the last moment the armistice commission was prevailed upon to withdraw the order (if something similar had been done with the Vix note in Budapest, three months earlier, the Hungarian tragedy would not have happened), and the wisdom of this course appeared immediately. The soldiers did not join in the riot. Unemployed and invalids took part, but in small numbers. The whole *Putsch* had not more than five thousand to ten thousand people behind it, which meant that, in a city of two millions, the communists were an insignificant minority, only important in the chaotic conditions of the first post-war months. But, worst of all, a big rift had opened in the party leadership itself. Most of the higher party officials were thoroughly frightened by the prospect of a rising without or almost without arms, against overwhelming odds. The partisans of Dr. Bettelheim later on accused the opposing faction of having informed the police of the details of the preparations. Anyway, the whole leading staff of the party was arrested on the eve of the action, only Dr. Bettelheim himself escaping. Next morning communist demonstrators made an attempt to release them by storming the jail, but they were met by police, about twenty were killed, and the demonstration dispersed. The factories had not moved. Dr. Bettelheim was caught a few weeks later and soon released, without a trial. The communists were no longer dangerous and the socialists did not want to make martyrs. Soon the fall of the Hungarian dictatorship deprived the Austrian communists of all support and authority; they remained an insignificant sect as long as the Austrian republic existed.

The defeat of the Vienna rising broke Kun's last hope. The Hungarian Soviets were now doomed, because the country was against them. Still, events dragged on. On June 24th a counter-revolutionary conspiracy came to a head in Budapest.

The Danube monitors revolted and shelled the seat of the government. They were driven away. The cadets of the officer school had risen with them, but were overwhelmed. Worse, a battalion of exclusively proletarian composition had joined in the revolt and a few engineer workers had helped the monitors, confidently assuming that they would be supported by Johann Haubrich, the commander of Budapest. The rebellion was crushed within a few hours, but it was followed by the biggest peasant revolt seen by the Hungarian dictatorship. During their retreat to Yugoslavia, the monitors had touched the district of Kalosca and Dunapataj, a strongly Catholic region. A few days later the peasants of the district rose, this time not with rifles only, but with cannon, mysteriously acquired. Again the revolt was crushed; Szamuely was sent to the unhappy region and performed a few of his worst feats. But terrorism was no longer any use. Harvest time had arrived and with it village after village was faced with the fight for the preservation of its crops.

All this was awful enough, and if the historian had simply to tell the tale it would be a tale of horrors. But we live in a time of incensed imagination, cleverly exploited for political purposes. Even among horrors infinitely worse than those perpetrated by Szamuely in Hungary, even concerning questions such as terrorism in present-day Spain, the observer must come to the conclusion that the crimes of both sides have been considerably exaggerated. In the case of Red terrorism in Hungary figures are available, and though they are hotly contested they convey clearly the main outlines of the real picture. The Reds state that altogether they executed 234 people, by trial and sentence and by executions on the spot. The Whites give the figure as 578. The truth must lie somewhere in the middle and the discussion of the evidence is without interest. The main fact is this: terrorism in Hungary, however cruel, was not what it was in Russia, in Spain, and in China; it was not a popular affair, not a wholesale killing of the aristocrats, the rich, and the priests. It was an administrative business, and if the figure of several hundred executed within four months is high, it is still not 1 per cent of that achieved by both camps in Spain in the first four months of the civil war. On the other hand, there is no doubt that the

Hungarian Whites, after their success, perpetrated a considerably higher number of murders. It was different in Russia, where terrorism was popular and where the Reds killed many more people than the Whites—partly because they had a better opportunity for doing it.

But the crisis which had been subdued for the moment in the rear spread to the front. Kun attempted to seek relief in a new campaign, this time against Roumania. In the meantime, the workers had almost completely left the army, which now consisted only of nationalist middle-class people and country-folk. The latter were disinterested, the former element had become definitely hostile. Treason was ripe everywhere. Of six divisions going into the new campaign, three, in a confidential message of counter-revolutionary commanders of the Reds to the headquarters of the Whites, were described as safely 'White'. This turned out to be true. The chief of staff of the G.H.Q., Colonel Franz Julier, was conspiring with the Whites; so were one or two division commanders. Some troops simply went over during the first fights. Others withdrew from the battlefield, declaring that they did not want to fight. It was not due to defeat; on the contrary, the first moves of the Red army had been successful. It was a deliberate mass strike of the soldiers. The faithful troops were sent about wandering, without aim, over the battlefield. Finally, the Roumanians broke through the lines, and, within a few hours, the Red army, so glorious a few months ago, disappeared from the scene.

The Roumanians approached Budapest. A few months later, in Russia, General Youdenitch was not merely to approach, but actually to enter, the suburbs of Petrograd. He met a stiff resistance and was driven out by the rapidly mobilized workers. But no workers could be mobilized in Budapest. The Soviet was convoked, on August 1st, to listen to Kun's declaration: 'The proletarian dictatorship ought to have met a different end, if only we had had self-conscious and revolutionary proletarian masses at our disposal . . . I would have wished the proletariat to fight upon the barricades, had wished it to die rather than to relinquish its domination. But I considered: shall we, without the masses, go to the barricades, alone? . . . The proletariat was dissatisfied with our domination, already it shouted in the factories, in spite of all our agitation: "Down with the dictatorship!" . . . Now I realize that we have tried in vain to educate the masses of the proletariat of this country to be self-conscious revolutionaries.' There was never a more comprehensive admission of failure. And for at least a year the communists maintained that the lack of decision of the masses had brought the dictatorship down. Only later did they completely forget that the conditions they had created themselves brought the masses to the brink of revolt, and then started charging it all to the 'betrayal' by the socialists. The socialists may have been wavering and unreliable, but the dictatorship broke down primarily not because the socialists did not want it but because the workers, 'in spite of all our agitation', did not want it. They had never been seriously revolutionary. The experiences of the dictatorship had made them anti-revolutionaries. This is certainly not an exaggeration in the light of Kun's own farewell statement: in the factories the workers shouted 'Down with the dictatorship'.

Kun abdicated and a government formed of trade-unionists took over with the double intention of negotiating peace with the Roumanians and carrying through democratic elections. During the last weeks the socialists, through Boehm, who had become Hungarian minister at Vienna, had negotiated with the Allies, and they now hoped, not without reason, to find the necessary backing in London and Paris. But developments in Budapest moved too swiftly. Almost immediately after his abdication, Kun had to ask for diplomatic protection because he felt his life in Budapest unsafe; he got the train to the frontier he had asked for himself and his associates, sacrificing Szamuely, who committed suicide. A terrific popular reaction against Bolshevism was afoot. Already during the last weeks of the dictatorship the country had been swept by a wave of violent anti-Semitism. Most of the Bolshevik and left socialist leaders and a considerable percentage of their executive staff had been Jews. In a country where the Jews had never been regarded as part of the nation anti-Semitism was therefore the natural form of reaction against Bolshevism. The Whites exploited this feeling cleverly and ruthlessly. In the following weeks Hungary saw real pogroms, and Jews who had not the slightest connection with Bolshevism were murdered. The Roumanians entered Budapest. The trade-union government was openly disregarded by the whole country and by its own civil service. After only five days it had to disappear before a *coup de main* of the Whites. And then the country which had suffered the horrors of the Kun régime was thrown into the convulsion of the opposite White terror. A few people were executed after a regular trial, but infinitely more died without any trial. Bolshevism could never again get a foothold in the country, partly on account of ruthless persecution, but mostly because it had lost all prestige among the workers. And the labour movement as a whole never recovered from the stroke.

CHAPTER VII

THE GERMAN REVOLUTION

Even more than by the Hungarian disaster the early history of the Comintern was determined by the German revolution. As a power Germany is infinitely more important than Hungary. It is doubtful, however, whether the thing called the 'German revolution' of 1918 deserves the name of a revolution at all. The forces which later joined the Comintern meant little in the convulsions of 1918–19. Germany, for orthodox pre-war Marxists, was the classical land of the impending proletarian revolution. It was the strongest industrial power of Europe, had a big, supposedly revolutionary labour movement, and was now shaken by the terrible aftermath of defeat. It ought to have been the ideal starting-point for world-revolution outside Russia and for years was regarded as such by the Comintern. In reality, it was nothing of the kind.

During the last months of the war, disgust with the fighting and with the autocratic régime had swept almost every class of the population, but the political parties felt themselves bound, as good patriots, to support a continuance of the war to the bitter end. This created a big cleavage between masses and leaders, such as occasionally occurs at turning-points of history, and was to influence deeply the thought of German revolutionaries for years. For this pacifist and republican trend the U.S.P., the group of socialist pacifists which had created an independent party in 1917, was a very inadequate expression. The U.S.P. was essentially a party of the more advanced socialist elements among the workers; the pacifist movement, in those final months of the war, swept the nation as a whole, carrying with it elements which were neither socialist nor labour nor even progressive; the Bavarian peasants, perhaps the most conservative element in all Germany, expressed this enmity against war and monarchy in particularly violent forms; a few months later they were again the vanguard of counter-revolution.

In the last days before the end all Germany seemed to have become revolutionary, because all Germany sympathized with the pacifist and republican programme of the U.S.P. The majority socialists withstood the wave till the end; even on November 8th they still issued leaflets for the war and the dynasty. In the meantime, the U.S.P. leaders stood quietly by, making peaceful propaganda and nothing more. A few extremists were in contact with the Soviet embassy, and had received money which they used for buying revolvers—while the Berlin garrison was ready to mutiny against the officers. The small Spartakusbund could do nothing but issue leaflets, which were increasingly violent in tone, but had little effect. Liebknecht had been released from prison in October, only to quarrel immediately with the less advanced leaders of the left wing of the U.S.P.

During the last days of the war Germany was shaken by a number of violent mutinies in the armed forces. The first of these, and the most far-reaching in its effects, was the revolt of the navy, at Kiel. The revolutionists have later attempted to describe the revolting sailors as conscientious revolutionaries; but the protocols of a Reichstag investigation, admirably interpreted by Professor A. Rosenberg in his work on *The Origins of the German Republic*, have amply proved that such was not the case. The sailors simply mutinied against the attempt of the officers to make the fleet perish—gloriously, as they saw it— in a last battle in the Channel. Unwillingly, the mutinous sailors found themselves in possession of the town. They elected a sailors' council, which did not issue a single political slogan and submitted without much difficulty to Gustav Noske, a very anti-revolutionary social-democrat. From Kiel revolt spread southward, and on the 7th November reached Munich, where a movement of war-tired and anti-Prussian peasant soldiers brought the local leader of the U.S.P., Kurt Eisner, into power. It was a big misunderstanding.

Berlin was still in the hands of the Kaiser. Here, divergences among the revolutionaries were strongest. The one group which had clearly outlined plans for the next few days were the 'Revolutionary Shop-stewards'. They prepared the general strike which broke out on November 9th. At the last moment the majority socialists joined and put themselves at the head of the movement. The garrison went over without a shot; the Kaiser had to abdicate. Then the shop-steward committee set out to form the Berlin Soviet, which must now be elected. But here they failed. They had attempted to capture the presidium by surprise, but the majority socialists had the majority of the meeting of the factory representatives of Berlin, which met on November 10th. Majority men and U.S.P. people together formed the new central council of the Berlin Soviet.

Already on this 10th November the majority socialists had the workers more or less in hand again. The monarchy was swept away; and the armistice was concluded the day after. The chief aims of the masses had been achieved. On 19th January 1919, in the elections for the constituent assembly, the workers gave the majority socialists five times as many votes as the U.S.P. The workers simply did not want a revolution. But that did not mean, naturally, that they wanted to revert to the old yoke; they expected a substantial improvement of their lot. Trade-union membership within one year increased to eight millions, four times what it had been before the war. Claims for increased wages were raised everywhere, claims, which, in substance, were impossible of achievement after the country had been bled white through war and defeat. This raised a considerable amount of friction. With an intact administration, army, and police, it would have meant little, but precisely these requirements of ordinary government were absent, for a time. This meant that minor frictions developed into serious troubles. No serious revolutionary intention was implied, however.

In the meantime, the socialist leaders had to decide on a course of action after the war. On November 9th majority socialists and independents had formed a joint government, but they disagreed as to the measures to be taken. The majority people had one thing in mind and achieved it at a stroke: they put into effect all the claims of the trade unions, from the eight-hour day to the legalizing of the shop-stewards.

They were convinced, however, that, for the time being, it was impossible to nationalize industry. They concentrated therefore on something else, which had far-reaching consequences. They put one Dr. Koeth, a lieutenant of the leaders of the heavy industries, in charge of demobilization. He simply demilitarized the factories and restored private property, wholesale.

This implied failure—due to socialist theory even more than to socialist practice. The socialists had never been able to imagine the coming of socialism otherwise than by big measures of expropriation. They had gradually come to the conclusion that the attempt to manage through the state almost the whole of economic life was a wild and impracticable idea. They felt it the more strongly now that they were in the position to carry it through. A lively debate of politicians and economists ensued, arguing about the limits of nationalization, and ending in highly technical considerations as to which branches were 'ripe' for it and which not. In the end nothing came of it. The socialists suddenly found themselves without an ideology, beyond the sheer demands of trade-unionism; this amounted to complete collapse—a collapse not then visible, but which has since taken shape in the uncontested victory of the Nazis. But even the workers were not really interested in the problems of nationalization; they felt that it hardly meant direct increase of wages for them, which was the only immediate interest of the majority.

In reality, there was such a wealth of tasks to perform that the socialists, even had they been an inspired instead of an utterly uninspired movement, would have found it difficult to cope with them all. Now was the chance to break the economic and political power of the Prussian Junkers by a sweeping agrarian reform in the eastern provinces; and now was the moment, not to expropriate, but to subject the private owners to a planned economy in the interests of the community as a whole. The second task has been dealt with by the Nazis in their own way. The socialists, however, fallen from the heaven of their Utopia, did not see the way towards a constructive and inspiring policy in real life. They confined themselves to a very narrow interpretation of the change which had occurred and thus themselves drove the vague aspirations of the masses into the channels of simple claims for increased wages which could not be fulfilled.

Thus, without any well-defined aim, waves of riots spread over the country. They were made considerably worse by the desire of the troops to go home. The government found itself without an army and had soon to call for volunteers. They were forthcoming, but only out of the groups most closely connected with the *ancien régime* and most inimical to the republic. Gustav Noske as war minister gave Germany an army as reactionary as that which had been broken in 1918.

Against the destruction of the rudiments of a workers' domination which had been created during the first days of the revolution, the majority of the workers put up no staunch resistance. The National Workers' and Soldiers' Council voted itself out of power by a big majority, deciding to hold the polls for the constituent assembly at the earliest possible date. It was not the revolutionary mood of the workers that was causing the trouble, for there was no such mood. The trouble was the capacity of small groups of revolutionaries to break the peace without adequate resistance and to make use, in doing so, of the vague unrest of the masses after the war. Against this, during December 1918 the government took a number of strong measures. The U.S.P. ministers disapproved of these measures and left the government. But they had no policy of their own.

In the middle of this stalemate the revolutionaries struggled helplessly. They were convinced that this was the opportunity for a socialist revolution, but, seeing that they could not obtain within due time a majority of the population, not even of the workers, they interpreted the Russian experiment, which they admired, in a peculiar way. Lenin had driven out the constituent assembly and imposed, instead, a Soviet régime identical with the rule of the Communist Party. For them the main teaching of Russia therefore consisted in this, that for a time a minority rule must be imposed by force of arms. This view induced them, logically, to make repeated attempts at a *coup de main*, a policy of *Putsche*. There were two groups among them, or rather three: the first and strongest group consisted of the Revolutionary Shop-stewards, who were members of the U.S.P., and, together with a few left-wing Reichstag deputies, constituted the left wing of that party; there was, moreover, the Spartakusbund with Karl Liebknecht and Rosa Luxemburg. There was finally the group at Bremen, inspired by Lenin and Radek, but led by a few less-known people. Between these groups there existed at first no profound divergence of opinion. Such divergences were soon to arise. Nevertheless, the whole position was wrong. The Revolutionary Shop-stewards, who wanted a socialist revolution, should have belonged to the same party as the Spartacus men; whereas it was contrary to political logic that they should be within the same party with Kautsky and the U.S.P. parliamentarians, whose wishes did not go beyond a parliamentary republic.

This left, revolutionary wing of the labour movement had one strong personality to lead it and this a woman: Rosa Luxemburg. It is time to say something about this extraordinary person. After her gruesome death at the hands of inflamed government officers a small volume of letters of hers, written from prison to Karl Liebknecht's wife, was published and made a strong impression, even upon her adversaries. In the violent propaganda of those days she had been represented as a fury, a witch, an evil spirit. Now suddenly Germany had to realize that it had killed one of its finest human beings. First of all these letters, which do not contain a word of politics, showed a personality of an extraordinary width of interests; in prison, she followed up her chief hobby, the study of zoology, especially of bird life, and at the same time translated Russian poems into German. But, more striking, the spirit revealed in these letters was nearer to the spirit of Gandhi than to that of Lenin. This woman, herself a hunchback, was filled with a profound love and commiseration for all human beings; her chief happiness was to listen to the song of the blackbird outside her prison. In unforgettable lines she describes her suffering in watching the beating of a buffalo which had been brought from Roumania to Breslau. Her letters abound in poetical memories, quotations, the sweetest consolation for Liebknecht's wife, whose husband was in jail. One might be inclined to ascribe this universality of compassion, which is perhaps the most outstanding feature in Rosa Luxemburg's more intimate life, to the thwarting of her own aspirations to happiness by her physical defect, but this was not the case. More than once in her life she had been deeply loved, in spite of everything, and for more than a decade she was united by the deepest of bonds with Leo Jogiches, a leader of the Polish revolutionaries before the war, and her collaborator in the Spartakusbund during the war. Moreover, she was loved and admired, not only in the closer circle of her friends, but wherever she came, a woman annihilating the handicap of physical deformity by the sheer charm of her sweetness, her understanding, and her warm-heartedness.

Unlike Lenin she was not a person with a single aim. She had a very wide culture and learnt foreign languages not, as did Lenin, primarily in order to understand foreign news-papers, but in order to understand foreign poetry. This implies that her approach to the labour movement was deeply humanistic. She was not the type who cares only for the starving little children in the backyards of proletarian districts; hers was not a cheap sentimentality. She wanted socialism, not so much in order to allay suffering as to enhance the force and joy of human life. But the human aspect remained always paramount; she would never have been able to put up with vileness in order to further her cause. This made Bolshevism, with its ruthless methods of wire-pulling, antipathetic to her from the outset. Not a moment in her life did she waver from her antagonism towards it. What would she have thought of the later Russian developments?

Yet this sensitive woman had a man's fighting spirit and a man's intellectual approach to things. Her bent of mind was strongly theoretical in the Western sense of the word, much more so than that of Lenin. Where Lenin never wrote a word without a practical purpose, one watches Rosa Luxemburg involving herself in abstract and intricate arguments about the accumulation of capital and trying to find a mathematical formula for the objective limits of capitalist progress. She failed in an attempt which Lenin would never have undertaken.

This theoretical bent sometimes brought her into sharp conflict with Karl Liebknecht. About Liebknecht little is to be said. He was never a Marxist, not always a revolutionist, but always enthusiastic. Before the war he had dabbled in anti-militarism, in the youth movement, in the anti-religious movement. The war drove him to despair; with his great devotion to his cause and his strong character he became inevitably the spokesman of the masses. When he came out of prison his one thought and his one belief was that the heroic devotion of a vanguard was needed and would be sufficient to bring about the revolution. To that sort of enthusiasm Rosa Luxemburg, profoundly balanced, pondering, observing, starting from the rigid assumptions of orthodox Marxism, was impassive. Moderation in the very centre of the storm was, in spite of the notoriety adversaries had given her, her most outstanding characteristic. But this moderation was combined with an unlimited belief in humanity, an almost Rousseau-like optimism.

Where the socialists had buried their revolutionary convictions, where Lenin, instead of the belief in the proletarian revolution, had put his hopes in a centralized group under his leadership, Rosa Luxemburg almost alone continued to believe in the proletariat. We have quoted, in the chapter dealing with Bolshevism, her criticism of Lenin: the masses must not be ordered about by an 'infallible' central committee. They must learn from their own experience, their own mistakes. Revolution must be the result of their increasing political understanding. She believed, in short, in the spontaneity of the proletarian masses.

This view, besides the individual psychological motives which may have determined it, grew out of the structure of the Western labour movement, as a revolutionary must see it. In Russia Lenin could praise the wisdom of a centralized bureaucracy, because it was his own. Bureaucracy in the West had not evolved out of secret groups of revolutionaries, living on secret funds, but out of the unions and the parliaments, where, obviously, it was filled with a mentality directly opposed to revolution. In the West, it remained to be decided only whether the masses were permeated by a similar spirit. If the answer was in the affirmative, then it was all up with the proletarian revolution. The hope lay in a revolt of the masses against the leaders, and two trends, very powerful in 1918, seemed to justify Rosa Luxemburg's assumptions just at the decisive moment. The one was the deep cleavage which had arisen between leaders and masses towards the end of the war. She did not see, as few saw at the time, that this was not due to any difference of political outlook, but simply to unbearable physical sufferings on the part of the masses during the war, bound to disappear with it. The second argument was derived from the very violent strike movements and riots which broke out precisely among those strata which had been least organized and most backward before the war. Whole regions, such as the Ruhr, Upper Silesia, central Germany—all of them mining districts—which had hardly been touched by socialism before the war, now entered the movement and sided, at once, with the radical wing. Rosa Luxemburg and her followers were inclined to mistake the lack of discipline, the Utopian hopes and the violence which inevitably go with the infancy of the labour movement, for decided and reliable revolutionism. But if this appreciation was not realistic and was bound to lead to failure in the end, Luxemburg's immediate aims were more realistic than those of any of her collaborators. Where they had all lost their heads and hailed the day of the final success, she alone saw clearly that the greater part of the workers were— for the time being, as she thought—with the majority socialists and not even with the U.S.P., not to mention her own group. She decided to wait, therefore, to make use of every opportunity to increase the scope for the fight of individual groups, to use every event to teach the workers revolution, but she did not want to be drawn prematurely into a decisive battle. 'The Spartacists must not take power before the majority of the workers have clearly understood the issue and follow us,' she repeated again and again. But her whole following was filled with the conviction that a small group of decided men could establish a minority dictatorship, and *then*, power in hand, convince the masses. Had it not worked perfectly well in Russia? It was useless to hint that there might be differences.

Thus Rosa Luxemburg was pushed into a triple adventure, in which she perished: the adventure of a schism, of unwarrantable slogans, and finally of a military *coup de main*. As to the split, it is doubtful whether she wanted it but certainly she did not resist it. The small group of personal adherents of Lenin and Radek in Bremen, here as everywhere intent upon forming independent communist parties as quickly as possible, brought what pressure it could to bear upon the Spartacists, threatening to proceed with the formation of a party of its own. They found support with Liebknecht and the majority of the

Spartacists, who did not understand the hesitations of Rosa Luxemburg. On December 24th, after a serious clash between government troops and revolutionary sailors in Berlin, the U.S.P. members left the Cabinet, which, naturally, worked to reconcile the divergences between the moderates and the extremists within that party. Precisely at this moment a conference of the Spartakusbund was called in Berlin, in order to set up a party of their own. The U.S.P., it was thought, would never be or become truly revolutionary. It was necessary, therefore, now the Spartacists could act in the open, to proceed, the earlier the better, without taking account of those waverers. The history of the foundation of the Communist Party of Austria repeated itself. In their conference of 31st December 1918 and 1st January 1919 the Spartacists established themselves as the 'Communist Party of Germany'. But the masses remained outside.

During the year 1919 and later it became a habit, in Germany, to call every revolutionary a 'Spartacist'. Thus an entirely mistaken idea about the strength of the Spartacists was created and things were attributed to them in which they had not so much as participated. Even within that minority of workers who fought for revolution in 1919 the Spartacists were a very small number. At the first national Soviet congress in December 1918 they had ten seats out of several hundred; none of their leaders, not even Liebknecht with all his popularity, had won a seat. In the second Soviet congress, in April 1919, a single Spartacist took part. The Spartacists were non-existent among the masses, or nearly so. They did not participate in parliamentary elections in 1919. But when, in June 1920, for the first time they participated in a general election, they won two seats, out of a total of nearly four hundred, and polled four hundred thousand votes. This was after twenty months of revolution. It gives a fair idea of the real importance of that insignificant sect credited with such tremendous deeds and misdeeds.

Whence this weakness? It was closely related to the method which was adopted in forming the party. There was only one organization in Germany which could command the allegiance of considerable numbers of revolutionary workers; the Revolutionary Shop-stewards. They were prepared to join in the formation of the new party, but Liebknecht and his men, scenting opportunism and the danger of weakness everywhere, had preferred to launch the party without so much as asking Richard Mueller and his people about their opinion. The latter, though resentful, nevertheless opened negotiations. But they put two demands which went to the root of the political problems confronting the new party: its members must remain within the trade unions and the party must participate in the elections. The constituent congress of the party refused to do either, overruling by a big majority the opposite view of Rosa Luxemburg and her friends.

We have repeatedly pointed out that, during the war, the Spartakusbund had only a few hundred members, and those mainly old, experienced party workers. But immediately after November the party, now legal and accessible to everybody, had been swamped with naïve and enthusiastic elements without any background. The masses who tended to the left went to the U.S.P. It was mostly the 'crazy fringe' which joined the Spartacists, and some of the newcomers were more than doubtful elements. On the whole they were sincere and self-sacrificing, but politically impossible. For them the communist programme of Soviets was a dogma. They were miles away from the misgivings Rosa Luxemburg had expressed, behind closed curtains, about the complete abolition of democracy in Russia. For them the very virtue of the Soviet régime consisted in the fact that it was a dictatorial rule of the minority. And loyalty to the Soviets meant for them abstention from parliament. Here all the older leaders of the new party disagreed, with the one possible exception of Liebknecht. But the constituent conference of the party was swept along by the vote of the newcomers, and, with a strong majority, decided not to participate in the elections.

Why had the great majority of the workers proved to be opportunist? Because, was their argument, they had been caught by the ideology of progress within capitalism, represented in parliamentary and trade-union work. Therefore the bureaucracy of the unions and the parliamentarians embodied the very essence of opportunism, and it was necessary to oppose to those bureaucracies a party directly led by the workers themselves. Down with parliament, down with the unions, down with every bureaucracy! These were the slogans which, at the time, made a man a communist. Neither was this an attitude limited to Germany. The Austrian communists, the Hungarians after the fall of the dictatorship, the Finns, a considerable part of the Dutch, and that socialist group in Italy which was nearest to the Comintern took the same line; and so did the majority of the small communist groups in England and a considerable section of the socialist left in America.

This attitude involves a strange contradiction. The young enthusiasts opposed the true class-consciousness of the masses to the corruption of the bureaucracies. At the same time, they were well aware within themselves that the masses were not with them but precisely with those bureaucrats. Hence their conviction that a minority dictatorship was necessary, so strangely contrasted with their equally candid conviction that the coming dictatorship must be a rule, not of leaders but of the 'masses themselves'. But this sort of contradiction was inevitable within a movement which, while believing itself the expression of the class-consciousness of the proletariat, had little essentially in common with the proletarian masses. It was this which led people to swing from one extreme to the other, to believe at the same time in the dictatorship of a small minority—the majority would never have 'guts' enough—and in a dictatorship without leaders—experience has proved that all the big bureaucratized mass organizations degenerate. The height of contradition was reached in the attitude towards the Soviets; when the majority of these Soviets proved to be not even for the U.S.P. but for the right-wing socialists, most of the Spartacists in the provinces repudiated the Soviets themselves and launched the slogan of the election of true, revolutionary Soviets, which meant Soviets elected not by all the workers, but by a small revolutionary minority.

The problem was most acute in so far as the trade unions were concerned. They had been the backbone of patriotism during the war and were the stronghold of a moderate policy now; but at the same time they grew at a breath-taking speed. True, the strike-movement grew even more rapidly than the unions. Starting from this latter fact, the eager young revolutionaries fell into the delusion that the trade unions had had their day. They opposed to the supposedly backward unions new types of industrial organizations, modelled after the pattern of the American I.W.W.; not organizations varying according either to industries or to crafts, but 'one big union', built upon a revolutionary programme. This spoilt their last chance to get a foothold within the mass movement. Only in the Ruhr, where the old unions had never really taken root, the foundation of a new miners' union was, for a time, a success. The Revolutionary Shop-stewards refused to join the new party on account of its repudiation of every mass organization. A certain compensation was found in the fact that, in spite of the official break, contact between the Spartacists and the left-wing Independents remained fairly close; the party, which had no strength of its own, could exert a certain influence by persuading the 'Independents'.

So it did, and after only a fortnight of life had met a crushing defeat. The government had proceeded far enough with the formation of new troops for it to take decisive action in the first days of January 1919. It dismissed Emil Eichhorn, a left-wing 'Independent' and chief of the Berlin police. As the police had arms and other means of coercion at its disposal, this was felt as a serious stroke against the extremists, which, in fact, it was. Eichhorn refused to withdraw and the Spartacists, together with a small number of left-wing Independents, launched a revolutionary movement and formed a government of three, of which Liebknecht was a member. But things were hopelessly muddled from the beginning. The masses, which had not been ready to take part actively in a Soviet revolution, were upset by the stroke and ready to fight in defence; it is doubtful how far they would have gone had the leadership been adequate. But it was not. Big demonstrations were called and the government withdrew from its ordinary offices into the suburbs. Thus, the immediate object of action was removed and nobody knew what to do next. The masses stood helplessly about and finally dispersed. Groups of Spartacists decided to capture, of all possible objectives, the offices of *Vorwaerts*, the paper of the majority socialists, much hated by the left-wingers; but the premises were without either military or political importance and no attempt was made to disturb the preparations of the government. The revolutionary junta sent a group of workers with orders to take over the Ministry of War, which had not been evacuated by the government. The leader of the group went into the building and there the officers in charge called his attention to the fact that his warrant, signed by the revolutionary junta, lacked an authoritative stamp. The man, a worker who had never been in politics before, went to fetch the stamp but changed his mind on the way, went home and remained in bed. This story stands for hundreds of similar ones, which characterize the German revolution.

Then, having completed preparations, the government struck. Picked troops, formed of old officers, students, etc., entered Berlin. No mass resistance was offered. Groups of Spartacists, numbering a few hundred, offered an heroic defence without any tactical or political plan. The *Vorwaerts* premises were defended with particular stiffness and a considerable number of the defenders were murdered after they had capitulated to the besiegers. Then the town was slowly occupied, district by district.

Rosa Luxemburg had foreseen but not forestalled the disaster. She knew that the masses were 'not ripe' for this rising, but, at the same time, had decided that she must not leave the fighters alone. After the débâcle she refused to leave Berlin. The fury of the counter-revolution was unleashed. The communists had no adequate underground organization, and the hiding-place of Luxemburg and Liebknecht was at once denounced to the troops. They were found, and killed in the most atrocious manner. They were the first of a long list of communist leaders to be murdered in Germany, but no loss the party and the International ever suffered was so full of disaster as this. With the destruction of Luxemburg and her personal circle German communism lost the one capable set of leaders it had. A leadership is not formed within a year or two. Those who had stood at the head of the party had been selected, in the socialist movement of pre-war times, over a long period. And the formation of a new leadership out of the younger generation which served as rank and file in 1919 was forestalled by later developments of the Comintern, which was incompatible with the formation of an independent leadership. Perhaps the loss for the International was even greater. With all her illusions, Rosa Luxemburg was close to the realities of the Western labour movement. All the other Western leaders of standing and capacity saw the incompatibility of Bolshevism and the West, and refused to join the new International. Luxemburg also saw the incompatibility, and was nevertheless ready to make an attempt at co-operation. Looking backward upon her role and attitude, one finds it difficult to believe that anything but a break could have been the end of her relations with the Comintern. But in the meantime she would have been the one person able to balance and withstand the influence of the Russians. She alone might have had the authority and strength to carry those she had persuaded to co-operate with the Bolsheviks with her when she broke with them. All the others who later took that step were officers without troops. She might have left at the head of an army; which would have been of incalculable consequence for the unity of the German workers when they attempted to withstand Hitler. But she died, and Leo Jogiches was killed a few weeks after her.

The tragedy of Berlin repeated itself all over the Reich. The ruthless actions of the newly formed Reichswehr under the socialist Noske drove the workers to fury; so did the thwarting of their illusive hopes as to a comfortable future, and the breaking of their strikes. From this, the U.S.P. profited much; it set out to grow from a small minority into the majority of the German socialist movement. But the Independents, though deeply dissenting among themselves, were essentially a party intent not on revolutionary combat, but on constitutional opposition; and only a small minority of the leaders joined the Spartacists in their attempts at armed resistance. Again and again, when it came to fighting, the majority of the workers remained at home, and small minorities were cruelly destroyed, as in Berlin. There are not many industrial districts in the Reich which have not seen this piecemeal destruction of the revolutionary movement.

Most bitter of all the defeats was that at Munich. Bavaria, from the first days of the revolution onwards, had lived in practical independence from Berlin and therefore the 'Noske régime' had not been introduced there. But the country was agricultural, the workers had been educated in a tradition of reformism and were overwhelmingly for the majority socialists. Kurt Eisner, the local leader of the Independents, stood at the

head of the government, but the U.S.P. had only three seats in
the Bavarian diet. This could not continue. Eisner was assassinated by an officer and the country was faced by the choice
either of going back to constitutional methods and abandoning
every idea of a swift move towards socialism—which would
have corresponded to the real balance of forces—or of trying a
minority dictatorship. The latter alternative was chosen, and
a Soviet republic was proclaimed on 7th April 1919. What
exactly preceded this act will perhaps never become quite
clear. A considerable number of majority socialists participated in the attempt, some of them undoubtedly in complete
sincerity; but the War Minister, Schneppenhorst, a member of
the party, who had played the extremist in the preceding
negotiations went, after the proclamation of the Soviets, directly
to the north and started organizing the punitive expedition
against Soviet Munich. What, in Munich, was at first called a
'Soviet' government was a strange thing indeed. It was a
coalition of a section of the majority socialists who were
opposed on principle to any dictatorship; of the Independents, who, after the death of Eisner, were weak; and of a
number of representatives of that 'Bohemia' whose chief
centre in Germany at the time, was Munich. Among this
latter element Gustav Landauer, anarchist, dreamer, and
historian of literature (he had written a remarkable study on
Shakespeare), was the outstanding figure. The proclamation
of the 'Soviet' republic had nothing to do with the workers. It
was the result of negotiations among these strange partners
behind closed curtains. And support, at the beginning, was
much stronger in 'Bohemia' than among the workers themselves. This made of the first phase of the dictatorship sheer
comedy. While the majority socialists did not know what to
do, Ernst Toller, a young poet who was a member of the
U.S.P., and Gustav Landauer dreamed of the creation of a
new brotherhood of mankind. In the meantime the Foreign
Secretary of the new dictatorship chose to declare war on the
Pope. It appeared afterwards that he had passed some time
in an asylum, to which he returned, if I am not mistaken,
after the tragi-comedy had come to an end. Even after the
catastrophe, *Die Internationale*, the theoretical organ of the
German communists, spoke of a 'dictatorship in the Café

Stephani [the main Bohemian café] and the surrounding districts'.

The communists, under the leadership of Eugène Levinè, a Russian who in his native country had had wide revolutionary experience, simply laughed at the fantastic play which was enacted on the Munich stage, and refused to participate. Soon, the whole thing collapsed. After only six days, on April 13th, the 'Republican Guard', an armed troop under the influence of the majority socialists, expelled the Soviet government and was about to restore the previous government, which had withdrawn to Bamberg, in northern Bavaria. To the communists this relatively harmless end ought to have been a godsend, as the Berlin leadership itself pointed out after the disaster. It was obviously a mild affair and the communists ought to have welcomed the opportunity to escape from a hopeless situation, in which otherwise they would have been involved. But they chose to act otherwise. It was not their 'Soviet republic'; on the contrary, they had laughed at it. Now that it was too late, they decided that a communist party could not let it be overthrown without resistance. They mobilized their members—relatively numerous in Munich—and defeated the counter-revolutionary rising.

As a consequence they found themselves at the helm, and started to organize both economic life and defence as ruthlessly as they could. It was the same story as in Budapest. They had no real backing among the natives of Bavaria, which is very strongly regionalist. Their chiefs and many of their adherents were 'foreigners', in Bavarian terminology, i.e. Jews, Berlin people, with a number of Russians, mostly war prisoners. They were far from instituting a régime of terrorism; it has been proved since that under their régime not a single adversary was court-martialled or killed. But they made a considerable number of arrests, talked much of terrorism, suppressed newspapers, and in other ways offended the pacifism of both the workers and the intelligentsia. Their rule lasted only two weeks. Ernst Toller overthrew the communist government by a vote of the Soviet, and what was called a 'dictatorship of the natives', of the true-blue Bavarians, was formed. It lasted only a few days. The government troops, reinforced from Berlin and Stuttgart, had encircled the town, and stormed it, on

May 1st with little resistance. In the last hours things escaped the control of Toller and the others and seven or eight hostages were shot; a senseless crime, perpetrated by uncontrolled soldiers, which incurred a terrible penalty. The 'Whites' celebrated their victory by an awful massacre, in which people were shot without so much as establishing their identity; among them a group of twenty-one Catholic workers, who had assembled for a fraternity social. Landauer was killed, Levinè sentenced to death and executed. Many other leaders received heavy sentences. The army was the real ruler, and one year later, during the 'Kapp *Putsch*', the legal government was overthrown by officers and students, and an extremely reactionary government installed by force. Hitler, then, found his first scope for action in Munich, which had passed through the 'Soviet' tragedy.

Munich marked the end of the first phase of the German revolution. For many months to come there was little fighting in Germany, for the forces of the right had gained enormously in strength. On the left the masses drifted slowly and inconclusively towards the Independents. The young Communist Party, however, was a heap of ruins.

After the death of Luxemburg, Liebknecht, Jogiches, and Levinè, a young lawyer, Paul Levi, was the uncontested leader of the party. The Russians had sent Radek, but he had been caught and jailed shortly after the January rising in Berlin; Levi could lead the party without any serious competitor. He was undoubtedly a brilliant man, equally proficient as a speaker, a writer, and a debater. He had a considerable amount of political insight. Emotionalism he despised, and it was probably this that had made him valuable to Rosa Luxemburg when she first made his acquaintance. He was defiant in temperament, disregarding authority and advice; essentially a deep pessimist. As Luxemburg, he was not of single purpose. Very rich, widely read, and cultured, he was an eager collector of Chinese pottery and was apt to forget politics in the admiration of a piece of jade. The other leaders never forgave him his aristocratic tastes, and he was never popular among the masses; but his outstanding gifts gave him pride of place.

Levi saw the situation clearly, and, as most congenital pessimists, rather enjoyed the hopeless difficulties which faced him when he took over. The party was thoroughly defeated, and that by its own mistakes. It had gone to decisive battles with incredibly small forces. Levi decided to put an end to this, and during all his subsequent career as a communist one of his chief cares was never again to allow a section of the party to involve itself in a fight which was disproportionate to its forces. This naturally entailed a considerable amount of caution, unpalatable to the party, which grew more excited the more hopeless the situation became. Levi saw, moreover, that the movement had been narrowly defined along the wrong lines. All hope lay in winning over a considerable section of the Independents and he set out to achieve this. But in order to achieve this and so become a real mass movement, the party must get rid of that sectarianism which was unacceptable to the leaders of mass organizations. The party members must join the trade unions again and the party must stand for election. This, naturally, provoked furious resistance, which was not unwelcome to Levi. He was of the opinion that the crazy fringe which formed the bulk of the membership was altogether a bad basis for a reasonable policy; the less of it remained in the reorganized party the better.

With these convictions Levi convoked the second congress of the party—the first after the foundation conference in Berlin in January—at Heidelberg, and there, in October 1919, he met the delegates with a surprise. He submitted 'theses'—i.e. doctrinal statements, a term to become very frequent later on —expressing the necessity of co-operation with the old unions and of voting for parliament. The 'theses' had not been published before the conference and the districts had not voted upon them when the delegates were named. This had been Levi's intention. He put an ultimatum, asking for acceptance of the theses without any further ado and declaring excluded all those who voted against them. A considerable number of delegates voted against, not on grounds of principle but on grounds of the procedure, which was indeed unwarrantable. This made the number of exclusions only more considerable. The party was split and those who had seceded were left to form their own organization, the 'Communist Workers'

Party of Germany', which never achieved much and soon disintegrated.

The party was now ready for negotiation with the Independents. But it was hardly a party any more. Of the few workers it had had most had seceded. A few districts, such as Chemnitz and Würtemberg, had remained faithful to Levi, but most of the Ruhr, all Hamburg and Bremen, and, most important, Berlin, was lost. With such an organization the left-wing Independents saw no need to negotiate, and thus it happened that the Independents, without caring for the small communist group, negotiated directly with Moscow. It was a step most hateful to Levi, who, a true disciple of Luxemburg, wanted to limit the influence of the Bolsheviks in the West. Until then the influence of the Bolsheviks over German affairs had been indirect only, working through the vague prestige of the Russian revolution. Now, for the first time, they came in direct and close contact with an important mass organization of the West. This opens a new chapter in the history of the German and the international labour movement. But before the Russians had achieved anything, a big crisis ensued in German home politics and revealed, once more, the hopelessness of the position of the small Communist Party.

On 13th March 1920 General Lüttwitz, with Reichswehr troops, invaded Berlin, declared the democratic government deposed, and put into power a certain Dr. Kapp, an extreme reactionary. The army had organized under cover of serving the republic and now felt strong enough to overthrow it. Not all the generals joined, the bourgeois parties remained hesitant, the government fled to reliably republican Stuttgart, and the T.U.C. proclaimed a general strike. The response was tremendous. The German proletariat rose in the most powerful mass movement it ever saw.

The movement was almost overwhelmingly republican and democratic in character. It started in an attempt to save the republic, and, in spite of all efforts of the extremists, collapsed as soon as this aim had been achieved. The masses obviously valued precisely that bourgeois democracy and that 'treacherous' semi-socialist government which the extremists had taught it to despise. Karl Legien, head of the T.U.C., and arch-traitor according to the communists, remained in Berlin while the government fled—he thoroughly disapproved of their flight—and, a septuagenarian with a price on his head, courageously led the strike movement from a cellar in a Berlin suburb. In the Ruhr the workers rose indiscriminately, and defeated and disarmed the military. In Chemnitz, the only district where communists had real mass influence, a sort of joint provincial Soviet government of majority socialists and communists was set up, under the leadership of Heinrich Brandler, a communist. In Leipzig, the Independents, who there dominated the labour movement, fought for days. In Hamburg and in the south fighting was unnecessary.

The Communist Party headquarters in Berlin had an attitude of their own. Looking at the streets of Berlin, which, during the first hours, were rather calm, they decided that after all the proletariat had accepted their views and dropped the socialists. Joyously they issued a leaflet asking the workers not to strike in defence of the 'Noske government'. Nobody paid attention and the local strike and fighting in Berlin began under the leadership of the Independents. Levi was not in Berlin and therefore could not forestall what his lieutenants did in his absence. On the second day of the general strike communist headquarters came round and joined.

After four days of vain attempts, the counter-revolutionary government resigned, under the pressure of the strike, of the disagreement of the military leaders among themselves, and of the wide-spread risings of the workers all over the Reich. The problem of the formation of a new government now arose. It was a decisive moment in the history of the German republic. Everybody was agreed that the old coalition of majority socialists with Catholics (formed after the elections to the Constituent Assembly) could not continue; the War Minister, the socialist Noske, was not unwarrantably held personally responsible for the *coup d'état*; he had shown a marked preference for monarchist officers and thus played the Reichswehr into the hands of the counter-revolutionary group. Now the Reichswehr had been beaten by the general strike, under leadership of the German T.U.C. During these days Legien and the T.U.C., victorious in face of tremendous odds, were the only generally recognized authority. Legien was anything but a revolutionary, had been, in fact, one of the leading patriots during the war, and had always stood for co-operation with the employers in industrial matters. But he hated and despised the Prussian-sergeant mentality which had been characteristic of the Noske régime and wanted to make something out of the victory of the workers. One thing he saw clearly: in Germany, only the workers were sincere democrats. Therefore, if the republic was to become more than a mere name the workers must govern at least for a time. A general election was necessary, and, with appropriate tactics, they might hope for a joint majority of the right-wing socialists and the Independents. Legien approached the leaders of the Independents in order to form a joint Labour government.

Hardly anybody dared doubt the sincerity of the old man who, at the end of his career—he died the year after—threw overboard so much for which he had stood and set out on a new course. Neither then nor later did the communists pretend that it was a trap or a manœuvre. The programme of the new government was obvious: nationalization of the mines, improvement of social legislation, republicanization of the civil service, thorough reshuffling of the army, an agrarian reform against the Junkers in the east. It was a moderate programme as the outcome of civil war, and just the sort of thing which had a real chance of success. Had Legien's plan been realized, it might have changed the fate of Germany. The right wing of the Independents wanted to test Legien's sincerity. They agreed that he should be Premier, but asked for the majority in the government and a few key positions; Legien agreed at once. He wanted to give the majority people a lesson and show them that, if Noske and his people beat down the workers, the trade unions could co-operate just as well with the other wing of the labour movement.

In the decisive conference on 18th March 1920 two representatives of the communists were present, Jacob Walcher and Wilhelm Pieck, both close followers of Levi and therefore rather inclining to the 'right wing' of the party. The conversation was frank. They were told freely that their organization meant very little for the moment, but that if the Independents joined the government they would be at least a left-wing opposition in the Reich and therefore have a chance to become a mass party. What would be their attitude in such circumstances? It would obviously be hopeless for the new government to carry out its intentions if, while reorganizing the Reichswehr, it was forced at the same time to beat down *Putsche* from the left: this was just what, one year before, had helped to inaugurate the Noske régime.

Walcher saw immediately that the fate of the negotiations was partly in his hands and decided—Pieck was of little account—that the communists must facilitate the formation of a Legien government. He gave a pledge to the effect that the communists would not attempt to overthrow by force a Legien government, as long as it kept to its own programme. He described the policy the communists would follow in such an eventuality as 'loyal opposition'. Walcher was a Würtemberg engineer, a workman of exceptional trade-union experience and knowledge of the masses; he was not a theoretician. He formulated his ideas in rather clumsy terms, speaking of a period of democracy in which no class would dominate. Such a praise of full democracy was the unpardonable sin among communists, and Walcher was severely upbraided for it by Lenin, when the latter learnt the text of Walcher's declaration. But, at the same time, Lenin agreed with Walcher's policy. At the party central committee, however, there was a storm; how could socialists be trusted? Was it not an axiom that they always betrayed? Even if Legien was sincere, how could he carry out what he intended to do? Was it not evident to every Marxist that democracy can only work against, never for, the workers, it being the 'dictatorship of the bourgeoisie'? Walcher seemed to have forgotten the A B C of Marxism.

But before communist headquarters had a chance to rectify Walcher's policy, the whole scheme was destroyed from another quarter. The character and structure of the Independent Party had been in transformation all through the year 1919, and now this process came to a head. The party which had originally consisted of old pre-war left-wing socialists, mostly of a very moderate type, had absorbed, after the revolution, many of those young elements which had joined the socialist movement at the moment of its greatest power. This element was politically nondescript and certainly had no settled political convictions. But it was excitable and the repeated defeats of 1919 had driven it to the left. Very few of the old leaders of the left wing made common cause with these new elements, but a number of young people who had come to the surface during the revolution brought the masses with them, especially in the mining districts of the Ruhr and of central Germany. Whether this new element would be any good for the formation of a revolutionary party remained to be tested. In the meantime a left wing was formed from it, and, under the impression of growing reaction, this numerous movement rapidly evolved towards communism. Thus the German communists for the first time had the opportunity to become a real mass movement. The Kapp *Putsch* had both enormously increased the strength of this left wing of the Independents and widened the schism from the official leaders of the party. Now, during the negotiations for the formation of a Legien government, the new group for the first time interfered as a major political force.

This group repeated the arguments of the left-wing communists *fortissimo*. They went so far as to threaten a split of the party if the Independents were to form a labour government together with Legien. They were convinced, for no particular reason, that a coalition with the majority socialists could only end in disaster. Had it not done so in 1918? To them the failure in 1918 seemed to be wholly due to the mischief done by the leaders of the majority socialists. They were impassive to the arguments which went to show that the situation was different; that in 1918 the armies of the Allies stood at the gates and had now demobilized; that the masses had been starved, and now had tolerably good food; that the fight had been between wholesale nationalization and private property, whereas this time the aim was to carry through a limited and constructive programme; that the workers had had no experience of the republic, but now knew better what they wanted; that the labour government had been founded on the downfall of the old régime, whereas now it would issue from the biggest victory the German working class had ever won; that the very fact of Legien's change of front showed that the majority socialists were not the same as in 1918. It was all in vain.

What was at the back of the minds of the left-wing Independents? Their openly expressed conviction was that nothing could be done within a democratic régime; which meant, in practice, the same principle as that held by the crazy extremists of the Communist Party before they were expelled, at Heidelberg. The left-wing Independents contended, in effect, that within a democratic régime Legien would always have the better of them; in other words they did not believe that the workers, by themselves, wanted the revolution. In this they were right, and they were right, in consequence, in believing that, in the end, the coalition would serve those who stood for reform as against those who stood for revolution. That even so mean a thing as a thorough democratization of Germany could have been a valuable achievement was an idea completely anathema to them. But they would never admit their own doubts, so obvious in their behaviour, and preferred to mislead themselves and others in a wild-fire of revolutionary slogans. Only the dictatorship could help the proletariat; they must fight only for that and avoid everything which could draw the proletariat to the course of worthless reform.

The left wing of the Independents, on this occasion, showed that it not only substantially agreed with the communists, but even with their left extremists. That this did not necessarily mean that a section of the proletariat had become more revolutionary is evident, yet they were already strong enough to bind the hands of the party as a whole. Legien's offers were turned down. Thus the majority socialists were faced with a decision: either to leave the government entirely to the bourgeois parties immediately after the greatest success of the workers, or to form a new coalition with the left-wing parties of the bourgeoisie. They chose the second course. Legien and all the other leaders were permanently disgusted with the left wing. The latter, who had always described the coalition of socialist and bourgeois as 'treachery', thus forced the majority socialists, who still led more than 50 per cent of the socialist workers, back into that very treachery; and yet they could go forward in self-righteousness, repeating frequently: 'Social-democrats can only betray.'

They could not, however, escape one problem the solution of which they had made almost impossible. There were districts in the Reich which, during the days of the fighting, had established a sort of proletarian dictatorship, notably Chemnitz and the Ruhr. These dictatorships must now be given up without resistance, or a fight continued against hopeless odds. In Chemnitz, to the repeatedly expressed satisfaction of Lenin, Brandler chose the first alternative. He managed to uphold Soviet rule in his town and district for more than a week after the end of the general strike, and then, when he saw himself completely isolated and surrounded by the Reichswehr, accepted an agreement by which the Soviet government was peacefully dissolved. The skilful execution of this difficult manœuvre predestined Brandler to the leading position which he was soon afterwards to assume.

But in the Ruhr things were definitely out of hand. Part of the territory held by the improvised Red army of the Ruhr was controlled by the Independents, who followed a policy similar to that of Brandler in Chemnitz. The western part of the region, with Essen and Duisburg, had fallen into the hands of elements which, while calling themselves communists, refused to take orders from the party. The situation of this isolated outpost grew hopeless when the left Independents failed to help them. They had attempted to continue the general strike, in Berlin, after the formation of the new government, in order to help the Red districts in the Ruhr. But the Berlin workers thought that with the withdrawal of Kapp the thing was settled and followed the advice of both majoritarians and right-wing Independents to resume work. Already it was clear that the left-wing Independents had no secure following. The new government, however, did want to put an end to the fighting. Representatives of the Red zone in the Ruhr met members of the Prussian government at Bielefeld, and an agreement about the peaceful dissolution and disarmament of the Red army was reached. Levi went to the Ruhr and strongly advocated acceptance, which proved so successful at the same time in Chemnitz. But he did not convince the extremists of the Ruhr.

The local Reichswehr did their best to make a peaceful settlement impossible. Only two weeks before they had been seriously beaten by unarmed workers. Now, having reverted to the service of the government which they had just attempted to overthrow, they were eager to take their revenge. They formulated the conditions for the handing over of the arms of the Red army in such a way as to make their fulfilment very difficult. In many quarters this was interpreted as a sign that the Reichswehr did not accept the idea of a peaceful settlement, and, once the arms were given up, would proceed to a massacre. This gave an easy chance to the extremists of the left, who wanted to persuade the workers to continue the fight. In the end, chaos ensued. Part of the workers gave up their arms, part did not. The Reichswehr entered the Ruhr and beat down what resistance there remained. The communist movement in the Ruhr was shattered. The rising in the Ruhr had been as big a military success of the workers as the general strike was a success in the field of industrial action. But as the success of the strike had been wasted by the failure to form a labour government, so the military success in the Ruhr was undone by the inability of the Ruhr workers to retreat in order when resistance was no longer possible. The first attempt of the German right to take power had led to complete defeat. Yet the aftermath of the crisis was such that the victory of the workers was turned into disaster and the Kapp *Putsch*, though failing in its immediate aims, marked a turning-point in German history. The workers had wasted their last big opportunity.

CHAPTER VIII

THE FOUNDATION
OF THE COMMUNIST INTERNATIONAL

During the revolutionary convulsions of 1919, the Communist International was founded.

Immediately after the revolutions of November 1918, Lenin had decided that now was the crucial moment for launching the slogan of the new international. All through the war he had stood for schism, not only from the patriots, but even from the pacifists. Now he set out to put his aim into practice. The war prisoners, some of them now trained communist agitators, were sent home with that aim. According to Lenin's wishes, and in the way already described, they founded the communist parties of Hungary and of Austria. But in Germany they found their work not so easy. There, the Spartakusbund had few members but a strong group of self-confident and able leaders: Liebknecht, Luxemburg, Jogiches, Levinè, Levi. Liebknecht's attitude is not known, but all the others were against Lenin's plan, some of them passionately so. They did not want an international in which the Bolsheviks would have all the power; they wanted a new revolutionary international, but would not form it before at least some strong revolutionary mass parties existed in the West. Luxemburg especially was convinced that without this being achieved before the foundation of a new international, the very fact of the foundation of an exclusively Bolshevik international would deter important sections of the revolutionary movement in the West.

No contact or almost none existed at that time between Russia and the victorious countries. In Germany, the most important of the defeated countries, Lenin could get no safe foothold on account of Rosa Luxemburg's opposition. This

seemed a serious obstacle indeed. But Lenin regarded Luxemburg's hesitations as sheer opportunism and decided to go
ahead. The work of preparing the new international was done,
quite naïvely at that time, by the Ministry of Foreign Affairs.
Chicherin launched a wireless appeal for an international
conference. Rosa Luxemburg's counter-stroke was to send two
delegates, Levinè and Eberlein, to this conference, but with a
mandate to oppose the formation of the international and to
refuse to join it, if it should nevertheless be founded. This was
on 12th January 1919, amidst the turmoil of the January rising.
Three days later Rosa Luxemburg was dead. Almost her last
act had been one of defiance of the Bolsheviks.

Levinè was stopped at the German border but Eberlein got
through, a feat achieved by few. It was very difficult to reach
Russia at the time, and even those who had wanted to attend
were not always able to do so. Thus the Bulgarian Tesnyaki,
one of the few organizations which had decided to join, were
represented, not by their own men, but by Rakowski, who at
the time was organizing civil war in the Ukraine. One American delegate had got through, but both Britain and France were
only represented by people living in Moscow, and no organization in those countries could be regarded as safe for the new
international. Both the Swedish and the Norwegian left were
represented, however, the latter preparing itself to take definitely the leadership of the Socialist Party of that country. Italy
and Switzerland were not represented but believed to be more
or less friendly. Holland had a delegate, representing the group
of Pannekoek and Gorter, mentioned in a previous chapter.
No Austrian delegate was present at the beginning, and Hungary was represented by a refugee living in Moscow. Hungary
was not regarded as important at the moment. A glowing
account published in *Imprecorr* five years after the event tells
how the news of the proclamation of the dictatorship, first in
Budapest and then in Munich, electrified the conference; but
the memory of the author has let him down. The conference
ended on March 7th, while the Hungarian dictatorship was
proclaimed on March 21st, and the Munich dictatorship on
April 7th.

In fact, Lenin knew that it was impossible to form an international without the Germans. But there was Eberlein, with

his imperative mandate against it. All the delegates united their efforts to convince him. At first he kept to his orders, however, and the conference, instead of acting as first congress of the Communist International, had to sit as a preparatory meeting only. But on the third day arrived the Austrian delegate, Steinhart, a brilliant speaker and an enthusiast (he has long since left the Comintern). Steinhart had travelled seventeen days, he had crossed the lines of both the Whites and the Reds at the danger of his life, and now he gave a highly coloured and emotional account of the struggle of the Austrian proletariat, which, he believed, was on the point of establishing a dictatorship. He impressed the conference deeply. Under the pressure from all sides, Eberlein gave in and consented to abstain from voting. Then the International was founded and a few basic planks of the platform were laid down; essential among them was the principle of the Soviet dictatorship and the duty of severing in every country all ties with both patriots and pacifists. As the newly founded International stood, there could be no doubt as to its leadership. Compared to the small groups which had joined them, the Russians were like giants to dwarfs. Moscow became the seat of the International, and Grigori Sinovjev was made its president.

It was hardly a happy choice. In the whole Bolshevik Party there was probably no man so like Bela Kun as he. A brilliant speaker and debater, he had the gift of dealing with various sorts of people, but an innate duplicity and love of double-dealing and intrigue very soon disgusted the most enthusiastic. He was notoriously anything but courageous, but, as is so often the case with excitable types, was capable of the wildest overrating of chances and unable to admit failure. He had made his career in the party by boundless submission to Lenin, who found him useful because he repeated the master's ideas *à la lettre*, but with a polemical and literary gift which Lenin did not possess. But he had refused to follow Lenin during the decisive days, and in November 1917 had twice publicly rejected responsibility for the Bolshevik *coup d'état*. This man, who was not deemed suitable for a major office in the Soviet state, was made head of the Communist International.

There was, however, no idea of Sinovjev leading the International alone. Radek and Bukharin were supposed to co-operate in every important decision. Bukharin knew the Scandinavian labour movement from his own experience, but was otherwise handicapped by his lack of linguistic ability; moreover, he was weak. Lenin appreciated him mostly as a man with gifts for abstract theory. Bukharin had opposed Lenin during the crisis of the Brest-Litovsk peace negotiations, where he defended resistance to the end; a course appropriate to what the French call a *grand cœur*, but which would have brought down the Soviet régime within a fortnight. Generally speaking Bukharin was to be ranked high by moral standards, but was no politician. He had a particularly unhappy tendency to swing from one attitude to the opposite one and to carry each of his varying attitudes to extremes. For years he was regarded as the incarnation of the extreme left within the International, to become later the incarnation of the extreme right.

Radek was of a different mould. He was a pupil not of Lenin but of Rosa Luxemburg, which meant that he was not used to submission and that he was used to close contact with the Western labour movement. It was his profound knowledge of the latter, especially of German socialism, which gave him prestige. Altogether Radek was a man of political qualities. Together with his wit, which has won him international fame, he had immense powers of application and a real thirst for detail. He was not the sort of man to be satisfied either with theoretical generalizations such as Bukharin loved, or with rhetoric in the vein of Sinovjev. He was clever and thoroughly undogmatic. Already in 1919 he had attempted to establish contacts between the Soviet Union and big German industrialists, a task which, at that time, almost every other member of the party would have regarded as a defilement. He was a cynic. The one thing this brilliant man lacked was character, that deep-rooted moral balance which draws an undefinable line between what is right and what is wrong. Radek was too clever to be either heroic or even consistent.

Sinovjev, Bukharin, and Radek formed the real day-to-day leadership of the Comintern. Occasionally Trotsky, while burdened with immense labours, lent a hand, especially in matters concerning France. Decisions of paramount importance were, of course, submitted to Lenin. Thus the leadership of the International was entirely in the hands of the Russians, Radek being regarded as a Bolshevik and being a member of the Russian party. At the same time the Russians had not set free a single man of paramount capacities for this work. Of course the people who really counted at that time, Lenin, Trotsky, Sverdlov, Dzershinski, Krassin, Chicherin, Kamyenev, and many others were overwhelmed with work; but there is no safer symptom of the real scale of values of a movement than the decision as to what is of essential and what of minor importance in an emergency. The Russians sincerely believed that they were working for world revolution and regarded their own revolution as part of it. But the choice of the men they delegated for the task proved that, unknown to themselves, they were Russian nationalists who regarded—already!—the other parties as auxiliaries in their cause.

Immediately after the first congress of the International the combined offensives of Youdenitch and Denikin closed the doors of Europe to Russia. During the whole decisive period of civil war the Russians hardly attempted to influence the policy of the Western communist movements. It would have been very difficult, technically, and moreover there was no time for it. We saw how the movement fared without their intervention. But while, in practice, there was very little activity —except for the occasional sending of jewels and money—there were the wildest dreams. The Russians, completely cut off from the rest of the world, saw events as they wanted to see them and as the revolutionary atmosphere of their own country suggested them to be. Trotsky, in the gazette of his armoured train, wrote an article in which he claimed to see the Red army, after defeating the Whites, conquer Europe and attack America. And Sinovjev, in number 1 of the *Communist International*, prophesied that within a year not only would all Europe be a Soviet republic, but would already be forgetting that there had ever been a fight for it. Such wild prophecies contrasted blatantly with the real insignificance of the forces the International had at its command outside Russia in 1919. In Hungary only the impotent debris of a party; in Austria and Germany groups less than 5 per cent of the socialist parties of their respective countries; in England and France as good as nothing. The Balkans seemed more hopeful, only to become a scene of defeat after a few months. The delusion of the Moscow leaders—including, of course, Lenin—was comprehensible in the circumstances, though it was dangerous. But it remained even after the blockade. When the material rampart was taken away, the Russians surrounded themselves with a spiritual rampart of their own making; anyway their mentality was so different from that of the West as to make a correct appreciation of its politics very difficult for them. And the atmosphere of a dictatorial country, strictly severed from all alien currents of thought, did the rest. Those who saw the world abroad generally saw it only from the communist point of view, living exclusively among communists, who were often only an infinitesimal fraction of the population of their respective countries. But this belongs to a later phase.

If the hopes of Moscow at that period had little in common with reality, its influence was not, however, limited to the very narrow circle of those who had adhered to the Comintern at the first world-congress itself. The general prestige of the Russian revolution was strong though vague, not only at the time. The newly founded organization of the Comintern also made some progress during the year 1919. A considerable number of recruits came in and strengthened the belief of the Russians that world revolution was quickly approaching. Only they did not always mean what the Russians believed them to mean. Lenin had conceived the Comintern as a body united in doctrine and action and strong through its unity. But the recruits to the Comintern during this first year of its existence came from the most varied quarters, and the conversions were effected for very divergent reasons and on varying and sometimes contradictory assumptions.

Of all parties and organizations which adhered in 1919 only a single one wanted to become what the Russians thought was a real communist party. This was the party of the Bulgarian Tesnyaki, which by tradition had been closely allied with the Bolsheviks since its foundation. Bulgaria was the smallest of all the Balkan states (with the exception of Albania) but at least the Tesnyaki, after 1918, rapidly beat their reformist competitors within the labour movement and became the only considerable labour party of their country. Their example exerted a decided influence upon both the Yugoslav and the Roumanian movements. Both the Roumanian and the Yugoslav socialist parties adhered a few months later, after having expelled a few right-wingers. But both, in contrast with the Bulgarian communists, were forced into division again after the second world-congress, and soon sank into insignificance.

The second adhesion to the Comintern after the first congress was that of a movement which had never had close contacts with Russia: the Norwegian Labour Party. This had one thing in common with the adhesion of the Bulgarian Tesnyaki; the Norwegians too controlled the bulk of the labour movement of their country, but it was a very small country indeed. Otherwise there was some contrast between the Bulgarians and the Norwegians. While the former were revolutionaries who had evolved under the constant influence of Russian Bolshevism, the latter were not even Marxists. It has been described, in a previous chapter, how Martin Tranmael, the leader of the Norwegian left, created a very peculiar blend of Western reformism and anarcho-syndicalism and won over his party to it. The Norwegian left, which was against civil war, against ideological unity, against centralization and discipline, against the subordination of the trade unions to the political movement, was the antithesis of Russian Bolshevism in every respect. Its adherence to the Comintern was based upon a mutual misunderstanding and did not last for long. But how was it possible to overlook such glaring contrasts?

In this respect the Norwegian left did not stand alone. During the first year of its existence the Comintern exerted a very considerable influence upon the anarcho-syndicalists all over the world. The small group of Dutch extremists who adhered to the Comintern at the first world-congress had collaborated, as described in a previous chapter, with the Dutch anarcho-syndicalist trade unions throughout the war and continued to do so, with the full assent of the Comintern. In France, large groups of the there numerous anarcho-syndicalists within the trade unions sympathized with the Bolsheviks earlier than any other section of French labour, and when, two years later, the French trade-union movement was split, they sided with the communists. The Spanish C.N.T. (Confederación Nacional del Trabajo), the strongest anarcho-syndicalist organization of the world, adhered to the Comintern during the first year of its existence, a fact strangely contrasted with the present heated enmity of the two. In the United States sympathies for the Russian revolution, and accordingly for the Comintern, were very weak within the trade unions of the American Federation of Labour but very strong among the small but active 'Industrial Workers of the World'. Most of the small groups in Britain which adhered to the Comintern were influenced by the anarcho-syndicalist ideas of the American I.W.W., notably the Scottish Shop-stewards.

Why did these groups so intensely sympathize with the Bolshevik revolution during its first stage? First of all, because the anarchists, since the time when Bakunin, the founder of anarchism, had fought Marx, had predicted that the socialist mass parties of the West would 'betray'. In this basic matter anarchists and Bolshevists agreed. The anarchists had always stood for revolution, though some of them wanted this revolution to be achieved, not by bloodshed but by the peaceful means of a general strike; this did not apply to all anarcho-syndicalists, least of all to the Spanish movement. Thus, in more than one respect, the Bolshevik revolution in Russia was the fulfilment of the dreams of international anarchism. Even its form appealed deeply to them. We have already mentioned that Bakunin was the first Russian revolutionary to conceive the idea of a revolutionary movement led and directed by a small circle of selected conspirators, but carried on by the spontaneous rising of the largest masses. Finally, the Soviet régime had something deeply akin to anarchism. Had it been a persistent reality, and not an incident in the evolution of a party dictatorship, it would have been anarchism in full. For the Soviets, elected by the masses, directly responsible to them, getting no special reward for their work, locally and regionally independent, must be and were the ideal of anarchism and anarcho-syndicalism. Accordingly Lenin, as early as 1917, had expressed in *State and Revolution* the idea that Bolshevism, on the international battle-field, must seek the alliance of the best elements of the anarchists against the socialist traitors.

But it is obvious that the successes the Comintern scored in this milieu could not last. Not a single one of the anarchist contacts thus established lasted for more than two or three years. The anarchists broke with the Comintern in disgust as soon as the dictatorship of the party, the Cheka, and the Red army had fully developed; admiration turned into deep hatred.

Another recruit, much more important than any other, came from Italy. Here the Socialist Party adhered *en bloc* immediately after having received the news of the first world-congress of the Comintern. Italy was one of the largest of European countries, and the Italian Socialist Party, which had opposed the war from beginning to end, won tremendous influence after its conclusion. Italy in 1918 remained almost as shattered as Austria and Germany. For two years after the war things seemed to move in the direction of a revolution and the Socialist Party seemed to be the force of the coming day. During 1919 and 1920 the Italians were the chief force of the Comintern in the international arena. But this adhesion was based as little upon a real agreement of views and methods as that of the anarcho-syndicalists. In spite of a considerable number of national peculiarities the Italian socialists, on the whole, were a typical Western socialist party, with a reformist right wing, a middle group, and a small, revolutionary left wing. Internationally Lenin had founded the Comintern in order to get rid of the influence of both patriots and pacifists over the labour movement. But nationally, in Italy, the split, which was the *raison d'être* of the Comintern, was not effected. It can be said, without exaggeration, that in the Italian Socialist Party there was hardly a single man who agreed with the Bolsheviks. The majority of the Italians rejected absolutely the idea of purging the party of the reformists and 'traitors'. And the small left-wing minority rejected activity in parliament, and on many other points agreed with that German 'ultra-left' wing which was excluded, a few months later, at the congress of Heidelberg. This state of things continued in the Italian Socialist Party all through the years of revolutionary excitement.

Had the Comintern taken action the difference would have become apparent at once. But it took care not to do so. Being unable to take a hand in Italian affairs themselves, the Russians welcomed the adhesion of the Italian socialists without looking too closely. Altogether they had naïve illusions in those days. They were convinced that the proletarian revolution was afoot all over Europe and sweeping everything before it. Forgetting all their doctrines about the treacherousness of the socialists, they took—as Sinovjev confessed later on—even D'Arragona,the ultra-moderate leader of the Italian trade unions, who has since become a Fascist, for a real Bolshevik. They were thrown hither and thither between extreme diffidence and naïve confidence.

CHAPTER IX

FACTIONS

Very naturally, the different types of communist parties had a very different inner life. Adhesion to the Comintern changed nothing, in substance, in the views and methods of the Italian and Norwegian socialists. But it was a very different matter with those parties which, by their very formation, had accepted the communist principle of a party purged from all deviations and all opportunism. These parties naturally displayed, at an early stage, all the characteristics of a communist party and it is important to study their structure. The historian of the Comintern is faced with two assertions about its 'régime' which he must subject to careful consideration. The first one is that the communist parties have evolved their specific peculiarities under pressure from Moscow. The other contention, still more far-reaching, which to-day is maintained by Trotsky and his followers, suggests that the present 'régime' of the Comintern is due to its degeneration under Stalin. It is only the more interesting to investigate the inner life of a communist party in 1919, before Moscow did exert any serious pressure upon it. The Hungarian and Austrian communist parties provide suitable examples, not for their numerical strength, which was insignificant, but on account of their typical evolution after the end of the Hungarian dictatorship.

As soon as the leading group of Hungarian Soviet leaders was safely in exile, it split into socialist and communist sections. The communists had the better of it within this small group. A number of leaders who before the dictatorship had been outstanding social-democrats now joined the communists, among them Dr. Eugen Varga, the economist of the party, who was to become chief economic expert of the Comintern, Dr. Eugen Landler, former leader of the railwaymen, who was to become the chief of one of the two factions fighting within the Hungarian Communist Party in exile, and Joseph Pogany, previously president of the soldiers' Soviet, who was later to serve the Comintern in high capacities in many countries, notably in the United States. But in spite of this success feuds soon broke out within the communist group itself.

The real leader of the Vienna group of Hungarian communists—which was all-important because contact with Hungary could only be established through Vienna—was Dr. Georg Lukacz, who during the dictatorship had been People's Commissar of Education. He had had a Heidelberg training and was incontestably a leader in German sociology, specializing in remote problems of the sociology of art, where he has given proof of outstanding theoretical gifts. Very naturally Lukacz, who from a strongly convinced Hegelian idealist had become a fanatical Marxist during the war, was mostly interested in the theoretical aspect of things. His anti-materialistic and essentially aesthetic bent of mind had not changed; as it was before in the pure theory of art so it was now in the pure theory of communism that he was interested, firmly convinced as he was that a close group of absolutely safe communists was the essential condition for success. He was one of the first men to study, in the West, Lenin's theory of the 'vanguard', of the organization of professional revolutionaries, and to draw, in a sensational article about class-consciousness, the logical conclusion that the proletariat had no 'proletarian class-consciousness' but must get it through the leadership of intellectuals, who by theoretical understanding have learnt what the class-consciousness of the proletariat *ought* to be. There is no doubt that Lukacz only expressed what was implicit in Lenin. At the same time such an attitude meant complete severance from the labour movement. A small group of about thirty people sat in Vienna cafés and flats and learnt orthodoxy.

But there was more than that in the newly-formed 'close, pure party'. The spirit of this group has been described in an interesting article by Ilona Duzcinska, an apostatical member, in *Unser Weg*, March 1921:

'A representative theoretician who was perhaps the sole

brain behind Hungarian communism', says Ilona Duzcinska, 'at a decisive moment answered my question as to whether lying and cheating of the members of the party by their own leaders were admissible by, this statement: Communist ethics make it the highest duty to accept the necessity of acting wickedly. This, he said, was the greatest sacrifice revolution asked from us. The conviction of the true communist is that evil transforms itself into bliss through the dialectics of historical evolution. (That this morality of the type of Nechaev is, *inter alia*, based upon admiration of Dostoevski, will surprise nobody.) This dialectical theory of wickedness has never been published by the theoretician just mentioned, nevertheless this communist gospel spread as a secret doctrine from mouth to mouth, until it finally was regarded as the semi-official quintessence of "true communism", as the one criterion of a "true communist".' So far Duzcinska. Lukacz, to-day, is an emphatic admirer of Stalin, whom he has praised for many years, not only as the greatest living statesman but as the greatest living philosopher. This in another man's mouth would doubtless be base adulation, but Lukacz is certainly in deadly earnest, and his appreciation, after all, is only a logical conclusion from his starting-point.

The strange development of this group of refugees cannot be understood without interpreting the secret doctrine of wickedness in the light of another doctrine of Lukacz which he has given full publicity. This is the identification of the truth and the party. The proletariat does not really know its interests and its historical task; therefore the party must carry the proletariat along a course which it would not follow by itself. In this basic assumption there is nothing which goes beyond Lenin. But where, then, is the criterion of truth, if it is not in the proletarian class-consciousness? The criterion lies in the true 'line' accepted by the party. But, again, the ideological purity of the party can only be safeguarded from above. Therefore the orders from above are the safeguard of truth. After all, if the central committee is infallible and the ordinary members children in need of a guiding hand, it is only natural that it should be necessary to mislead both the masses and the less initiated members of the party itself.

Those who want to get an inkling of the very peculiar

atmosphere reflected in Lukacz' line of thought must go to the collection of his papers and articles published in 1923 under the title *History and Class-consciousness*. They will be struck by the strange merging of the highest type of philosophical and critical analysis—especially of the history of dialectics—with the crudest adoration of the changing orders of a central committee. Lukacz has carried the theory of an almighty central committee, against which Rosa Luxemburg had forewarned the Marxists in 1904, to the last extreme. And reality soon fell into line with the wildest dreams of the ideologists. In the meantime the first steps of this development were made outside the real labour movement, and were proclaimed in a vocabulary unintelligible not only to workingmen, but to any mortals who had not enjoyed a Heidelberg training.

Against this club of rigid logical philosophers rose Kun. He did not object to their moral doctrines, but to the highbrow atmosphere, to the complete severance from the problems of the average worker, to the intellectual conceit, which was patent in the behaviour of Lukacz and his group. It was the year 1920; the Comintern had gained in strength, and Kun went to Vienna with a Comintern mandate to reorganize the party. He encountered fierce resistance from the side of those who were to be ousted and who had more than one grudge against Kun from the days of the dictatorship. Then Kun chose to try a simple device. He offered money, not to Lukacz and Landler, but to a number of second-rank leaders of the opposition against his rule. He had miscalculated, however, because his adversaries, though partisans of wickedness in theory, hated the sordid in practice. The offer was not only declined but made public throughout the organizations of the Hungarian communists, and finally published by Duzcinska and in a number of other pamphlets.

But the opponents of Kun had no means to fight him successfully. They had doctrines and allegiance in common with him. They stood, as he did, for the doctrine of the closed, pure party of revolutionaries; for indifference to moral means, inside and outside the party and for absolute obedience to their superiors. And it was Kun and not Lukacz who had a mandate from Moscow. To the complaints about Kun's attempts to bribe his own party Moscow remained entirely insensitive. But Kun's adversaries did not want to give in, and a fierce factional fight between two personal cliques which differed somewhat in psychology, but neither in doctrine nor in practical politics, went on for at least eight years and made every serious attempt to resume underground work in Hungary futile from the outset.

This sort of factional fight was to become characteristic of communism, both inside and outside Russia. There is no party in the Comintern—with the one very significant exception of the British party—which has not been rent asunder several times by these factional fights, of which the crisis of the Hungarian party was the first notorious instance. A good deal of the history of the Comintern consists of the story of these sometimes very unpleasant rivalries, where the personal merges indiscriminately with the political. Austria was the next example.

The factional struggles in Austrian communism, which were to last for ten years, are less interesting than those of Hungary. To the Hungarian fights the personalities of Kun and Lukacz give colour; the background of an historical defeat adds a tragical touch; and the ruthless logic of Lukacz's thinking gives them a meaning beyond the narrow circle of those who joined in the fight. All that was completely absent in Austria. There, after 15th June 1919, after the *Putsch* had been defeated, the various coteries within the leadership simply started to accuse one another of having betrayed the cause, not in the metaphysical sense in which later most communist leaders of the world were one day to 'betray' their cause, but in the common meaning of the word: they charged one another with having informed the police. Into this atmosphere no change was introduced by the splitting of a small section of left-wingers from the socialists. On the contrary, the newcomers started fighting with the old guard, and party affairs were soon in such a muddle as to make the situation hopeless; no political difference could be discovered in a purely personal fight, which nevertheless was carried on with ferocious passion. The result was that during the fifteen years of its legal existence the Communist Party of Austria could not secure a single seat in parliament.

The whole affair would deserve no mention had it not repeated itself in almost every party. In the Communist Party of the United States, for instance, for many years a fierce fight was afoot between one 'group Foster' and another 'group Ruthenberg'. The Comintern stated officially, on several occasions, that it was impossible to discover a political meaning in this bitter antagonism, and forbade the continuation of the well-organized factions. They were continued, nevertheless, in the Hungarian, the Austrian, the American, and many other parties. It is therefore essential to probe somewhat more deeply into the reasons of these cleavages. The Hungarian feud, being perhaps the worst of them all, is particularly significant because it started without any intervention from Moscow. The innate law of the life of an ordinary communist party can thus be studied, in the Hungarian case, in almost ideal isolation from disturbing factors.

In the Hungarian as in the Austrian and many other cases the root of the evil was obviously the failure to achieve the aims the party had set itself. A certain amount of personal antagonisms and struggle between various 'sets' of leaders is a normal feature of the life of every political party. These antagonisms are more or less obliterated, for obvious reasons, in times of success, and become more acute in times of failure. And the first determinant of the fierce antagonisms which every communist party harbours within its own ranks is constant failure to achieve its aims. This, with a communist party, is almost unavoidable. For the primary contention upon which the Comintern and all its sections are constructed is this: revolution would be possible if only the socialists would not 'betray' it; revolution is an immediate aim of the present period. It is true that this basic contention, which was a dogma until 1934, has been more or less abandoned since—and one of the immediate effects has been the lessening of feuds inside the parties —but this will concern us in due time. At present we are confronted with the position during the first fifteen years of Comintern history. During this early period, the *obiter dictum* of socialist betrayal was coupled with this other assertion: *Therefore* we must build up a reliable, revolutionary communist party, as the best guarantee of victory. If failure came instead of victory, it was because the particular communist leaders involved were no good, had 'betrayed' in the same way as the socialists. The leading groups of defeated communist parties constantly hinted at major social facts as an explanation of their defeats: the masses were unwilling to make a revolution, or its enemies were too strong. But every such assertion was invariably turned down and branded as opportunism (except when, in later years, Stalin occasionally could not deny his personal responsibility for defeat). All that is certainly not Marxist. Whereas Marxism tends rather to over-emphasize the 'objective' factor, the automatic processes in society, as against the will of the individual and of small groups, this communist neo-Marxism believes in the saving power of small communist parties, provided they are truly revolutionary; there seems to be an assumption, never openly asserted, but always implicit in practical decisions, that the masses will surely follow the party, provided only it is the right sort of communist party. The inevitable result is that leaders and leading groups are made responsible for events which they were, in fact, quite unable to avoid.

What, moreover, in the eyes of the average communist between 1919 and 1934, was a 'success'? Not such as a democratic socialist would interpret it. The socialists, generally speaking, were satisfied—and sometimes altogether too satisfied—if the party grew in membership and polling strength and if the lot of the masses was improved. These would not be criteria acceptable to communists. The improvement of the material life of the masses might only foster a 'worker's aristocracy'. And the party might grow and win parliamentary seats precisely because it was in decay and falling into 'opportunism'. The test of real success, in communist eyes, could only consist in a tangible approach towards the revolutionary conquest of power by the party. But this aim proved everywhere to be unattainable. Thus the aims are always put much too high, sometimes as high as Utopia itself. The parties, whose *raison d'être* was not the day-to-day struggle for the interests of the wage-earners but revolution, expected that revolution almost from year to year, and were naturally deeply disappointed again and again. Trotsky, who still maintains the views which the Comintern held a decade ago, gave an instance of this sort of Utopianism as late as June 1936, when, after the French stay-in strikes, he published an article entitled 'The French Revolution Has Begun.' What could he do afterwards but look for the 'traitor' who had ruined a revolution which, in reality, had never existed?

The double Utopianism which believes that everything can be achieved in the nick of time, and that success or failure depend upon the quality of the 'vanguard', naturally claims scapegoats every few years, or even more frequently. And it makes little difference to what aim this Utopianism is applied. It is as rampant in the claims and plans of the Stalin régime in Russia as in the world-revolutionary dreams of the Comintern before, and of its dissidents after, 1934. But with time it becomes increasingly difficult to find scapegoats. Every defeat and delusion, whatever else it may achieve, naturally tends to drive one set of leaders outside the party, or at least out of leadership, until every possible opposition is excluded. What does remain then? As nobody any longer dissents and nobody therefore can be charged with any responsibility, however understood, nothing remains but to invent scapegoats where there are none. The Utopian says: When once we have created that iron cohort of revolutionaries which is able to lead the revolution—or the 'workers' republic', where revolution is already achieved—then everything will be all right. The 'iron cohort' *is* finally achieved, i.e. every inkling of opposition to the orders of the infallible centre is beaten down, its standard-bearers excluded, jailed, shot. But in fact nothing is changed. It appears only more glaringly that communism, a Utopia based upon the belief in the omnipotence of the 'vanguard', cannot live without a scapegoat, and the procedures applied to detect them, invent them, accuse them, holding them up to opprobrium and destroying them, become only more cruel and reckless. Thus the highest Utopia, the semi-religious belief in a society freed from oppression and exploitation and based on solidarity alone, paradoxically leads to an orgy of self-destruction of the leading group amid crimes and horror such as no bourgeois society has ever witnessed. The enthusiastic belief in the rapid approach of the millennium has never been without a vengeance.

In this atmosphere it is not of primary importance whether the scapegoat is sentenced on personal or on political grounds. The antagonisms within communist parties frequently defy any attempt at a political interpretation. More than passing disagreements within 'bourgeois' parties normally correspond to real divergences of views within its ranks. First the party follows a policy which a part of the members and followers find incompatible with their own ideas; then follows a struggle, sometimes ending in a split. But in a communist party there is invariably first the struggle and sometimes a split, and the reasons come afterwards. More than once desperate attempts were made to formulate the content of this or that disagreement which had or was about to split a communist party; both sides were unable to say what really divided them. The one thing which it was possible to say was that party affairs went wrong; and as the very suggestion that basic elements of communist policy might be unrealistic itself constituted the crime of treason, nothing remained but to find an explanation either in the individual wickedness or in minor tactical mistakes of certain leaders.

Therefore the factional fights within a communist party are invariably more cruel and ruthless than similar fights in other, less Utopian movements. A man who, working within the party, is personally guilty of the failure of the revolution to come, is, in fact, worse than an open enemy; against him, every weapon is admitted, nay, is obligatory. He is a 'traitor'; for in the communist mentality, every failure—not objective failure, but failure of the reality to comply with the Utopia—supposes a traitor. It is naturally not certain in advance who is the traitor. First there is the betrayal, permanent and overt through the fact of failure itself; later it will be decided who has betrayed. This means that the apparent tactical reasons for a split are never quite so real as they appear from outside. There are, even in a communist 'iron cohort' and 'monolytic vanguard', inevitably minor differences of opinion, which can serve as a basis of accusation. But the fierceness of the 'purge' never corresponds at all to the width of the real divergence. It is proportionate, not to the real rift of opinions within the party, but to the width of the gulf between the Utopia and reality. On the other hand, personal antagonisms within a communist party are never quite as personal as they seem to be; for the personal inability of a group to lead means that it has 'betrayed', with all the duties of savage repression incumbent, in consequence, upon its personal adversaries. It is impossible to understand the following story without keeping this constantly in mind.

The basic law of a communist party is therefore to proceed through a series of 'purges' of 'traitors'; this, in the end, has helped first Moscow, later Stalin, to establish absolute domination within the Comintern. But it is not due to Moscow; it is implicit in the general 'ideology' of the movement. It is always difficult for the uninitiated to understand the mentality of a group of millenarians. Yet without the realization of the basic elements of their particular psychology no understanding of their history is possible. This is what makes the Comintern so puzzling, what drives judgements about it from one extreme to another; there is hardly a leading man in world affairs who did not regard the communists alternately as hopeless and insignificant Utopians and as dangerous, unscrupulous, and hard-boiled realists. In reality they are both at the same time. And as this book is written, the merging of the two aspects has taken on breath-taking dimensions. Yet there is no difference of principle between Bela Kun, who in 1920 attempted to bribe leading party members to betray their political convictions and personal allegiances, and the things which we are witnessing to-day. Only the methods have been refined, and have, in consequence, become more successful.

It is noteworthy, however, that all this does not apply fully to the English Communist Party, which in this respect is an outstanding exception among all parties of the Comintern. The changes of tactics which were imposed from above upon the British Communist Party, as upon other parties, were here effected without victimization, with only one or two exceptions. By an astute combination of extreme compliance with stubborn camaraderie the leading communist group in Britain managed to hold together. This would have been entirely impossible if only a minority of the leading personnel had approached the repeated heavy failures of communism in Britain with an ordinary communist mentality. The fact is that there was not a single leading or secondary figure within the party which could be used for the purpose of starting one of the usual fights. In practice, the English communists, from an early stage onwards, regarded themselves mostly as a group which gingered up the trade unions; material advantages for the workers they did not disregard; revolution remained a somewhat remote ideal; it did not induce them to despise the humdrum practicalities of the life of the workers, or to regard them only as means to be used for the revolution. The typical English empiricism was visibly rampant even among the English followers of Lenin, and the gap between Utopia and reality was therefore considerably smaller than it was for Continental, Russian, or Eastern communists.

To sum up the whole situation of the Comintern in 1919 from a somewhat different angle, it may be said that it consisted of three elements of very different character: first there were small sects directly founded from Russia, mostly by war prisoners, and financially entirely dependent upon Moscow; the Hungarian party, before and after the dictatorship, and the Austrian party were typical. Secondly there were small sects which had arisen in their respective countries before or during the war, without interference from Moscow, but now loyal; such were the German Spartacists, the Dutch group of Gorter and Pannekoek, the small sects which were about to adhere in Britain; some of them needed money, but none brought the Comintern increased influence in the West. Finally, there were a few big mass parties, notably the Bulgarians, the Norwegians, and the Italians, which had adhered formally, but did not accept money and did not obey Moscow in the least. The left wing of the Swedish socialists, which adhered at an early date, lies between the last two groups. It had emerged from a split out of the old Social-democratic Party during the war, but in spite of being a relatively small group was far from being homogeneous in the Bolsheviks' sense, and very far from listening to orders from Moscow. Friendly advice from Russia was defied, at that period, by even the most obsequious followers. Did not Kun openly refuse to follow Lenin's suggestion to set up an independent communist party during the Hungarian dictatorship? And so uncertain were ideas about discipline, even in Moscow, that the *Communist International* simply published, in No. 2, 1919, both Lenin's wireless message about the matter and Kun's refusal.

CHAPTER X

MOSCOW SPLITS
THE WESTERN LABOUR MOVEMENT

In the last chapter we took our examples from very small communist sects, to whose history we will not return. The importance of the history of these sects lies in the fact that they show the living principles of communism as if in a laboratory, undisturbed by any outside influences. The same trends reappear in the history of the larger parties, but diluted through the broader life of the post-war mass movements, whose influence even the rigid doctrinairism of a communist party cannot fully avoid. But in 1919 there were not yet any real communist mass parties. Their formation was due to the radical change of the structure of the international labour movement in 1920.

In January 1920 Russia concluded peace with Esthonia and thus got direct access to the West. At the same time the labour movement in the Allied countries, which had been strongly under the influence of victory in 1919, became more restive, and the Comintern won real access to France, to Czechoslovakia, and, to a certain extent, to Britain. Finally, the movement to the left within the German U.S.P. reached its climax at that time. These movements to the left brought the Comintern into contact with forces very different from those it had hitherto met. During 1919 the following of the Comintern had been very small indeed in most countries, and in those countries where mass parties had joined, the influence of the Comintern was more formal than factual. None of the mass parties which had joined had split, as Lenin must have wished from the beginning. But now, in Germany, France, and Czechoslovakia, left wings evolved within the old socialist movements and did not simply want formally to adhere to the Comintern but agreed with the idea of a split in order to get rid of the influence of the anti-revolutionaries. Be it noted at once that this movement towards a split and towards the Comintern took strength after the decisive battles were over. All over the Continent 1919 had been the really revolutionary year. If, during 1920, and not earlier, masses turned towards the Comintern, it was because they felt they had been beaten and were looking for a new and purer movement, which would not betray them.

All that provided a new basis for the international action of the Comintern. But the Russians were forced to act, perhaps even before they might otherwise have done, by the actions of their adversaries, the socialists. The old socialist parties had met, in March 1919, at a conference in Berne, with the aim of reconstituting the old, 'Second' International; this had been one of the reasons for the haste with which the first congress of the Comintern was convened. In August 1919 the socialists held a second international conference, at Lucerne. But if Berne was no success, Lucerne was a failure. Dissensions between the patriots and the pacifists rather grew instead of diminishing after the war. The issue of the war itself was over, but instead came the growing radicalization of both the German Independents and the French socialists. The latter, with the support of a considerable number of other parties, refused to adhere to a rejuvenated international, unless it condemned formally the war policy of the patriots. About this claim the international conference split and the left wing of the socialist international, the pacifists, tried a policy of their own. At the head of this left wing stood the Socialist Party oi Switzerland.

The Swiss Socialist Party had never succeeded in winning over the majority of the workers in that thoroughly bourgeois country. Very naturally the socialist minority of the workers tended to the left, and, having only a very limited influence upon national affairs, could be trusted to go in for any experiment in reorganizing the International. Robert Grimm, the strongest man of the party, had crossed swords with Lenin at Zimmerwald and Kienthal and did not think much of the Bolsheviks; he had had a big conflict with them during a stay in Russia, in spring 1917. His opposition to affiliation was strengthened by the behaviour of the German and Austrian communists, their rejection of Parliament and of the trade unions. And finally the Swiss labour movement was beaten twice in its own country, first in the general strike of November 1918, which we have already mentioned, and a second time during an attempt to carry through a general strike in August 1919, on the basis of a purely local conflict in Bâle. The Swiss workers were tired of revolutionary tactics.

Now the constitutional machinery of the Swiss Socialist Party was as complex as the machinery of the Eidgenossenschaft itself. The directory of the party had voted affiliation to the Communist International by a narrow majority, but when the question came to the referendum of the membership it was already September and the motion was defeated owing to the impression of the defeat the movement had recently suffered. Grimm immediately took the opportunity to launch an alternative scheme. He suggested the 'reconstruction' of the International on a broader basis, a platform which would admit all parties which had rejected 'social-patriotism' during the war or repented after it.

The scheme was launched at a favourable moment. As a result of the break which had ensued after the Lucerne conference, a considerable number of socialist organizations all over the world were wavering, as far as international relations were concerned. None of these organizations was eager to join Moscow. If even Rosa Luxemburg had disliked the idea, it can be imagined what were the feelings of others, less advanced in their views than she. Thus a big phalanx was created both against reunion with the impenitent 'social-patriots' and against a dictatorship of Moscow over the labour movements of the West. The idea was to form an international of which the Russians should be members but not masters, and whose headquarters should be somewhere in the West. The French Socialist Party, during the last months of the war, had voted *en bloc* against the credits, and was therefore the natural centre for such a movement. The Swiss and the French socialists, and the German Independents acted in concert, and the two latter about the same time, claimed admission to the Comintern, as they stood. The 'reconstructionist' movement was materially supported by the Austrian socialists, proportionally the strongest labour party of the world, by the socialist parties of Finland, Esthonia, Latvia, and by the German socialists in Czechoslovakia. A big section, probably the majority, of the British Independent Labour Party could be trusted to join in case of success. The American socialists were clearly for 'reconstruction'.

On the other side, the side of the social-patriots, the partisans of the Second International, stood the British Labour Party, the German majority socialists, the socialist parties of Belgium, Holland, Denmark, and Sweden, the Czech Socialist Party in Czechoslovakia, and the Hungarian Labour Party. The situation in Poland was not clear, and Spain was still wavering. The chances of the partisans of the old Second International and the 'reconstructionists' seemed to be about equal. But it must be taken into account that, while the political Labour Party in Britain stood for the right wing, the trade unions at that time were increasingly tending to the left, so that no decided opposition would probably come from Britain. As for Germany, the majority socialists were the backbone of the international right wing but they were losing ground every day to the Independents. Grimm's idea had a fair chance of success.

Almost immediately the movement produced defections within the Communist International. The Italians, very busy at the time with the surge of the mass movement at home, held back, but it was ·well known that their adherence to the Comintern was intended to favour just such a reconstruction as was now to be tried. The Scandinavians were more outspoken. They suggested that an international conference between the Russians and the reconstructionists should be held somewhere in Scandinavia, not in Russia; the Russians refused flatly and a violent quarrel between party headquarters in Moscow, Stockholm, and Oslo followed. The one noticeable result of the failure of the Scandinavians was a declaration of Grimlund, one of the leaders of the Swedish communists, in the social-democratic paper in Reval, urging the reconstructionists to join the Comintern *en bloc* in order to break the preponderant influence of Moscow. Thus Moscow, apathetic in the international labour movement up to then, was forced to act by the action of the other groups of the socialist left.

Without a moment's hesitation Moscow decided to counter the efforts of the reconstructionists by splitting the labour movement all over the world. The idea, certainly, was not a new one. The reconstructionists, in essence, were a block of the revolutionary and the pacifist elements, the latter strongly prevailing, against the patriots. They made an attempt to carry on the old Zimmerwald policy with the one difference that the pacifists, in summer 1915, had been a small minority, whereas now, after the war, they were on the point of becoming the majority of the international labour movement. But Lenin already in November 1914 had proclaimed the necessity of forming a new international to the exclusion of both patriots and pacifists. At the time that had been a failure. In Zimmerwald and Kienthal the Bolsheviks had, in fact, collaborated with the pacifists, for the simple reason that otherwise they would have remained completely alone. In March 1919 the foundation of the Comintern had been an attempt to narrow the fold of those with whom the Bolsheviks were prepared to collaborate. But again this intention had failed: the two strongest adherents of the Comintern outside Russia, the Italians and the Norwegians, both united pacifists and revolutionaries in the fold of one party. All that had been tolerable and tolerated as long as things remained in suspense. But this time the international realinement was to be clearly decided for many years to come. And the Russians did not hesitate as to the lines on which they wanted this realinement to take place.

The trend of their ideas was simple enough. The leaders of the German Independents, the French and Austrian socialists, had been not for, but against, revolution during the decisive months of 1918 and 1919. Hence an international in which they would play the lead would be no good. Hence the necessity of splitting the labour movements of their respective countries. This implied that the broken particles which would join the Comintern would be at the mercy of the Russians. This need not even have been the primary aim intended. But it was almost coincident with the aim of forming what Lenin thought would be a really revolutionary international. It had dawned upon him, from August 1914 onwards, that only a strict selection and rigid education in revolutionism, such as made the Bolshevists what they were, guaranteed success, not only in Russia but everywhere. No similar organization existing outside Russia it was only natural that the Bolsheviks should take the lead and perform the task of education. The success of their revolution seemed to prove that they, and they alone, were right; and the material power and prestige they had thus won gave them overwhelming superiority over any opponents.

Was their action determined by the interests of Russia as a state? This idea is sometimes expressed in the Western labour movement. Closer investigation rather tells against it. At the end of 1919 and the beginning of 1920 Russia was still in bad straits and the Bolsheviks needed support from the West more than ever. Such support had been forthcoming, notably from England. The actions of the British T.U.C. and the 'Hands off Russia' committees had done a great deal to forestall and thwart intervention in the Russian civil war. It was obvious that there were reasons why the British labour movement gave more help to Russia than any other. The wave of sympathy was very strong all over the world of labour, but on the Continent, and especially in Germany and Austria, it had been balanced by the attempts to force the Continental labour movements into the channel of Russian methods. The fight against the communists at home had forestalled the fight for the Soviet Union. In England the Communist Party had not yet been formed. Precisely for that reason the sympathy of large sections of the British workers for the Soviet Union, strengthened by the 'labour unrest' of the epoch, could transform itself into practical action. How important this friendly attitude of the British movement seemed to Moscow—as, indeed, it was—is evident in the attempt to get control of the *Daily Herald*, which, at the time, made such a big stir.

If the Russians, instead of seeking friendly relations with the labour movements of other countries, now set out to split them, they must make the social-democrats their irreconcilable enemies and thus deprive themselves of the one support abroad upon which they could have counted, had they renounced the idea of an international split. It is true that a German revolution would have been a still bigger help. The Russians were far from realizing the factual situation in Europe and were full of revolutionary dreams; but this millenarian belief in revolution is itself sufficient proof that, at that time, they did not yet conceive the idea of a possible contrast between the ideals of the Russian state and the ideals of revolution. Russia would soon bring the world the revolutionary gospel and the revolutionary millennium; only, in order to achieve it, all people must submit to the Russian lead. It is the Islamic idea of a holy war, expressed in terms of historical materialism. The idea of Russian domination over the labour movement was so intimately knit together with the belief in the redeeming powers of the Bolshevik creed and the Bolshevik creed only, that every doubt and every rebellion seemed to Lenin and his followers the essence of blasphemy, to be rewarded with immediate excommunication. There was no rift yet between belief and political interests; therefore the Russians, like most genuine crusaders, were able to unite the most sincere enthusiasm with the most unconcerned disregard for the means they were employing in the pursuit of the holy end. But their enthusiasm and their revolutionary delusions would have availed them nothing, had not the swing to the left come to their help within the German and French movements.

The German Independents got a harsh reply to their call to the Bolsheviks and other 'social-revolutionary organizations' to join in a new international: 'The workers in the U.S.P. must understand that a working-class party cannot facilitate the development of the proletarian revolution without breaking with such right-wing leaders' as had led the party during the war and the revolution. These leaders of the U.S.P. (continued the reply of the Comintern) hold the same fatal views as the leaders of the majority of the French Socialist Party, the American Socialist Party, and the British I.L.P. A long series of mistakes of the leaders of the Independents is enumerated: their idea that the support of the majority of the people is necessary for the establishment of the proletarian dictatorship; the difference these leaders make between the use of force, which they do not reject, and revolutionary terrorism, which they do reject, in contrast to the Bolsheviks; their lack of readiness to face civil war; their lack of understanding of the necessity of wrecking the machinery of the bourgeois state; their hesitancy in speaking openly about the inevitable difficulties and sacrifices of the revolution; their petty-bourgeois insis-

tence upon the safeguarding of democratic liberties; their lack
of understanding of the distribution of the large estates among
the peasants; their useless attempts to win the lower middle
classes before the revolution, while, in the Bolshevik view,
these classes would only join the revolution after it had won;
the lack of disruptive activities in the army; their vague talk
about 'nationalization', where a clear-cut fight for expropriation without compensation would be necessary; their rejection
of an alliance with the Spartacists; their reluctance to break
once for all with the Second International; their silence about
the traitorous part of the workers' aristocracy; their indifference to the colonial revolutionary movements; their constant
collaboration with such traitors as Friedrich Adler and Karl
Kautsky and the part they allowed the leader of the right wing,
Rudolf Hilferding, to play within the U.S.P. 'The E.C.C.I.
[Executive Committee of the Communist International] holds
the view, that, in the interest of the success of the international
proletarian class-struggle it is not permissible to create anywhere, under whatever pretext, another international association of the workers, which would not be revolutionary.' All
parties which have broken with the Second International are
invited to Moscow.

Negotiations ensued and the leaders of the German, French,
British, and American left-wing socialists soon realized that
the Russians meant what they said. It was obvious that an
international split on a large scale had become inevitable.
Lenin and his followers cleared the ground for this impending
split. Experiences both in Germany and in Switzerland, and
occasionally in other countries, went to show that the strongest
barrier between the small communist groups and the big left-
wing socialist movement was the attitude of the communist
left wing to parliament and to the trade unions. Thus it was
necessary to get rid of the nuisance of the 'ultra-left' within the
communist parties, who opposed work in parliament and within the unions. As for Germany, the ruthless action of Paul Levi
at the Heidelberg congress in October 1919 had solved the
problem. Now Levi's action was extended to the International.

Difficulties were particularly great in England and America
but for quite different reasons. In America the American
Federation of Labour, the association of the craft unions, had

never made a serious attempt to organize the workers in the big industries. It did not desire to do so. All 'progressive' elements were therefore opposed to Samuel Gompers, the leader of the A.F. of L., and his organization. They maintained that the big industries could only be organized outside the fold of the A.F. of L., and that therefore work in the official unions was useless. Though this was an exaggeration, it contained more truth than similar contentions in Europe; even to-day under President Franklin D. Roosevelt, the attempt to organize the big industries has produced a split within the American trade-union movement. Being hostile to the A.F. of L., the incipient communist movement in America had fallen under the influence of the small but active I.W.W. (Industrial Workers of the World), which was strongly tainted with anarcho-syndicalism.

In England the situation was different. Here the unions did not organize only a small minority. They were more representative of the labour movement as a whole than those of any other country. At the same time, they were the very incarnation of that spirit of gradual and constitutional progress which was directly opposed to the ideas of communism. Work in these unions seemed hopeless to the English communists. There did not yet exist a communist party, either in Britain or in the United States, only small groups who wanted to merge and form a communist party. The strongest of them, in Britain, evolved from the Scottish Shop-steward movement of the war. The Scottish Shop-stewards had opposed the official unions, not without success, and anti-trade-unionist ideas were in consequence popular among them. Anti-parliamentarianism was a natural extension of their anti-trade-unionism. But it was opposed by at least some of the small groups who were going to form a communist party in Britain. The Comintern supported the latter in their fight against the anarchist tendencies.

The action of the Comintern against the 'ultra-left' was really the first direct interference of the Comintern with the life of the communist parties abroad. It led to what is perhaps the most interesting theoretical debate which ever took place inside the Comintern. At that time arguments were still fresh and lively, and no military discipline hampered their flow. In defence of work in parliament and within the unions Lenin himself took up his pen, overwhelmed with work as he was, and wrote his *Left-wing Communism, an Infantile Disease*, published in May 1920. The protagonist on the other side was Hermann Gorter, the Dutch poet and Marxist, who replied with an *Open Letter to Comrade Lenin*. Gorter had been to Moscow and talked to Lenin; and, a clear-sighted man who saw the reality of human beings, he had come back horrified by Lenin's lack of genuine interest in the problems of the West. 'This man I expected to be and to feel himself the generalissimo of the world revolution; but I had to realize that Lenin thought constantly of Russia and saw all things only from the Russian point of view,' so Gorter told his closest political friend, Anton Pannekoek, who has retold the story to me. Lenin saw things exclusively from the Russian point of view, to be sure, but not so much from the point of view of the interests of the Russian state—he was sometimes ready seriously to impair those interests for the sake of the international revolution—as from the point of view of the absolute value of the Russian experience. 'This has been done in this or that way in Russia; therefore you will best do it in the same manner,' ran his argument in substance; and after his death the Comintern was to follow the same course, only more crudely.

Very naturally, the discussion between Lenin and Gorter turned on the value of the Russian experiment for the West, and that is what gives it a wide interest even to-day. *Left-wing Communism* is perhaps the most powerful thing Lenin has ever written, because it is almost free from those philosophical and economic generalizations which were not Lenin's strong point. It is a handbook of revolutionary tactics and as such can sometimes be compared, for force of argument, realism, directness and convincing power, with Machiavelli's *Il Principe*. Here a great master of politics speaks, sometimes condescendingly, sometimes angrily, to young pupils who will not listen to reason, and makes a laughing-stock of their 'supernatural nonsense'. Lenin starts from the assumption that 'some elements', as he modestly says, of the Russian revolutionary experience, are of international value. In fact, he assumes that all essential elements of Bolshevik principles, tactics, and organization must be transferred to the West. 'We in Russia . . .'—'Russia' is the third word of the pamphlet.

Lenin starts with the problem of leadership. Have you ever seen, can you imagine, a mass party without leadership? It is the problem of the mass movement which he raises, his eyes fixed upon the impending split in Germany and France. Do you think that parliament exists less and that the masses look less upon what happens there because you refuse to go to the polls? And how do you imagine you can lead a mass revolution without having first won over the trade unions? There, within the unions, are the masses of the workers, with their inevitable limitations and backwardness. You fancy you will rule nations and at the same time confess you are unable to win over a single union?

Thus the main argument of this remarkable book. At one stroke Lenin's tactical genius unveils the essentials of the attitude of the opposition: sectarianism. But he is perhaps not quite as clear-sighted in interpreting the reason which makes his opponents talk 'supernatural nonsense'. He believes it to be an 'infantile disease'. In fact, it is nothing of the sort. During the next fifteen years the communists in the West were unable to conquer one single union. And in consequence the views held by the 'ultra-left' opposition proved to be anything but an infantile disease. In slightly disguised form, they came back and haunted and sometimes dominated the Comintern throughout its existence. Lenin knew perfectly the conditions of a successful social revolution. But he did not fully understand the mentality of the Western labour movement. His opponents said: 'From the viewpoint of revolution the trade unions are hopeless.' Lenin answered: 'If that were true, there could never be a social revolution.' That it actually *is* true, and that *therefore* there can be no social revolution in the Marxist sense in the West, he would never admit.

It is essentially this, though in a slightly different form, which Gorter stresses in his answer. He starts from the conditions of the Russian revolution, a revolution of the whole people, led by the Bolsheviks, but carried out by soldiers and peasants. In the West, Gorter points out, the peasants are a bourgeois element and so is the intelligentsia, so are the lower middle classes. Against the *people's* revolution in Russia Gorter puts the future *proletarian* revolution in the West, which will be a revolution of the proletariat against all other classes. In this

struggle the proletariat will be alone, quite alone; no manœuvring therefore, and less necessity for leadership. But the full,
enlightened class-consciousness of the proletariat is of infinitely
greater importance in the West than in Russia. This proletariat, however, moves in a much more bourgeois atmosphere.
Therefore the educational tasks take pride of place. The
organization of the revolutionaries will be small, for a long
time, but pure. It will act as a model for the class, which will
slowly follow. Gorter's view of the difficulties of a social revolution in the West is infinitely nearer to the facts than Lenin's
belief that only a revolutionary party using appropriate
tactics is needed in order to reach the goal. But at the same
time Gorter's view implies a denial of the existence and even
of the possibility of a socialist revolution within this generation.
Again, Gorter, in his pessimism, was to be justified by the
event as against the optimistic Lenin.

Practically, the matter was settled, partly by a split and
partly by authority. The German partisans of Gorter's views
had already seceded at the Heidelberg congress. Gorter,
Pannekoek, and a small group in Holland left soon afterwards.
The English and Americans were persuaded to change their
views at the second congress of the Comintern, mostly by the
personal authority of Lenin.

This second world congress of the Comintern started in
Moscow in July 1920. It was no longer a small gathering. The
war with Poland was going on, but other frontiers were open.
There were delegations from the three communist mass parties
outside Russia: Italy, Norway, Bulgaria. There were delegations from the other Balkan countries. There were the small
communist parties of Germany, Austria, and Hungary; there
was a delegation of the socialist left in Czechoslovakia. Representatives of the German Independents and of the French
socialists were present for the purpose of negotiations. Delegates represented the adherents of the Comintern in France,
and the various British and American groups. And finally the
most important Asiatic countries were represented, with the
Indian Manabendra Nath Roy as the outstanding personality
among the Orientals. Lenin laid enormous store upon these
delegates from the Far East. He saw the world revolution as an
international crisis, with Russia at the centre: on the one hand

the proletarian movements of the West and America, on the other hand the national risings of the East.

Most of the debates turned on the problem of the 'ultra-left', and it was made obligatory for all communist parties to participate in parliament and work within the trade unions. But there was, most urgent though less mentioned in public, the problem of the Communist Party of Poland, which was strongly represented. It had emerged out of the union of two groups, as told in a previous chapter. Now the Soviet armies were rapidly advancing towards Warsaw and the Polish communists were to show what they could achieve. Hopes ran high. Everybody expected a quick collapse of Poland and the German communists prepared to launch big revolutionary activity as soon as the Red cavalry appeared on Germany's eastern frontier. These expectations are naïvely revealed in Sinovjev's opening speech, which, at the same time, is a document suggestive of the incapacity of these out-and-out revolutionaries to learn. Sinovjev referred himself to the failure of his prophecy of last year, that at the time of the second congress all Europe would be sovietized, and then continued:

'A German bourgeois professor has concentrated on this sentence and a few days ago I read an article where he ironically states: Well, then, the second congress will soon be opened. More than a year has passed. It does not seem that the Soviets have finally won in Europe. But we can quietly reply to this learned bourgeois: Perhaps it is so, perhaps we have been carried away; probably, in reality, it will need not one year but two or three years before all Europe is one Soviet republic. If you are so modest yourself that one or two years' delay seems to you extraordinary bliss, we can only congratulate you for your moderation.'

And further in the same vein. In the light of the Polish campaign this was meant in full earnest.

But in the general enthusiasm the Polish delegates remained sceptical. They were asked whether the Polish proletariat would rise at the moment of the approach of the Red army to Warsaw. They flatly denied it. Tukhachevski, military commander of the campaign, was naturally for the offensive, Trotsky, chief of the Red army, was hesitant, but Lenin drove the offensive eagerly forward. He was convinced of the rising of the Polish proletariat, in spite of all warnings that nationalism and hatred of Russia would unite all classes at the moment of a national emergency. In fact, what the Polish delegates had predicted, happened. The national proved to be stronger than the social motive in Polish hearts. And the attempt to carry revolution into the West with Russian bayonets failed.

The chief business of the world congress was the negotiation with the representatives of the German Independents and of the French socialists who attended the congress; in other words, the preparation of the international split. The real issue had been cleared before. The negotiations between those parties and the Comintern at the congress were manœuvres intended to impress the masses at home. The Russians had a clear line of action. They were convinced that all European leaders were useless, that it was desirable not to take a single outstanding personality of the Western labour movement into the fold of the Comintern. The absolute rule of the Russian Bolsheviks would be only the better established for it, and their absolute rule was, they sincerely believed, the one safeguard of real revolutionism. Therefore they tried to make the conditions of admission as acceptable as possible to the masses and as unacceptable as possible to the leaders. The Western left-wing socialist leaders, on the other hand, stood for 'reconstructionism', for an international as broad as possible. They were ready to swallow a lot in order to bring it about, and, if break there should be, they wanted to put the Russians in the wrong by obvious readiness for compromise.

The Russians had put the points they had enumerated in their answer to the Independents into a set of eighteen conditions, which were to be accepted or rejected. The delegations of the U.S.P. and of the French socialists were ready to accept these ultimative conditions. Then the Russians introduced new conditions, which were absolutely unacceptable to the leaders: periodical purges—so old is the idea of the 'purge'—in every communist party, which meant a repeated split every few years; and a nominal exclusion of all the outstanding leaders of the reconstructionists—Hilferding and Kautsky in Germany, Longuet in France, Ramsay Macdonald in England; for the first time they included leading members of their own

Italian section—Turati and Modigliani were to be excluded from the Italian Socialist Party. It was a clever move intended to separate the fate of the leaders from the decision of the masses which had hitherto followed them.

But then, by one of those sudden moves which so often in the history of the Comintern have thwarted well-thought-out plans, they themselves brought down half the edifice they had built with so much effort. And the mistake was made precisely where it ought least to have happened after all that had passed before: the Comintern attempted to split the international trade-union movement. What led them to attempt it will probably never become quite clear. In the answer to the Independents the trade-union question had not been mentioned, but in the meantime the attempts which were afoot in Europe to reorganize the Trade-union International had led to success, and the reconstructed International of the trade-unionists established itself at Amsterdam, uniting in one fold the adherents of the old Second International and of 'reconstruction'; from the moment of its foundation it wielded, under Edo Fimmen's leadership, considerable authority. The Russians saw that here was their strongest enemy in the ranks of the International labour movement, and they eagerly threw themselves upon it.

An international of the 'Red' trade unions was formed in Moscow at the time of the second congress of the Comintern, and Losovski was put at its head. He was a Russian, had been an active Menshevik till 1919, and had then become Bolshevik; he had a certain amount of knowledge of the French labour movement from the times when he had been an exile. Otherwise nobody took him very seriously. This man was set upon the strongest and most solid alliance of the international working classes. The foundation of the 'Profintern' (the Russian word for the Red Trade-Union International) clashed directly with Lenin's orders to remain within the existing unions. It was explained that national unity could well be combined with an international split. But nobody believed it, and in fact the international split was followed by national splits in several countries. Now this idea of the foundation of a 'Red' international against 'Amsterdam' provided the leaders of reconstruction with a decisive argument. Of all national trade unions only the Bulgarians definitely affiliated with the Profintern.

The eighteen conditions had become twenty-one, the famous 'twenty-one points'. And all over the industrial world workers were going to decide, in the autumn of 1920, whether they would accept them or reject them. In their final form they can be summed up as follows: Point 1, after an introduction about the necessity for all Comintern parties to be truly communist parties, goes on to say that the whole press of every party must be directly under control of the central committee. The task of the press and of communist agitation in general is clearly expressed: 'Wherever the communists get access, they must expose systematically and mercilessly not only the bourgeoisie, but their agents, the reformists of all shades, as well.' Point 2 formulates the general aim of the impending split. The communists must strive systematically to remove both reformists and 'centrists' (the adherents of 'reconstruction') from all more or less responsible positions within the labour movement and replace them with reliable communists, 'without taking offence at the necessity to replace sometimes, especially in the beginning, "experienced" opportunists by simple workers from the rank and file'. Point 3 obliges every communist party to organize an underground machinery besides the public activities of the party. Point 4 makes it a duty for every communist party to disorganize, as much as possible, the army of its respective country. Point 5 insists upon the necessity of work among the peasants, a point amply elaborated in a special set of 'theses' voted by the second world congress. Point 6 emphasizes for a second time the necessity of fighting not only against the patriots within the labour movement, but against the pacifists as well. Point 7, elaborating the preceding point, contains one of those additions which the representatives of the reconstructionists found unacceptable. It insists 'unconditionally and as an ultimatum upon the break within the shortest delay' with both the reformists and the policy of the middle group. 'The Communist International cannot put up with notorious opportunists, such as are represented by Turati, Modigliani, Kautsky, Hilferding, Hillquith (the leader of the American socialists), Longuet, Macdonald, and others, claiming the right to be members of the Communist International.' Point 8 proclaims the duty of all communists to help the revolutionary movements in the colonies of their respective countries. Point 9 formulates the necessity for the communists to work within the trade unions with the aim of overthrowing their reformist leaders. For this purpose the communists must organize nuclei within the unions and other non-party working-class organizations which must daily 'unmask the betrayal of the social patriots and the waverings of the middle-group people'. According to point 10, all communists must 'emphatically urge the break with the yellow Amsterdam International' and advocate support of the Red trade-union international. (The word 'yellow', which is used about the Amsterdam International, would seem to mean, in the ordinary language of the labour movement, that this International is either paid by the employers or consists of unions which are paid by them; it is not surprising that the trade-union leaders among the German Independents and other 'reconstructionists' took this insulting denial of good faith in a bad way.) Point 11 establishes the strict subordination of the parliamentary groups of the various communist parties to their respective central committees. Point 12 is of cardinal importance for the structure of the nascent communist parties: 'In the present phase of acute civil war a communist party will only be able to do its duty provided it is organized with the highest possible degree of centralization and keeps iron discipline; the central committee, backed by the confidence of the members, must be invested with complete power, authority, and the most far-reaching qualifications.' Point 13 concerns the periodical purges of the whole party membership. Point 14 obliges all communist parties to support 'every Soviet republic'. According to point 15 all parties which join the Comintern must subject their programmes to a revision; the new programme will be subject to the approval of the E.C.C.I., of the Comintern. Point 16 establishes the rule that the decisions not only of the world congresses but even of the executive committee of the Comintern overrule decisions of the national parties. Point 17 specifies that every party adhering to the Comintern must call itself officially a 'communist party'. The press of these parties, according to point 18, must publish all important documents of the Moscow executive committee. The last three points concern the procedure of the split within those parties which want to adhere. Such parties must accept or reject the twenty-one points at an extraordinary congress to be held within four months from the second world congress. At least two-thirds of the members of the central committees of those parties which join must have voted for affiliation before the second world congress; the E.C.C.I. has power to grant exceptions to this rule. Finally, those who reject on principle the twenty-one conditions, and especially those delegates of the impending extraordinary congresses who vote against them, must be excluded from their respective parties before the latter will be admitted to the Comintern. These, then, were the twenty-one points which were to be made the basis of the split of the international labour movement. Within the German U.S.P., the British Independent Labour Party, the French, Swiss, Spanish, American, and a number of other smaller socialist parties, these points were discussed by all members in the following months. No split of the socialist parties was involved in Bulgaria, the Baltic states, in Sweden and Norway, in Poland, in Austria, or in Italy, where communist parties already existed. But this did not mean that the twenty-one points had no importance for those countries. On the contrary, it was here that they were most rigidly applied. Parties such as the Norwegian and the Italian socialists, which had hitherto been members of the Comintern by a simple act of adherence, were to be transformed into true communist parties by the acceptance and rigid execution of the twenty-one points.

Sinovjev went personally to Germany, where the decisive congress of the Independents met in October 1920 in Halle. Levi's clever tactics and Sinovjev's tremendous oratory had the better of Hilferding's prophecy that the split would not lead to revolution, but only to a weakening of the German labour movement. The congress, after days of excited and turbulent debates in which outstanding figures of the labour movement of almost every important country participated, gave the communists a comfortable majority of eighty votes. The U.S.P. had swollen to 800,000 members, and the increase of communist strength seemed to be enormous. The split, naturally, would extend to all local branches, and if the result there corresponded to that of the Halle congress the success of the communists would be great indeed.

The result did not correspond, however, and that mainly on account of the trade-union problem. For the backbone of the party of the Independents was the strongest and most militant of all the German unions, the engineers'. And as soon as Losovski, who was co-delegate with Sinovjev, had uttered so much as a word about fighting the Amsterdam International, a storm was raised at the Halle congress which spread to the local branches. The bulk of the active trade-unionists simply refused to follow the left wing into the camp of the Comintern. Of the 800,000 members of the U.S.P. not more than about 300,000 finally joined the Comintern, bringing the United Communist Party of Germany (which emerged out of the union of the Spartacists and the left Independents) up to 350,000. About a third of the old party made an attempt to continue, but, in 1922, consented to merge with the majority socialists. Hundreds of thousands of the rank and file dropped out of politics completely. As against the million or so which the remnant of the Independents and the majority socialists had enrolled between them, the communists were still a minority, though no longer a negligible one. But the chief result of Halle and its aftermath was a considerable strengthening of the right wing within the labour movement.

In France the split was executed on different lines. The French Socialist Party had never split, but with less than 200,000 members it was far from controlling the masses of the French workers, the more so as the percentage of intellectuals and lower-middle-class people within the party was very high and the trade unions were strictly severed from the political movement. Within the party a small group, under the leadership of Loriot and the Russian Boris Souvarine, stood for unconditional affiliation to the Comintern. A minority, under Renaudel, Pressemane, and Blum stood absolutely against affiliation. But the party was dominated by a middle group, led by Frossard, Cachin, and Longuet. Political opinions within the party had not been cleared, as in Germany, by two years of revolutionary struggles. There was no chance for the Comintern to win anything but a very small section of French socialism, if it relied on only the decidedly communist elements.

Thus the Comintern tried to split the middle group and was successful. It was easier in France, because the problem of Amsterdam *versus* Profintern was less important in the French socialist movement, which counted few trade-unionists in its ranks. All the Comintern had to do was to close its eyes to the 'opportunism' of certain leaders. By doing that it obtained the adhesion of both Cachin and Frossard; the former had been the chief intermediary between Mussolini and the French Government during the war, the latter was later not only to revert to the Socialist Party, but to lead a split away from it to the right, joining the semi-Fascist Doumergue Cabinet in 1934. None of them was indeed a very reliable revolutionary, but at the moment they were very useful. The congress of the French Socialist Party met at Tours, in December 1920, and there the Comintern won a big majority, carrying with it about 150,000 party members. To be a communist was cheap, in France, where no revolutionary fight was afoot; and as to the meaning of the word 'discipline' in Comintern vocabulary, the French had as yet no notion; later on they were to find it little to their taste, even less so than others did.

In Germany the very idea of splitting the trade unions was hopeless. But in France, where the C.G.T. (*Confédération générale de Travail*) was hardly stronger than the Socialist Party and had, moreover, a strong anarcho-syndicalist element in its ranks, a split ensued. Leon Jouhaux, the leader of the C.G.T., had gradually carried it away from anarcho-syndicalism, had struggled to bring it into line with the trade-unionist movements of other countries, and had been a patriot during the war. He had met strong opposition, but most of the leaders of that opposition, with Merrheim at their head, did not go over to the Communists. After the war a wave of radicalism swept through the French unions, just as it did through the Socialist Party. Jouhaux was afraid of losing his majority and being overthrown. He chose to split rather than to await the stroke. In certain branches, and particularly among the railwaymen, revolutionary committees had been formed. Jouhaux issued an order prohibiting the adherence of any unions, and the dissidents were excluded in batches. It might have been easy for them to avoid the stroke, strong as they were, had they complied with the rules laid down by Jouhaux, and they might have beaten him in the end. But this did not occur to them; every temporary retreat was 'opportunism'. Thus Jouhaux had an easy task. The excluded groups formed a new centre, the *Confédération générale de Travail unitaire* (C.G.T.U.), which grouped communists, anarchists, and syndicalists together. Losovski in Moscow was satisfied. Profintern had now at least one mass organization in the West. But in France there was soon disappointment. The split drove many thousands away from the unions. The C.G.T.U. had soon to acknowledge that, being weaker than the united C.G.T. of earlier days, it could not fight better than the reformists; and in the end the fighting power of the unions was rather diminished than increased.

The whole split in France had taken place under the cloud of a series of defeats, the last and most important being that of a strike of the railwaymen early in 1920. Labour unrest in the Allied countries had developed later than among the Central Powers, but naturally the aftermath of the war made itself felt here as there. The forces of the existing order were stronger, however, and the convulsions much less critical. On the other hand, developments in France were similar to those in Germany in that the split ensued after the decisive defeat of the post-war movement. The Comintern won direct influence only after the movement had overflowed its mark and ebb had followed high tide. The movements which, united, had met defeat split in mutual reproaches about the causes of defeat.

This was perhaps even more sharply outlined in Czechoslovakia. There the Comintern found a double inheritance. The German socialists in Czechoslovakia had found themselves in the united national front of the German minority against the Czech majority at the moment when they were incorporated into the new republic. But when it became obvious that the new state was a *fait accompli* German socialism in Czechoslovakia split naturally into one group which tried to collaborate in the new state, and another one which wanted to revert to the old, intransigent class-struggle. No practical issue of revolution existed; only a very strong tradition of intransigent Marxism of the German type. Practically all the elements which, in Germany, had formed the U.S.P. were ready to join the Comintern in Czechoslovakia.

But among the socialists of Czech nationality the position was different and supremely paradoxical. There, the majority had co-operated with the Czech National Committee during the war and was now, after the successful national revolution, a mainstay of the new state. But a minority, under the leadership of Šmeral, had sided with the Hapsburgs, being the one force among the Czechs which, till the end, had not participated in the fight for national liberty. Now, after the war, Šmeral found himself isolated and in dire need of support. To think of him as a revolutionary was preposterous. Having stood at the extreme right wing of the movement, he was and continued to be an active enemy of revolutionism. But revolution was not a practical issue in Czechoslovakia. Therefore Šmeral did not find it difficult to don the robe of the revolutionary and turn towards the Comintern.

He was helped, in doing so, by the policy of the official Czech socialists. During the war they had merged with the other national forces so as to be almost indistinguishable from them. The republic had been greeted by the Czech workers with tremendous enthusiasm; they had not felt that anything had remained undone. After a time this enthusiasm naturally subsided, everyday antagonisms between the labour movement and the other parties were again preponderant, and every disillusionment worked against the out-and-out patriots and for Šmeral. Had Šmeral attacked the new state, not ten per cent of the Czech proletariat, which, all in all, loved the republic, would have followed him. But he did nothing of the kind and, clever and unprincipled tactician as he always was, won the majority of the Czech workers.

On this occasion, as in the case of the split in France, Sinovjev demonstrated that he regarded revolutionary purity as sometimes less essential than obedience. Frossard was no revolutionary; Cachin was suspect; Šmeral was a notorious antirevolutionary. But they were ready to obey Moscow, and were therefore useful. Yet the split and the formation of a communist party in Czechoslovakia, which proceeded under such favourable auspices, was not to be accomplished without a heavy shock. Unrest, as in France, had been slight in 1919, but grew in 1920. It found an outlet in the split of the socialist movement. When the left wing had won a majority in Prague it took over the *Narodni dom*, which was, at the same time, the party office and a vast popular establishment. But the right wing, before losing the majority, had put the property deeds of the premises in a form which placed the personal property right of representatives of the right wing beyond doubt. The party was ejected from its building, a row with the police ensued, blood was shed, and, within a few days, in mid-December 1920, Czechoslovakia was faced with a general strike to decide the ownership of the *Narodni dom*. It was a most unhappy issue. The workers rose against what seemed to them an act of unwarrantable violence. But naturally the socialists and the non-socialist labour organizations—very strong in Czechoslovakia—abstained. The left-wing socialists, just about to form their ranks, could not provide adequate leadership. The issue of the *Narodni dom* was narrow but there was nothing else to place in its stead, and the dispute was expressed in different slogans in every town. What applied to slogans applied to tactics; they varied from armed risings to exclusively economic strikes. It was easy for the government, which had proclaimed martial law, to beat down the movement town by town. A good deal of blood was shed, and the strike was called off. Bitterness between the two wings had grown tremendously, and the split was a fact; but the Communist Party of Czechoslovakia, as that of other countries, was formed out of the shattered ranks of a beaten army. More than a year was needed for the left wings of the German and Czech socialist parties to form themselves into communist parties and merge into one body for the whole republic. Subsequently, the socialist trade unions were split, under circumstances and with results very similar to those in France; and the Profintern had a second mass organization in the West.

In Switzerland the defeats of 1919 had been enough. But when it became clear that the efforts of the 'reconstructionists' were going to fail the central committee of the party once more voted affiliation to the Comintern; not for long, however. The twenty-one points frightened even the most decided partisans of Moscow, and the party remained independent and unshattered. A small group of a few thousand members, with an influence less than negligible, and only in the town and Canton of Bâle, formed a communist party.

To finish our survey of the European continent: in Austria and Holland the puny communist parties remained what they were. In Denmark and Belgium similarly unimportant parties were formed under great difficulties. In Spain, Yugoslavia, and Roumania the weak socialist parties were split, on the twenty-one points, and still smaller communist parties emerged beside the socialists. The Hungarian party existed only among the exiles.

Nevertheless the Comintern could be satisfied with the results of its 1920 campaign. It held the whole of the socialist movement in Italy, more than half in France, Czechoslovakia, Roumania, and Bulgaria, noteworthy minorities in Germany and Poland, and outposts in all the other countries. Internationally, it was a minority, but one which certainly had a chance, given adequate strategy. The first approach to tactics must recognize that the revolutionary era, for the time being, was over; the Comintern, however, was a revolutionary organization.

Before describing the consequences of this contradiction we must say a few words about the origins of communism in the Anglo-Saxon world. Only a few words, because at that time communism was in those countries in no respect a serious power. In Britain the twenty-one points were laid before the conference of the I.L.P. at Southport, and a small minority joined the communists. About the same time the many small communist groups merged into the Communist Party of Great Britain, after considerable difficulties. Finally, they adopted Lenin's programme of work in Parliament—mostly a wish and not a reality—and within the trade unions, which was to become much more important. The birth of the Communist Party in England was thus very different from that in most countries of the West; almost everywhere the party had emerged out of a split. In Britain it mainly emerged out of unification. On the Continent Comintern taught its adherents to be doctrinaire, because this was the way to sever their ties with the socialists. In England, compared with the small sects out of which the C.P. emerged, the latter was a mass party and its foundation a step away from sectarianism.

Among the injunctions Lenin had given the party when it started was that to join the Labour Party. Here again, as in every other respect, British communism differed from its Continental counterparts. They had to fight away from the reformists; here it was to approach them. There were obvious motives for this peculiar policy. The argument stressed by Lenin was that the Labour Party was not a party in the Continental sense, but a loose confederation whose constituent elements kept complete liberty to say what they thought. But this, important as it was, was certainly not the only motive force behind this decision. Lenin laid enormous store upon Britain, starting from Marx's saying that a revolution which halted on the other side of the Channel would be mere child's play. And while revolution in Britain seemed second only to revolution in Germany in international importance, the forces of revolution in Britain were very small. Lenin probably thought that it was preferable to delay somewhat the complete break between communism and the bulk of the British labour movement, and to let the former gain strength before it faced isolation. Nor was the friendly attitude of the British labour movement towards Russia without importance. But here, as in other non-Russian problems, Lenin suffered from illusion. The Labour Party simply refused to admit the Communist Party, and there matters remained. During the big crises from 1921 to 1926 the question of communist affiliation never touched more than a small fringe of left-wingers within the Labour Party.

Things were different in America, where the split proved to be disastrous for the socialist movement as a whole. In America the labour movement was weak and the Socialist Party was only a small minority within the labour movement. Before and during the war both membership and polls of the socialists had grown regularly. The majority of the party was left, a fact natural enough in a movement with only a slight hold upon the masses of the workers. Thus, when the question of the Communist International first arose the left wing within the party won big majorities. But 1919 was a bad year for American socialism; after the war, the trend was heavily against it, and it was cruelly persecuted and shattered. Then came the twenty-one conditions of the Comintern, which made things worse. A considerable part of the membership was organized in national sections, mostly of eastern European origin, which were strongly under communist influence. These sections seceded, siding with communism, but cutting practically all links with the American labour movement, while at the same time refusing to submit to the discipline of the new Communist Party. After the split the American party collapsed and only the debris remained socialist or reached the Comintern. Within the communist movement the fight between the Anglo-Saxons, who, under the leadership of John Reed, formed the 'Communist Workers Party', and the national minorities which formed a 'communist party' continued. It needed all the efforts of the Comintern to bring the two parties to accept unification. Hardly had it been achieved when the young party was driven underground by a combination of persecution from without and romanticism within. Fierce factional fights tore the underground party asunder, and almost destroyed it at its very birth.

CHAPTER XI

NEW BROOMS SWEEP CLEAN

At the beginning of 1921, for the first time, Moscow had real mass parties at its command, as it never had during the decisive revolutionary years. It was prepared to launch them into the fight, but at the very moment that it set out to do so, the power of the young mass movements was broken by a series of catastrophic events. It needed only two years to destroy all or almost all the results of the second world-congress.

The second world-congress had laid down the twenty-one points, and by splitting the Western labour parties Moscow had shown that it meant to force their application through. Also the twenty-one points were to be enforced upon those parties which had adhered to the Comintern in 1919. For at that time Moscow believed absolutely in the world revolution, and the first step in this direction had to be the creation of genuinely pure communist parties. Of the early adherents the Italian Socialist Party was by far the most important.

This party was in reality pacifist, not revolutionary. Italy had emerged from the war more in the position of a defeated than in that of a conquering nation. It was shaken by severe convulsions. But the whole machinery of the labour movement, and the mentality of the masses that supported that labour movement, made revolutionary action impossible. In the summer of 1919 shops were sacked all over the country; the Socialist Party remained inactive. Soon afterwards, the peasants, living under semi-feudal conditions, rose in many provinces and began to re-distribute the land. But the movement, if supported at all, was supported rather by the Catholic Party than by the socialists. In the meantime, however, the country was swept by enormous strikes. The strike weapon, being familiar to the labour movement, was made use of to the full, and employers were forced to pay ruinous wages. Occasionally troops mutinied, and during the summer of 1920 it was felt that a revolution was approaching.

The socialists emerged from the general elections of 1919 as the strongest party. They were thus confronted by an important decision. The right wing of the party, under Filippo Turati, urged that the party, in accordance with its strength, should form a coalition cabinet. But to the majority, led by Serrati and Lazzari, the idea of a coalition was anathema. They therefore insisted that the party remain in opposition. An impossible situation was thereby created which contributed a good deal to the rise of Fascism : those who had the strength refused to govern, while those who were thus obliged to take up the responsibility lacked the necessary power. At the same time, the group around Serrati refused to take concrete steps in the direction of revolution.

There did not exist within the Socialist Party any revolutionary group at all, with the exception of the leaders of the youth organization and the provincial organization of Turin. But among what was called the left wing, those groups were a small minority. The majority of the extremists, under the leadership of Bordiga, a man of culture and temperament, devoted and sincere but utterly unpolitical, belonged to the international ultra-left, which wanted to boycott the Parliament, to build up a small but pure communist party, and prepare for a revolution in the far distance. This passive extremism was simply the reflection of the fact that a genuine revolutionary movement, in spite of turmoil and excitement in the country, was totally lacking.

In such conditions the party entered upon the decisive battle, unaware, moreover, that it was the decisive battle. In August 1920 the Amalgamated Engineers announced a policy of passive resistance all over Italy in order to enforce a claim for increased wages. The trade unions, generally, sympathized with the right wing and by no means wanted a revolution ; but, conscious of their strength, they intended to squeeze the employers as best they could. The method of passive resistance was chosen because a strike involving hundreds of thousands would have proved too costly. Unexpectedly, the exasperated employers retaliated with a lock-out. The financial position of the engineers was at once desperate, and in order to give their action more weight and to counter the lock-out the workers entered the factories and remained there. To-day we should call it a stay-in strike, of which, in fact, it was the first example. Other groups joined, and the movement, to the surprise of its leaders, took on the colour of a general expropriation of the factories by the workers. The anarcho-syndicalists, not a negligible factor in Italy, pushed the socialists further along this road, and the workers, not content with having the factories in their hands, started to work them.

This was well enough for a week or two. But in the long run it would not do. The occupied factories were cut off from supplies of raw materials, from bank credits, and from their markets. One choice only remained: to go forward to socialist revolution or retreat. A joint conference of trade-union and party leaders was called. Serrati had not yet returned from the second congress in Moscow. The union leaders were almost unanimously against revolution; the party leaders were divided among themselves, but, as is the case in most crises, not along the lines of division one would have expected. Later communists voted against, and later anti-communists for, revolution. But the opposition of the unions decided the issue. The decision was transferred to them. They negotiated with the government, which, though sparingly, made promises. The factories were evacuated. Giolitti, the old and experienced Prime Minister, had never wavered in his conviction that the trouble would ultimately end in this way, and he had refused to take the factories by armed force.

If there was any country in the West with conditions similar to those prevailing in Russia, it was Italy, where the peasants were not conservative, where the intelligentsia was largely socialist, and the south deeply disaffected. But Italy remained a country of the West. Its labour movement was educated in the Western tradition. This, and not the economic structure, proved to be finally decisive.

Reaction set in almost immediately. The threat of revolution had been proved non-existent; but the employers were frightened and insulted, and the government with them.

Police measures multiplied, and Mussolini's star rose, meteor-like.

These were the circumstances in which the Italian Socialist Party had to decide about the twenty-one points. The defeat weighed the scales heavily against the Comintern. It was impossible to let the issue turn upon the occupation of the factories and the failure to transform this situation into a revolution, for to follow such a course would be to place some of the closest adherents of the communists under the ban. The party had therefore to decide about the twenty-one points as such. In particular it had to decide about the exclusion of the right wing, which included Turati and Modigliani. It was known that the trade unions were absolutely against Moscow, that they were the strongest force in the workers' movement, and that they would back the right wing in the event of a split. Serrati, the leader of the centre group, had also had enough. He came back from Moscow disgusted with many things, and especially with the intention of the Russians to control the movements of the West. His disgust hardened to a firm decision when he saw that following Moscow would mean severing himself from the trade-union leaders. Revolution was no longer a practical proposition, so at least the movement should be spared the intolerable blow of a big split. He confronted Moscow with the following alternatives: either to abandon its intention of excluding the right wing or to lose the party as a whole. Together with Turati and the trade-union leaders, Serrati had the confidence of the overwhelming majority of the labour movement. Thus the Comintern was forced to rely upon what remained: the small group in Turin, and Bordiga and his friends. In other words, the Comintern, having lost the allegiance of all the level-headed elements of the Italian movement, had to rely upon precisely that lunatic fringe of anti-parliamentarians which it had just excluded in other countries. This meant that the new Communist Party which would issue from the split would inevitably be still-born.

The delegates sent by the Comintern to the decisive party congress, convened at Leghorn in February 1921, were entrusted with ample powers to judge and decide by themselves. This, from the beginning, was one very objectionable feature of the Comintern 'régime'. The various delegates were given the widest powers, with very little control from above; but the national parties were expected to submit unquestioningly. The delegates chosen for the Leghorn congress were Matthias Rakosi, known to us from the Hungarian dictatorship, a man of fiery revolutionary temperament but without discrimination; and Christo Kabakchiev, the theoretician of the Bulgarian party, who, from the heights of his Macedonian revolutionism, looked down upon the labour movements of the West. Levi, too, was present. Kabakchiev, from the outset, made matters worse by invariably insulting the majority as opportunists, social-patriots, traitors, and by insisting upon the acceptance of the twenty-one points, including the immediate exclusion, not only of Turati, and Modigliani, but of all their friends. This made attempts at negotiation, begun by both Levi and Serrati, hopeless. Serrati was even ready to concede the exclusion of all those who would vote against the twenty-one points; but then all the right-wingers would have voted for them. Thus the issue had to be fought out to the bitter end. The party was split, the communists obtaining about a third of the votes. Even this was no true picture, for the masses were much more for Serrati and against the Comintern than the activists who had voted at Leghorn. The whole bulk of Italian labour left the Comintern. Within the Socialist Party the rift between Turati and Serrati, between those who wanted to participate in the government and those who rejected participation, continued; while outside, the Fascists were smashing the labour movement. The Comintern had lost the one big country in which it had dominated the labour movement as a whole, and the men who, a few months ago, had been carried in triumph shoulder-high by the workers of Leningrad and Moscow were now insulted as traitors.

The Leghorn split had an unexpected sequel, much more catastrophic for the Comintern than the Italian débâcle. Rakosi and Kabakchiev felt that there were people in the West who were insufficiently impressed with their tactics at Leghorn. They went straightway to Berlin and there dictatorially demanded that the central committee of the German communists, Levi and his group, should endorse their action. This Levi, Clara Zetkin, and most of the leaders who had come over from the Independents, refused to do. Levi, on the contrary, thought that Leghorn had been a crime and that if the Comintern continued in this way, there would soon be no single mass Comintern party left in the West. The issue, a life and death one, was clearly between a mass party and a narrow though pure party. Meeting stout resistance, Rakosi did not shrink from saying that the German party was obviously not yet a true communist party and that it probably stood in need of further splitting. The authority of Moscow was strong; Levi was personally very unpopular on account of his wealth and aristocratic way of living; and the ex-Spartacists disliked the ex-Independents. Rakosi obtained a narrow majority in the central committee. Levi, Zetkin, and their followers resigned from the leadership, and Levi left on holiday for the south.

He had gone no farther than Vienna when he was forced to return. Something more than unexpected had happened. Rakosi had gone home and in his stead Sinovjev had sent Bela Kun to Germany. By this time it was mid-March 1921. Bela Kun had just had time to witness, in Russia, the greatest crisis of the Soviet régime. The civil war over and the Whites defeated, the Russian workers had revolted against the intolerable sufferings imposed upon them by the party dictatorship and the economic situation. Lenin has repeatedly insisted that at that moment the majority of the peasants were opposed to the Communist Party and that the majority of the proletariat at least wavered. The Petrograd proletariat declared a general strike, which was followed by an armed rising at Kronstadt, the heart of the 1917 revolution. The slogans essentially reduced themselves to a demand for the restoration of the power of the Soviets, from which the communists were to be excluded. The revolt was drowned in blood. Economic policy was changed overnight and free trade partly restored, to combat existing famine conditions. It was the beginning of the so-called N.E.P., the 'New Economic Policy'. Economic grievances once relieved, the political system remained stable, but it had been shaken to its foundations. Kun, hysterical as usual when confronted with danger, had gone to Germany convinced that the Soviet Union would founder unless revolution in the West came to its rescue.

As usual, Kun's powers were ill-defined, while his excitement was easily transmitted to the German communists. The new united party which had emerged out of the union of the Spartacists and the left Independents was now three months old and had not yet effected anything spectacular. It was felt that, unless it was to fall to pieces, or rather to continue along the old, opportunist lines, something must be done. The new central committee which had come to power a few weeks previously, after Levi's withdrawal, felt that it was its special duty to tear the party away from opportunism. At the right moment an international crisis occurred. French troops, because Germany had failed to comply with certain disarmament clauses of the Treaty, occupied Düsseldorf. The Bavarian government refused to carry out orders from Berlin to disband its secret army. At the same time the date of the referendum in Upper Silesia, which was to decide whether that region should go to Germany or to Poland, was approaching, and fierce armed struggles were being waged sporadically in the contested province. In reality, all these were minor events. The Silesian referendum was carried through with surprisingly little trouble. The Bavarians did not submit, but nor were they punished. After a time the French evacuated Düsseldorf. But the heated and angry imagination of the people who, in Berlin, wanted to do something to save Russia and to make their own party revolutionary regarded these events as portents of an approaching breakdown of the bourgeois régime. They decided to 'take the offensive'.

They were not given the opportunity. In all probability, the social-democrats, through the Prussian police, whom they controlled, had come to know the prevailing mood at communist headquarters. Who were they to interfere if the communists wanted to break their own necks? There was one district in Germany at this time in which almost the whole population was communist, a queer district at that, the copper-mines of the Mansfeld region. This district had been Luther's home. Luther's father had himself been a Mansfeld miner. It had persisted as one of the most religious and conservative districts in all Germany; before the war only company unions had been admitted in the mines, and the workers themselves had sometimes beaten almost to death the social-democrat agitators who had tried to break through into this forbidden region. Immediately after the war this part of the country, in which before an absolute and naïve belief in 'Kaiser, Volk, und Vaterland' had prevailed, went wildly to the left and became a communist stronghold. The ordinary unions, naturally, were still anathema to the Mansfeld miners, with the difference that now they hated them for 'left' instead of 'right' reasons. Hoersing, the social-democratic governor of the province, at this point sent police into the mines, justifying his action by the provocative explanation that as almost all the miners were thieves it was necessary for the police to protect the mines from the general robbery.

The Mansfeld miners had plenty of rifles and a few machineguns left over from the time of the war and the Kapp *Putsch*, and they immediately rose in revolt. As far as their own district was concerned, the rising was not unsuccessful; for many days they put up a stiff defence against overwhelming odds. Naturally enough, the communist headquarters saw in all this their opportunity to start the offensive upon which they had decided only a few days before. The problem was simply one of extending the Mansfeld rising to other districts. They had, in fact, during the first days, an important success. The Leuna factories near Halle, only a few hours away from Mansfeld, joined the revolt. These were Germany's biggest chemical factories, employing between ten thousand and twelve thousand workers, and had had a political evolution not dissimilar to that of Mansfeld. But with this the successes were already at an end. In Hamburg the communist minority of the workers for a few hours occupied the shipyards, a sanguinary clash with the police being the only result. In central Germany Max Hoelz made the countryside unsafe for a few days. He was a sort of German Robin Hood, a worker who had never been politically awakened before the war, who had lived in England and had come back with a strong dislike for Prussian manners and conditions. The war had then kindled his wrath, and now, at the head of a band a few dozen strong, he perambulated the hunger districts of central Germany, conquering for a day or so now this, now that small town. He was a hero of popular legend, unable to submit to the discipline of any party. (Years later, after having passed several years in jail, he joined the Communist Party and then went to Russia, where he disappeared.

It was explained, in answer to inquiries from friends, that he had been drowned while bathing in a river.)

This by itself was not an insurrection that possessed even the slightest chance of success. There must be more. But all the fiery appeals of the Communist Party were unable to raise an echo among the workers, who had not risen even for more important issues than the occupation of a few copper mines by the police. Kun and the central committee were therefore driven to attempt to obtain by force the collaboration which the workers would not give willingly. The party launched the slogan of a general strike, and as the factories did not move, communist unemployed were sent to drive the workers out of the factories. The attempted rising against the police degenerated into a fist fight between employed and unemployed. Thus, on Maundy Thursday, the following cable came from Moers, Rhineland:

'The Friedrich-Albert-Huette in Rheinhausen, owned by Krupp, was the scene of heavy fighting on Thursday between communists who had occupied the plant and workers who wanted to go to work. Finally the workers attacked the communists with clubs and forced their way into the plant. Eight men were wounded. At last Belgian soldiers interfered, separated the fighters, and arrested the communists. The communists who had been driven out later returned with reinforcements and again occupied the plant.'

Levi, who quotes the cable on page 40 of his pamphlet against the rising, adds the following comment: 'Even more pathetic reports arrived from Berlin. We learn that it was a terrible thing to watch how the unemployed, crying loudly at the pain of the thrashings they had received, were thrown out of the factories.'

Thus the alleged offensive of the working class, undertaken in its name by the Communist Party, at once transformed itself into a fierce fight of the communists, with the unemployed as their battering-ram, against the workers. But this phase was also over and done with after two or three days. Kun and his lieutenants then thought of something different. On March 19th the enlarged regional committee of the Communist Party in central Germany was convened at Halle. 'We saw clearly', reports X, military commander of the party in that region, 'that a commotion all over Germany could never be unloosed by Hoersing's decree [the police occupation of the Mansfeld mines], but that it was necessary to bring about a provocation and that the famous first shot must be fired from the side of the enemy. . . . The mood of the workers of central Germany was so unsatisfactory that the opinion prevailed that artificial means must be used in order to inflame the people. . . . [A member of the Berlin central committee] suggested that, if no other method could be found, comrades X and Y should be arrested in order to bring the Halle workers out into the streets. The most popular leaders must then disappear, and the story be invented that they have been liberated. Attempts must be made to incite the workers by assassinations [*Attentate*] until they start to fight.' (In the report there follows a lengthy description of plans to blow up two wagons of communist hand-grenades and cartridges, so that it can be explained afterwards that the ammunition had belonged to the Fascists, and so that stories can be spread about the deaths of hundreds of workers in the accident.) 'The comrades—with the exception of A and B—agreed. . . . Then C and D suggested that our own party offices should be blown up during Wednesday night, supposing that this would rouse the workers more than anything else; the party could then say to the workers: "Look, they destroy your property." I opposed the motion and suggested that the ammunition depot be blown up instead. It was decided that the depot should be blown up at two o'clock at night, and the co-operative [the same building as the party premises] at half-past two.' But the attempt, the report explains, failed twice on two consecutive nights, although undertaken seriously. Another leader, discussing the possibility of blowing up the party premises during the daytime, adds to his report: 'in that event about twenty of our best comrades would have been victims of the attempt, but this consideration Comrade Z [the representative of the central committee] pushed aside with a move of his hand.' On this occasion the good sense of some of the local people prevailed and the attempt was carried out at a time when no loss of life was threatened. In Breslau, the local committee too attempted to blow up part of its own premises and, for some reason about which we can only speculate, chose to begin with the toilet of its office. A lengthy debate ensued as to whether, in order to add to the psychological effect, it should be blown up while somebody was there. Finally, this motion was negatived, though dynamite was actually applied. The toilet went into the air without any sacrifice of life and without other than ridiculous after-effects. A more serious matter was that dynamite attempts were made upon railway lines, attempts which, conceivably, may have been made without authorization from the party, but which were credited to its account by the infuriated railwaymen.

All these efforts availed nothing. In the second week of the rising, Mansfeld was subdued, the Leuna works were stormed, isolated revolts on the part of small communist minorities in other towns were easily dispersed, while the workers remained indifferent and disgusted. The Mansfeld organization was shattered to pieces, and within a few years Mansfeld became again what it had been before, the *eldorado* of the company unions. The disaster was almost equally great in other districts. The party had entered upon the 'action' with about 350,000 members. During the fighting and the ensuing weeks, it declined to 150,000 members. For the time being the communist mass party in Germany had practically ceased to exist. Thus, while at the close of 1920 the Comintern had had two powerful movements, in Italy and Germany, at its disposal, it had been successful, in less than half a year, in wrecking them both. In their disappointment great masses had joined the communists. But disgust with the failure of their hopes and illusions was something quite other than a readiness to fight, and when that passive disgust which had carried them into the communist ranks was mistaken for readiness to fight the house of cards tumbled and only ruins remained. At the time it seemed a tremendous lesson, of universal application, which would never now be forgotten. Everybody in the Comintern believed that never again would a similar experiment be attempted, and that the communist parties would now settle down and try to win over the majority of the workers.

The demonstration of its consequences, openly and impressively, would really have been the first condition for the learning of this lesson, and this Paul Levi intended to do. He thought that so tremendous a defeat could not be hushed up. He believed, moreover, that what had happened was at least as much a moral as a political issue, and that the party, and world communism as such, could only clear itself from its responsibility by speaking openly about what had happened. A straightforward confession was in his opinion the only means by which the party could cleanse itself. He therefore published the pamphlet entitled *Our Road*, from which we have quoted above, about the fight between employed and unemployed. The central committee's reaction to this was to exclude him at once from the party. They considered that they had done very well, and that the 'offensive' had to be resumed at the next opportunity. Meanwhile, however, a violent crisis shook the party. The U.S.P. leaders who had come over a few months ago joined Levi, one after another, and with them went a number of the old Spartacists. In Moscow Sinovjev began by supporting Kun, but about six weeks after the débâcle, in May, Clara Zetkin went to Moscow and placed authentic documents proving the complete isolation of the party, the strange methods of Kun and his lieutenants, and a number of other facts, before Lenin. Kun was immediately disavowed, and the theory of the 'offensivists' rebuffed. But Levi was neither acquitted nor recalled into the party. Lenin quite openly stated that Levi had been right upon every point, but—he had betrayed the party by writing his pamphlet against the rising. The Bolshevik conception of discipline, which refused to allow the public discussion of issues which the central committee had not expressly submitted to public discussion, prevailed.

Even now the matter was not yet at an end. *Vorwaerts*, the Berlin social-democratic newspaper, had obtained possession of many of the reports, containing both assent and criticism, which had been sent to communist headquarters from the scene of the fighting. Adroitly, *Vorwaerts* published these documents in small batches. The party leaders began by denying everything: the whole story of provocations and dynamiting was a police ruse. Many even of the higher party officials believed this. As time went on, with the *Vorwaerts*' disclosures continuing, and official documents emanating from the communist machine appearing in the columns of that newspaper without a *démenti*, hesitations appeared even among the most faithful. Finally, the general secretary of the party, Ernst

Reuter-Friesland himself, turned about. He had been a man of the left wing and very much in favour of 'offensive' tactics. But in December 1921, when *Vorwaerts* published the worst documents of its collection, he declared himself convinced and left the party. No further choice was left the central committee. Knowing, more or less, the nature of the documents which *Vorwaerts* still had in the dossiers, and unable to deny their authenticity, the Communist Party itself published all the incriminating papers disclosing its activities during the rising. It is from this official collection that our quotations about the dynamite and assassination attempts of the rising are drawn.

When the storm broke and everyone, Lenin included, turned against the German central committee, its leaders began to see their mistake. They had already driven away hundreds of the most experienced members of the party staff. But, finally, the central committee came round, and the men who had had the biggest share in the rising, Heinrich Brandler, August Thalheimer, and Paul Froelich, were from this time onwards the strongest advocates of caution and delay. The later history of the right wing within the Communist International cannot be understood unless it is realized that almost all the leaders of the right wing had begun as leaders of the extreme left, but had never recovered from the shock of the disaster of March 1921.

CHAPTER XII

UNITED FRONT

The disaster of March 1921 had its effects not only on the German communists but on the Comintern as well. The whole policy of international communism was changed within a few months. A world-congress had to meet every year, according to a statutory rule religiously observed during the first years. Lenin used the third world-congress, which met in Moscow, in the early summer of 1921, for the change of tactics he thought necessary. The new policy inaugurated at that congress can be summarized in one sentence: the Comintern, for the time being, renounced attempts at armed risings and acknowledged the necessity of a longer period of preparation. March 1921 had shown that the time was over when the risings of small communist minorities met with any sympathy, however small, among the workers. A peaceful mood was now dominant and the workers positively hated the communist attempts at violence. As long as the majority of the working class was not won over for communism, no communist rising could henceforward be anything but an adventurous *Putsch* with disastrous consequences. Even the Comintern must recognize that the revolutionary period was, for the time being, over. It was convinced, however, not without reason, that this pacific atmosphere would not last for ever, that the new stability was only relative and temporary, that new economic and social crises would come.

Facts spoke too strongly in favour of a more cautious policy to allow any serious doubt. Nevertheless, Lenin met furious resistance from the majority of the Western communists when he proposed the new tactics at the third world-congress. There were many communists in the West who believed that there was no real need for further moderation, that the policy of the March rising had failed only because it had not been carried through uncompromisingly; those extremists contended, and some of them contend even to-day, that the one reason for the change of policy of the Comintern was the change of policy of the Russian state. It is true that at that period Russia too underwent one of the biggest changes in its revolutionary history. The Kronstadt rising, which had inspired so much terror in many leading communists in February and March, had been defeated. But its military destruction had been preceded by big political concessions to the disaffected masses. The 'New Economic Policy' had been introduced, the peasant had been allowed to keep the greater part of his harvest and to sell it as best he could, free trade had been partly restored, and attempts were made to win the help of foreign capitalists for the work of reconstruction. The latter attempts failed completely, but they were a strong factor in Russian politics in 1921-2. Civil war was over. In Russia the atmosphere was more peaceful, and with its neighbours Russia sought peaceful and friendly relations and even economic collaboration. In spring, 1922, Russia, at Rapallo, signed an informal alliance with Germany. France was regarded in Moscow as the chief adversary.

It is a matter for speculation what might have happened had these milder trends in Russia coincided with a period of acute revolutionary tension in the West. Very likely the end of the period of civil war would have inclined the Russians towards less extreme methods, whatever the situation abroad. Russia was tired. It did not want more heavy fighting, and the moods prevailing in Moscow were naturally transmitted, directly, to the Comintern, whose leading men were all Russians and saw the world with Russian eyes. Moreover, the conditions of a totalitarian dictatorship which, after Kronstadt, had been definitely established, tended to cause misunderstandings. The Russians were inclined to regard every divergence of opinion as inadmissible, and thus shut out, artificially, every independent source of information. They had to rely, therefore, on their own inspiration, which they instinctively drew from what they saw around them. During their own civil war they had seen the whole world in flames. After its end they suddenly understood the lack of revolutionary conditions in the West.

But whatever the influence of the latest developments in Russia may have been, at that moment their appreciation of the Western scene was for once adequate. At the third world-congress Lenin insisted strongly upon the necessity to win over the *gros*, the great majority, of the workers. 'To the masses!' was the slogan finally adopted, after long debates, by the congress. But in carrying the new policy through, the Russians stood almost alone. In spite of their recent defeats, the Western communists stood flabbergasted at the change. A very few months ago they had split away from the big mass parties and formed communist minority parties; one of these parties had attempted to fight in a really revolutionary manner, so they thought. And now Lenin said they had been merely foolish, and told them so with his usual rudeness.

Kun, being chiefly responsible for the disaster, naturally refused to admit his guilt and insisted that the old tactics had been and continued to be the only real communist tactics; he was followed by the Hungarians and the Austrians. That would have mattered little. But there was the rump of the Italian party, the small section of the movement which had remained in the Comintern after the Leghorn congress; for Bordiga and his people, who held a firm grip upon the Italian party, the very idea of becoming the majority was a pollution of communist purity. In Germany views were divided. But those who were willing to accept Lenin's views were precisely those who, being against the March revolt, had been for Levi and were therefore suspect of treason. The bulk of the Germans violently defended what they had done. In Czechoslovakia, England, and the United States communist parties were still in the process of formation, and Lenin could not yet expect real support from those countries. The French and the Norwegians, for reasons soon to be explained, held back cautiously. Lenin put through his views, after long debates, by a considerable majority, but this was a majority based upon the authority and the pressure of the Russians. After the exclusion of Serrati and Levi, there was no man left to withstand them. The formal majority, however, did not imply real assent. There remained parties, such as those of Belgium and Holland, which never really accepted the idea of winning over the masses, shutting themselves up in voluntary sectarianism. Many other parties, not to say all of them, accepted the task in general; but they shrank from its practical implications.

Immediately after the third world-congress, Radek, now the chief adviser of the Comintern in matters concerning the West, set out to give the new policy a concrete form. In order to do so he drew upon the inheritance of Levi. Shortly before he had resigned Levi had drafted an open letter to both the majority socialists and to the rump of the Independents who remained after the Halle split, and to a number of other organizations. He suggested joint action of all political and industrial labour organizations for concrete, immediate, non-revolutionary aims such as the defence of the eight-hour day—a very important issue in Germany at the time—against wage reductions, against unfair taxation, and a number of similar slogans, culminating, characteristically, in the suggestion of an alliance between Germany and Russia. The open letter had been turned down by all the bigger groups to which it was addressed. But that was only what Levi had wanted. He had seen clearly enough that now, and only now, the aftermath of war and revolution would have to be cleared up and that the question remained of paying the bill. With Germany being bled to death by the war, low wages, long hours, and heavy taxation were clearly inevitable—unless, the communists said, the capitalists were expropriated. The socialists of both dispensations did not want social revolution, so they must agree to accept heavy sacrifices in the name of the workers. But for that they had no mandate. The workers who had not wanted to fight for revolution would surely fight about wages, hours, and taxes. And as they wanted to fight for these immediate objectives, against the wishes of their leaders, a rift would open between masses and leaders, and the former would gradually come over to the communists, who would lead them to revolution. These tactics were now tried again, in Germany, and transferred to other countries. The new methods were described as the tactics of the 'united front', and their aim was described by Radek as being to convince the socialist rank and file that 'their leaders do not want to fight, not even for a piece of bread'.

After the third world-congress the leaders of the German party, with Brandler, Thalheimer, Walcher, Froehlich and others, were gradually convinced of the advantages of this method. Radek and Brandler, with the assent of Lenin, pointed out very correctly that no success was possible without the masses, that the masses could only be won, in the present period, by appealing to their immediate interests, and that being enrolled or following the lead of the reformist parties, they could not be expected to follow the communists directly, without previous proof that their own parties refused to lead them in the struggle for their immediate interests. But that did not mean that the men who had opposed and continued to oppose the new tactics were simply fools. They declared that the communists, if they limited themselves over a considerable period to the immediate practical day-to-day tasks of the labour movement, would soon be identical with ordinary reformists. And this was no mere empty talk. In the West there existed in fact a contrast between revolutionary and non-revolutionary methods, which in Russia had never existed.

One of the chief reasons for this was the existence of democracy in the West. There existed, after 1918, in all countries of the West, constitutional machinery through which the workers could put their claims. Such machinery had never existed in Russia, where every fight for the most moderate issues had immediately confronted the workers with the power of the state. In the West the socialists, when pressed by the masses to co-operate with the communists, simply answered: 'All right, provided the communists are prepared loyally to employ all available democratic means.' The primary democratic method, however, is the capture of government by means of the vote. The communists, when offering a united front about legislative matters to the socialists, had to answer the query: 'Are you ready to form with us a democratic government, if our combined efforts win a majority?'

Here things touched at once the root of the matter. In *State and Revolution* Lenin had put forward the view that democracy is only the 'dictatorship of the bourgeoisie'. A democratic government could not possibly help the workers; it could only betray them. The betrayal of the socialists consisted largely in the forming of and participation in democratic governments. There existed an absolute contrast between a democratic and a Soviet government. People who took Lenin's views seriously could not but conclude that the communists, if they formed a democratic coalition with the socialists, would be just as bad as those traitors themselves. The dilemma was irresolvable. If the communists wanted to offer a united front to the socialists they must co-operate with them on the basis of democracy, i.e. precisely on the basis they had always rejected. They must either remain pure revolutionaries and not win the masses; or win the masses, not for revolution, but for the defence of their immediate interests within democracy. Is this not a rigid argument inconsistent with the transitions from one order of things to another which always happen in politics? It would have been, indeed, in a country where the general trend was towards proletarian revolution. But in the West it was generally fully sufficient for the socialists to point out to the workers that this or that action implied unconstitutional methods, in order to deter them. In such an atmosphere, to work on the basis of democracy meant to capitulate to the socialists. And the real dilemma was between remaining revolutionary or winning the masses. The left wing chose the former, asserting that, when conditions grew intolerable, the workers would find the communist view justified and change their minds; the right wing chose winning the masses, asserting, light-heartedly enough, that once the masses were won it would be easy to carry them into revolution.

In the meantime, at the end of 1921, the problem of a socialist-communist coalition had become very acute in Germany, in two provinces. In the provincial diets of Saxony and Thuringia the socialists and communists together had a majority, and the socialists, rather to the left in both districts, were ready to co-operate with the communists. Thus the problem of the coalition government and of the united front in general merged with the other problem of the divergences within the socialist parties. Were the left wing socialists better than the right? Could communists collaborate with them? Or were they just such traitors as the right-wingers, even more dangerous on account of their pseudo-radical phrase-making? This too entered into the heated debates between the partisans and the adversaries of the new tactics within the communist parties.

To the practical problem of a coalition the communists, hemmed in by the dilemma outlined above, were simply unable to give a clear answer. Instead they found an ambiguous formula which, while covering their dogmatic qualms, might or might not open the road to coalition. They launched the slogan of a 'workers' government'. But what was the 'workers' government'? Was it a democratic coalition between socialists and communists? Was it a coalition between socialists and communists, but based upon Soviets, provided there were socialists ready to join in such a government? Was it simply another word for the 'dictatorship of the proletariat'? About this there was serious disagreement, which did not halt before the doors of the Russian central committee. There, generally speaking, Lenin, Trotsky, Radek, Bukharin, tended to the right in problems of united front tactics, while Sinovjev saw the danger of opportunism as the greater menace. On one occasion he went so far as to define the 'workers' government' as a simple 'synonym of the proletarian dictatorship', which would have stultified the united-front tactics as a whole; it brought him a serious rebuff from Lenin.

Among the national parties the introduction of the new tactics brought about a series of crises. The Italians, while accepting the united front in words, did not apply it in practice. For the Bulgarians its execution was unnecessary because they held already the allegiance of a large majority of the Bulgarian proletariat. But serious conflicts were raised in Norway and France. In both these countries the leaders of the communist parties were at odds with Moscow for reasons which had nothing to do with the problems of a united front. Tranmael in Norway, just as Frossard in France, found it convenient to accuse the Comintern of treason to its principles. Why, then, had they split the international labour movement the year before and imposed the twenty-one points, if now they proclaimed a return to the principles of democracy? In Norway Tranmael consistently maintained that, after Kronstadt, the Bolsheviks had ceased to be a revolutionary party and that revolutionaries could no longer accept their lead. But in fact the rupture between the pacifist syndicalism of Tranmael and the Comintern was bound to come.

The real grievances in France were of a different order. The communist party which had been formed after the congress of Tours was communist only in words. Complete liberty of opinion continued. The many municipal councillors of the party voted and administered in their towns as they pleased, in the usual manner of French left democrats, displaying the tricolour and indulging in patriotic propaganda when they pleased. The journalists of the party press wrote what they thought, occasionally attacking Soviet Russia, the Red army, the Red terror. Worst of all, the communists within the C.G.T.U., the Red trade unions, in the old tradition of the French labour movement, claimed complete independence from the party in their trade-union work. After, as before, the congress of Tours, the number of working-class members of the party was very small. A sort of sensation was produced when, at the first close inquiry into the situation of French communism, it was found that many active members were freemasons. Thus some of the leading communists, while rejecting the discipline of Moscow, had accepted the very rigid discipline of the French freemason, where all shades of the French left, in the widest interpretation of the term, co-operated.

It is useless to follow the details of the factional struggle which ravaged the French party between the congress of Tours in December 1920 and the beginning of 1923. On the one side stood the old partisans of the Comintern, Souvarine, Loriot, and their following, who defended Moscow's policy: strict discipline and ideological unity, exclusion of the dissentients, subordination of the unions to the party, united-front tactics with the socialists. Against them stood the old men of the moderate socialists, Cachin and Frossard, who had only come over to the communists at the last moment. Now, again, Cachin submitted in the end, whereas Frossard, the general secretary of the Communist Party, left it at the beginning of 1923, and after a short time became one of the leading socialists. With him left most of the 'politicians', journalists, municipal councillors, and the like. The party was almost wrecked in the process. From 150,000 members it had sunk to 50,000, thus experiencing gradually the decline which the German party had experienced, catastrophically, within a month. But, as in Germany, so in France, the year 1923 marked a new upward trend. Precisely the withdrawal of Frossard and his followers gave many revolutionary trade-unionists confidence in the party. Hitherto they had despised 'politics' in true syndicalist manner, regarding them as the job of careerist intellectuals. Now they believed there was a chance to make the Communist Party into a real working-class party, a thing which had never yet existed in France. Two of their most outstanding leaders, Monatte and Rosmer, joined the party, which with their help won complete control of the C.G.T.U., the Red trade unions.

One must constantly keep in mind these conflicts, both in the Russian central committee and in the communist parties abroad, in order to understand what the new phase really meant for the Comintern. The period of united-front policy, paradoxically, was a period of the growth of rigid centralization of the Comintern under the lead of Moscow. In itself the slogan, 'To the masses!' implied a lenient régime within the communist parties. It was no use trying to win the majority of the proletariat if, at the same time, the communist parties were split in such a way as to reduce them to insignificant sects. During these years the Comintern took care not to repeat the mistake of Leghorn, which had ruined Italian communism. This was the chief reason why the crises in the Norwegian and in the French party were allowed to drift on, endlessly. The effect, in the end, was not altogether different from that of Leghorn, though it was reached by longer detours. For the new tactics made the communist parties into a thin wedge between 'sectarianism' on the one side and 'opportunism' on the other. Every wrong step implied falling into one of these two capital sins. How could the Russians have given liberty to the national parties to make up their own minds, from their knowledge of their respective countries, about the border-line between the two? Most of these parties were not at all what the Russians called 'real Bolshevik' parties, and at Moscow the conviction held that, left to themselves, they would immediately relapse into their traditional Western opportunism. But had they been thorough Bolsheviks it would have helped them little. For the Russians themselves seriously disagreed on every important step of the united-front tactics, which, in fact, were self-contradictory. In such a position, only an infallible authority could draw the boundary line between Bolshevism and 'deviations', a term first introduced into Comintern affairs at that time, and which was to win tremendous importance; it had long been current among Russian Bolshevists. Thus united-front tactics implied a fight against deviations, or, in other words, implied heresy-hunting, which, in its turn, created innumerable conflicts, and made a purely disciplinarian concept of unity of action more and more prevalent.

The most outstanding feature of this rigid 'régime' was the international generalization of every slogan. 'Workers' government', for instance, was a slogan with a meaning, though a dubious one, in Germany. But what could it mean in Austria, where the socialists had more than 40 per cent of the total vote at general elections, the communists, however, less than I per cent, and not a single parliamentary seat? What could it mean in the United States, where socialists and communists would not have been able, with their joint forces, to win more than a single seat in Congress? Nevertheless, the Austrians, as the Americans, as dozens of other parties, were ordered to apply the new slogan. Otherwise they would have been suspect of not accepting the new tactics which the third world-congress had laid down. It was a very queer situation, but, given the starting point of communist ideas, an inevitable one. The communists had given religious value to the application and rejection of certain tactics. To enter a democratic government, to conclude this or that compromise, was treason. But such religious rigidity in tactical matters was incompatible with tactical flexibility such as the Russians themselves admitted as necessary after the end of the revolutionary period. The contradiction between these two viewpoints could only be solved by mechanical obedience to orders from above. Continual changes of tactics, mechanically ordered from Moscow, became inevitable. And tactics having an importance quite incomparable with what they mean in any other movement, and being the chief measure of orthodoxy, theories had to be created every time in order to prove that the new tactics were within the scope of the accepted dogma. It was only logical that, in due course of time, these theories too were adopted and their acceptance enforced from above. Thus it happened that, after a time, not only contradictory tactics, but with them contradictory theories, were enforced from Moscow every day.

One of the most significant moves in this direction was the extension of the slogan of a 'workers' government' to 'a workers' and peasants' government', which was proclaimed in 1922. No immediate practical issue had forced the attention of the Comintern upon this problem. The inclusion of the peasants as an element in the 'workers' government' was simply an attempt to extend the scope of the communist mass parties beyond the borders of the real proletariat. Lenin and the other Russians felt very strongly that one of the reasons for the failure of revolution in the West had been the complete isolation of the proletariat from all other classes. As had become usual and already almost axiomatic, the Russians tried to cure this defect by applying their own methods to the West. The Bolsheviks had won by making an alliance with the peasants. The Western communists must try to do the same. No doubt this was, from the communist point of view, highly desirable, but it could not be taken for granted that what had been possible in Russia was possible in the West. Already in 1920 Herman Gorter, as against Lenin, had pointed out the impossibility of a workers' and peasants' alliance in the West as one of the chief reasons why the Russian revolution could not be taken as a model. Now the communists experienced the accuracy of Gorter's forecast in their own failures.

In 1923 a Red peasant's international was founded in Moscow, in order to simplify the task. But not in a single country did the communists succeed. Failure was due to two very different sets of reasons in two different sets of countries. In Russia the Bolsheviks had won over the peasants, because the peasants in fact though not by law, were still serfs under the feudal domination of the landlord, whom they hated as nothing else on earth. The Bolsheviks had abolished serfdom and removed the landlord. Nothing similar existed in the United States, in France and Germany, not to mention England. There the farmer was property-minded, because he had property, and he simply did not listen to the communists. The position was different in such countries as Hungary, Poland, parts of Italy, and the Balkans, where the peasant was still heavily oppressed and not yet a conservative element. But in these countries the difficulty lay with the workers. The Russian worker, generally, came from the village, with which many ties continued to connect him. The union of workers and peasants constituted the mass of the 'toilers'—a word much used in communist vocabulary—or of the people. Of all European countries only Spain shows a similar relation between workers and peasants. Everywhere else, in the backward countries, the workers had fallen much more strongly under the spell of the town civilization than the peasants. In Hungary the workers had simply refused to collaborate with the peasants, whom they despised. In Italy Serrati had furiously opposed the idea of an alliance between workers and peasants, in Bulgaria the Tesnyaki, the truest of the true, had rejected co-operation with the very advanced Peasant Party of Stambuliiski and were soon to reject it again, to the despair of Moscow. Even where property interests did not stand in the way, the union of workers and peasants, so easy to effect in the primitive conditions of Russia, proved impossible in the more varied social conditions of the West.

In the meantime the tactics of the united front, with all their dangers, contradictions, and undesirable consequences, were far from being a complete failure. They had their most natural application on a ground where most of the difficulties for communist dogma were absent, in work within the trade unions. To strive for better conditions of work was clearly no deviation from true communism. Therefore the slogan 'To the masses!' for a long time found its most adequate application within the unions. Owing to active trade-union work the English party grew into a consistent body; for the same reason the German party gradually recovered from the disaster of 1921. In France, it is true, no such effects were to be expected, because here trade-unionism as a whole had received a terrible blow in the split of 1921. In France the first general elections after Tours took place only in 1924; they showed that the socialists, who, after Tours, had been a small group of officers without troops, had again become considerably stronger than the communists.

The year 1922 brought an opportunity to apply the tactics of the united front on an international plane, and, at the same time, to make them serve the immediate interests of Russia as a state. After the international split the 'reconstructionists', i.e. the remainder of the German Independents, the French socialists, the Austrian socialists, the British I.L.P., and other smaller groups had formed an international between the second and the third, generally called 'International $2\frac{1}{2}$'. 'International $2\frac{1}{2}$' now called for a conference of all three Internationals, in order to agree upon a common policy of all working-class organizations. The Comintern eagerly accepted. It suggested a common fight for certain immediate demands of the workers, mainly for the defence of the eight-hour day and against unemployment, and linked these slogans with specifically Russian claims: international help for the famine districts —it was the year of the big drought and thousands of peasants were dying from starvation in the Russian south-east—recognition of the Soviet Union and re-opening of economic relations. It was obvious that the Russians wanted to win the support of the socialists for the impending Genoa conference with the Western powers; but at the same time they wanted to create difficulties for the socialists by the discrediting of their leaders in such questions as the eight-hour day and the fight against unemployment. The two aims were incompatible. And the hesitation whether to use the Comintern to win the help of the socialists or to destroy them remained a permanent feature of Comintern policy. They wanted both to have the cake and to eat it. They wanted to continue their revolutionary policy, but at the same time to enjoy the fruits of a non-revolutionary policy.

With such suggestions the Comintern delegates—Radek, Clara Zetkin, Frossard—went to the conference of the three Internationals early in April. But there Vandervelde, three times premier of Belgium and chief representative of the Second International, had prepared a counter-stroke. Support Russia? Well and good! But only if it brought its political system into line with that of the democratic West. Vandervelde put down his conditions: liberate Georgia, which in spring 1921 had been overrun by the Red army, against the patent will of the majority of the population, which was Menshevik, but, most of all, anti-Russian; freedom of the press and propaganda for the non-Bolshevik socialist parties in Russia; finally, liberation of the leaders of the Russian 'socialist-revolutionaries', who were just about to be tried for high treason. Naturally, a heated discussion ensued about these demands. Radek thought co-operation important enough to make concessions on minor points. He granted the admission of a neutral commission of inquiry to Georgia and the admission of European counsel to the trial of the socialist-revolutionaries, among them Vander-velde himself. He pledged himself, moreover, that in this case the death penalty would not be applied. In exchange the Second International accepted the creation of a commission of nine members, three of each International, in order to prepare demonstrations for the slogans which the Russians had sub-mitted and to consider the possibilities of further united action.

The Comintern had tampered with Russian affairs! This was different from manœuvring with the socialists in the West. Lenin and Sinovjev immediately protested, the former writing an article entitled 'We Paid too Dearly'. The foreign counsel were admitted to the trial in Moscow, but treated in such a way that after a few days they left under protest, declaring that they could not fulfil the task of defending the accused. The pledge concerning the death penalty was kept. The commis-sion to Georgia, however, never took shape, because neither the Second nor the Third Internationals any longer wanted the committee of nine, which was broken up after two months. But if direct negotiations with the chief socialist parties on an international scale had failed, local co-operation with the socialist left was sought only the more eagerly.

After the conference of the three Internationals, the official leadership of the socialists remained deaf to all appeals for co-operation. 'First stop slandering and disrupting the socialist parties' was the constant answer; and that it was to remain till Hitler. If the question of responsibility is raised there is hardly a doubt that both sides were equally responsible. Both manœu-vred. Neither wanted sincere collaboration. As to the com-munists, Lenin had written in *Left-wing Communism* that the collaboration they offered the socialists—in the passage con-cerned with the British Labour Party—would support the reformists 'as the rope supports the hanged man'. But the appeal, which was rejected everywhere by socialist head-quarters, found willing support in certain German provincial organizations. This was largely due to the unification of the socialists and Independents into one united social-democratic party, which took place in summer, 1922, and drew after it the merging of the Second International and the 'International $2\frac{1}{2}$' in spring, 1923. Now hundreds of thousands of former Independents were members of the united party and many of them were more sympathetic to the appeals of the communists than headquarters in Berlin. The dividing-line between the adversaries and partisans of the united front was, however, not completely coincident with the old dividing-line between Independents and majority socialists. The partisans of the united front were strongest in Saxony and Thuringia, where socialists and communists together held majorities in the provincial diets, a fact which both parties would have liked to turn to the advantage of the labour movement.

In January 1923 the congress of the Communist Party of Germany met at Leipzig. Two weeks before, the French had occupied the Ruhr and produced a big political and economic crisis in Germany, but the Leipzig congress did not care overmuch for that; the eyes of Radek, Comintern delegate in Germany, and of the national party leaders were fixed on collaboration with the left-wing socialists in Saxony and Thuringia. At the head of the party stood Heinrich Brandler, with August Thalheimer as first lieutenant, notably in matters of theory. After his brilliant achievements in Chemnitz during the Kapp *Putsch*, he had taken part in all the crazy activity of March 1921, but, as he said soon afterwards, was 'not going to commit twice in his life the same mistake'. He had, however, learnt his lesson decidedly too well, from the communist point of view. Brought to trial in June 1921 for the crimes of March he had defended himself by radically denying all intentions of the party towards revolutionary action. His words were soon refuted, when *Vorwaerts* started publishing his dossier. But what Brandler had said in court stood. He had gone so far as to contend that a dictatorship of the proletariat could be established by peaceful means.

Brandler saw one thing with the singleness of purpose which distinguishes both the great and the narrow: no revolution in Germany without winning over the majority of the trade-unionist workers! Those workers believed in democracy. And Brandler set out to explain to the party that, in order to win over the majority it must 'start from the illusions of the workers with a decent standard of living'. The whole tragedy of revolution in the West was in these words. The dominating 'illusion' of these groups was democracy, and so Brandler proposed to make use of democratic 'illusions'.

'The workers' government', said the final resolution of the Leipzig party congress, 'is neither the same thing as the proletarian dictatorship, nor is it an attempt to bring this dictatorship about by peaceful parliamentary means; it is an attempt of the working-classes to carry out a working-class policy within the framework and, for the time being, with the means of bourgeois democracy, backed by proletarian institutions and mass movements.' This was a clear announcement of the party's readiness to co-operate with the socialists in a democratic coalition government. It was a prospect already very attractive to the left of the Socialist Party and likely to win over its majority. But, at the same time, it was a wholesale recantation of all the basic principles of communism. It threw a queer light upon the alleged character of the united-front tactics as a manœuvre. Such a manœuvre could only end in sincere and complete collaboration with the socialists, in other words the manœuvre would inevitably become earnest. In the light of later German events there will probably be few people—except the partisans of Fascism—who would not regard the achievement of such a task at that time as a great blessing and the failure which overtook the attempt as a catastrophe for German democracy. But it was unacceptable from the communist point of view. Whereas very often in the history of the Comintern intentions most seriously announced turned out, in the end, to be sheer manœuvres, here, for once, the irony of history had willed it that a manœuvre should become bitter earnest.

But, naturally, this called forth violent opposition. In Germany a left wing formed under Maslow and Ruth Fischer in Berlin, Thaelmann in Hamburg, and others, who opposed Brandler's policy and set against it that old policy of a fight to the finish with the socialist traitors. Again Radek and Sinovjev quarrelled; Radek, not quite so extreme in his right wing views as Brandler, wanted to include a few members of this left-wing opposition in the central committee. Sinovjev, criticizing Radek, wanted a still stronger representation. The struggle was bound to be transferred to the international arena.

A few weeks after the Leipzig congress, the congress of the Czechoslovak party met at Prague and emphatically endorsed, under Šmeral's leadership, Brandler's policy. Thus the old fight between the ultra-left and the right had reappeared. The twenty-one points had not killed 'opportunism'. Lenin's pamphlet on left-wing communism and the exclusion of all the ultra-lefts had not killed the ultra-left tendency. They were both implied in the situation, ineradicably; for the International, unable to win the majority of the workers for its programme, could only waver between sectarianism and adaptation to the socialists.

But at this juncture two sudden crises interfered and brought the Comintern again, as in 1921, to the threshold of the abyss.

CHAPTER XIII

BULGARIAN INTERLUDE

The first blow came, quite unexpectedly, in Bulgaria. We have followed the history of the Bulgarian Tesnyaki to the end of the war and to their adhesion to the Comintern, early in 1919. At the end of 1919 Stambuliiski, the leader of the Peasant Party, had obtained by peaceful means what he had failed to obtain in September 1918 by insurrection. A government of the Peasant Party was formed and under Stambuliiski's rule Bulgaria became, in fact though not in name, a very advanced peasant republic. These were good times for the Bulgarian communists. Apart from occasional slight intervention, the government left them full liberty, a thing unheard of for a revolutionary party in the Balkans. They now grew splendidly, until they had obtained absolute domination of most trade unions, a fourth of the total vote of the country, and the domination of many municipalities.

Since the defeat of the second Balkan war in 1912, the Macedonian refugees, numerous, cohesive, and of boundless courage and fighting spirit, had always been a big factor in Bulgarian politics. Late in 1922 Stambuliiski effected a friendly understanding with Belgrade, which thwarted the hopes of a fight to win Macedonia for Bulgaria. The central committee of the Macedonian revolutionaries immediately sent a final warning to Stambuliiski, and the Macedonians joined hands with the conservative parties against the Peasant Party. Months of eager preparation on both sides followed. Finally, on 9th June 1923, the Macedonians rose, which was a surprise neither for Stambuliiski nor for the communists, nor, for that matter, for anybody else in Bulgaria. It appeared, after a few hours, that the Macedonians had won over the whole army and police. In Sofia Stambuliiski was immediately defeated. Fighting in the villages continued for a few days, ending with the death of Stambuliiski. Resistance was slight; large strata of the peasantry seem to have been dissatisfied with Stambuliiski's rule, which protected the large rather than the small peasants, without gaining, for all that, the sympathy of the conservative forces.

What was the attitude of the Communist Party in this emergency? To the surprise and anger of the whole International, it proclaimed neutrality. In one Bulgarian town, in Plevna, the communists had risen against the *coup d'état*. The central committee disavowed the act, and this in spite of a fairly obvious fact: the coup of the Macedonians and the military was not simply directed against the Peasant Party, but against democracy as such, against political liberty, which had been ample under Stambuliiski.

It was not the first time that a communist party had to take stock of an attempt to overthrow democracy. In Germany, the Kapp *Putsch* had been such an attempt, and the Communist Party's first reaction to it had been a manifesto declaring democracy as indifferent to the workers. Two and a half years later Mussolini entered Rome. This time, the communists had fought Fascism, for there was a considerable difference between the German and the Italian event. Kapp had attacked the government and, to begin with, had left the workers alone, exactly as Zankov, the leader of the Macedonian coup, did in Sofia; Mussolini, on the contrary, had started by beating down the workers, and by doing so had captured the government. But when Fascism had finally won in Italy, the Comintern failed to understand the bearing of the event. Bordiga proclaimed that the Fascists would soon make an alliance with the forces of bourgeois democracy. Others, such as Sinovjev, contended that Fascism was essentially a sanguinary repression of the proletariat which was to come, inevitably, in all countries whether formally democratic or not. The crucial importance of the fight between democracy and Fascism was not understood, could not be understood by an organization which loathed democracy, regarded it as the 'dictatorship of the bourgeoisie', and was, at the same time, itself moving towards a political régime as totalitarian as that of Fascism.

In Bulgaria this indifference was driven to an almost incredible extreme. A manifesto of the party, issued immediately after the coup, called the counter-revolution a 'fight of the cliques of the rural and urban bourgeoisie for power', and added that 'the toiling masses in town and country will not participate in the fight which has broken out between the urban and the rural bourgeoisie, because such a participation would mean that the exploited fight the battles of their exploiters'. Not without reason the Bulgarian communists called themselves proudly 'Tesnyaki', which means, 'The narrow-minded ones'. It was the one moment in all the history of the Comintern in Europe when the slogan of a united front of workers and peasants would have had a concrete meaning. And it is difficult to say whether, to talk in Comintern vocabulary, the passivity of the Bulgarian communists was a 'right' or a 'left' deviation. The manifesto, with its disparagement of democracy, was very left; but the absolute inaction revealed rather the eagerness of an organization with strong unions, big 'people's houses', considerable funds, and a large staff to avoid fighting with a strong and ruthless adversary. Blagoyev, the founder of the party, had advised passivity; but he was a dying man. Kolarov, to a certain extent his successor, was in Moscow. Chiefly responsible for the action taken on the spot were Dimitrov, the later president of the Comintern, then general secretary of the Bulgarian party, and a certain Lukanov.

But the practical attitude of the Bulgarian communists disagreed with the united-front policy prevailing in Moscow, and Sinovjev almost openly accused the Bulgarian communists of having sympathized with the counter-revolutionary coup. Quoting an official statement of the Bulgarian party to the effect that 'the masses in Sofia met the coup with a feeling of open satisfaction', Sinovjev upbraided his Bulgarian subordinates for even now, after the coup, 'attacking the fallen Stambuliiski government more than the Whites'. Exactly in the same way, even in the day of the Kapp *Putsch*, the German communists had attacked Noske more than Kapp. Exactly in the same way, during Hitler's rise, they were to attack the socialists more than the Nazis. The gist of it is that there is no

such thing as an 'education' of masses to revolutionary traditions. A mass party, in normal times, must carry on normal,
non-revolutionary activities. And acts, not words, decide. The
Bulgarian Communist Party proved to be just as non-revolutionary, in the hour of trial, as any socialist 'traitors' could
have been. The only difference was that, in contradistinction
to these 'traitors', they could grandly justify their passivity
on the score of contempt for bourgeois democracy.

The pressure of Moscow would not have availed against a
party financially independent and strongly rooted in the
Bulgarian masses. After two weeks, however, the victorious
military government of Zankov started severe persecution of
the communists. The spirit of resistance among the masses had
been broken very quickly, and the counter-revolution could
now proceed quietly to the destruction of its second opponent,
the communists, after having destroyed its chief opponent,
Stambuliiski. The communists saw that they could not continue to exist legally. And then the feeling of impending catastrophe, together with the pressure from the Comintern, which
wanted to 'correct' the 'deviation' of June, produced a frightful cataclysm. The communists, who had not been ready while
the masses were in movement, decided to fight, in self-defence,
when there was no longer a chance. Instead of going immediately underground, which would have been the one way out
after the decisive mistake of June, they prepared a rising. This
their adversaries naturally learned, and on September 12th
the whole leading staff of the party, hundreds of people, were
arrested. The party had entered into negotiations with the
Peasant Party, or what remained of it, in the last weeks, but
now it rose, isolated and disorganized. Not a single town participated in the rising. A few villages rose, but mostly isolated
small groups of party members which were forced, almost
immediately, to retreat to the mountains. There, for about ten
days, they carried on guerrilla warfare, or, to use the usual
Balkanic expression, a 'Komitatshi' war. But they were soon
defeated and dispersed.

Now the Zankov government had what it wanted. A terrific
persecution followed, comparable in extent and cruelty only
to the White terror in Hungary. Arrests, tortures, official and
unofficial executions drove the party to despair. Very natu-

rally, the unity of the party broke under the strain. Feeling the whip of the dictatorship upon their own bodies, the members accused Kolarov—who had come back to Bulgaria and participated in the fighting—Dimitrov, and the rest of the leaders of having failed to lead them to the fighting in time. A left wing, under the leadership of two former officers, Minkov and Jekov, evolved and gradually got out of hand, while the party was wrecked by persecution and dissension. The Zankov government was disliked and hated by the common people and in this atmosphere the Minkov-Jekov group, throwing off the skin-deep Marxist varnish of the Bulgarian mass movement, turned towards attempts to murder the leading men of the régime. In April 1925 the Minkov-Jekov group executed what has probably been the biggest coup of the kind in all history. They blew up the Sofia cathedral while the whole government was attending service, together with the king. But, as by a miracle, all the decisive people were saved and all the main perpetrators of the attempt were caught. Minkov and Jekov were killed without trial, a number of executive members of the conspiracy were hanged. Then the White terror was unleashed with doubled strength, revelling in torture which it is impossible to describe.

If the defeats of June and September 1923 had discredited the old leaders and the right wing of the party, the cathedral affair discredited the left. For a time the old group of leaders took over again, but only debris were left of the relatively strongest of all Comintern parties and only the gradual and partial restoration of democracy, owing to disagreements in the camp of the counter-revolutionaries, gave it some scope for action. It never again attained its original strength. And the rifts within the Comintern, to be related later, shattered the party for a second time.

CHAPTER XIV

GERMANY IN 1923

The Bulgarian disaster could be interpreted as an isolated case, and was felt to be such among communists abroad. Incidentally this had happened to one of the most important sections of the Comintern, but the Bulgarian party had not been strongly controlled by Moscow, and the Comintern was not directly responsible for the defeat. A few months later, however, an apparently similar disaster befell the German party, upon which Moscow had set the biggest hopes and which it had kept directly under its thumb.

The occupation of the Ruhr by the French in January 1923 led immediately to a disastrous devaluation of the mark. In the economic decay which befell the country, worse than during the war, the original generous impulse towards a united national resistance against the invaders languished. And, after a few months, Germany found itself on the brink of dissolution.

Neither Brandler in Berlin, with his advisor Radek, nor Trotsky or Sinovjev in Moscow, had realized the full importance of the Ruhr crisis in the beginning. Lenin was a dying man and no longer of any account. How far Moscow was from a correct appreciation is shown by one incident which a few years later became public knowledge. The Rapallo treaty between Russia and Germany contained a secret clause which pledged the Red army to maintain ammunition factories of the Reichswehr in Russia, thus enabling the Germans to circumvent the disarmament clauses of the Versailles Treaty. In accordance with these arrangements the Red army delivered shells to the Reichswehr throughout the year 1923. Here the left hand was clearly ignorant of the activity of the right. The

Russians relied on the antagonism between France and Germany, France being at that time their chief opponent. The Ruhr crisis was welcome to them and they did everything to strengthen the resistance of the Germans.

For months the political and economic disintegration of Germany was proceeding without the Communist Party and the Comintern preparing for anything serious. But, with the mark falling and hunger again stalking through the workers' homes, as during the war, the masses drifted away from the democratic parties which had promised recovery through social peace. The movement was twofold: the fringe of the Social-democratic Party turned towards the communists. The masses which had followed the bourgeois democratic parties joined the monarchical nationalists, the many armed corps of the right, and the rising Nazi movement. The disintegration of the régime was obvious. In August a long series of economic strikes extended until it involved a large part of German industry, and at the same time the industrial movement became more and more political in character. Finally the movement culminated in what was almost a general strike, carried on until the existing government resigned. It had been a coalition of all bourgeois democratic parties, without the socialists and without the right, with Chancellor Cuno at its head. After his withdrawal the socialists entered the coalition, Stresemann became chancellor, and took over the Foreign Office, and the new government set out at once to put an end to the Ruhr crisis, to come to an agreement with France, and to stabilize the mark. Such had been the aim of the general strike, and the workers were satisfied. The movement had reached and overstepped its mark. After the withdrawal of Cuno and the formation of the new government there remained only a few minor strikes. On the whole, the workers looked for an immediate improvement of their lot by the impending stabilization of the mark, the more so because at that moment inflation, which had originally produced a delusion of good business, had already realized all its bad effects and led to a widespread and rapidly increasing unemployment.

But the issue was not so simple as it appeared to the masses in August. Since the end of the war Germany had lived on the fallacious quicksands of currency devaluation, which had hidden behind astronomical figures of prices and wages the real impoverishment of Germany through the war. It was now necessary to cut the losses; in order to stabilize the mark both public servants and private employees must accept very big cuts. The transition to normal conditions could not be effected without additional months of a 'crisis of stabilization', additional months, hence, of sacrifice and starvation. This gave the right a splendid opportunity. The socialists in the government were confronted with much the same problem as that which brought down the British labour government of 1931. Either they must themselves carry through the cuts, which would give the right a splendid opportunity to denounce them; or they must refuse to co-operate and let in the extreme right. It is difficult, nay, impossible, to carry on a democratic government with starving people. Moreover, the right, during the months of conflict with France, had acquired even more arms than it already had, with the help of the Reichswehr, who wanted to create secret reserves in case of a war. There were days of anxious waiting when nobody could say whether the government would stand or whether a military, semi-Fascist dictatorship would take over. At the end of September the conflict with France was provisionally settled; but after, even more than before that settlement, Germany lived in a revolutionary atmosphere, the parties behind the régime losing ground, and the extreme parties of both the right and the left growing rapidly.

Gradually the German Communist Party and the Comintern became alive to the seriousness of the situation. In July Moscow made a big attempt to use the Comintern once more as a means of its foreign policy, or, more exactly, to evolve a method which would suit both Russian foreign policy and the German Communist Party at the same time. In 1922, only a year before, the Comintern had still tried to come to an agreement about certain matters with the Second International. Now the socialists in Germany mattered little; they were, in 1923, on the downward trend. But the nationalists mattered. So Radek, on a solemn occasion, launched an appeal to them from Moscow, suggesting a common front between communists and revolutionary nationalists. One of the latter, A. L. Schlageter, had attempted to blow up a railway line under

French control in the Ruhr, had been caught, court-martialled, and shot. Radek took the fate of this young adventurer as his point of departure: 'Where will the way of these young people lead?' he asked his Moscow hearers: There are only two ways for Germany: with Russia against France or with France against Russia. If Germany chooses the second alternative, the national ideals of the activists of the right will prove shallow phrases; only if Germany, in its fight against the imperialism of the Western powers, joins hands with Russia, will German nationalism have a chance. But to join the struggle of all the oppressed involves a complete break with capitalism at home. Choose then!

On the basis of this speech by Radek the Communist Party started a so-called Schlageter campaign, which led to a number of public discussions between leading communists and outstanding Nazis—notably Count E. Reventlow—about the aims of the impending German revolution. But the political effect was very small. The Fascist wave, expressed in the Nazis and a number of similar organizations as well as in the formation of numerous secret armed corps, grew continually, and the communists failed to produce a major split in the nationalist ranks. For this there were many reasons of an idealist kind: anti-patriotism and anti-nationalism together with the class-war idea had been the theme of communist ideology throughout, and German revolutionary nationalism, since 1919, had arisen in direct, sometimes in armed, opposition to these tendencies. Moreover, the groups most liable to Nazi agitation in the early period were precisely those strata of intellectuals and lower middle-class people who felt themselves superior to the proletariat and hated the idea of submitting to its lead. But there were more direct reasons of a material and political character which accounted for the communist failure. Everybody knew that a communist revolution implied a fight with the armed forces of the state, the Reichswehr, which was not in the least touched by the communist agitation, and most of the police forces of the various 'states' which composed the German republic. To these forces the communists, after the thorough disarmament of the population in 1920, could oppose next to no arms. The Nazis, on the other hand, counted upon the direct co-operation of the Bavarian provincial government at Munich, and upon the friendly neutrality of the Reichswehr. For the moment they were mistaken. When, on 9th November 1923, Hitler finally unfolded the banner of revolt, both the Bavarian government and the army failed him and he was heavily and quickly defeated. But, at the time, everybody felt that the Nazis, the Bavarian government, and, to a limited extent, the Reichswehr, or at least part of it, belonged together, an idea which, as events in 1933 proved, was not absurd; even in 1923 they would certainly have co-operated against a communist rising.

Thus, while the front of the nationalist forces grew incessantly, the proletarian movement reached its climax and overstepped it in the August strike. Social-democracy was undoubtedly in disintegration. The older members held firm, but the masses of the followers drifted away; at the same time the communist ranks were swelled, not so much by converts from the socialists as by masses hitherto unorganized but now driven into action by the economic and political crisis. About August and in the following months the communists probably had a stronger following than the socialists, but at the same time millions of workers, who had hitherto believed in democracy and democratic socialism, simply withdrew from the political arena. A few months later, during the winter of 1923-4, the unions lost no less than four million members, half of their total membership; an undeniable symptom of the general decay of the labour movement.

Hence the general situation after the August strike was this: politically, the forces of democracy had united and formed a joint government combining all parties from the socialists to the 'populists', the party of Stresemann and of heavy industry; but, at the same time, these parties were rapidly losing their support among the masses. It was obvious that soon a government of the right would step in, with powerful mass support and complete backing by all the armed forces of the Reich. On the other hand, the labour movement, in spite of its hectic outbreaks, was in a state of disintegration, which did not, however, affect all its sections equally: the unions suffered most, the socialists heavily, while the communists grew rapidly.

Towards the end of July and during the first two weeks of August both the German central committee under Brandler and the Comintern had become aware of the impending crisis. They decided that the moment for revolution was approaching. All the symptoms, they thought, were there: the parties of democracy declining, the whole people, in all its classes, suffering and in a state of excitement and readiness to fight. So far the analysis was not wrong. Moscow and Brandler omitted only to ask themselves whether this semi-revolutionary movement drifted mainly towards communism. In fact the rapid growth of the militant right—of which the Nazis were the most extreme, but not the most numerous element—the failure of the communists to break their ranks, the obviously successful pressure of the right against the existing democratic government, ought to have shown them that the growth of the Communist Party was only a minor and incidental factor in a movement which, if carried on to its logical end, could only lead to the victory of Fascism. This was overlooked at the time, but is clearly apparent to-day; in the light of Hitler's final victory in 1933 the crisis of 1923, with its culmination in the unsuccessful Hitler *Putsch* at Munich, appears as a prelude to the final Nazi revolution. The year 1923 stands to 1933 in Germany much as the abortive Russian revolution of 1905, which culminated in the unsuccessful rising of the Bolsheviks in Moscow in December, stands to the victory of Lenin in 1917.

But why could not the communists profit from the deep psychological crisis of the masses as the right did? There are several answers: one is obviously that somebody within the communist ranks 'betrayed', and the investigation must go on to find out who was the traitor, a question which has obviously as many answers as there were leaders implied. Another answer, and, in our opinion, the correct one, is that the communists had no chance to break into the ranks of the right, which, held together by their caste-dislike of the workers, and by the feeling of strength deriving from their close connection with army and state, was indifferent to communist agitation. The author himself actively participated in the 'Schlageter campaign' of that year and was struck by the self-assured feeling of the young university students of various nationalist organizations, who did not doubt that they were infinitely stronger than the communists; which was only the truth. And the weaker side never exerts attraction over the stronger one.

In 1918–19 feelings such as caste-dislike of the workers and anti-semitism had receded far into the background and everybody was prepared to accept, if not the dictatorship, then at least a strong preponderance of the socialist parties. By 1920 the labour movement had been already so far discredited as to give a small nucleus of national revolutionaries the self-confidence necessary for trying the Kapp *Putsch*. The act proved to be premature, the conspirators were heavily defeated by the general strike, and once more the proletariat had a chance. Failing to form a labour government, it failed to take the opportunity. And, in the following three years, with their sufferings, the spinelessness of the democratic parties before French pressure, and the slow retreat of the socialist movement, the right had learned actually to despise both the socialist and communist parties and the workers. It was difficult to remedy this situation now, after the chance for the proletariat to take the lead in transforming society had been wasted between 1917 and 1920. The communists, least of all, were able to see and to believe that the tasks which the proletariat had failed to achieve—the task, namely, of organizing national recovery after the war on the basis of a planned economy and a strong centralized state—could be achieved by other classes and groups. Thus they stared, hypnotized, upon the minor reshufflings within the labour movement and failed to see that Fascism, for the first time in Germany, was approaching power.

A number of secondary facts and mistakes then turned the miscalculation into catastrophe. Only a very few weeks before the Cuno strike the communists, realizing the seriousness of the political crisis, began preparations for a rising. Before these preparations had taken shape the labour movement was again in decline, a fact which the communists failed to notice. To make things worse a method of which nobody would have dreamt a year or two before was employed: Brandler and a number of other leaders were called to Moscow, and there, with Russian slowness and inefficiency, the plans for the coming German revolution were laid down in endless debates. It was the beginning of October before Brandler came back to Germany. By that time the coalition government was increasingly threatened from the right, but had found stability in its efforts to stem the ebbing tide of the labour movement. The contest with the French in the Ruhr had been provisionally settled, martial law had been proclaimed, and the executive power entrusted to General von Seeckt, chief of the Reichswehr.

The party, in the meantime, had undergone a deep transformation. As soon as the order to prepare for a rising had reached the lower staffs of the party, early in September, the party had practically broken off contact with the masses and concentrated exclusively upon military preparations, which, in fact, were play-acting. There could not be serious military preparations, because there were no arms. Official data of the Comintern later on spoke of six hundred rifles which the party owned in Saxony, which was intended to be the centre of the rising; they would have been put out of action within a few hours. In order to spare the forces for the decisive moment the party itself occasionally discouraged sections of the workers from striking. But this was not the decisive factor. The authority of the Communist Party, considerable as it was among the workers in these months, was not strong enough to stem powerful spontaneous movements. If the number of strikers had declined rapidly since August, it was because the workers had already spent their strength. Moreover, the withdrawal of the communists from the labour movement contributed to the process of disintegration. A party which, during the decisive weeks of a supposed revolutionary crisis, could completely withdraw from the working class and transform itself into a big military conspiracy was, in fact, what Rosa Luxemburg had said in 1904 the Bolsheviks would be, not a movement of the proletariat itself, but one attempting to dictate to the workers. The features which Luxemburg had criticized in the early years of Bolshevism had grown to real incongruity among the imitators of Bolshevism in the West.

When Brandler came back he saw one thing clearly enough: there were no arms. He sensed that something was wrong, that the party was weak compared with its enemies. But he failed with the rest to see the reason. Accustomed to manœuvres with the left-wing socialists, he believed that these were the pivot of the situation; if they joined hands with the communists in the rising it would have a chance of success, not otherwise. In reality, the left-wing socialists were quite a minor force, with a regional following of perhaps half a million workers in Saxony and Thuringia. Even if not merely the left but all socialists had joined, this would not have diminished by one inch the certainty of defeat at a moment when the trade unions were breaking to pieces, the workers and unemployed turning their backs on politics in their millions, and all other classes rapidly uniting against the labour movement, which had no arms and was confronted with both a big popular movement of the right and the armed resistance of the Reichswehr. But while the Comintern as a whole mistook the approach of Fascism for the approach of communism, it was only natural that Brandler should ride his own particular horse, the left-wing socialists. The communists intended to enter the Saxon and Thuringian provincial governments; these had hitherto been formed by the left-wing socialists with communist support. Surely the government of the Reich would not tolerate an attempt of the communists to form strongholds in central Germany? But the left-wing socialists, it was supposed, would defend the governments of which they themselves were partners and out of this defence the rising in the Reich would develop. Later on, when this plan had been partly executed and led to disaster, all concerned in its elaboration tried to throw the responsibility upon the other man. In fact all the men primarily concerned, Sinovjev, Trotsky, Radek, Brandler, shared equally in the responsibility for the plan of insurrection. There were minor disagreements, but on the main point, that the rising should take place within a few weeks and start from defence of the Saxon government, which the communists were to join, there was no disagreement whatsoever. Stalin was not yet interested in international questions; he took occasional part in the decisions but without influencing them; a letter of his has survived, in which he warns the Comintern leaders not to precipitate the rising.

Brandler was the only one of the leaders concerned who felt that something was wrong. In order to bring the socialist left-wingers really into line with the communists he wanted a few weeks of political campaign before the communists should join the Saxon government. But there was no time; the right was visibly preparing to take power and the left had to act as quickly as possible. When Brandler learned that there were only six hundred rifles, he decided, under pressure from Moscow, to join the Saxon government at once, in the hope of getting control of the arms of the Saxon police. He had not time to achieve even that. After a few days, the Reichswehr entered Saxony. There was no spontaneous resistance. The workers accepted the fact without even so much as deep emotion; the entry of the communists into the Saxon government was far from catching their imaginations, and they were disheartened by repeated defeats, growing unemployment, and many years of underfeeding. On October 21st a conference of trade-unionists, co-operative men, and other representatives of working-class organizations met at Chemnitz, in order to discuss technical problems of the Saxon government; many of the participants were left-wing socialists. Before this conference the communists formulated the proposal for a general strike, to oppose the Reichswehr. Not one hand applauded among the socialists; they felt the helplessness of the workers against the arms of the Reichswehr, and the hopelessness of a general strike at the very moment of a sudden and catastrophic growth of unemployment. Even the general strike would have been a failure. Then Brandler saw, in the faces of the left-wing socialists, what he ought to have seen without them: he and his party were isolated. He withdrew the motion of a general strike. The Reichswehr entered Dresden and threw the ministers out of office. The Saxon episode and the dream of a proletarian revolution in Germany were at an end.

While the masses, during October, had fallen into despair and indifference, the Communist Party had been in feverish excitement, expecting every day to receive the order to rise. At the Chemnitz conference, the couriers were ready to bring the watchword to the provincial capitals. One courier started too early and a section of the Hamburg organization rose. About two hundred and fifty men who had obtained rifles by surprise attacks upon the police stations, they fought heroically for three days. In the two or three districts where the fighting went on part of the population gave the communists a certain amount of underhand support. But the big masses of the Hamburg proletariat remained completely indifferent. It was the final proof that the chance of a proletarian revolution had existed only in the imagination of the communists.

The party did not at once realize what had happened, that it had suffered a big setback. To so many illusions it now added one more: it refused to see the importance of the Saxon affair, treated it as an insignificant episode, and continued to keep the temperature of the party at boiling-point, in expectation of an impending rising. In the meantime the socialists were forced out of the Reich government and Brandler and his immediate friends started to talk of the 'Victory of Fascism over the November republic', thus showing only once more that they did not know what Fascism was. In fact, during these months Stresemann, by a mixture of energy and supreme skill, avoided the Fascist danger and integrally restored democracy. During this process the Communist Party was banned; there was no possibility of resistance to even this stroke, and the party was allowed to revive after a few months.

Then, during the winter of 1923-4, it dawned upon the party that it had been very definitely defeated; that all its illusions about the impending proletarian revolution had been cruelly destroyed. A violent psychological crisis overcame the party. The sudden economic crisis had given the employers a chance to purge the factories of party members, and most of them found themselves unemployed instead of in power, as they had expected. At the same time, the party as a whole felt that the era of revolution was at an end, that this time it was a decision for good. Thus they started furiously to seek after the traitor who had ruined the proletarian revolution for which, in reality, all through 1923 there had never been a chance. It was the last time that the membership of the party gave a free verdict, uninfluenced by bureaucratic pressure. In fact, the authority of the party machinery was simply swept away in the storm. 'Brandler has betrayed us', was the cry of the members; he had become the best-hated man in the German party. The left wing, under Maslow, Fischer, and Thaelmann, had never suggested a rising during all these months. But now it was the left which profited by the disaster. Brandler had not started the revolution because the left-wing socialists had failed him. Only an opportunist could deal with those opportunists. The communist left had always struggled against a broad application of the united-front tactics. Now the overwhelming majority of the members saw the left vindicated by the event. Brandler had tried to use the left-wing socialists for his aims, but he had only achieved dependence on them.

The crisis would have been bad anyway, but it was enormously exacerbated by the sudden eruption of fierce factional struggles in Russia. Lenin died in January 1924, while Sinovjev and Stalin on the one hand and Trotsky on the other crossed arms for the first time. The German events played a big part in the sudden outbreak of dissension in the Russian Communist Party. It was felt that the restoration of free trade and of economic liberty to the peasant—the N.E.P. in a word—was slowly strangling socialism in the country, that the rich peasant, the 'kulak', was becoming slowly stronger than the government. The whole old guard of Bolshevism had hoped keenly for help from the West; they had got defeat instead of relief, and now it became inevitable to decide for good whether the party should go with or against the peasant. Thus Russian Bolshevism was drawn into a deep crisis by the defeat of a revolution which had only existed in the imagination of its adherents.

The crisis both in the German and in the Russian communist parties was increased by the fact that this time the immediate responsibility of the executive committee of the Comintern—of Sinovjev and his staff—was undoubtedly implied. Defeats before 1921 could not be laid at the door of the Moscow leadership, which, at that time, was not in a position to lay down the law. The disaster of March 1921 had been met by the exclusion of those who had given warning—Levi and his group—but at the same time by the recalling of Kun and his henchmen, who were primarily responsible. In this the method later employed by the Comintern after defeats had already been foreshadowed: the supreme leadership at Moscow was kept out of responsibility, in a sort of assumed infallibility; and the executive organs had been subjected to severe chastisement, while those who had openly criticized the Comintern policy were excluded. But then Kun had really been more responsible than Sinovjev, and Levi had really broken the established rules of communist discipline. Again, the Bulgarian catastrophe of the summer of 1923 had happened against the orders and instructions of the Comintern; again, the authority of the Comintern was not involved. In the German defeat of

October 1923, however, it was. Every detail of the plan had been worked out in Moscow and every detail of its execution had been supervised directly by Moscow. If those who had brought about the defeat were traitors, then Sinovjev was the arch-traitor.

But this did not only involve his own personal position. His downfall at the time would have meant a catastrophe for the party leadership, which was fighting against Trotsky, with Sinovjev as front-rank leader. Moreover, the idea of an international centralized organization was jeopardized. Every Western group of leaders had proved unsatisfactory and opportunist and just now the defeat of Brandler was a new justification of the contempt the Russians had for the Western labour movement. If the Russian leadership itself was impaired, what barrier against opportunist deviations remained? Who could lay down the line of action and see to the purity of international communism, if one of the leading men of Russian Bolshevism itself had failed in a decisive moment? Thus the very fact of the patent responsibility of Sinovjev for the defeat forced the Russians towards the claiming of papal infallibility. It was established before Stalin so much as cared for Comintern affairs.

All responsibility was thrown on Brandler, the group which had worked under his leadership, and upon Radek, who had been representative of the Comintern in Germany during the decisive months. Minor points of view worked in the same direction. Sinovjev, as described in previous chapters, had always been sceptical and hesitant as to the value of the united-front tactics with the socialists, which Brandler and Radek had sponsored. Though he had himself contributed to their failure in the German case, he now returned to his old attitude. The formula he gave was that the 'united front from above', i.e. negotiations and agreements with the socialist leaders about common actions, was admissible only in exceptional cases. Normally, the communist parties must limit themselves to the application of the 'united front from below', with the simple socialist party members, without any contact with their leaders. But in fact the 'united front from below' was only a diplomatic way of saying that the communists must return to their old tactics of denouncing directly the socialist leaders and asking the socialist members to join the ranks of the communists.

Naturally the fight between Brandler and his opponents in the German party was embittered by this volte-face of Sinovjev. It was embittered, moreover, by the transference of Russian dissensions into the Comintern, which, on this occasion, took place for the first time. Radek was a partisan of Trotsky, in Russian matters. In German matters there existed a far from negligible disagreement between Radek and Trotsky. Radek was convinced that a rising had been out of the question in October. Trotsky was one of the few people in Russia who believed that it had been possible. Trotsky and his group have later posed as the specific standard-bearers of international revolution as against the Russian nationalism of Stalin. But during the 1923 debates Radek and Trotsky immediately buried their serious disagreements about Germany, in order to oppose a united front to Stalin and Sinovjev in Russian matters.

This union between Trotsky and Radek seemed very dangerous to Stalin and Sinovjev. Trotsky notoriously commanded the unqualified allegiance of the leaders of the French communists, Souvarine, Loriot, Rosmer, and Monatte. Radek was very closely allied with Brandler and his group in Germany. Would the two strongest parties of the Comintern pronounce themselves for the Russian opposition? While the representatives of the German and other communist parties stayed in Moscow, in the winter of 1923-4, and discussed the German defeat, both Russian factions carried on intensive lobbying among the international delegates. At first the German left, under Maslow and Ruth Fischer, had sympathized with Trotsky's case; but then they realized that Trotsky had little backing in Russia and that an unreserved pronouncement against Trotsky would win them the support of the Comintern in Germany. They made the pronouncement. A French group allied to them made a similar pronouncement, and Brandler was deposed in Germany, Souvarine and his group in France. Thus the Comintern had become an instrument in the Russian internal feuds; a fact more important even than the defeat in Germany which had brought this fact about.

CHAPTER XV

WAVERINGS

The fourth world-congress, at the end of 1922, had not been very important. But the fifth world-congress, in summer 1924, was an event of primary importance in the history of the Comintern, because it had to deal with the aftermath of the German disaster. It happened to be the last congress held at a regular interval from the preceding one; during the next year the outbreak of fierce fights within the old guard of Bolshevism made the statute of the Comintern, as so many other communist statutes, a scrap of paper.

The fifth world-congress marked a turn to the left. The habit of automatically extending the same policy to almost all communist parties of the world had made great strides since 1922, and it was regarded as a matter of course that the new, more extreme policy should be international. As usual, it was formulated in a general theory. The slogan of a 'workers' and peasants' government' was dropped, or rather explained away as a synonym of the proletarian dictatorship. The 'united front from above' was dropped too, and only the 'united front from below' was still permitted, which, again, was only a polite formula for breaking with the united-front tactics as a whole. The theoretical explanation given for it was the following: It would be all right for various working-class parties to co-operate; but, unfortunately, the socialists happened to be no mere working-class party. They were the 'third party of the bourgeoisie'. For the character of a party does not depend on the social structure of its membership, however proletarian it may be, but on the character of its policy, which where the socialists are concerned is invariably bourgeois.

The new tactics, like the preceding tactics of the united front, were carried to their logical end in Germany. There the new leadership, under Maslow and Ruth Fischer, made it their chief task to wipe out all 'opportunist' heresies. Every contact with socialists was regarded as such a heresy, and a severe régime of oppression of every opinion in favour of such a policy was introduced into the party. The first consequence of the tendency to the left was a tightening of party discipline and a restriction of liberty of thought. Up to then those who had accepted the basic principles of communism had been allowed considerable liberty in discussing tactics. That was so no longer now that 'Brandlerism', i.e. the defence of the old type of united-front tactics, was denounced as almost as bad as social-patriotism itself.

The most difficult problem facing the new tactics was that of work within the trade unions. If the socialists were bourgeois, then the trade unions, with their large socialist majority, were certainly bourgeois too. Such was the view of most of the rank and file of the German left-wing communists, and, in consequence, they urged the party to drop work within the unions and form revolutionary unions of their own. But what, after all, had been the use of the exclusion of the ultra-left in 1919, if, five years later, the same views were again voiced with the same strength? Relapses into the most extreme sectarianism seemed to be inherent in the structure of communist thinking. The drift away from the unions, in Germany, was intensified by their heavy collapse in the winter of 1923–4, when they lost no less than four million members. Even very moderate Russians, such as the leader of the Russian unions, Tomski, thought that the German unions were lost and that it was as well to proceed with the creation of independent communist unions. But it was then realized that the breakdown of the official unions had its limits; they still kept four million members and remained the greatest working-class organization in Germany. Lenin's teachings in *Left-wing Communism* were remembered, and finally, under pressure from Moscow, the German left agreed to remain within the official unions. This, however, was not carried out without difficulties. A number of communist trade-unionists broke away from the official policy of the party, creating miniature revolutionary unions of their own. The party saw the danger of losing every foothold within the official unions if this went on unchecked, so, after discussion had proved to be unavailing, a considerable number of these revolutionary unionists was excluded. After establishing a rigid régime against the partisans of Brandler, the new leaders of the German party had to establish an even more rigid régime against dissentients within the ranks of the left wing itself. Yet the end was not achieved. There were no trade-unionists within the party who were not either for secession or for Brandler. The new central committee refused to employ 'Brandlerites' in important trade-union work. Thus this work, in fact, broke down. The German T.U.C. held triennial congresses. At the congress of 1922 the communists had eighty-eight delegates; at the congress of 1925 they had four.

Together with the breaking away from the socialists and the unions went attempts to infuse new revolutionary spirit into the masses. The party attempted repeatedly, with little success, to disrupt important gatherings of the reactionaries. In the course of these attempts a semi-military organization, the 'Red Front', was created. It won considerable popularity among the masses, being almost the only thing which, among the elements of the new policy, was successful. Those who remained with the communists preferred fights with their fists to fights with the ordinary political means. It must be said that, in this sense, the Red Front has been a pace-maker for Hitler's storm troops, which many of the Red Front men joined before and after 1933. At the same time the political influence of the party declined irremediably. At the general elections of May 1924 the party had had three and three-quarter million votes; at the general elections of December of the same year it polled two and three-quarter million votes; at the presidential elections of April 1925—which, it is true, took place under somewhat peculiar conditions—it polled one and three-quarter million votes. Decline was rapid indeed. After the stabilization of the mark the bulk of the workers cared more than ever for their immediate interests and nothing else; the Communist Party, however, had never cared so little for them. In 1923, possibly, more revolutionism might have helped the communists; in 1924 and 1925 left extremism was definitely out of date.

The swing to the left, as explained repeatedly, originated in the German disaster of 1923, and it was in Germany that the decisions of the fifth world-congress had their biggest effects. But these decisions included other countries too. With three or four exceptions, the swing to the left was effected everywhere, and everywhere it had more or less the same consequences. It would be impracticable to describe the change in detail, country by country. Only the most important aspects of the new policy must be mentioned.

By far the most important result of the fifth world-congress was that change of régime which we have described in Germany. The conception of opportunism had been considerably extended and the scope of liberty of opinion within the party had been narrowed accordingly. The fight against opportunism, by reaction, had called forth a revival of the old views of the ultra-left, and the fight against these had again contributed to the stiffening of party discipline. Most important of all, the Russian factional struggles, which during these years went from bad to worse, mingled with the divergences of views in the West; this not only made the issues more important, it distorted them, because the issues in the West were fundamentally different from those in Russia and were nevertheless identified with them. For all these reasons the years 1924 and 1925 are years of continual crises and exclusions, and the years between 1926 and 1928 were to be even worse.

The first of these crises belongs rather to the old period than to the new. The Norwegian rift came to a head during the year 1923. Since Russia was on the way to a totalitarian dictatorship and, at the same time, increasingly dictated policy to the parties of the West, Tranmael had made up his mind to break with Moscow. This was the time of the united-front policy and of relative leniency. But the hesitations of Moscow merely gave Tranmael his chance, at the congress of the Norwegian party in February 1923, to gain control of all important jobs within the party; he won this decisive victory by temporizing in all matters of principle. Once he had a sure hold of the party machinery he turned to the offensive, frankly refusing to carry out any order from Moscow. It was only too true that Tranmael, as Radek said during these discussions, had entered the fold of Comintern with a false passport, that he had never been a communist. But the misunderstanding had been on both sides, and now, at the split in November 1923, Tranmael carried a big majority with him. What remained of the communists disappeared during the following years. At the general elections of 1924 the communists still won six seats; a few years later they held only one seat in parliament. Norway had been the last country where a party affiliated to Moscow controlled the majority of the workers. That was done with, now.

The crisis in Poland which immediately followed the Norwegian split was already of a very different character. Poland in 1923 had passed through events similar, in many respects, to those of Germany in the same year. Inflation had led to violent mass movements and to a rapid progress of the parties of the right. In the meantime, the communists had practised their united-front tactics and not prepared for a rising. Then, unexpectedly, in November 1923, a spontaneous rising broke out in Cracow and lasted a few days. The communists were entirely unable to interfere. Unfortunately, the leading group of the Polish communist parties, close disciples of Radek and Rosa Luxemburg, sided with Brandler in German and with Radek and Trotsky in Russian matters. They were denounced as opportunists; the old guard of Polish revolutionism, which had a tradition of decades, was overthrown within a few weeks, and a new group of young men put into power within the party.

In France things were less dramatic, but the effects of the crisis went even deeper. The leading group, with Souvarine at its head, sided decidedly with Trotsky. Souvarine, one of the most far-sighted men in the Comintern, as early as 1924 spoke of the end of the revolutionary era and the 'degeneration' of the Soviet régime in Russia. That was too much; he was excluded, the first man to be excluded on account of lack of submission to Stalin. But the case of Souvarine was not a personal matter. The sense of intellectual liberty is deeply ingrained, in France, as a result of the revolutionary traditions of 1789. Not only Souvarine spoke of the degeneration of the Soviet régime. Whether there was real degeneration or whether, under Stalin, all the intrinsic trends of the dictatorship came simply to the surface, is no matter of discussion here. Anyway, earlier than in any other country, as soon as serious dissensions started in Russia after the death of Lenin, large groups of communists in France felt that this was no longer the régime they had admired. Thus a considerable section of the French communists sided with Trotsky, mistaking him for a champion of liberty against Stalin. Souvarine was followed by Loriot, and both were joined by the group of revolutionary trade-unionists under Monatte and Rosmer. The workers who had joined the party after the exclusion of Frossard left it again. The continual flow of members and leaders out of the party left it no peace for many years, and it did not find its feet again before 1935. To this day French public opinion has proved to be more sensitive to the dictatorial, terrorist methods and to the general moral ambiance of the 'Soviet' régime; sensational defections for these reasons, such as the recent one of André Gide, have never failed to occur in France. Most of those who left did not stay long with Trotsky, but, having seen what the dictatorship really meant, turned away from communism completely.

The crisis within the German party, though complex enough had less far-reaching effects, because in the case of Brandler Russian problems were not directly implied. Brandler and his group, even after they had been excluded from the Comintern many years later, always sided with Stalin in Russian affairs and changed their mind only in 1937. Therefore Brandler, in 1924, when exclusions were still the exception, was spared. He was called to Moscow and forbidden any interference in German politics.

Much more dramatic were the consequences of the new policy in Sweden. There the man who had led the party with such conspicuous success during the war, Z. Hoeglund, still stood at the head. He had been long convinced that the revolutionary period was over, that a practical policy was necessary, and that the dictatorship of Moscow in the Western communist parties was intolerable. The split in Norway completed his disgust. He simply refused to accept the new policy laid down by the fifth congress, contending that it would reduce all communist parties to the size of the Communist Party of Austria. There remained nothing but to exclude him, which, given his prestige, meant a major split. About one-third of the members of the already small party resigned. But after Hoeglund's exclusion new leaders under Kilbom took over, and, following a very independent policy which was far from being left wing, brought the party new strength; it grew even beyond the strength it had boasted under Hoeglund.

There remained Czechoslovakia, where Šmeral could really not continue as the leading man under a left régime in the Comintern. But in Czechoslovakia more than anywhere else the elements for an alternative leadership were absent. A majority within the central committee for the newly founded left wing was obtained under strong pressure from Moscow, but after a few months a number of the new leaders had to resign, because their conduct of finances had not been un-objectionable. A new leadership, out of certain elements of the old leadership together with men from the new left, was formed, but the party was badly shattered.

These shiftings of personnel were by far the most important aspect of the turn to the left in most parties. The change of policy was nowhere so clearly outlined as in Germany. Relations with the socialists, it is true, were broken off everywhere. But in only a few countries did the left wing undertake real adventures with more or less consent from Moscow. It is true that at this time the attempt on the Sofia cathedral was executed and led to a fearful massacre of communists. The rising in Esthonia, too, deserves mention, because it was undoubtedly planned with the assent of Moscow. The Esthonian, as the other communist parties of the Baltic countries, was in gradual decline, owing both to persecution and to the increasing appeal of the socialists to the workers. In 1924 persecutions in Esthonia became particularly cruel, and a number of death sentences were carried out for reasons which would by no means be regarded as adequate in democratic countries. As in Bulgaria in September 1923, so now in Esthonia in December 1924 the communists rose, not because the country was ready for a revolutionary crisis, but simply in self-defence. Being no more than three hundred, the insurgents had a few initial successes in Reval, the capital, owing to the advantage of surprise. But after only a few hours everything was over. It was a classic example of a hopeless *Putsch*. The persecutions, naturally, were intensified after its failure; and the rising itself had provided a suitable occasion to institute a military dictatorship.

The failures in Bulgaria and in Esthonia were among the chief reasons which brought the policy of the fifth world-congress to an end.

Before describing the new turn to the right, however, it is important to emphasize that the fifth world-congress, though officially marking a turn to the left, had excepted from it several big countries. Even in more than one respect it had marked a definite turn to the right. During the year 1923 a number of chances for the Comintern had appeared on the horizon which it did not want to forgo. In the international trade-union movement, in the British trade unions, in China, in Yugoslavia, and in the United States, movements which seemed to provide a big opportunity for the tactics of the united front had arisen. In responding to these movements in 1923 the Comintern had been well within the scope of its general policy. But it maintained its friendly attitude even in 1924, after the change to the left.

Most immediately important among these changes was the one going on in the trade-union movement. There the English, together with certain leading men of the Amsterdam International, had more or less suddenly broken with the German majority socialists and attempted to create a unity movement with the Russian unions which we will describe in a later chapter. Suffice it to say here that the Russians eagerly entered into negotiations for international trade-union unity. At the same time they started co-operating with the Chinese national revolutionaries, with the party of Kuomintang. All of which called forth strong resistance from the German left, but they had to give in to the decision of the Russians.

The policy of the Comintern in Yugoslavia and in the United States was even more remarkable, because in both cases the Russians, through the farmer movement, sought contact with groups which were not even socialists. In Yugoslavia, after the defeat of the communists in 1920, the Croatian Peasant Party, a party of regional and Catholic opposition against the centralizing tendencies of Belgrade, had advanced much. Its leader, Stepan Radič, a clever demagogue, thought it useful to threaten Belgrade with social revolution. He went to Moscow and joined the Peasant International. Sinovjev was altogether enthusiastic, convinced that the Yugoslav revolution was near and that it would be a Red revolution. The contradictions in the minds of the Russian leaders were remarkable: on the one hand, they chased even right-wing communists, because they were opportunists and traitors; for they were convinced that only a pure communist party could make revolution. On the other hand, they trusted in leaders such as Radič, who had never pretended to be even a socialist. For the Russians believed in two contradictory conceptions at the same time and with equal vigour: in the constant approach of revolution, and in the constant betrayal by all and everybody. In the case of Radič, where they certainly ought to have believed in treason, they happened to believe in revolution. But Radič, having obtained his aim, went back to his country and there joined the reactionary government.

In the United States the communists hoped to put themselves at the head of the movement for a farmer-labour party initiated by the La Follettes. They hoped to play, within a coming farmer-labour party, the role of ginger group which the British I.L.P. had played in the Labour Party. But besides the sanguine over-estimate of the whole venture, they misinterpreted their own position. When the La Follette conference finally met, at St. Louis, it speedily removed the communists. The La Follette movement, at that time, was no great success anyway, but it would certainly have been a wholesale failure had it allowed the communists to put their stamp on it. The communists failed to see the difference between the role of a ginger group played by the I.L.P. in the history of the English labour movement, and the role they themselves wanted to play in the United States. Though the I.L.P. was more advanced in its views than the non-socialist trade-unionists of the end of the nineteenth century, it was not a revolutionary but a constitutional movement, and therefore acceptable to the trade unions. It was a very different matter with communism. But, in spite of the defeat at St. Louis, the communists in America for years continued to agitate for a farmer-labour party.

Thus the years 1924–5 in the history of the Comintern present a far from coherent picture. In many countries a violent change of communist policy towards left extremism had been effected precisely at the time when every revolutionary chance had vanished from the horizon. Essentially the turn to the left in Germany, France, Poland, Czechoslovakia, and a number of other countries was a measure of despair. The attempt to win, through the indirect methods of the united-front tactics, the majority of the workers for a communist revolution had failed conspicuously and led the communist parties into a very dubious position. Now, after the failure had become clear, the parties were driven to a policy which, if containing very few chances of success, at least seemed to guarantee communist purity. But in countries such as England, China, the United States, and Yugoslavia, where a more broad-minded policy seemed still to hold out serious chances of success, the Comintern did not stop at applying exactly those 'opportunist' policies of the united front which elsewhere it condemned ruthlessly.

But there was more than one weakness in this attitude. First of all, the Russians were never able to realize the hopelessness of their revolutionism in the West. When they saw the conspicuous failure of the German left wing to bring about those successes which had been denied to Brandler, they did not think that there was no chance for communism in the West; they sought the men who had 'betrayed' and naturally found them among the existing leaders; disgusted by defeat, they turned down the very left-wing leadership they had helped less than two years ago to put at the helm of the Continental parties. Distrust between Moscow and the German central committee of Maslow and Fischer was inveterate; the German left, since the introduction of the N.E.P. in Russia, had been very critical of the Soviet régime; since the third world-congress it had been very critical of the Comintern. Maslow and his group were altogether inclined to think that in the West communism must be, not less extreme, but more extreme than in Russia. He was inclined to think, moreover, that this Russia, where the rich peasant seemed to be more important every day, was not a good leader of the Western revolutionary movement. Part of these bad feelings had been smoothed out when, in 1924, the German left wing had for a time forsaken Trotsky and his cause in order to be entrusted with the leadership of the German party. But the Russians never felt quite safe with Maslow and his group, because he had won the party by mass support after the defeat of 1923, and over their heads. Now they started pushing the German party to the right. The party congress which met at Berlin in June 1925 was summoned to resume serious trade-union work, to entrust with this work a few Brandlerites, those being the only people who were able to do it, and to take a few members who inclined towards the right wing into the central committee.

The Berlin congress refused and the representative of the International was shouted down. There was open conflict between Moscow and the leaders of the strongest of its parties abroad. At once Maslow and his men came back to their old view: Russia, degenerating under the pressure of the kulak, the rich peasant, was pushing the Comintern to the right. And the emergence of this view made the issue one of life and death both for Moscow and for the left wing of the Comintern. It so happened that just at that moment Russia won new importance in the eyes of the more advanced elements of the Western labour movement. During 1923 and 1924 Russia had visibly recovered from the after-effects of war, civil war, and famine. In 1924 an official delegation of the British trade unions had gone to Russia and brought home an enthusiastic report. The official British delegation was followed by a stream of unofficial delegations from other countries. Broad strata which were absolutely non-revolutionary in their own countries started sympathizing with the Soviet Union. The same feeling was still stronger among those groups of the labour movement, principally among the left-wing socialists, which, while sympathizing with revolution, felt that for a long time to come there was little chance for it. In 1919, at the height of the revolutionary wave, even Bela Kun had refused to follow closely the Russian model; with the receding of the revolutionary fervour, admiration of and belief in the Soviet Union became the one remaining consolation of the advanced left. The Russians violently accused Maslow and the communist left wing generally of a treasonable disparagement of the achievements of the Soviet Union.

Summer 1925 was a moment of relative calm within Russia; the conflict between Stalin and Trotsky had come to rest, for the time, with the defeat of the latter. The conflict between Stalin and Sinovjev had not so far come into the open. Yet

Stalin, in autumn 1924, had taken a definite stand to the right by proclaiming his famous theory of 'socialism in one country'. It is impossible to contend, as Trotsky does, that it is an anti-Leninist theory. Lenin, in the last year of his activity, had come to believe that Russia had everything which was necessary for the construction of socialism, and if there was any innovation at all in Stalin's theory it was only that he expressed clearly what Lenin had expressed very cautiously. Stalin's policy implied increased concessions to the rich peasant. The practical meaning of the new slogan was that Russia, though an agricultural country, could build up socialism with the help of the rich peasant. As is well known, Stalin himself started to root out the kulak a few years later, during the first Five-Year Plan. One should never attribute too much importance to either Stalin's theories or Stalin's day-to-day policy. He is one of those men to whom it does not matter that he will do to-morrow the contrary of what he did to-day and who will calmly persecute all those who repeat to-morrow what he himself ordered them to say to-day. Anyway, at that time a conflict between the right wing, the friends of the rich peasant, with Stalin and Bukharin at their head, and the partisans of the undiluted dictatorship of the proletariat was inevitable.

Stalin very cleverly won allies abroad for the impending battle, declaring himself consistently for the right wing in all Comintern affairs. But with supreme skill he left the final step of destroying the left-wing leadership of the Continental communist parties to Sinovjev, who had a right to predominate in these matters, as president of the Comintern. The German central committee was ordered to Moscow and there the members of the committee were given the choice either of forsaking Maslow and Ruth Fischer, their leaders, or breaking with Moscow. With the revolutionary fervour in the West definitely at an end, no communist party could have lived without the financial support and without the prestige of Moscow behind it. The German central committee, the leading group of the German left, split, and those who had submitted, with Ernst Thaelmann at their head, formed the new central committee and at once started to fight fiercely their old masters Maslow and Fischer. An 'open letter' was sent to the members of the German party, asking for a thorough change of party policy, for serious work in the trade unions, for a more friendly approach to the socialist workers, a less rigid régime of heresy-hunting within the party, and, last but not least, absolute allegiance to Moscow. Sinovjev had carried the day over the German central committee. He had dethroned his only possible allies.

For it was the end of August when the open letter went to Germany, and at the same time the left-wing groups were broken up all over the Continent. And it was only four months later, in December 1925, that the storm broke in Russia, that Sinovjev openly declared against Stalin on the question of the rich peasant, and was defeated without difficulty. Had he stood firm for his friends in Germany, France, Czechoslovakia, and other countries during the summer he might have put himself at the head of the Comintern, whose president he was, against Stalin. But Stalin is at least a first-rate tactician in the intrigues of party machinery. He had discredited Sinovjev with the international left wing before attacking him in Russia.

The outbreak of dissensions among the old Bolshevik guard in Russia added a new fierceness to the tactical fight within the Comintern itself. During the second half of 1925 the left-wing leaders had been evicted everywhere from their leading positions, but there was no talk yet about exclusions. The scene changed, however, after the fight in Russia had come into the open. Now the left wing of the Comintern parties loudly accused the reaction, the peasant régime, the betrayal of the party leaders in Russia, as the reason for the turn to the right in Comintern affairs. And, by reaction Stalin was driven to the use of those fierce methods which he has applied since the days of these struggles. The régime, in Russia, was now practically totalitarian; and the Russian totalitarian régime reacted with the highest penalties it could inflict against all those communists abroad who attacked it. During these struggles the rule that every serious dissension within the Comintern must lead to exclusions was first put into effect.

It is useless to follow the involved history of these feuds. In Russia Sinovjev, after his initial defeat, joined hands with Trotsky, and the two during 1926 and 1927 fought a losing struggle for life and death against Stalin. The fiercer the fight in Russia the fiercer its reflex in the communist parties abroad.

Sinovjev was formally relieved from Comintern work at the end of 1926 and Bukharin took his place. The International left split under the menace of exclusion into many groups. Exclusions were not yet a matter of course. Convinced communists still regarded them as almost equivalent to a death sentence. Most of the oppositionists tried to evade the bitter necessity of leaving the party and attempted to find some compromise between their convictions and the official 'line'. But they found their hands tied by their profound conviction that it was treason to the cause not to speak up about what they thought was patent degeneration of Russia and of the Comintern. In the end all opposition groups were excluded. Shortly after Trotsky and Sinovjev were excluded in Russia, at the end of 1927, the purge had come to an end among the oppositionists abroad.

The losses inflicted upon the various parties by this purge were different, both in quantity and kind. Some movements, and especially the Communist Party of France, suffered a real disaster, losing most of the men who counted. Losses were great, though not catastrophic, in Germany, substantial in the United States, but small in Britain, in Sweden, in Czechoslovakia, and, at that time, in China. The moral loss was altogether enormous. Not that the rigid narrowness and the revolutionary romanticism of the left had much to commend it. But here those who stood by their convictions were thrown out and those who submitted took their place. It was a process to be repeated twice during the following years, until the Comintern was completely purged of all those who could possibly have an opinion of their own. The immediate effect was to defeat the good advice of the 'open letter' as to less rigid methods of ideological discipline. Ideological freedom was certainly a good thing had everybody been agreed about everything and ready to accept everything; but such was not as yet the state of things. And could you seriously suggest allowing people to call themselves communists and claim, at the same time, that the policy of the Comintern was wrong? In Berlin, especially, the left wing was strongly entrenched and could not have been ousted without violent measures. Once for all, during those fights, it was decided that it was not permissible for a communist to differ from the opinion of his superiors.

As to policy, it naturally tended to the right rather after than before the crisis. But a fact already visible in 1924 repeated itself now on a larger scale. Then, already, the fierceness of the factional fight and the scale of the reshuffling of the leadership in various parties far exceeded the real change of politics. Now this was even more so. Naturally, the united-front policy in Britain, the United States, and China could now be followed with still less hesitation. (The alliance with the Croat peasants in Yugoslavia had already been a complete failure.) In Poland too, where the right wing, dating from the times of Rosa Luxemburg, had always been strong, a more or less complete return to the old united-front tactics was effected. The Swedish party, which had never been left-wing, found it easier now to work according to the convictions of its leaders. And in Italy a considerable change was effected, too late, however, to influence events. After endless negotiations, and against strong resistance from the left extremists under Bordiga, the repentant left-wing socialists under Serrati had finally been admitted into the fold of the Comintern, a broken handful. Under the increasing pressure of Fascism the party, nevertheless, melted away. Bordiga, who had taken sides for the Russian opposition with his usual violence, was excluded, and his followers with him. And, with the help of the repentent socialists, a new central committee was formed which, for the first time, accepted the united-front tactics in earnest. When in 1927 the socialist trade unions were officially dissolved the communists made a serious attempt to reconstitute them underground; the attempt was however, defeated, by the Fascists.

Little was changed in Germany, France, or Czechoslovakia. Here the new leadership was simply a fraction of the old one, who had broken with the friends of the Russian opposition, but not broken with their tactical views. Thaelmann, for instance, was certainly convinced that Maslow was a traitor because he accused the Soviet Union of degeneracy. But, at the same time, he believed that Brandler was a traitor because he had co-operated with the left-wing socialists. The Russian conditions increased this hesitancy. Stalin, while fighting against Trotsky and Sinovjev, pushed the Comintern to the right, but he did not want it to go too far. He was preparing his own fight with the Russian right, with Bukharin and Rykow, after clearing his account with the left. Had the communist parties abroad been in the hands of convinced partisans of the moderate wing it would have been a serious danger for Stalin. Thus the communists abroad were encouraged in their waverings, and a double-faced policy ensued. A few of the less outspoken elements of the right wing were introduced into the various central committees, where their influence was carefully balanced against that of the old left-wingers. Work in the trade unions was resumed, but within narrow limits; co-operation with the socialists was effected occasionally. The most important example was that of a common campaign in Germany for the expropriation of the former monarchs of the twenty-two German states; the referendum on the matter was narrowly defeated, but the poll in favour of it had been so high as to represent a big success of the united labour movement. But then this policy was dropped. Continual hesitations, continual changes of policy led naturally to growing distrust between those who, coming from the right wing, wanted to revert to the old united-front tactics and those who, coming from the left wing, did not want to do so at all. The swing to the right in 1925 was as little consistent in itself as the swing to the left had been in 1924. In fact, nobody in Moscow saw the way to revolution.

In the meantime the new policy brought as many catastrophes as the old one. Almost at the same time disaster came to a head in Poland and in Britain. Poland since the war had gone from one crisis to another. The year 1926 was particularly critical and among general disintegration the star of Marshall Josef Pilsudski, the leader of the Polish legions during the war, rose high. Pilsudski had started as a socialist, had fought as a terrorist against Tsarism before the war, and was still violently opposed by the parties of the right. In May 1926 Pilsudski rose against the conservative government and carried the army with him. After a few hours of fighting in the streets of Warsaw he was master of Poland. The communists had regarded the whole affair as a fight of the 'left' against the 'right', and, applying carefully the tactics of the united front, had fought in Pilsudski's ranks. They expected it to be the beginning of revolution. A revolutionary movement there was indeed, as in Germany in 1923; but as in Germany it happened to be not a proletarian, but a semi-Fascist revolution. This was clear almost immediately, when Pilsudski threw the very communists who had fought for him into jail, and started to abolish democracy.

The communists had helped a semi-Fascist dictatorship into the saddle! It was only natural that a fierce factional fight broke out within the party. The leaders who had applied the united-front tactics defended what they had done, which after all was an impossible position to take. The left attacked them because they had applied these tactics, sticking to their dogmatic conception of Bolshevik purity. But neither side understood that Fascism, as in Italy and later in Germany, did not come as a force of the right, of conservatism, but as a revolutionary movement, though of a very peculiar kind. Thus the factional fight within the Polish party went on, aimlessly, exclusively fed by memories of the past; for there was no doubt that in future Pilsudski, now dictator of his country, must be fought.

But during these very days of May 1926 the British branch of communism had equally collapsed, and this was of far greater importance.

CHAPTER XVI

GENERAL STRIKE IN BRITAIN

Originally the English Communist Party had found it difficult to establish itself. On the one hand its ranks were filled, at the beginning, with all sorts of pacifists, active but unrevolutionary trade-unionists, and people who did not know very well themselves why they were communists. A considerable number of left-wing politicians, such as Mellor, George Lansbury, Ellen Wilkinson, Philips Price, and trade-unionists such as David Williams, leader of the transport workers, A. J. Cook, leader of the miners, Purcell, sometime chairman of the T.U.C., were at one time communists, only to leave the party on different occasions. On the other hand the sectarian, anti-trade-unionist, anti-parliamentarian tendencies were very strong in the beginning. Both tendencies were, however, overcome surprisingly soon. The non-revolutionary elements left as soon as the revolutionary meaning of communism became clearly apparent; and the common sense of the race, together with the pressure of Lenin and the Comintern, soon made short shrift of left extremism. It is remarkable that the English Communist Party, in contrast with almost every other communist party of the world, never relapsed into the 'infantile disease' of left-wing communism after it had once overcome it. (What looked like a relapse into left extremism between 1929 and 1934 was forced upon the majority of the leaders against their will, from Moscow.) Two or three years after its foundation the English Communist Party, which had largely been formed out of syndicalists who despised the existing unions, became outstanding within the Comintern for its relative competence and seriousness in industrial matters.

As soon as the party had coalesced into a somewhat coherent body the peculiarities of the policy of the British labour movement made themselves felt very strongly. The number of workers ready to pledge themselves to violent revolution was very small. In England proper the party never won any direct mass support; what masses it controlled came from Wales and Scotland; and even there the influence of the communists was limited to narrowly confined regions. On the other hand, there was no such abyss between the communist workers and the ordinary members of the Labour Party as existed between communists and socialists on the Continent, and between communists and the average workers in the United States. The Labour Party refused to admit the Communist Party. But for many years individual communists remained members of the Labour Party through their unions, and, occasionally, were nominated as parliamentary candidates. Still stronger was communist influence within the trade unions. Not that any single major union has ever been under communist leadership or domination! But there was a widespread feeling, in the years following the war, that the unions ought to follow a more militant policy, and many of those who rejected the communist ideas about civil war and dictatorship welcomed the communists as useful allies in the elaboration of a new policy for the unions.

The hand of the communists was considerably strengthened by the disaster of 'Black Friday' in spring 1921. The mine-owners had attempted to cut the miners' wages. The miners had relied upon the 'triple alliance' of their own union with the railwaymen and the transport workers. At the last moment their allies had failed them, David Williams, the communist leader of the transport workers, being among those chiefly responsible. Williams was immediately excluded from the party, but that did not affect the result of the fight. Frank Hodges, chairman of the miners' union, strongly advised his men to accept defeat, and for the moment there was no choice left but to submit. The outcry for a more militant leadership was general.

Those who were asking for more aggressive tactics did not always realize what this meant. It is certain that the standard of living of the workers in the unsheltered industries tended to decline after the war. It had gradually but continually risen during the preceding period and the shock produced by the sudden change of the trend was naturally very strong. This change of the trend was inevitable, because Britain had become inferior to a number of foreign competitors in certain trades; in the case of mining the decay was largely due to the supplanting of coal by oil. In fact, the miner's wages could have been upheld only if wages had been made independent of the state of the industry, independent of good and bad business; in other words, only a complete abolition of capitalism could bring about such a result, and that implied revolution, which does not mean that even revolution would in fact have led to the keeping of the existing standard of living. But the militant movement within the trade unions refused to see those wider issues. As it was, trade-union militancy in a period of decay of the unsheltered industries was a dangerous playing with fire.

Neither the communists nor the militant trade-unionists realized whither they were drifting. For a couple of years they seemed to have smooth going. First, the communists launched the 'minority movement' within the unions. Though not a single one of the big unions adhered, and though, in consequence, its strength as an organization was negligible, the 'minority movement' and its continual agitation for a new, militant leadership and for greater centralization and unity of action of the unions, proved to be a considerable factor in determining union policy. The communists scored a big success when, under the pressure of the left wing, Hodges was not re-elected as leader of the miners and A. J. Cook was chosen instead. Cook himself was perhaps rather inferior in knowledge and political shrewdness to the average trade-union leader, but he was a highly emotional agitator of the revivalist type, whose oratory strongly appealed to the miners, who felt the basis of their existence shifting under their feet. And behind Cook stood his old personal friend, Arthur Horner, a communist and chairman of the South Wales district of the miners' union. Horner undoubtedly knew more than Cook and was able to take the lead where Cook was lacking. Then, in 1924, when the agreement of 1921 expired, the question of the miners' wages came up again, and this time the triple alliance, which had collapsed in 1921, stood the test. On 'Red Friday' the owners had to give in to the pressure of the triple alliance, the government being unwilling to face a general strike. It was to some purpose that labour had just secured a parliamentary position strong enough to put it in power for a time. That too was a symptom of the rising of the tide, originating in the menace to the standard of living of broad strata of the workers; though the Labour Party at that time stood considerably to the right of the more important unions and its leaders opposed the drift to the left as best they could. 'Red Friday' enormously enhanced the pressure of the militant elements within the unions, and their prestige became stronger still when, in 1925, after the fall of the labour government, the agreement for the mines was prolonged for nine more months under pressure from the conservative government. Everything seemed possible if the workers only willed it.

Thus, to the surprise of the whole world, the English trade unions, with their reputation of being the most conservative labour organization in the world barring only the American unions, suddenly became the extreme left wing of the non-communist labour movement. And it so happened that during the year 1923, which was decisive for the turnover of the unions to the left, this trend received support from abroad. The Amsterdam International of trade unions at its foundation in 1920 had been a very conservative body, but, with defeat in Germany, in Italy, and in many other countries some of the leaders had grown very suspicious as to the validity of reformist tactics. Chief among the critics was Edo Fimmen, a Dutchman and leader of the International of transport workers, who was then president of the Amsterdam International. In 1923, Fimmen declared publicly against reformism, nationalism, co-operation with the bourgeoisie, and for an attempt to conciliate the Amsterdam International and the Russian labour movement. It is not necessary for our purpose to follow in detail the criss-cross play which ensued within the Amsterdam International. Fimmen had to resign his chairmanship at Amsterdam, but kept his position with the International of transport workers. Other international trade-union organizations followed his lead. The unions of certain countries such as Austria were dissatisfied with the altogether too pacific and conservative spirit of Amsterdam. Out of all these elements grew a fairly strong movement for reconciliation with the Russians, for 'international trade-union unity'.

In May 1924 the congress of the Amsterdam International met at Vienna, and there, to the surprise of all concerned, the change of mind of the English unions became apparent. When the motion for reconciliation with the Russians came up the German delegation tried to counter it by a long tale about communist attempts to split the Continental labour movement. It was a dramatic moment when from the benches of the British delegation came shouts of 'What have you done with Liebknecht and Rosa Luxemburg?' To the German attacks against the Russian movement the leading British trade-unionists had replied with the charge of the communists that in 1919 Noske and his men had known of and agreed to the assassination of the two main leaders of German communism. The motion for reconciliation was turned down at the Vienna congress. But the next result was that the British T.U.C. took independent action and approached the Russians directly.

It was a favourable moment. While the English had moved considerably to the left, things in Russia were going heavily to the right, and the two movements seemed to approach a point where they could easily agree. Sinovjev, to be true, was still in office, but behind his back the alliance between Stalin and Bukharin, the trend to the right, which was to mark the next few years, was developing. And one of the strongest supporters of this course was Tomski, the leader of the Russian unions. Tomski did not care much for revolution. He thought, as Bukharin and Stalin did, that communism was dangerously isolated and that an alliance with so strong a labour force as the English unions would be useful. Moreover, such an alliance could only strengthen the drift to the left, which was already strong at that time within the English unions. It was difficult to say how far this drift would carry the movement. Right through to revolution? The Russians, to whom the political climate of England had always been a book with seven seals, did think it would. But even if it did not, such an alliance would mean a great opportunity for the strengthening of the English Communist Party on the one hand and a big chance for Russian foreign policy on the other. Were not the unions a decisive factor in British policy? The Russians were unable to see that the policy they followed must drive the unions into a dangerous conflict with the state, which they had no chance to win; and that in consequence their policy would lead, not to an improvement, but to a very considerable deterioration of Anglo-Russian relations. As always, hopes in Moscow were sanguine. Visibly, they thought, the British labour movement, which up to then had been in the rear, was coming to the forefront of the revolutionary struggle. If all hopes had been deceived in Germany, England now seemed to offer a greater, a more splendid hope.

After the Vienna congress the delegation of the British T.U.C. went to Russia and returned with a favourable report. The visit led to the formation of an Anglo-Russian committee for trade-union unity. The immediate aim of the joint committee of the Russian and English trade unions was to bring about international trade-union unity against the resistance of the right wing of the Amsterdam International, which was led by the German unions. But the remaining attributions of the committee were ill defined. It was interpreted as a big move to the left within the English unions. But the Amsterdam International, in spite of its prestige, had no means to determine the policy of the national unions which were affiliated to it; and the English, in spite of their sympathy for Russia, were determined from the very outset not to allow the Russians to interfere in their own affairs.

All the leading men in Russia agreed about the importance of the new step. Sinovjev, at the fifth world-congress, ranged himself beside Bukharin and Tomski in defence of the new policy. Hasty as ever, he told the congress that revolution in Britain might come just as well 'through the door of the unions as through the door of the Communist Party'. If this was true, then it was difficult to see why the labour movement had been split all over the world, because socialists could only betray. Sinovjev's words actually implied an abandonment of the mainstays of the communist faith. But there was no trace in Russia of opposition to these views. Trotsky, who in later years was so emphatically opposed to the policy of the Anglo-Russian committee, did not say a word against it at the time of its foundation. Only Losovski, the chairman of the Red trade-union International, was unhappy. If international trade-union unity became a reality then his own International was done with. He did his best to obstruct the plan; and Sinovjev, whose policy was always two-faced, defended together with Losovski the independence of the dissident communist unions in France and Czechoslovakia, while emphatically preaching international unity and collaboration with the English. On the other hand, the continued existence of dissident communist trade-union centres gave a strong case to the reformist opponents of international unity on the Continent. The divergence of views evolved into a real subterranean fight between Tomski and the Russian unions on the one hand and Losovski and the Red trade-union International on the other. When, at the end of 1925, open fight broke out between Stalin and Sinovjev, the latter espoused Losovski's cause and started opposing the unity slogan. But he did so in vain; Losovski did not dare to support the Trotsky-Sinovjev opposition and remained faithful to the leading group of the party.

All seemed to go well abroad, however, until the militant policy of the British unions reached its climax in the general strike. The English Communist Party grew slowly in numbers; the minority movement grew considerably in influence; the T.U.C., in 1925 and 1926, was definitely under the sway of the left wing; and, within the Amsterdam International the English fought for international unity, vainly but valiantly, at the head of the left wing.

Then came the general strike and within a fortnight the results of three years' work were swept away. It is not within the scope of this study to discuss in detail the history of this strike; the main fact, in our context, is that from the very moment of the outbreak the communists lost all influence over events. Their own forces were much too small to take the lead and the T.U.C. no longer listened to their advice. It had all been very well as long as militancy meant spreading slogans and occasionally throwing the menace of a general strike into the balance of important negotiations. But the real general strike was another thing. The unions felt the majority of the nation roused against themselves, not because it had made up its mind against the claims of the miners, but because the T.U.C. was suspect of having allied itself with the forces of international revolution. The T.U.C. did everything in its power to allay the suspicion and one of the most outstanding leaders of the left wing, George Hicks, moved and carried the rejection of the money the Russians had offered to support the strike. There was probably not a single leader not thoroughly frightened by the dilemma which had suddenly become a reality: to start revolution or to accept defeat. The frivolousness of the idea of going to the length of semi-revolutionary measures in the defence of wages became suddenly apparent. For a general strike is essentially a semi-revolutionary measure and therefore only appropriate in a big political crisis, such as had arisen in Germany at the moment of the attempt of the army to overthrow the constitution in 1920. Revolution was out of the question; therefore defeat was the only remaining alternative. After a fortnight the leaders decided to drop the aimless struggle. The miners carried on for months, until they were thoroughly beaten, Cook discredited as a leader, and the strongest position of the left wing completely shattered.

The communists witnessed a considerable increase of membership in the months following the general strike; especially, and almost exclusively, in the mining areas, where the miners flocked to the party as long as the struggle continued. But this was a small consolation in the face of the complete change of mind of the labour movement as a whole. Immediately after the strike the right wing, represented by Citrine, Thomas, and their friends, and helped by H. Smith, the new leader of the miners, got the upper hand. The rules barring the communists from the Labour Party were made more rigid; measures were soon to be taken within the unions against the minority movement. And finally, even the communist membership within the mining areas collapsed. The party had won about six thousand miners in these months, but they were naturally carried away by the general mood of depression after the defeat. Faced with a certain amount of pressure from the mine-owners, the miners left the Communist Party in thousands a few months after they had joined it; it had nothing to offer them.

The dream of a social revolution in England was over. The sudden break in the rise in wages and their downward trend after the war had produced a major crisis. This crisis was of a character wholly new to the English working-men, and in fighting it they applied means which Continental movements, more experienced in that sort of thing, would have shrunk from using. But with all its effervescence, the movement had stopped long before it had so much as approached revolution. It was proved once more that, whatever happens, the workers of modern industrial countries are never revolutionary of their own accord, and the English experience had given particular emphasis to one of the chief reasons: in such an attempt the workers would be isolated, a helpless minority against the nation as a whole. Britain, it is true, is a country where the majority of the population consists of wage-earners. But that does not imply that they all feel, or are ever likely to feel, themselves 'proletarians'. A movement such as the general strike met the definite disapproval of the majority of the community, a majority which had every means of coercion, and this settled the matter, as far as England was concerned. The British labour movement, as in other countries, never recovered from the blow it had received in its semi-revolutionary attempt.

From the Moscow point of view, however, now, if ever, was the moment to speak of socialist betrayal. But nothing of the kind happened. The struggle between Stalin and the left was at its height. Admission of failure would have meant the admission that the Russians had made an alliance with opportunists abroad; at that time, while the factional struggle was raging, this was still a serious charge. Thus, paradoxically, the Russians for a long time did everything in their power to diminish the importance of the defeat of the British T.U.C. in the eyes of the Russians and of the communists abroad. This put the new right-wing leadership of the English unions in a difficult position. They wanted to break with the Russians as quickly as possible, but the Russians did not give them a chance. For more than a year the English delegates, with Citrine at their head, displayed open contempt of the Anglo-Russian committee, dropping *de facto* the struggle for the admission of the Russians to the Amsterdam International and turning down every suggestion of the Russians. But it was not until June 1927, when diplomatic relations between Russia and Britain were broken off in connection with Chinese affairs, and the British T.U.C. refused to oppose the policy of the Conservative government, that the Anglo-Russian committee finally came to an end. It was only a few months later, after the final defeat of Trotsky and Sinovjev, that the effects of the failure of the Comintern in the attempt to co-operate with the English unions made themselves felt, in a new turn of Comintern policy, this time towards the left. But in this turn-over Chinese affairs were more important than previous defeats in England. We must now leave, for a time, our account of European communism, and turn our eyes to the East.

CHAPTER XVII

THE COMINTERN
AND THE COLONIAL PEOPLES

Of all the many attempts of the Comintern to influence events outside Europe and the United States only its interference in the Chinese revolution has won historical importance. But the role of Russia and the Comintern in that revolution is unintelligible, if considered as an isolated fact. It is only the most important application of general ideas which have been equally applied by the Comintern in other colonial and semicolonial countries, though with less important effects. We must therefore give an outline of the colonial policy of the Comintern.

The origins of that policy date back to pre-war times. Lenin was deeply impressed by the Persian revolution of 1908 and the first Chinese revolution—the overthrow of the Manchu dynasty and the creation of the Chinese republic—in 1911. The socialist parties of the West paid scant attention to these movements, which, as they rightly contended, had little in common with the European labour movement. For Lenin, such an attitude was one of the clearest symptoms of opportunism. Labour or not, the East, from Turkey to Japan, was entering on a revolutionary era. This was bound to have a revolutionizing effect upon the West, such as had—according to Lenin—the Russian revolution of 1905; the revolution in Russia had not been proletarian either.

Then came the war, an 'imperialistic' war in Lenin's view, fought largely for the redistribution of colonial empires. This gave the imminence of colonial revolutions new importance. The bourgeoisie of the leading industrial nations was faced, according to Lenin, by two enemies: its own proletariat at home and the colonial masses which strove for liberation from the yoke of imperialism. The two were natural allies. Only those sections of the working classes of the West which directly or indirectly profited from imperialistic exploitation of the colonies could refuse to accept such an alliance. Only the social-patriots and the representatives of the workers' aristocracy could despise the revolutionary movements of the colonies. Here Lenin's colonial policy was closely knit with his views on the reasons for the decay of pre-war socialism. It was closely linked, on the other hand, with his views on the policy socialists ought to follow towards movements of national liberation. Though the defence of nationalism was hardly compatible with socialist internationalism, Lenin, pushing aside all objections of principle, had from the earliest days of his career insisted upon the right of every nation to acquire complete political independence if it so desired. He had stood for the right of the national minorities in Russia to secede from the Russian empire. Great realist as he was, he had very soon acknowledged the supreme importance of nationalism in our time. It was only logical to apply the right to independence to colonial peoples just as much as to those of the West.

In practice, the application of this general view in the complex concrete national problems of our modern world proved to be very difficult, and it was almost impossible to evolve a consistent policy. Generally speaking, the Comintern has in most cases supported national minorities against national majorities, though by various means. In Ireland, to take one instance, communism almost merged with the most advanced sections of Irish nationalism, though it never won real influence in that country. In Czechoslovakia, on the other hand, the communists never supported the claims of the extreme wing of the German nationalists for separation from Czechoslovakia and reunion with the Reich. Naturally, things became even more difficult where the Soviet Union was directly concerned. Russia always supported, through the medium of the Comintern, the claims of those national minorities who wanted to join the Soviet Union, such as the White Russians and Ukrainians in Poland. On the other hand, Russia itself, as a 'Soviet' state, just as under Tsarism ruthlessly conquered and suppressed those nations which wanted to secede from Moscow. The conquest of Baku without so much as an attempt to ascertain the will of the population, the ruthless suppression of Georgia in and after 1921, the conquest of Outer Mongolia, bear witness to the limitations of the principle of self-determination, in the interpretation given it by Soviet Russia, as soon as Russian interests are concerned.

But the question of national minorities was not the essential problem of the Comintern's colonial policy. The struggle of those big nations who were or seemed to be natural adversaries of imperialism was much more important. The chief interest of the Comintern, as far as national problems were concerned, was concentrated upon such countries as China, India, Persia, Turkey, Egypt, Syria, Korea. These countries seemed to provide a suitable ground for a big attack upon imperialism.

Let us just mention, shortly, a border case between national minorities and anti-imperialistic nations: the black race, which, in most parts of Africa and some parts of America is a majority, without, however, having a state of their own. The Comintern has made considerable efforts to organize the Negro, but with much less success than is generally supposed. There was an enormous amount of talk about work among the Negroes in the Communist Party of the United States, but in fact, in 1928, at the sixth world-congress of the Comintern, not more than fifty (!) Negroes were reported as having joined the Communist Party of that country. Things did not improve when the communists tried to make up by extremism what they lacked in efficiency. In 1929–30 the American communists launched the slogan of an independent Negro republic in the south of the United States—which might or might not drive out the whites—but without any success. The number of Negro members of the party has probably somewhat increased since, but communist influence among the American Negroes is still negligible. Here, as everywhere, the basic traditional loyalties of the working population proved to be stronger than communist slogans. Co-operation with the black people was as unacceptable to the average American worker as it was unacceptable to the Negro to join an organization led by whites and not specifically devised for the defence of his own interests. These may be prejudices; but they are certainly very strong historical forces.

The situation was very similar in South Africa. Here, too,

the protocol of the sixth world-congress—the latest document containing reliable information about the subject—states with regret that hardly any black people are members of the tiny Communist Party of South Africa. The big riots in the mines of the Rand in the first years after the war partly originated among the whites, and here there was probably a certain though not a very considerable amount of communist influence. But as far as risings of the black people were concerned, it is evident from the many reproaches directed from Moscow at the South African communists that the latter had no real influence on events. The black people might talk vaguely of communism, a communism of their own making, only slightly connected with the teachings of white extremists; practical influence of the Communist Party on the Negro there was none.

And this statement does not apply only to South Africa, or, for that matter, only to the black race. Generally speaking, in the colonial countries big communist efforts brought about very little, with the one exception of China. Where communism became an element of native risings, it was mostly a communism which had little practical connection with Moscow. This was notably the case in the country where the communist movement, next to China, won most importance, in the Dutch East Indies. Java, after the war, had witnessed the simultaneous rising of Javanese nationalism and of the labour movement. The latter was inspired by the example given by the few white workers of the country. But while the white unions in Java were naturally moderate, the coloured unions, notably the union of railwaymen, which arose after the war, tended to be more radical and called themselves communist. The new nationalism which arose about the same time was essentially part of the political revival of Mohammedanism. It received a peculiar stimulus from the struggle against the immigrant Chinese merchants, who had monopolized most of the good jobs. At one time the union of the Javanese nationalist Mohammedans, the Sarekat Islam, counted more than a million members. But soon a split arose. The Sarekat Islam was a movement mainly intended to safeguard the interests of the smaller Javanese merchants. When the question of a revolutionary fight in alliance with the workers and the peasants arose the movement split and only a minority went to the left. In the meantime a communist party had been organized, with the very active participation of Sneevliet, one of the leaders of the Dutch communists at that time; he has long since been excluded. There was very little contact with Moscow, however, and after the expulsion of Sneevliet from Java the movement, having lost all links with European thought and European tactical experience, was communist only in the vaguest sense of the word. The split in Sarekat Islam gave the government a chance. While trying to conciliate the moderate wing a ruthless persecution of the radicals began. As in Bulgaria in September 1923, so in Java in spring 1926, the communists rose arms in hand, not because the tide of the revolutionary movement was rising, but, on the contrary, because, in isolation and under persecution the party was menaced with destruction. Attempts at Batavia were defeated within a few hours. In the east of the island, in the province of Soerabaja, unrest and occasional risings continued for a few weeks, mainly on account of the lack of roads, which delayed military action. Soon, all was over. Communism never again became a force in Java; its defeat went so far that in 1930, when the sailors of the *Seven Provincien*, a battleship of the Java navy, mutinied because their pay had been reduced, the communists were not able to influence the event in any way.

But communist work in British India was still more ineffectual. There, the communists had a very capable leader in the person of Manabendra Nath Roy, a descendant of a Brahminic family, imbued with the finest tradition of both Hindu and European culture, a man who had made an independent study of Marxism, had a wide outlook, and was regarded by Lenin as the best representative of colonial revolutionism. (He was excluded in 1929 as a right-winger.) But Roy achieved nothing. It took the Comintern nearly ten years to form a communist party in British India, and then it was a party with hardly any following. As in most oriental and tropical countries, communism in British India is a vague ferment somehow influencing the thought of most politicians of advanced opinions. But real influence of the Comintern, in the sense in which it exists in the Western labour movement and in China, there is none. For in India more than anywhere else communist ideology, however much adapted to the traditions of the soil, clashed with all the loyalties of religion, caste, and nation which are so strong in the life of that big country.

During the first years of its existence the chief attention of the Comintern, as far as the colonial problem was concerned, was not directed towards any of the countries just mentioned. It was directed towards the near and middle East, towards Turkey, Persia, and the Arabic-speaking countries. And here, where interests were strongest, failure was more complete than anywhere else.

In order fully to understand the problems which faced the Comintern one must go back to its origins. The Soviet Union had quite a number of Mohammedan people within its borders, and in spite of the resistance of the Mohammedan lords and clergy was quite successful in winning some of them for the régime. It is true that it is very difficult to judge the final results of Soviet policy among these peoples. Turkistan, where most of them live, has been closed to foreigners as rigidly as Formosa has been closed to foreigners by the Japanese, and much points to the conclusion that, in Russian Turkistan, there is continual unrest. There is no doubt, however, that in certain regions lying close to both Turkey and Persia, and notably in Daghestan, the Soviet régime, after much and cruel fighting, *did* win the allegiance of the population, and that naturally provided a suitable basis for work beyond the border.

Upon this work the Soviet government laid great store from the very beginning. Till as late as 1924 the Soviets regarded Britain and France, which had organized intervention during the civil war and might start organizing new attacks at any moment, as their chief enemies. And, besides Germany, the Moslem peoples of the Near East seemed to be the only possible allies in a fight with the great powers of the West. Persia, during the war, had been shaken by quite a considerable anti-English movement. Only a few months after the armistice Kemal started organizing armed resistance in Anatolia against the intention of the Allied Powers to prepare for Turkey the lot of Persia, to transform it into a *de facto* colony. Very soon, too, profound antagonisms between both Britain and France on the one hand and the Arab national movement in Palestine, Syria, and Arabia proper on the other became apparent; in Egypt these antagonisms had existed before the war. Finally, Afghanistan was about to enter a period of convulsion and an anti-British party was visibly making headway in Kabul.

The Soviets and the Comintern did not hesitate to make use of these movements for their own purposes. They did everything in their power to effect alliances with Kemal in Turkey, with King Amanullah in Afghanistan, with Riza Khan in Persia, with the leaders of the Arab national movement in various countries. And finally, in 1924–5, they supported to the best of their ability the struggle of Abd-el-Krim in northern Morocco against the allied armies of France and Spain. This policy, however, raised a doctrinal question of wide significance. Most of the movements concerned were led by the clergy and the big feudal landowners; others, as that of Kemal in Turkey, of Riza in Persia, of Amanullah in Afghanistan were progressive in the sense that they wanted to break the power of the Mohammedan clergy and to modernize their respective countries. But none of them was really democratic, and socialism and the proletarian class-struggle were quite outside their scope. Whenever rudiments of a proletarian movement appeared, they were all inclined to suppress it with the cruelty peculiar to Asiatic politics. The problem was particularly acute in Palestine, the one Asiatic country which, from 1920 onwards, started to evolve, on the basis of Jewish immigration, a strong and powerful labour movement of the European type. Here the Arabs, in fighting the Jews, implicitly fought for the destruction of the one movement which was likely to spread the ideas of modern trade-unionism and European socialism in the Near East. But the Jewish labour movement in Palestine belonged to the Second International, and Zionism as a whole was regarded as an ally of Britain. The Comintern did not shrink for a moment from inciting the Arabs, under the leadership of the Mufti of Jerusalem, to fight and destroy the unions of the Jewish workers.

But it would be a mistake to assume that here the Comintern simply subordinated the interests of the labour movement to the interests of the Russian state without caring for socialism and Marxism. The final effect of their policy was certainly to do everything in their power to help Turkish pashas, Persian imams, and Arab muftis to fight a fight whose social implication, from the communist point of view, was more than objectionable. But they had reasons of doctrine behind their activity. To realize it one need only compare their policy in the East with that in the West. In the West, too, Russia had constantly desired and at times achieved co-operation with the antagonists of Britain and France, with Germany and Italy. But this had not led to a dissolution of the communist parties in those countries. The Comintern had not given unreserved support to the Fascists in Italy, or to the Junkers and conservatives in Germany, as far as the home problems of those countries were concerned. On the contrary, there had always existed a certain contrast between Comintern policy and the policy of the Russian state in those matters; a contrast, which, in Germany, had culminated in the preparation of a revolution by the Comintern while the Reichswehr was receiving ammunitions from the Red army. The prevailing view in Moscow was that a revolution in one of the great countries of the West was the most desirable alternative, and that the Comintern must not be handicapped by Russian interests in working for it; but, pending the outbreak of such a revolution, Russia must naturally safeguard her own interests and make the best possible use of diplomacy and a policy of alliances. In the Near East, this cleavage between the Comintern and the Russian Foreign Office never existed. The doctrinaire reason for the difference between Eastern and Western policy was that, according to Lenin, world revolution must be essentially an anti-imperialistic revolution. The imperialistic bourgeoisie of the West would naturally rally to its cause all the forces interested in imperialism, and only a section of the working classes, of the lower-middle classes and the poor peasantry, would oppose it. But in the East all classes, including even the mullahs, muftis, and feudal landowners, suffered from imperialistic oppression, and were therefore natural allies of the international proletarian revolution. In theoretical debates Lenin preferred not to mention the alliance of the Comintern with the religious and feudal elements, speaking only of alliance with the progressive bourgeoisie. But in practice, as certainly as the Mufti of Jerusalem and Abd-el-Krim, the chieftain of the Rifi tribes in Morocco, are not progressive bourgeois, equally certainly the Comintern allied itself with all anti-French and anti-English forces, of whatever social description.

At the second world-congress, in 1920, the colonial pro-gramme was one of the chief items of the debates. Here Manabendra Nath Roy, opposing Lenin to a certain extent, raised the question of the social antagonisms within the anti-imperialistic movement in the East. According to him the irruption of modern industry into the East was bound soon to produce an alinement of forces considerably nearer to the typical situation of the West than that existing in the East before the war. The bourgeoisie, while growing richer, would somehow coalesce with the feudal classes and both together would tend to come to a compromise with the Western imperia-lists against the proletariat and the peasantry. Only these two latter classes would really lead the anti-imperialistic struggle. The main task, therefore, was not so much to support the ephemeral fight of feudal elements, muftis, and pashas against the great powers of the West, but to form and strengthen com-munist parties.

So far Roy. What was the reaction of the congress to this view? One might expect either acceptance or rejection. But neither happened. The Comintern in public opinion has often been credited with an extraordinary rigidity, and there is undoubtedly much in the accusation. But not less remarkable is the desire, always strong in Russian politics, to eat the cake and to have it at the same time. In the West this tendency reflected itself in such extraordinary ideas as to make an alliance with the German Reichswehr against the French, while preparing the overthrow of the same Reichswehr by the German communists. In the East the same tendency to obtain incompatible results at one and the same time reflected itself in the vote of the second world-congress. Both Lenin's 'theses', which aimed at the unconditional support of the struggle of all Eastern nations against Western imperialism, and Roy's 'theses', which insisted upon the hopelessness of such a policy, were voted together by the congress. Thus, the Comintern would attempt at the same time to support Kemal, Riza, and the Mufti of Jerusalem, and to overthrow them. The root of the later catastrophe in China lies in this duplicity, in this child-like conviction that your adversary will not understand your intentions, though you express them quite openly, that he will continue to co-operate with you as long as *you* want it, and allow himself to be overthrown when it suits *you*.

But long before this policy was finally doomed through the experiments of the Comintern in China, it failed in the Near East. The corner-stone was Turkey. Turkey, in those years, was regarded by the Russians as a very close ally. But they were inclined to overlook the fact that they needed the alliance much more than the Turks. Before Russia's alliance with Germany, through the Rapallo treaty in 1922, Turkey was the one possible ally of Russia in its all-round isolation. And Turkey was a military power of increasing strength and importance. The Turks, on the other hand, did not long remain in isolation. Already during their fight with the Greeks in Anatolia, between 1919 and 1922, very close, though unobtrusive, links had been established between Ankara on the one hand and Rome and Paris on the other. The Russians provided Kemal with war material in the early stages of the struggle, and he could not have won the war without their support. But he did not so much as consider giving in to the political tendencies of communism.

This led to a catastrophe for the young weak Turkish Communist Party. Immediately after the second world-congress, in September 1920, the Comintern had convened a congress of the oppressed peoples of the East at Baku, a city at the same time Mohammedan and proletarian. By far the majority of the delegates came from the near and middle East. Sinovjev harangued them in one of his most brilliant addresses, which carefully avoided the thorny problem of internal dissensions within the Mohammedan movement. For a few months, the Comintern believed that it had really and successfully laid its hand upon the anti-imperialistic movements of the East. It was mistaken and was very soon to become aware of the mistake. The Turkish delegates who had assisted at both the second world-congress and the Baku congress went quite openly back to their country. They were stoned by the population in every village they passed through, finally arrested, tortured, and thrown into the sea. The Comintern had to choose between Kemal and the Turkish communists. For the first time the interests of Russian foreign policy actually involved the existence of a communist party. The Russians chose Kemal in preference to Turkish communism. Never again was the Turkish Communist Party supported in earnest and in the later congresses and meetings of the Comintern no Turkish delegates took part. Again, the Trotskyists, at present, are quite wrong in attributing the rise of this kind of 'opportunism' to Stalin. The decision about Turkey was taken while Lenin was formally and actually at the head of the Soviet state.

The Turkish affair had an aftermath, which showed very clearly the limitations of communist chances in the East. Enver Pasha, the real dictator of Turkey during the war, had been forced to take flight after the armistice, had tried to establish a Turkish state in Turkistan, and, finally, after a very chequered career, of battles, victories, defeats, and almost miraculous escapes such as are the proper lot of a hero of oriental legend, had made his appearance at the Baku congress. He was too compromised to be simply admitted by the Comintern as an ally; during the war, in alliance with the German generals, he had established a régime of violence against the Arabs, upon whom the Comintern laid great store. Thus Sinovjev moved and carried a resolution asking Enver to give real proofs of his conversion to revolutionism before being admitted into the fold of the committee for anti-imperialistic action which had been created at Baku. Enver wavered; but when, finally, he realized that at home the Russians were as much anti-Moslem as anti-Christian and that they wanted to use him as a tool only, he rose against them in Russian Turkistan, carried on a guerrilla fight, and was finally killed by Red troops.

The case of Enver then repeated itself on a larger scale, though in less dramatic circumstances. Kemal, without shunning Russian support, managed within two years to make himself quite independent of it, carrying out a very clever policy of balance of powers in the Near East. Then the experience of Turkey repeated itself in Persia. The Soviets had occupied Ghilan, the Persian border province, and organized there a Soviet régime. They had to evacuate Ghilan in 1921 in order to win the alliance of Persia. They renounced every attempt to strengthen Persian communism for the same reason.

Again this was done with the direct co-operation of Lenin and without any protest from the side of Trotsky. With the overthrow of King Amanullah, Russian influence in Afghanistan declined. In the Arab-speaking countries the Russians were not faced with independent powers, but only with national movements, and this might have given wider scope to communist agitation, which need not have been hampered here by considerations of Russian foreign policy. But the communist parties of Syria, Palestine, and Egypt never prospered. The movement in those countries was essentially religious and racial and in both respects the communists could not compete with the local priesthood and the local feudals. In the end Russia got a very limited and uncertain amount of support in the Near East, and the Comintern, after a big start at Baku, withered away both in the near and middle East.

Let us add, for the sake of completeness, that the Comintern met a similar fate, though for different reasons, in the Far East. The leader of the Japanese communists, Sen Katayama, figured as a big personality at Comintern congresses as long as he lived. But almost all his political career before he went to Moscow had been spent among Japanese workers in the United States. The Japanese labour movement has remained very weak to this day, in the unpropitious atmosphere of exalted patriotism which is characteristic of modern Japan. Most of it has been definitely patriotic. Marxism won a considerable amount of authority among intellectuals, but very little among the workers. The Communist Party has been shattered by incessant factional strife. So has, to an even higher degree, the Communist Party of Korea. Neither ever became a considerable political force.

CHAPTER XVIII

THE CHINESE REVOLUTION

If the Comintern all over the colonial and tropical world has never managed to obtain general practical influence, China is an exception. Not even in Germany has communism played a part so important as in the Chinese revolution. The interference of the Comintern in China was on a larger scale than any other it achieved.

Why was China so much more open to communist influence than other Eastern countries? Other semi-colonial and colonial countries were beset with the same social and national problems: subdued to the foreigner, powerless, in a state of disintegration, the peasantry starving. In Japan and in Turkey communist ideas broke against the proud tradition of a people of conquerors and rulers. Among Hindus a movement openly opposed to caste and ritual has no chance; among Mohammedans atheists are regarded as criminals. Confucianism in China undoubtedly has played an important part in finally stopping the communist advance; but Confucianism, not so much a religion as a code of behaviour, has not at its disposal an organization similar to that of the Mohammedan churches or taboos similar to those of the Hindus, the former barring communist ideology, the second barring the very idea of the abolition of classes. It was the lack of strong religious barriers which opened the way for communism in China.

The revolutionary movement in China, as that in Russia, originated in the intelligentsia. The Chinese intelligentsia suffered deeply from the ignominy to which the oldest civilized race of the world had been subjected, at the hands of the 'southern barbarians'. It is this Chinese nationalism which animated the whole of the Chinese revolutionary movement, communists as well as the left and the right wing of the nationalists. It is the national motive which was most stable among the shifting policies of Chinese communism, and which brought it its most important leaders and supporters.

As the revolutionary movement in Russia, so the nationalist movement in China had its origin in the contact with the West. The first reformers, at the end of the nineteenth century, hoped to Westernize China, and to make it powerful again and able to resist foreign aggression; they attempted to carry out their reforms with the help of the Manchu emperors. But soon reaction set in, the progressive emperor was overthrown, the queen dowager called in the superstitious and fanatical 'Boxers', and the end was a hopeless and disastrous war with the West, ending in all-round defeat in 1901. Since then China has been *de facto* a joint colony of the Western powers and of Japan.

The defeat of the reformers and the Boxer war marked a turning-point in the history of the Westernizing elements in China. Until then those exerting Western influence had been mostly moderates; now it had been proved that reform in co-operation with the Manchus was impossible, and the reformers became revolutionists. Secret societies, with varying aims, had always been a marked feature of Chinese political life. Some of them were founded to defend the peasants against the usurers; others, on the contrary, to defend the land-owning gentry against the poor peasants; some, to defend the southern provinces, Kwantung, Fukien, etc., against the domination of the Manchus; some to safeguard the common interests of the Chinese merchants abroad. But in the last decade of the nineteenth, and more so in the first decade of the twentieth century, the revolutionary, Westernizing, anti-Manchu spirit pervaded many of these societies, especially those of the foreign merchants in Honolulu, California, Java and other places, which had been closely in touch with the West. Very naturally, merchants who supported the revolutionary movement with their wealth found their closest allies among the students who had had a European training and among certain army officers who had been touched by Western influences while learning the Western art of war.

Sun Yat Sen, the leader of the later Chinese revolution, was and always remained the best representative of this type of early nationalist revolutionary. It is characteristic of him that all his life through Sun Yat Sen was searching for a formula for the renovation of China which would allow it to become thoroughly Westernized and at the same time to remain thoroughly Chinese. He had studied in America, and he loved and admired American institutions and technique. Yet he wanted a China where the old patriarchal virtues should remain intact; a China governed justly, everybody receiving just retribution according to his work and status; a China which, while introducing Western industry, would not introduce Western capitalism; a China without the class struggle; a democratic China, but without Western parliamentary democracy. Again: eat the cake and have it. Destroy the old China and leave it alive. But the contradictions in his views agreed well with the hesitations of the intelligentsia between old China and the West, and there is more than one chance that in the end the new China will in fact be something of a compromise between the two.

Sun Yat Sen was the founder of the Kuomintang, the 'People's Party', which to-day is the official ruling party of China. The communists have repeatedly very closely co-operated with the Kuomintang, sometimes have been members of it, and have accepted most of the basic ideas of Chinese nationalism and of the teachings of Sun Yat Sen. Both the Kuomintang and the communists, very naturally, consider Sun Yat Sen a political genius. But practically all those who have met Sun Yat Sen without being imbued with the admiration of the disciple for the leader, have drawn a very different picture; English 'bourgeois' observers agree with a detached and educated communist such as M. N. Roy about the outstanding feature of Sun Yat Sen's political activity: he was a schemer. He was continually brooding over conspiracies and alliances. He set hopes, inadequate hopes, upon every possible ally. He was deceived again and again; he shifted his basic views as often as an old ally had to be discarded and a prospective new one appeared upon the scene. While singleness of purpose, clear and definite knowledge about the essentials of the situation were the outstanding characteristics of Lenin, vagueness in practice and theory was always the outstanding feature of Sun Yat Sen. He alternately admired the United States, Japan, and Soviet Russia. He believed in the power of a small group of conspirators to change China; turned a bourgeois democrat; allied himself with various sets of ambitious generals, repeatedly surprised as often as they eventually pursued their own aims, and not his ideals: a very bad judge of character indeed. He would not have been deified by the communists had he not happened to be in alliance with them during the last two years of his life, a sudden convert to revolutionary mass movements, as he had been a convert to half a dozen other political systems before. But he was one of those men who are certain to be deified by their own people after their death because they express naively and unpolitically certain political ideals cherished by the nation. As long as such people live they are everybody's playthings; when dead they are everybody's heroes. As to Sun Yat Sen's political outlook and mode of approach to political matters Woodrow Wilson is perhaps the nearest parallel in the modern political life of a Western country.

Sun Yat Sen, after a considerable number of unsuccessful military attempts, finally succeeded in 1911 in overthrowing the Manchus, with very little resistance. The bourgeoisie of Shanghai and the south and many of the leading generals supported him. For a moment he believed he had already rejuvenated China. After a few months it became only too clear that the republic which had taken the place of the Manchu empire meant only chaos and the competing rule of rival generals in the various provinces. By the end of the World War China was in a state of obvious disintegration.

But the passive disintegration of a political régime is a splendid starting-point for the revolutionary action of small groups. In this case more than one element of the situation worked for revolution. The underground fight between the peasant on the one hand and the usurer, the administration, the local gentry, etc., on the other is as old as Chinese civilization. But the extortions of the militarists doubled and trebled the burden of taxation the peasant, already on the brink of starvation, was accustomed to bear; and, at the same time, the continual wars between the military governors and the rapid changes from one master to another in almost every province gave the peasants a chance to turn effectively to armed resistance. Peasant banditry increased rapidly. At the same time the disintegration of the régime brought the problem of foreign aggression to a head. Japan, during and after the war, laid hands upon the whole province of Shantung and from this basis dominated Manchuria and the whole north of China, mainly through one of the big 'militarists', Chang-tso-lin. Thirdly, the rise of industrial capitalism, notably in Shanghai, the building of railways, the extension of merchant shipping, created a relatively strong proletariat. Its frightful exploitation, the general political instability, the fact that most factory-owners were foreigners, combined to drive the young proletariat from the very beginning into a revolutionary attitude. First, the war between the Western powers, and later the example of the Russian neighbour, created a very favourable atmosphere for revolution among the intelligentsia. Later, this atmosphere was enhanced by formal concessions by the Soviets, who evacuated the Russian extra-territorial settlement in Tientsin but took care not to lose either the Manchurian railway or Outer Mongolia. Finally, the very fact of continual warfare represented an inducement for certain generals to ally themselves with the revolutionary movement as soon as this movement had become a political force.

As always in backward countries which tend to Europeanize themselves, the intelligentsia was the first to become vocal. It had already backed the revolution of 1911. Now the national plight of China was the thing nearest to its heart. In Russia the first revolutionary movements had been social from the beginning; in China they were inspired by nationalism. In 1919 the students of Pekin, and soon of other centres, started boycotting Japanese goods. The initiative evoked a strong response all over the country and must be regarded as the beginning of the great Chinese revolution. But the students alone, without any definite backing, were not able to resist in the long run the pressure of the militarists, who, in the north, were all of them more or less in the hands of the Japanese. In the meantime Sun Yat Sen had returned to Canton in 1917, after years of exile from China. Canton had always been a revolutionary town—the cradle of the national resistance of the southern provinces of China against the northern, barbarian, Manchu conquerors. But the revolutionary varnish was very slight. The generals of the province of Kwantung accepted the presence of Sun Yat Sen, because it gave them a certain amount of prestige. Otherwise, they did not care for his views, and as often as he made himself a nuisance with them, pleading for a policy of national unity and abolition of the ferocious rule of the army, they simply drove him away. Twice Sun was driven out of Canton; and he was still unaware of the splendid opportunities for his cause implied in the revolutionary movements in the north.

The Pekin intellectuals who had led the 1919 movement were forced by its defeat to consider attentively the basic problem of every revolution, that of the possible allies of the revolutionary intelligentsia. Had a strong bourgeoisie existed it would have certainly risen against the rule and warfare of the generals, which made production and commerce equally impossible, and against the rule of the foreigners, especially the Japanese, who, crudely enough, tried to push the Chinese out of every alluring enterprise. There was hardly any such bourgeoisie. Most of the factory-owners, almost all the ship-owners, and most of the shareholders of the railways were foreigners. The Chinese financiers, the 'comprador' class, were all more or less directly connected with some general whose wars they financed and from whose plunder they lived. Still less than in Russia could the intelligentsia rely upon an alliance with the bourgeois elements.

The natural ally of the intelligentsia was the people: the workers with their innumerable grievances and the peasants with their age-long feud against the administration and their new-born hatred of the army. For it was obvious that a strong China could not be created before the power of the generals was broken and national unity restored. Here the national ideals of the intelligentsia and the practical interests of the peasants agreed. If history were logical the intelligentsia must have evolved a theory based upon the struggle of the 'people' against its oppressors, disregarding class distinctions within the people; it would have been a theory similar to those of the 'socialist-revolutionaries' in Russia.

But history is not logical. China, as Russia, developed under the influence of the West, did not dare to evolve its own thought, was looking for enlightenment from abroad. The role which German thought had played in Russia was played by Russian thought in China. In revolutionary matters the Chinese naturally turned to their Russian neighbours and accepted, rather indiscriminately, the Russian version of Marxism. Characteristically, the birth of Chinese Marxism and communism is not linked in any way with the labour movement, but very directly linked with the literary movements of the Westernized Chinese intelligentsia. Chen-du-hsiu, the founder and, during the decisive phase, the leader of the Chinese Communist Party, was a man of fifty before he became a communist; he had been, during the earlier part of his life, the pioneer and leader of the Chinese literary *risorgimento*, the pioneer of a new literature based on Western models, and the editor of a paper called *Young China*. His first lieutenant, Li-tai-chao, was one of the leading professors of Pekin University, an economist. For them Marxism was the direct continuation of national revolutionism; the intelligentsia was going to find its ally, not so much, it is true, in the proletariat in particular, as in the people in general. But these were problems of the future. Initially the party consisted of a few dozen, and then a few hundred students, just as previously the revolutionary circles in Russia; there was hardly a single worker among them. And the first business of the new organization was not to organize masses but to liberate itself, in painful debates, from the presence of a welter of anti-political ideologies, among which anarchism was paramount.

One thing at least the fact of the foundation of a Communist Party in 1920 decided implicitly: the Chinese revolution would not be a fight of the whole nation against the foreigners, but only of its lower classes, to the exclusion of the militarists and the comprador class who financed them. But things did not at first go according to Marxist orthodoxy. The Chinese Communist Party had been founded in direct co-operation with representatives from Moscow. But, as in Turkey, Moscow wanted to achieve two aims at once, a Communist Party and co-operation with the militarists. The Communist Party, during the early years of the movement, seemed quite a minor force; the generals were very big forces and some of them were Russia's neighbours. True, some of them at least were agents of Japan, but this did not constitute a crime in the eyes of Moscow, as long as relations between Moscow and Tokyo were satisfactory; and they were, from the end of the Russian civil war to the Manchurian incidents of 1929. Moscow did all in its power to deprive the Chinese nationalist movement of its anti-Japanese character and to push it in the direction of an anti-British movement, though the points of divergence between Britain and China were insignificant compared with the Japanese danger. For years the Russians co-operated with General Wu-pei-fu, who, together with Chang-tso-lin, held Pekin. Wu-pei-fu was a ferocious enemy of the rising labour movement. Only later, when the nationalist movement grew stronger and clashed acutely with Wu did the Russians strengthen their ties with Feng-hiu-siang, another general of the north-east, a Christian who cleverly showed sympathy for the nationalist movement.

We must repeat: at that time the Kuomintang, Sun Yat Sen's Nationalist Party, nominally ruled Canton and the province of Kwantung, but was in fact a small group of ideologists without power, the real government of Kwantung being in the hands of militarists; and the Communist Party, hardly existing at all in the south, was in the north a circle of student conspirators without any influence whatsoever. But slowly the picture changed. The year 1922 saw the first big strike in China—there had been smaller strikes since 1911—the railwaymen of the Tientsin–Poukow line struck, not so much for better wages as for the recognition of a union they had formed. The movement was drowned in blood by Wu but made a tremendous impression. In Shanghai the textile workers started to organize; and in Hong Kong the sailors rose in a strike which closely resembled a revolt against the British. The strike lasted for many months and the strike committee, which was not tolerated in Hong Kong, went over to Canton. So did many of the strikers. They immediately strengthened the nationalist movement in Canton. Now, and only now, did Sun Yat Sen realize his opportunity. Here, and only here, might be a balancing power against both foreigners and militarists, an element able to stabilize his rule in Canton. After all, it was not he who had sought the support of the workers; they came, and only their coming made him aware of their importance.

But how to organize them? Sun Yat Sen throughout his life had borrowed every comma of his thought from some Western source, and he now looked for advice to the professional revolutionary organizers of the West. Here was a tremendous chance for Moscow. Canton was geographically remote from the Russian border, but if they succeeded in putting a reliable ally into power in Kwantung, it would enormously strengthen their position and the cause of revolution in China. It was the moment when the united-front tactics in the West were at their height. The idea of applying similar tactics in the East met no resistance. Adolf Joffe, one-time head of the Russian peace delegation at Brest-Litovsk in 1917, experienced diplomat and one of the closest friends of Trotsky, met Sun Yat Sen in secret conference at Shanghai in the summer of 1923. He gave detailed advice to his Chinese partner about the policy he ought to follow. This conference between Joffe and Sun resulted in a number of measures which, as a whole, have transformed the face of China. When Sun went back to Canton two Russian advisers followed him; Borodin, a close friend of Lenin and one of the chief agents of the Comintern, who in 1922 had represented the Comintern in Britain and there effected the turnover of the Communist Party to trade-union work, thus preparing the general strike; and General Galen-Bluecher, the most brilliant of all the Red guerrilla leaders of the civil war. Galen became chief adviser to General Chiang Kai-Shek, Sun Yat Sen's brother-in-law, who had just been named commander of the newly created military academy in Whampoa, which was to form officers for the intended revolutionary army of the Canton government. And Borodin became political adviser to this government itself. According to his suggestions, a trade-union council was formed in Canton, based upon the committee of the Hong Kong strikers. Out of these strikers and other elements of the same political opinions an armed workers' guard was formed in order to make the government independent of the whims of its generals. Peasant unions were created all over the province of Kwantung and the government tried to back them in the fight for lower rents. The Kuomintang called a congress, at which a central committee agreeing with Borodin's policy was elected; and the party launched a programme which, besides the national issues, contained strong pledges to both workers and peasants. The whole of these measures was called the 'reorganization of the Kuomintang'. As a result the communists individually joined the Kuomintang, while the Communist Party as such remained independent. Many of the Whampoa cadets, the chief military force of the movement, were communists; some communists were elected members of the central committee of the Kuomintang, whose majority consisted of members of the left wing of that party, favouring co-operation with the communists. Canton became a 'Red' city.

The Kwantung government and the mass of its adherents were far from being socially homogeneous. The general revolutionary atmosphere of Canton made it easy to win over the numerous petty bourgeoisie of that town, and even a considerable number of the landowners consented to the change, which they regarded as capable of bringing increased power to their beloved south. Many of the higher officers, too, had voluntarily submitted, not because they agreed with social radicalism but because the reorganization of the Kuomintang gave the Canton militarists the hope of playing, with Russian help, a role in Chinese affairs very different from the insignificant efforts of the previous Canton governments. From this lack of homogeneity arose divergences, both in China and in Moscow.

Rebellion came first in China. The foreign merchants and Chinese capitalists who had hitherto supported the Kuomintang seceded almost immediately. This element counted for something, not so much in Canton, as in Shanghai and farther north. The right wing of the Kuomintang, thus constituted, proceeded to a conference at the 'Western Hills', near Pekin, and seceded from the party. Sun Yat Sen went to the north in order to make the best of the situation there, but fell ill and died in Pekin in 1925. In the meantime a dramatic incident had happened in Canton. A secret society of the Canton merchants, the 'Paper Tigers', rose against the reorganized government, but was put down by the Whampoa cadets and the workers' militia. The government took a course even more definitely to the left. After Sun's death Wang-Chin-Wei, the declared leader of the Kuomintang left, became president of the Canton government. Borodin and, at his advice, Wang-

Chin-Wei, attempted to revolutionize Kwantung thoroughly before trying to extend the Kuomintang régime farther north.

In Moscow a certain amount of discussion had preceded the order to the Chinese communists to join the Kuomintang as individual members. Trotsky, much later, claimed to have voted against this step. But if he did so he did not mention the matter in public until 1926, when the situation had become very different. The very fact that Joffe, his closest associate, concluded the agreement with Sun, and that no quarrel between him and Trotsky ensued, shows clearly that no serious divergence of views existed between Trotsky and the other leaders of the Comintern upon the matter. If there is any truth in Trotsky's claim to have voted against the adhesion of the individual communists to the Kuomintang, he was certainly not opposed to a very close co-operation between the two parties. And, in fact, the policy followed by the Comintern was undoubtedly the only possible policy. As in other countries, so in China, the first stages of the revolution had to be carried through with the co-operation of all anti-militarist and—in the Chinese case—anti-foreign elements. The communists themselves could never have secured the support of the Cantonese petty bourgeois masses, of the Kuomintang generals, of many strata of the wealthy bourgeoisie, etc. The choice therefore simply lay between two things: either the communists must make an attempt to split the revolutionary movement from the outset, and then that movement would have remained ineffectual; the reorganization of the Kuomintang, the mass movements deriving from it, the conquest of China by the nationalists, would never have happened; or, if they had happened in spite of communist abstention, the communists, in a movement of mainly national impulses, would have remained an isolated sect. But very likely neither the Kuomintang nor the communists would have achieved anything had they not almost merged in the first stages of the movement. The Kuomintang, for the masses, was essentially a small batch of intellectuals whose national ideals they vaguely shared, but who were otherwise incomprehensible. The co-operation of the communists testified to the social, immediate implications of the movement, lower rents, and better wages, which mattered for the masses. But the masses alone would have been helpless without the upper stratum represented by the Kuomintang. The pact between communists and Kuomintang symbolized the co-operation of both the higher and the lower stratum in the national cause.

Under the impulse of the revolutionary measures of the Canton government the movement spread to the north. General Feng, without officially adhering to the Kuomintang, espoused the national cause, and at one time took Pekin. And then followed the spark which set the powder-barrel alight. On 30th May 1925 a military cordon at the international settlement in Shanghai fired upon striking and demonstrating textile workers. Immediately a general strike and a boycott of British goods followed in Shanghai. As the Russian revolutionary strikes in 1905, so the Shanghai strike of 1925 was paid for by the mill-owners themselves, as far as they were Chinese. The movement immediately spread all over China; students' demonstrations and revolts, boycotts, strikes. The Hong Kong strike was resumed on an even broader basis than the first time. British trade in Hong Kong was nearly ruined. And the generals at Canton started to talk eagerly of an expedition northward.

Though the union of communists and nationalists had been necessary in order to bring a broad mass movement into being, the very appearance of this mass movement shattered their alliance. After a few months the Shanghai Chamber of Commerce, the most representative body of the Chinese industrialists, sought and obtained a compromise with the administration of the international settlement. And in Canton the generals, landowners, and the moderates in general were thoroughly frightened by the revolutionary extremism of the movement. On 20th March 1926 something quite unexpected happened. Chiang Kai-Shek, the military commander of Canton, suddenly executed a coup against his own government. He dispersed the workers' militia, arrested many leading communists and communist Whampoa cadets, closed the offices of the trade unions, and even of the local Kuomintang, and was about to establish himself as military dictator. It was a turning-point of very wide bearing. How would the communists react?

The stroke was aimed at them. The natural reaction would

have been to go into hiding, to break with Chiang Kai-Shek, who had broken with them, and, backed by the big mass movement which was approaching its climax, to try to extend the revolution. Former revolutions in other countries had been faced by similar events. In every revolution there comes a point when the moderates are frightened by the progress of the extremists and openly turn against them. It is an inevitable process, and it has been invariably the moment when the revolutionary front, united at first, broke into two. In China, up to that moment, the difference between the Kuomintang and communism had been abstract and theoretical only. Now it had acquired concrete meaning; it was time, from the communist point of view, to proceed one step further. The communists need not have broken with those who had no desire to break with them; they would naturally have been driven to break with those who were about to destroy them.

Why did they not do it? Who was responsible? Not even Borodin was the decisive person. During those years the most minute details of the policy of the Chinese communists were directed from Moscow. Stalin, with his profound distrust of every living soul, did not allow any step to be taken without his personal orders and he did not see any difficulty in directing a revolution in Canton from Moscow: he had, however, considerations of his own. A break with Chiang Kai-Shek and an open struggle with all the moderates would entail a break with Feng in the north too. Then, Russia would be completely isolated in China, so far as the ruling powers were concerned; it would have to rely only on the revolutionary mass movement, with its dubious chances. The assets were big, the role of Russia in Chinese politics considerable. Up to then the interests of the Communist Party of China and of Russian foreign policy had coincided without difficulty. Now Stalin attempted to find an uneasy compromise between interests which were already divergent, a compromise which proved impossible.

And yet the way was open, would have been open at least, had there been no obstacles of an 'ideological' character. Chiang Kai-Shek proclaimed repeatedly that he was quite prepared to co-operate with Russia provided the differences between the Kuomintang and the Chinese communists could be solved, or the Kuomintang itself admitted, as a 'sympa-thizing' party, to the Comintern. For such an offer Chiang had very strong reasons. He could easily do without Borodin and Russian political influence, but he could not easily dis-pense with General Galen and Russian military and technical advice. Throughout the Canton crisis, and again during the 1927 crisis, Chiang offered much in order to keep Galen. The substance of his offer was that he would remain a reliable ally of Russia provided Russia left the Chinese communists to their fate. It was essentially the same policy as that followed by Kemal in Turkey six years earlier. Only the result would have been somewhat different. The Chinese communists, in an enormous country in disintegration and ruled by two dozen different rulers, and amidst a growing revolutionary mass move-ment, could better stand on their own feet than the Turkish communists. And Chiang, for many reasons, would find it more difficult to find alternative allies in place of Russia. To Stalin only two logical courses were open: either to drop the generals and support the communists, or to support the gene-rals Chiang and Feng, and drop the communists. Both courses promised a certain amount of success. The course he chose presented no chance of success.

Instead of accepting Chiang's suggestion, one way or the other, he attempted to force a compromise upon Chiang. Chiang was ready to compromise on account of Galen and the other Russian technical advisers and on account of the prestige he derived from continued collaboration with the Russians. But in Canton he had won the fight, for the moment, and the Russians must cut their losses if they wanted to con-tinue as his allies. The compromise which was reached in May 1926 was very unfavourable for Borodin. Wang-Chin-Wei, hitherto president of the Canton government and leader of the left wing of the Kuomintang, who had fled on March 20th, would remain in exile; Chiang was recognized as head of the Canton government. The workers' militia was not reorganized. The number of communist officers in the Whampoa academy and in the army was strictly limited. So was the number of communist officials in the administration. They were no longer allowed to keep leading positions within the party. On the other hand, they must deliver a list of their members into the hands of Chiang, in order to enable him to control the carrying out of the compromise. The communists, moreover, were not allowed to win over new members in the army or in the administration. As to the workers and peasants, no limits were put to communist recruiting, but very severe limits to the content of their slogans. They had formally to recognize Sun Yat Sen's programme of social peace and had to tone down their slogans until they became identical with those of the Kuomintang. They had coincided with the Kuomintang slogans ever since 1923, but then before Chiang's coup the Kuomintang had been much to the left, whereas now its slogans were severely revised and moderated. All the communists could now offer the peasants was a 20 per cent reduction of rents. They were not permitted to carry out an agitation against landowners in general, but only against 'bad landowners'. Last but not least they had to consent to Chiang's plan of an expedition to the north. They had opposed such an expedition because in their opinion the Canton base was not yet socially strong enough. If successful, the expedition on its way north would induce very strong conservative elements to join the Kuomintang and thus deprive it of its revolutionary impulse. But this was exactly what Chiang wanted. Military glory, nationalism, social conservatism strengthened through the adherence of many militarists of the north to the Kuomintang, would safeguard his rule and put him in a position to make short shrift with the communists. Every step to the north would make him more independent of them, bring nearer the day of the final break and the extinction of the communists. The Russians and the Chinese communists, in agreeing to help him on his march to the north, prepared their own destruction.

True, Stalin and his advisers had one hope: the northern expedition would be a failure and bury under its ruins the prestige of Chiang. Galen in particular was strongly convinced of this, and in order to save his own prestige remained in Canton when the expedition started. But of all men the Russians were the last who were allowed to make such a mistake. The northern campaign proved to be, not a military, but a revolutionary affair. Stalin, Borodin, Galen, Chen-du-hsiu had grossly underestimated the impulse of the movement. Wherever the Cantonese armies went the road was opened to them by revolution. The students and middle-class people greeted them as national liberators; the peasants saw here the enemies of the hated tax-extorting generals; the workers hoped for a big change in their existence. The soldiers of the anti-Kuomintang generals ran away or deserted. Soon provincial governors, seeing the hopelessness of resistance, went over with their armies and their provinces, but without changing anything in the territory they ruled. In December the Cantonese took Hankow, the Yang-tse capital, and the Kuomintang government moved thither.

This brought things to a head. Hankow, renamed Wu-han, was a new revolutionary centre. It had been taken by the 'Iron Division', the one communist army corps which still existed. In spite of all the restrictions imposed by the compromise of May 1926 the communists in their advance had made the best of the stipulations, and had organized in the regions where they passed peasant unions of a somewhat radical character. Notably in the province of Hu-nan the peasants started expropriating the land of the owners, with the connivance of the communists. Then, in January, the population of Wu-han, in a big rising, assaulted and took the Hankow British settlement. When the government moved from Canton to Hankow it went from a place which had become thoroughly conservative to a centre of revolutionary ferment. Borodin went to Wu-han and with him those members of the government who inclined to the left.

Chiang protested immediately. Shanghai should be the new capital, or Nanking; for the time being he regarded Nanchang, the capital of the province of Kiangsi and his headquarters, as the capital of Kuomintang China. If the revolutionary wing had witnessed a certain increase of forces through the northern expedition Chiang could point to a much stronger increase. He held control over Canton, over most of the army, and all the more conservative leaders joined him in Nanchang.

There is no need to follow the criss-cross of the negotiations which ensued between Wu-han and Nanchang. Chiang still bided his time, and Borodin, in an almost inexplicable blindness, and Stalin hoped for a continuance of the compromise while Chiang prepared the final coup. In February Chiang had approached Shanghai closely, but did not take it. The

workers inside the town rose, in order to drive out the commander of Chang-tso-lin, who held the town. They were
defeated, with the loss of many lives. Chiang hardly regretted
it. Since the affair of 30th May 1925 the Shanghai trade
unions had made tremendous progress and Shanghai had
become the centre of the Chinese labour movement. The
Chinese T.U.C. had its centre in Shanghai; it claimed to control two million members and was affiliated to the Red trade-
union International. Chiang had certainly no objection to
bleeding a labour movement of this type. After the February
defeat the Shanghai labour movement seemed to be crushed for
a time. But such was the *élan* of the revolutionary forces that in
March they rose again, and this time they succeeded in driving
out Chang-tso-lin's troops. During the last phase of the fight
Chiang triumphantly entered Shanghai.

Now Chiang had reached his goal; he could no longer
vacillate. Whatever nationalist bourgeoisie there was in China
was concentrated in Shanghai. Shanghai was the right place in
which to come to an understanding with Britain and to liberate
himself from the anti-English fetters which the Russians
had imposed upon him, only to their own advantage. Things
now move at a breath-taking speed. Chiang, at the very
moment of his entry into Shanghai, orders the workers to
deliver their arms to the army. The communists delay and turn
to Moscow; the local committee at Shanghai, feeling the axe
over its head, implores Borodin and Chen in Wu-han and
Stalin and Bukharin in Moscow to order the fight, which is
anyway inevitable. Instead, Moscow orders them to bury the
arms. The order is partly executed, partly sabotaged by the
organization. The communists are left almost without arms.
There are few parallels to this action in history. Had the
leaders in Wu-han and Moscow believed in Chiang they would
not have ordered the digging-in, but compliance with Chiang's
demand. But at that moment they were already aware that
something very serious was afoot. The meaningless order to
bury the arms simply signified that Wu-han and Moscow
realized the danger, but did not see a way out. And, in fact,
it was very difficult or impossible now to find it. In Canton and
Shanghai Chiang had all the trumps in his hands. Only
Wu-han was out of his reach. Defeat was almost certain, by

now. But the situation was made worse by the hesitating and two-faced attitude the communists took in front of the conflicts between peasants and owners which started to spread over central China. Then Chiang, having utilized his adversaries' indecision to the end, took action. Suddenly the Shanghai committee and all the known communists he could capture were arrested. The party had no choice left and rose, without arms, without organization, without preparation. The general strike broke down, the few nests where armed resistance was attempted were soon taken, and then an orgy of shooting, beheading, torturing, and all an Asiatic fancy can contrive in matters of cruelty ensued. A number of fighters and strikers were thrown into the boiling cauldrons of locomotives.

The Shanghai rising was immediately followed by open rupture between the Wu-han government and Chiang. Wang-Chin-Wei, the leader of the left wing of the Kuomintang, went back to China and became president of the Wu-han government. Open conflict broke out between the left Kuomintang at Wu-han and the right wing in Shanghai. Two communists joined the Wu-han government, and were restored in Wu-han to the position they had held in the Kuomintang in Canton before the coup of March 1926. But soon Wang-Chin-Wei and his men had to realize that a left policy was a thing more easily planned than carried out. Shanghai was the centre of the Kuomintang generals, who openly ruled there. In Wu-han civil revolutionary politicians ruled, but they were at the mercy of their generals. Apart from the 'Iron Division' Wu-han was occupied by a few Canton troops and numerous corps which had gone over to the Kuomintang during the northern expedition and whose leaders were absolutely unreliable. At the head of this group of generals stood General Tang-Shen-Shi, a man rather to the right of Chiang and who had conspired with the left-wingers for the simple reason that he found himself in Wu-han and wanted to use his position against Chiang, for his own personal ends. There was only one way to break his dominating position, that of unleashing the mass movement. But the moment this was attempted Tang would certainly throw out the Wu-han government, which was at his mercy. Already the tide of revolution, after the Shanghai disaster and a subsequent coup of the same order in Canton, had visibly reached and overstepped its climax. On the narrow territory of the Wu-han government, consisting mainly of the provinces of Hu-peh and Hu-nan, the help of Tang could not be dispensed with. Wang-Chin-Wei was wavering between him, or rather between the pressure of the upper-class officers, and the communists. In order to break the enchanted circle the communists suggested that the territory of the Wu-han government be extended. While Chiang stopped in Shanghai the Wu-han government tried to carry out the original plan of the northern expedition and to take Pekin. But in the meantime General Feng had openly declared for the Kuomintang, had come to an understanding with Chiang, and after a very involved criss-cross of intrigues barred the way to Pekin against the Wu-han troops. The issue could no longer be avoided. The peasants, trusting in the 'left' character of the Wu-han government, had risen all over Hu-nan, expropriating and killing owners and their guards, the 'min-tuan', the local gendarmerie. The question was decisively put to Wang-Chin-Wei and to the communists; for or against the risings. The answer was half-hearted. Punitive expeditions were sent to the revolting districts, in which the communists actually participated. But their participation was rather formal and the troops under communist command tended to fire into the air. On the other hand the communists obtained the dispersal of the biggest peasant troop by means of persuasion. Very naturally, this did not transform the landowners into communists. In co-operation with the landowners the whole garrison of Chang-sha, the capital of Hu-nan, rose against the peasant unions. Communists and other active members of mass organizations were massacred in their hundreds: the terror spread to the countryside. Tang-Shen-Shi refused to interfere. The Wu-han government had to capitulate to its commander-in-chief and the communists received an ultimatum bidding them agree with the measures of repression of the peasant movement. They rejected it, the communist members of the Wu-han government and of the party central committee resigned, Borodin went back to Russia; and then the terror was unleashed in repression of communists and left-wingers all over the Wu-han territory. The episode in Wu-han had lasted less than four months. A few months later Wu-han capitulated to Chiang and Wang-

Chin-Wei went once again into exile. The catastrophe of Chinese communism was complete and Chiang, its greatest adversary, triumphant.

The tremendous defeat had its effect on the Communist Party, which was nearly wrecked by the unimaginable tortures and persecutions to which the members were subjected. But the destruction of the party was not only physical. It had lost, once for all, the confidence of the workers. Wherever, in later days, the communists won a foothold, they were welcomed by a considerable section of the poor peasants; but the workers remained invariably indifferent. Instead of the Red trade unions the Kuomintang created official unions of the Italian type, which, there is no doubt about it, sometimes won the real allegiance of the workers. Occasionally these unions fought the communists, arms in hand. There was no longer any communist labour movement in China. For years the Chinese communists and the Comintern discussed how to win the proletariat again, admitting that they had lost contact with it almost completely. Then suddenly a certain Wan Min started writing articles about the big successes of communism in Chinese towns, claiming, at one time, no less than 60,000 urban members for the Chinese Communist Party. But there is also the report of Edgar Snow in his *Red Star over China*; Snow is the best expert on the matter and not suspect of an anti-communist bias. He simply calls Wan Min's reports 'fantastic', without any further comment.

The policy of the Chinese Communist Party was suddenly and entirely reversed after the Wu-han disaster, and a course of civil war against all sections of the Kuomintang was initiated by orders from Moscow. At the same time Chen and his friends, who had made no step without the assent of Borodin, who, in his turn had acted according to detailed orders from Moscow, were accused of opportunism. Stalin wanted a scapegoat and, of course, wanted a confession from his subordinates that all his orders had been right and only their way of executing them wrong. The Russian Borodin submitted without any qualms, and, after only one year of disgrace, was again appointed as an official of the Comintern, though in a less outstanding capacity. Chen, however, who had a standing of his own as the founder of *Young China*, which had preceded his communism, with the pride of a Chinese intellectual refused to be the scape-goat for a policy which others had step by step evolved. He was ousted from the central committee and retired into hiding, shutting his lips.

The problem of the real causes of the disaster remains, and much ink has been spent by all communist groups in attempts to solve it. Trotsky, as was to be expected, vehemently accused Stalin of having betrayed the old revolutionary communist tradition. But this tradition was never so outright and unquestionable as Trotsky would like to assume after being chased from Russia. In fact, Lenin had first evolved the policy of a close alliance with *all* sections of the oppressed nations, and it was he who first, in the case of Turkey, subordinated the interests of communism to the interests of the Russian state. When Stalin, during the whole course of the Chinese revolution, tried to square Russian and communist interests and to maintain an alliance with the Chinese moderates, he was only in the tradition of Lenin.

Anyway, nobody considered the establishment of a pure dictatorship of the proletariat in China. Even the left-wing communists saw that for such a task the Chinese proletariat was too weak. They suggested that the revolution should aim at a 'dictatorship of the proletariat and the peasantry', in other words a régime which would destroy the militarists, evict the foreign powers, abolish usury on the land, give protection to the workers, and create a centralized administration. The left-wing communists believed that for the carrying through of such a programme a break with even the left wing of the Kuomintang was necessary. It is doubtful whether such a policy would have been wise and whether the communists would have had any chance in a fight against all sections of the Kuomintang. While Trotsky accused Stalin of betraying the revolution, Chiang Kai-Shek accused him of subordinating the task of Chinese national liberation to that of social revolution. It would have been a consistent policy to submit to Chiang and to leave the Chinese communists to their own devices; it would have been equally consistent to drop Chiang, follow Trotsky's advice, and choose the dangerous course of intransigent revolutionism. But it was impossible to be the ally of Chiang and at the same time prepare his overthrow, or play with the idea of his overthrow at least. It is this mistake which goes through all Comintern history: the desire to eat the cake and have it.

In the initial stages of the movement this was not altogether obvious. But the coup of Chiang in Canton on 20th March 1926 put the choice before the communists. They refused to choose. They made a 'compromise' with Chiang which implied giving up their political and military independence. There was no further opportunity for them to break away from the chain by which Chiang held them without at once provoking a coup and frightful persecution. They had imagined that they would have the better of Chiang; but he was infinitely shrewder than Stalin and Borodin. Already they were his prisoners. He then manœuvred them into increasing difficulties, finally asking them to deliver even their arms. When they had done so he simply butchered them.

But this policy of compromise was not the simple result of the lack of understanding of foreign countries which Stalin shared with Lenin. Stalin has proved since that he is ready to forsake revolutionary policy completely. He could not do that, however, as long as the traditions of the revolution were strong and embodied in the powerful opposition of Sinovjev and Trotsky. Here the revolutionary past proved to be the biggest handicap of Russian policy, both at home and abroad, as it continues to be to-day. On the other hand, Russia was incapable of leading a revolution abroad. It had never been able to do so, because it had always identified Russian methods and necessities too directly with foreign ones. This tendency to transfer Russian methods abroad, always naïve and very strong, had even increased with the emergence of a completely totalitarian dictatorship under Stalin.

This dictatorship had at the decisive moment shrunk from advancing revolution. Isn't this a splendid confirmation of Trotsky's view about 'betrayal'? Hardly. The most revolutionary of revolutions cannot continue to be so indefinitely. The Russian revolution had ceased to be revolutionary precisely because, in many respects, its success had been so complete. A bureaucracy had emerged which had little in common with the Bolsheviks of the times of Tsarism. Again, the notorious 'betrayal'. Again, hardly. Socialism cannot help producing a bureaucratic system. How, in a system where everything is administered by the state, could the domination of the bureaucracy be avoided? Lenin had imagined that the Soviet system would avoid such a bureaucratic régime, but the Soviet system had never been a reality and Lenin and Trotsky had been chief among those who destroyed every vestige of it. Trotsky, in shouting about treason, simply accuses the unsatisfactory reality of the system which he has himself helped to create; seeing what he has done, he accuses everybody but himself on account of the failure of a philistine, peace-loving, bureaucratic totalitarian régime, with its incapacity to lead to revolution, to correspond to his dreams. Yes, the new bureaucracy had shrunk from revolution in China, had shrunk from its big international implications, had distrusted, hampered, destroyed the mass movement. But what else does this prove but the complete unfitness of the doctrine of international Bolshevism? In the West the Comintern had invented revolutionary situations where there were none. In China the Russian bureaucracy, the legitimate child of the Russian revolution, had wasted the one big revolutionary chance it had ever had.

CHAPTER XIX

THE CHINESE SOVIETS

From July 1927 onwards the communists found themselves at war with both the left and the right wings of the Kuomintang, which were about to effect their reconciliation. They had been subject to the most cruel persecution, a persecution of a truly Asiatic ferocity. In July the soldiers of Tchang-tso-lin broke into the Russian embassy at Pekin, with the consent of the diplomatic corps; the step was justified by its result. The Pekin committee of the Communist Party was in hiding there and the rules of extra-territoriality had been manifestly broken by the Russians. The captured Chinese communists were all executed, in the first place Professor Li-Tai-Chao, who was killed by slow strangulation. And as Tchang-tso-lin acted in the north, so did the Kuomintang generals in the Yang-tse valley and in the south. The communists could only choose between death without or after resistance. There was no chance of success. The workers had definitely turned their backs on the communists, the intelligentsia was falling off in numbers after the defeat, and the peasants, though easily inclined to revolt, were disappointed by the previous policy of the communists and the heavy suppression to which they had been latterly subjected and which increased every day.

In these circumstances Moscow decided to launch the civil war and the slogan of the Soviet régime, as a symbol of complete break with the Kuomintang. It was a step of far-reaching consequences for the Comintern. The alliance between Stalin and the right wing in Russia, whose leaders were Bukharin, Rykow, and Tomski, was drawing to its close. The crushing defeat of the right-wing policy in China hastened the rupture.

But here we are, for the moment, concerned only with Chinese events, which are intelligible without attributing too much influence to the Russian factional fights.

To the change of policy corresponded the change of leadership. There had always existed elements among the leading ranks of the Chinese communists who had disagreed with Chen and his friends. Some of them had entered the Kuomintang with reluctance; others had at least opposed the concessions made to Chiang during the later phase of collaboration with him. One of them, Tsu-Tsu-Bo, an intellectual from Shanghai, known at that time in Comintern circles under the Russian name of Strakhov, had been one of the committee of three which, together with Borodin and Roy, had been the real leaders of the party during the previous phase. Then there was Mao-tse-tung, son of wealthy peasants from Hu-nan, who had had a certain amount of university training, and Li-Li-Sian, a lower-middle-class intellectual from Hu-peh. These three henceforward were the real leaders of the party. Strakhov represented it at the sixth world-congress in 1928.

The one coherent military force of the party was the 'Iron Division'. This corps, after the failure of the expedition against Pekin, had been ordered against Chiang by the Wu-han government before the rupture with the communists. The Wu-han troops had slowly advanced against Shanghai and had taken Nanchang, the capital of Kiangsi. Their commander was one Yeh-tin, a confirmed communist. There was another army corps in Nanchang under communist influence, commanded by a certain Ho-lung, who had been an ordinary bandit leader of peasant origin, but had been converted to discipline and communism, and now brought his division over with himself. Both found themselves in Nanchang when they were faced with the rupture between Wu-han and the communists. At the beginning of August they rose in revolt against Wu-han, after they had received orders to that effect from the Communist Party. But they could not remain in Nanchang, where their rising called forth very little response and where they were surrounded by troops of both the left- and the right-wing Kuomintang. They hardly knew where to go. It was a hopeless enterprise. But finally they felt that Canton and Kwantung, the cradle of the revolution, would provide the best opportunitites. They left Nanchang for the south, and in a heroic march of eight weeks reached the southern coast. Communist sources agree that the country people remained passive at their sight. Finally, they threw themselves, surprisingly, upon the coastal town of Swatow, which they occupied. But English and American men-of-war interfered; they had no reason to love the isolated communists and helped willingly in their destruction. With their co-operation Swatow was recaptured by the Kuomintang after a few days and the communists dispersed.

A series of similarly desperate and aimless attempts might have followed, but insensate exaggerations soon brought things to a head in such a way as to enforce a complete change of tactics. The attempt to create Soviets in the big towns amidst the general indifference of the population spent itself in the one sanguinary catastrophe at Canton. The chief responsibility for this débâcle lies at the door of one Heinz Neumann (shot in 1937 in Moscow), a German. He came to China as representative of the Comintern when the turnover to the left was effected. He had been a Berlin student with gifts for writing and debate, had joined the party, and soon become one of the principal lieutenants of Maslow, the leader of the left wing. The gifted young man had poured scorn over the right, while Maslow was at the head. But, immediately after Maslow's fall he wrote a pamphlet against his master so full of vilification that the sudden change provoked the disgust of the betterminded.

Generally, for this and other reasons, Heinz Neumann was regarded as a man apt to do anything if it suited his career, his taste for adventure, and his craving for mischief. Now, after being squeezed out of the leadership of the German party for a time, he was sent to China, and there staged a rising in Canton. At least one of the best-informed authorities on the subject, Boris Souvarine, in his *Stalin* directly accuses Neumann of staging the rising for the sole purpose of sending a glorious bulletin to the fifteenth congress of the Russian Communist Party, which was sitting at the beginning of December 1927 and just about to exclude Sinovjev and Kamenjev and to confirm the exclusion of Trotsky. The defeat in China had been the strongest asset of the opposition against Stalin in these last months, and a splendid revolutionary rising would have been just the right thing to relieve Stalin from the charge of opportunism. The account of Souvarine may be somewhat dramatized. It must have been difficult to time the rising in Canton in just such a way as to make the cable arrive at the decisive sitting of the congress in Moscow, as indeed it did. But if this coincidence was due to chance, the general policy behind the Canton rising was not; Stalin undoubtedly wanted something spectacular in order to beat off his adversaries in Russia, and did not care about the aftermath of an ill-considered *Putsch* in China. Heinz Neumann, about whose character no single man in the Comintern had the slightest doubt, was deliberately chosen because his dash, his careerism, and his absolute lack of scruples made him the right person for the task.

Thus, a 'commune' was suddenly proclaimed in Canton, in the first days of December. But it lasted for exactly fifty-eight hours, and ended in devastating defeat. Heinz Neumann had miscalculated. The scheme had achieved its service at the decisive moment of the Russian party struggle, and after the defeat and its details had become a scandal in the Comintern, Stalin dropped Neumann as rudely as he had previously dropped Chen and Roy. What had happened? In Canton a political crisis had broken out in November and the right and left wings of the Kuomintang, or rather two militarists who claimed to represent those two tendencies respectively, had come to blows. Neumann took this opportunity, concentrated remnants of the troops of Yeh-tin, which had been dispersed at Swatow, and peasant 'partisans', i.e. small groups of peasants who had taken up arms, and entered Canton. He had established contact with the Communist Party there, and on the night before the rising the provincial committee of the Communist Party had appointed a secret group which it called a 'Soviet', whose very existence was unknown to the workers. The armed forces of the rising counted about 5,000, and they succeeded, at first, in taking the centre of the town by surprise. But exactly as in Sofia in September 1923, in Hamburg in October 1923, in Reval in December 1924, and in central Germany in March 1921, the workers remained indifferent. No mass movement had preceded the military coup and no mass movement was unleashed by its sudden outbreak. Only a very narrow circle of sympathizers joined the fighters; on the other hand important elements of the proletariat, notably the engineers, who had always been adherents of the Kuomintang, took arms against the communists. Nothing was needed but a swift concentration of troops, helped, again, by the warships of the great powers. Soon all was over and nothing remained of the Canton 'commune' but heaps of corpses. A frightful massacre swept away every communist and extended to all progressive elements; girls were killed for no other reason than that they wore bobbed hair. All members of the central and provincial committee of the party involved in the rising met their death; but Heinz Neumann escaped.

Among Chinese communists the memory of the desperate fight of the Canton rebels against overwhelming odds has been raised to the dignity of a heroic legend. But the political effects were disastrous. The party had lost all allegiance among the workers before Canton. The Canton adventure put the seal on this verdict; never again since then have the Chinese communists had the slightest influence over the Chinese labour movement. The Canton rising decided that, in future, the communists would be an organization of intellectuals leading peasants. In the biggest centre of its activity the Comintern had ceased to be a working-class organization at all.

While in December the Canton defeat marked the end of the communist labour movement in China, in November of the same year the foundations for something more stable had been laid. In Chalin, in southern Kiangsi, a peasant Soviet was created and maintained and extended itself in slow and adventurous warfare. The word 'Soviet' in this connection did not mean the same thing as that designed by that name in Russia. There have always been peasant risings in China, and in every big crisis they spread rapidly and sometimes reached an enormous extent. In the middle of the nineteenth century, such a peasant movement, called the Tai-ping, had formed in Nanking and in the south an empire of its own, with a dynasty, a religion, and a powerful army, opposed to the Manchu empire in the north, which it had resisted for sixteen years. The Chinese Soviets were essentially and even in important details a re-enactment of the Tai-ping revolt, only on a smaller scale. Against the inefficient Manchu administration the Taipings had conquered and held almost a third of China. Against the machine-guns and aeroplanes of Chiang Kai-Shek the peasant rebels had to hide in remote districts, far from the towns. They could not have done so much had they not been helped by the political and organizing experience of communist intellectuals. The risings were there without the communists. What the latter did was mostly organizing and educational work. 'Soviets' sprang up in many parts of China and many of them were suppressed as quickly as they had arisen. But in the end four Soviet areas of a somewhat greater extent defended themselves successfully for a couple of years, with their centres in southern Kiangsi, eastern Honan, northern Szechuan, and northern Shensi respectively.

The early history of the Chinese Soviets contains many unsettled points which may never be brought to light. Official communist and official Kuomintang sources are equally unreliable, and, as the Soviet districts were blockaded, no neutral evidence exists. Only the merest outline of the social and political character of the 'Soviet' régime is visible. The 'Soviet' movement seems to have been identical, originally, with what the communists appraisingly called peasant 'partisans' and the Kuomintang, more simply, 'bandits'. Banditry of expropriated peasants, in countries such as China, Spain, and many others, is not regarded as a dishonest but rather as a praiseworthy and heroic occupation. With the extortions of the various provincial generals, the burdens of the war, and the subsequent destitution of the peasants banditry had increased considerably. The creation of a 'Soviet' district meant nothing but that the communists had put themselves at the head of one or other of these peasant bandit movements and won with them a stable territory, however small. One of the first territories thus won was the Tin-kan-shan, an almost unapproachable mountain fastness in Kiangsi. But the very fact of the acquisition of territory naturally changed the movement of roving bandits, who made the countryside unsafe, into something different. Very little is known, unfortunately, about the original organization of the revolutionary territories. It is clear only that the partisans could hardly ever remain in the district where the revolts had originated. For the possibilities of creating stable régimes were dependent upon military advantages, upon remoteness and inaccessibility. Therefore half the history of the Chinese Soviets consists of marches, endless marches over thousands of miles, long before the 'great march' of 1934, which brought the whole of the Kiangsi group into Shensi. This implied not only heroic and romantic exploits. It meant, primarily, that the territory occupied by the Soviets was almost always conquered territory. The main forces of the Red partisans had been revolting peasants. But, in leaving their home districts, they had ceased to be peasants, even peasants in revolt and hiding, and become 'Red warriors'. The Red partisans during years of fighting and marching transformed themselves, with the help of the communist conceptions of discipline, into the 'Red army' which was the decisive force of the régime. The Red army was an army not quite like other armies. It came as the peasants' friend, it had a peasant ideology. But it was an army, not a movement of the villages. It could impose its revolutionary will upon them, whether they liked it or not, and sometimes it had to carry out measures which the peasants certainly did not like. It was menaced almost continually by famine, and the peasants had to feed it just as other armies. It tried to avoid the consequences—which implied and sometimes actually brought about armed clashes with the peasants —by transferring the burden of the war to the rich instead of to the poor. It is here that detailed evidence is most lacking and most necessary. The border-line between rich and poor is ill defined; the conception of a 'rich peasant' can extend so far as to include the ordinary peasant, but can as easily shrink so far as to mean almost nobody. There is reason to believe that, in the early phase, the practice approached the first, whereas of late it tended definitely in the second direction.

At first, it seems, the Reds, when taking a district, started by shooting all landowners and rich peasants, missionaries, gentry, wealthy merchants, gendarmes. But soon it became evident that difficulties arose. The chief task the Red army set itself was to spread social revolution, and the chief means of social revolution in the villages was the redistribution of land. This could not be carried out by the Red army without the help of the peasants themselves, who alone knew about the local property conditions. Even in the scanty evidence available, complaints occur about the ability of the rich peasants to get the better of the poor in redistribution. The difficulty was typical enough. A revolution exclusively based on the peasant has a definite meaning under the one condition that the peasant is a serf. If there exists a feudal landlord who commands the labour of dependent serfs, then the expropriation of this land-lord, the transformation of a feudal society into a society of free peasants, is a conceivable aim. But in China, during the last two thousand years, no feudalism had existed. The trouble in the villages was the frightful scarcity of soil, which was the basis of increasing indebtedness of the poorer peasants to the richer, and to the growth of an intolerable burden of usurious interest. But this could not be abolished by decree, for the poorer peasants were dependent upon the richer, who became usurers. Hence the hopelessness of an agrarian revolution with-out the help of the towns. Had the Reds been able to give the Chinese peasants better fertilizers, the peasants could have done without the help of others. As it was, the Reds, step by step, retreated before the rich peasants, finally renouncing any attempts at redistribution. It is the chief objection to Edgar Snow's otherwise so instructive account of the Chinese Reds that it does not study in the least the agrarian problem in the Soviet territory; yet the agrarian problem is at the very root of the Soviet régimes in China.

These difficulties exerted their pressure on the Soviet régimes, notably upon the strongest of them, the Kiangsi Soviets, where were assembled almost the whole of the party leaders with Mao-tse-tung as president of the provincial Soviet. At that time Mao-tse-tung did not yet hold the ideas he explained to Edgar Snow almost ten years later; the communists at that time were not content to rule remote peasant districts. All documents of the time are full of discussions about the relation between the peasant risings and the revolution in the towns, and of com-plaints that the latter did not proceed more quickly. The com-munists, though no longer in practice a party of the working class, still regarded themselves as a working-class party in theory; and the bad economic position of the Soviet districts, the insolubility of all their difficulties without the help of the towns, drove the Soviets on to an offensive policy. During the early years it was not regarded as sufficient or even as admissible simply to hold the mountain fastnesses the communists had occupied. These were regarded as nothing but military bases for an offensive against the big towns. Once, in 1929, the communists obtained a considerable military success by capturing Chang-sha, the capital of Hu-nan. But they were driven out, within two days, by the troops of the Kuomintang, with the help of British and American gunboats. Later attempts in the same direction failed, and led to very heavy losses, which the Soviets could not afford. It became apparent that the Soviet troops, excellent in guerrilla warfare as they were, were not up to large-scale military operations, which very often led to their complete annihilation.

One important element of these repeated defeats had its roots in the political situation. With the workers no political contact worth mentioning existed, and contact with the other urban classes was very slight. In 1929 the Japanese captured the Manchurian railway, hitherto in the hands of the Russian government. On that occasion Chen-du-hsiu, who had remained in hiding outside the Soviet districts and had not spoken since 1927, raised his voice. It was no use, according to him, to talk of Soviets and to create them in remote corners while the whole of the nation was further away from social revolution than ever. The national motive must again receive its due place, and an anti-Japanese campaign must be opened. The only reflex to this declaration was the exclusion of Chen from the party. To say that something was wrong with the policy laid down by Stalin was by now a *crimen laesae majestatis*. But the rejection of Chen's view was not only determined by the rule that every criticism must be impossible. The communists could not have executed any campaign whatsoever in the towns, because they were non-existent outside the Soviet districts. This was manifest when their sudden appearance in Chang-sha called forth as little response as their appearance in Canton two years before.

Thus the all-round failure of the attempts to carry the revolutionary movement beyond the borders of the Soviet districts created a crisis within the Chinese Communist Party and the Kiangsi Soviet government. The crisis seems to have been hastened by the first two 'annihilating drives' of Chiang Kai-Shek against the Soviets. These attacks made it more urgent than ever to be economical with the available troops and to stop all adventurous offensive enterprises. And, probably, it inclined the Soviet government at the same time towards concessions to the more wealthy peasant element. Anyway, in due course two conflicting lines of policy declared themselves. Li-li-sian, supported by Tsu-Tsu-bo and a very considerable part of the party and the army, insisted upon a continuation of the offensive tactics. Mao-tse-tung and the others resisted and carried their policy through. Thereupon, the partisans of Li-li-sian rose, in December 1931, in nine out of the fourteen counties of the Kiangsi Soviet territory and carried at least three divisions of the Red Army with them. The revolt was put down and drowned in blood. Even *Imprecorr* speaks of 1,500 arrests. Li-li-sian was called to Moscow, where he disappeared. Mao-tse-tung was henceforth undisputed dictator of Soviet China.

It had been again a decisive moment. Every attempt to carry revolution into the big towns from the Soviet basis was rigidly stopped. At the same time, a more moderate policy was definitely sponsored within Soviet territory, free trade of loyal merchants was admitted, small workshops no longer expropriated; more caution was advised in the redistribution of land. It had been an inevitable realinement. The continuation of the Li-li-sian policy of extremism against the wealthy peasants within the Soviet territory, together with military offensives, meant quick disaster under increasing pressure from the Kuomintang armies. The policy now followed on the other hand, meant nothing but a respite. A revolution which renounces offensive tactics is doomed. It would be interesting to know by what means party discipline was maintained after the catastrophe. In fact, the Chinese communists had reached the practice of shooting their own leaders a few years before it became habitual in Russia. At least the reality of the revolt of the Li-li-sian group is not open to doubt. But accounts of the police régime which evolved out of it are lacking. Edgar Snow treats the police régime as meagrely as the agrarian problem.

The reality of the Chinese situation was doubtless decisive throughout; but the mechanical imitation of Russian methods sometimes played its part, too. After the Wu-han catastrophe in 1927 contact between Moscow and the Chinese party had become difficult. This undoubtedly made for an independence of the Chinese Soviet leadership unusual in the Communist International. Moreover, the Chinese Soviets, as Snow has incontestably established, received very little material help from Russia and had resources of their own. Nevertheless, a certain parallel between Russian and Chinese Soviet policy is obvious. The first ruthless phase of conflict with the rich elements of the villages corresponds more or less exactly to the fight against the kulak in Russia, only that this phase started earlier in China. The later mitigation of the agrarian policy of the Chinese Soviets corresponds exactly enough to the gradual retreat from the policy of collectivization and aggression against the kulak in the Soviet Union. And while the agrarian policy of the Chinese Soviets reflects, somewhat mechanically, the Russian agrarian policy, the policy of the Chinese Soviets towards the Kuomintang was determined, through and through, by the turn to the left of the Comintern between 1928 and the beginning of 1934. In 1928, as will soon be described, the Comintern banned every attempt at co-operation with other, non-communist organizations of a socialist and progressive character. This policy, in China, was carried through much against the obvious interests of Russian foreign policy. When the Chinese communists, in 1929, on the occasion of the conflict about the Manchurian railway, and in 1931, when the Manchukuo puppet-state was proclaimed, refused to appeal to Chinese nationalism and to offer co-operation with the Kuomintang, they acted under orders from Moscow; but those orders ran directly counter to Russian interests and were uniquely dictated by the return to those principles of communist 'purity' which seemed abandoned since 1921 and 1925. This new dogmatic rigidity caused the Chinese Soviets to lose the last opportunity of survival as an independent force.

In 1933 the 19th Kuomintang Army, which had defended Shanghai against the Japanese in 1932, revolted in the province of Fukien against Chiang Kai-Shek on account of his unwillingness to continue the war with Japan. Fukien is a border province of Kiangsi and the Fukien rebels sought co-operation with the Soviets. This offer was a godsend. It gave the hard-pressed Soviets a sudden chance to extend their territory over a wide area, to win over modern military forces with excellent armament, and industrial centres which would have provided a basis for a much more progressive social policy. The offer was the more alluring because, in 1932, the Comintern had decided that the Chinese communists must again make the national defence of China against Japan one of their primary bulwarks. Nevertheless, the Fukien offer was rejected: no collaboration with Kuomintang forces! And then came the last disaster. The Comintern had sent a German officer, who was working under a Chinese pseudonym, while, on the other side, Chiang Kai-Shek employed the services of General von Seeckt, the former chief of the Reichswehr. The two Germans met in war, the one as a Kuomintang chief, the other as a Soviet chief. But Seeckt had the better of his adversary, who had abolished the guerrilla tactics of the Chinese and chosen to oppose the fifth 'annihilation drive' of the Kuomintang against the Soviet by a system of rigid trench warfare. The enormous superiority of the Kuomintang in material made this a hopeless strategy; the Kiangsi territory was gradually conquered by Kuomintang troops, tens—according to some reports hundreds—of thousands of people were killed, and finally the Red army had to evacuate Kiangsi. A similar fate befell the other smaller Soviet districts soon afterwards. The Red army set out on its 'great march', a feat of courage and tactical skill against which Xenophon's retreat with the ten thousand becomes a commonplace affair. Of 90,000 who had started upon the march through the whole of China 20,000 finally reached Shensi, the last Soviet base, near the Mongolian border. It was a heroic feat, but the political and military defeat of the Soviet movement was almost final.

The transfer of the Soviet base to Shensi did not in itself provide a solution. Shensi is socially and intellectually even more backward than southern Kiangsi, social antagonisms are less acute, scarcity of land plays a minor role. Shensi is altogether an inadequate base for a revolutionary movement of any kind; for many years indeed it was regarded as the province with a model administration, which avoided successfully all conflicts between peasants and militarists. On the other hand, Chiang Kai-Shek was not likely to stop before the Shensi Soviets in his policy of annihilating the communists. He had destroyed all the other Soviet districts; he would destroy this one. As communists, the Shensi Soviets would be doomed. But in the meantime much had happened. Hitler had come to power in Germany, Russia had become an ally of France, Britain had entered on a phase of conflict with Japan, the Comintern had dropped its purism and turned again to the right, and that to a degree never known before. As communists the Shensi rebels were lost. But what if they made an entirely new start and re-entered the scene, which they had left as Reds, with the blue flag of the Kuomintang? The story of this new venture belongs to an entirely different phase of Comintern policy which had, in the meantime, started in Europe. We must revert thither.

CHAPTER XX

THE LEAP INTO THE ABYSS

Summer 1927: defeat everywhere! There had been defeat in Germany in 1923, defeat again in 1924-5, from which the German party had scarcely recovered. The year 1926 had brought defeat in Britain; a few days later, defeat in Poland. The movement for international trade-union unity lay in ruins. In March 1927 came Shanghai, in June and July, Wu-han. And not a single success. The new turn to the right, timidly and inconsistently effected on the European continent, carried to great lengths in Britain, in the United States, in China, had led to catastrophe. Its continuation had become almost impossible. It was impossible to carry out a policy of alliance with any section of the Kuomintang, because all sections of the Kuomintang were equally severe in their persecution of the communists. It was impossible to co-operate with the T.U.C., because the T.U.C. made a laughing-stock of the Anglo-Russian committee, until the Russians were forced to dissolve it. All hopes, all attempts were at an end. Left policies had been tried and failed; right policies had been tried and failed. Only one thing could maintain the vanishing hopes of revolutionaries: in the dim future a new revolutionary wave might come. In the meantime, the Comintern had little importance. The Russians, after the Chinese defeat, were seriously losing confidence in it.

Simply to drop it was impossible. It was the moment of the fiercest fight against Trotsky; a dissolution of the Comintern would have looked like a wholesale confirmation of his accusations of treason. This might not have impressed Stalin very much, but there was something else: the fight with the right wing, with Bukharin, Rykov, Tomski, was to follow the defeat of the left wing, of Trotsky and Sinovjev. And here the situation of 1926 repeated itself. In 1926 Sinovjev had been at the head of the Comintern and Stalin had ousted him by overthrowing the left groups within the Comintern. Now Bukharin was president of the Comintern; again, he might conceivably have appealed to the existing right-wing leaders of the various communist parties, if Stalin went to the left. That Stalin had been doing very steadily since the end of 1927, disavowing the policy of concessions to the rich peasants and preparing the suppression of free trade, the reintroduction of the 'war communism' of 1918–21, the first Five-Year Plan. A conflict with Bukharin and his group about all this was inevitable. The conflict would inevitably extend to the Comintern. If a move to the left was effected in Russia a similar move would be effected within the communist parties. In order to beat Bukharin on the international field, the right wing of the communist parties must be thrown out and this squared fairly well with the fact that the defeats of the last two years had all been defeats of a 'right-wing' policy.

For the moment, Stalin, deeply discredited by the Wu-han catastrophe, had to cleanse himself from the charge of opportunism. A chance offered itself precisely at the moment when Borodin had to leave Wu-han and the policy of the Chinese communists was reversed. On 15th July 1927, for quite a minor reason, the workers of Vienna rose in revolt. The rising of this thoroughly socialist proletariat was a surprise to both the socialist leaders and the communists. Big masses were involved, but they had no arms, the socialists refusing to hand out their secret stores, in order to avoid civil war. After a few hours all was over. The Communist Party, practically non-existent as it was, had had no chance to interfere. It was immediately accused, from Moscow, of failure to form Soviets during the rising. The Austrian communists, far from being in a position to form Soviets, were unable to get a single municipal councillor elected in Vienna. But for Moscow it was a suitable occasion to demonstrate its thorough revolutionism, which had become somewhat doubtful.

The Austrian events were not unimportant. Immediately after the rising of July 15th the movement of the Heimwehren, a semi-Fascist military organization, spread all over Austria. It

was the first sign that in central Europe the period of democracy and moderation was over and harsher times were
approaching. The Heimwehren clamoured for a new constitution and for the abolition of democracy. In 1929 they very
nearly reached their goal, were forestalled once more, only to
obtain it finally in 1934, after the victory of Hitler in Germany.
During this long-drawn-out crisis the Austrian communists
definitely refused to defend democracy, describing every
attempt to do so as sheer treason. While, in reality, Fascism
was about to conquer the country, they continually talked
about the approaching proletarian revolution, urging the
workers to form Soviets; nobody listened. But the central
committee of the party was split and the right wing, which
stood for the defence of democracy, was excluded. It was the
prelude to all that followed in other countries.

The sudden reversal of tactics in China, the rupture of the
Anglo-Russian committee, and the Austrian affair, considered
together, represented already a big change of policy. But since
the beginning of 1928, when the divergences between Stalin
and Bukharin grew more acute, though they did not yet come
into the open, a general turn to the left was effected. The first
parties to be affected were those of England and France. In
Britain the break between the T.U.C. and Moscow had been
accompanied and followed by strict measures against the communists in the Labour Party and against the minority movement within the trade unions. It became very difficult for the
communists to comply with the statutes of these two organizations and remain communists. Starting from this situation the
British communists, against considerable resistance within
their own ranks, were forced to drop their fight for affiliation
to the Labour Party, and to oppose actively the trade-union
rules. By submission to Moscow they avoided a complete break-
up of the traditional leadership of the British Communist Party.

In France, for a long time, it had been the traditional policy
for all the forces of the left to give mutual assistance to one
another at the polls. There are two ballots in French general
elections. Hitherto, every party of the left had run a candidate
for the first ballot; at the second ballot, all forces of the left,
radicals, socialists, and communists, had traditionally united
against the candidate of the right, voting unanimously for the

candidate of the left party who had received the strongest vote at the first ballot. Now the French communists were ordered to drop this procedure and to maintain their candidates at the second turn. The communists had altogether sixteen deputies, and were a minor parliamentary force. But their new tactics at the polls menaced the left with the loss of about a hundred seats and were likely to help a majority of the right into power. There was little resistance within the French Communist Party against the new policy. By 1928 practically all leaders apt to display independence, such as Frossard, Souvarine, Loriot, Monatte, Suzann Girault, Treint, Paz, etc., had been excluded. The French communists simply obeyed. They accepted the description of the new policy as one of 'class against class'; this formula was intended to express the idea that there was absolutely no difference between Fascists and left-wing socialists, that they were all equally bourgeois, that the communists were the only representatives of the proletariat, that an alliance with left-wing socialists was an alliance with bourgeois elements and therefore a betrayal. All this the French communists took for granted. But outside the ranks of the party there was furious resistance. The sale of the party press dropped heavily and the first ballot already brought disaster. Then, suddenly, the communists changed their tactics. The slogan 'class against class', proved to be capable of interpretation. The communists, while still rejecting any co-operation with the socialists, concluded a close alliance, based upon all-round electoral co-operation at the second ballot, with the Catholics in Alsace. France was still regarded as an enemy by Russia: the German-speaking autonomists in Alsace were more or less dissaffected, and an alliance with them appeared much more tolerable than one with the socialists. As a result of this pact with the Alsatian Catholics the communists won three seats in Alsace and were able to put a communist into office as mayor in Strasbourg. They kept only six of their seats in the rest of France.

Czechoslovakia's turn came next. There the government had prohibited a festival of the communist sports organization and the party decided, in accordance with the new policy, to meet the prohibition with violence. A 'Red day' was announced and the revolutionary workers of all Czechoslovakia were called to Prague for a display of the forces of the party, in spite of the announcement that the police would use fire-arms. The Czechoslovakian party had never been a revolutionary movement, and now less than ever did the workers see any reason to risk their skins. Not five thousand appeared in Prague, and no demonstration took place. At that a furious protest came from Moscow. The old leaders of the party, those of the Šmeral group and those of the left who had come in in 1924, were held responsible indiscriminately. Šmeral submitted silently as ever, and was only summoned to Moscow, where he had to remain. But the traditional left wing resented the charge of being opportunists and protested that they had been asked to perform the impossible. All the leaders of the left, Neurath, Jilek, Bolen, and many others were thereafter excluded from the party. Again, a big slump in party membership and sales of the press followed.

During the previous years of faction fighting in Russia the world-congress had not been convoked. It was summoned in 1928, instead of in 1926, as it should have been to comply with the statute of the Comintern, which, since 1924, provided for biennial instead of annual congresses. Even now it was unable to decide anything. There still existed a certain balance between right and left, between Bukharin and Stalin. Stalin would never have allowed Bukharin to carry through his policy but did not want an open clash. The congress, therefore, was more or less a formal affair. Both sides prepared for the approaching decision. The programme of the Comintern was voted; it did not contain anything new compared with the viewpoints previously established. More important was the analysis of the present situation. Bukharin, executing the orders of the political bureau of the Russian party, submitted the thesis that the post-war world was entering into its 'third period'. The first period had been that of revolution, between 1918 and 1923. Then, as the fifth world-congress had stated, an era of democratic pacifism and of relative stabilization had come. This era was nearing its end. What was to come instead? Paradoxically, Stalin and Bukharin had accepted the formula of the 'third period', but put on it two mutually exclusive interpretations. To Bukharin the third period meant that capitalism was in a process of enormous expansion, which was a clear advance on the pre-war standard. To the left wing it meant the approach of a new revolutionary era. The acceptance of such a formula meant nothing if the interpretations given to it were strictly contradictory. But the lip-service to an elastic formula was a sign of submission. In the meantime, the exclusion of all right-wing elements was visibly approaching. Bukharin, who felt that soon the storm would burst, made use of the platform of the congress for what, as he knew, would be one of his last public utterances; he stood up to criticize the methods of exclusion and ideological dictatorship within the parties in his farewell speech to the congress: 'Discipline, in our party, is the highest rule. But I want to quote an unpublished letter which Lenin sent to me and Sinovjev. Lenin writes: "If you chase all intelligent people who are not very pliable, and only keep obedient idiots, then you will certainly ruin the party".' It was almost a declaration of war, but the issue could not be doubtful.

Stalin dominated Russia, and through it the Comintern. To facilitate the final destruction of Bukharin and his followers a war atmosphere was created. The break between Moscow on the one hand and London and Nanking on the other, together with a series of incidents, had created in 1927 a considerable war scare in Russia, which was never again to subside. It seems to belong, organically, to all totalitarian régimes. It seems strange to-day to remember that in 1928, according to the Comintern, Britain was about to fight Russia. It was the time when labour was preparing for its second turn of office, with a definitely pacifist programme. But this was what the members were taught; every other task was subordinated to the preparation for war and every opposition was denounced as traitorous at a moment when only a traitor was ready to deny the danger of war. In this atmosphere the final fight was prepared.

The storm broke in Germany, where, in September 1928, the right wing of the central committee managed for a few days to win the majority and to overthrow Thaelmann. On an order from Moscow the whole central committee voted for the repeal of this measure, and the right-wing leaders were excluded from the central committee. Then, a new, clearly outlined era of extremism was inaugurated in all communist parties.

This new extremism was inaugurated long before the world depression set in, though this depression gave it an enormous impulse. The main doctrine of the 'new' policy was the same as that of every previous turn of the Comintern to the left. Ordinary trade-union work and the ordinary parliamentary activities of the modern labour movement were again condemned as traitorous, as they had been by the ultra-left around Gorter in 1919–20 and by Maslow and his friends in 1924–5. Only this time the biggest economic crisis the world had ever experienced provided an ideal ground for the spreading of left extremism.

One reason obviously was the enormous amount of suffering to which almost every class and social stratum was subjected by the world depression, and which naturally created a widespread exasperation and readiness for violent means. But the effects of the world depression are not exhausted by such a vague description. Depressions, and especially an economic depression of such a scope as that of 1929–33, do not create readiness for every sort of fight. The masses of unemployed, who determine, more and more, in such a situation the views and actions even of those who have remained in work, are little adapted to continual, methodical fights for determined aims. They waver between short, wild, desperate outbreaks and complete apathy. They naturally distrust their own forces and look out for a saviour to do what they cannot do. They leave in millions their old organizations, partly because they cannot any longer afford the small expenses connected with membership, but mostly because they feel that these organizations are powerless to help them. Here, then, is the point where left-wing extremism of the type of 1929 meets admirably the mood of the workless. If the communist agitators tell the unemployed that the trade unions have betrayed him and are no good, he is ready to believe them. If they tell the worker who is still employed that the union—by betrayal, of course—cannot protect either his wages or his job, he feels that the communists are right—and leaves the union. Thus the turn of the Comintern to the left, which had originated in internal feuds rooted in its previous history, found an unexpected response among the workers as a result of the crisis.

The theory of the 'third period' provided general justification for the new policy. It was now definitely interpreted as implying the beginning of a new revolutionary era. The change of tactics had been a mild one at the beginning. But the new trend had its own momentum, which drove to ever more furious exaggerations, and additional factors worked to increase the original impetus. One of them was the resistance met by the new tactics among the right-wing elements within the communist parties and which merged with the bitter fight between Bukharin and Stalin in Russia. A second element was the first Five-Year Plan in Russia, with its fearful vicissitudes, the attempts to collectivize agriculture in one year, the driving out of millions of wealthy peasants to the arctic wilderness, the famine, the trials of alleged wreckers, etc. The specific atmosphere of the first Five-Year Plan, formed of a mixture of wild enthusiasm, cruel persecution, disregard for the suffering of countless victims, bureaucratic corruption and inefficiency— an atmosphere as un-Western as anything can be—transferred itself automatically to the leading Comintern men who were living in Moscow or in close contact with it, and brought this atmosphere of civil war in the midst of peace to the European communists. In the course of this crisis, Bukharin was ousted from the presidency of the Comintern. No new president was nominated. Stalin did not want to entrust anybody with this outstanding qualification. The real work was handed over to Molotov, a man who had never been abroad, and to a number of minor personalities such as Manuilski, Kuusinen, and others. The choice of this personnel was a clear implication that international communism was no longer regarded as important in itself, but as a minor dependency of the Russian state, directed not even so much along the lines of Russian *raison d'état*, as according to the necessities of Stalin's fight with his factional adversaries in Russia.

But, in Europe, a very propitious atmosphere for the new policy of the Comintern was created by the sufferings, the exaltations, the wild revolutionary illusions, and the deep and growing despair brought about by the world depression. These paroxysms provided a suitable atmosphere for the growth of Fascist mass movements all over the world, and the rapid growth of Fascism, with the menaces and the seductions it entailed for the various communist parties, added, in its turn, to the general hysteria of the Comintern machinery and the machinery of the various communist parties. At no moment, however, did Moscow take practical steps for the preparation of a revolution in the West during this period, which proves that it did not regard it as a practical proposition. But the trend to the left which had been created within the communist parties suited it well.

The new policy started from the usual starting-point of all previous turns to the left, the rejection of alliances with the social-democratic and labour leaders. This naturally implied a rejection of co-operation with their respective parties. But soon this was insufficient. In the new extension of left extremism the German communists, as usual, went farthest. It had been customary in Berlin on May 1st to gather all workers in one big demonstration under the banners of the trade unions. The individual political parties had been free to participate in these demonstrations under their own banners. Now, in 1929, the communists decided to start a demonstration of their own which, in the opinion of the police, very likely implied the danger of violent clashes between socialists and communists. The police were only too right; such clashes continued throughout the following years, until both parties met in the jails and concentration camps of Hitler. The police president of Berlin, the socialist Zoergiebel, reacted to the communist plan of a separate demonstration by prohibiting all processions on Mayday, thus depriving communists and socialists alike of a right they had enjoyed since the revolution of 1918. The socialists submitted, but the communists attempted resistance. The police made use of their arms, and one working-class district of Berlin, Neukoelln, was covered with barricades for two days. But while a small stratum of communists resisted the police, the communists' appeal for a general strike all over the Reich found a response—in one single factory of sweetmeats. The average worker did not feel at all implicated by the attempt of the communists to settle their own accounts with the socialists and the police.

Similar events occurred in Paris on this May-day of 1929, with the difference that here the socialists were not involved. Processions on May-day had always been prohibited in Paris. Once, in 1919, the socialists had attempted to break through the prohibition, but had been defeated. Now, in 1929, the communists came back to the charge, but they met complete disaster. For years the socialist press had mentioned one name in the highest circles of the Communist Party as being a police spy; but the man had always accepted every order from above and was therefore regarded as very useful. Anyway, whether the charge was true or not, the police proved to be in possession of the complete lists of the party; all active members of the party in Paris, to the number of three thousand, were arrested on April 30th and released again on May 2nd. No demonstrations had taken place. All over the world the new tactics suffered similar defeats on this May-day.

The effects were very serious. The very helplessness and lack of strength which had been displayed on that occasion drove the communists to fury. Up to that day the communists had always attempted to draw a line of division between the socialist leaders and the average socialists and trade-unionists, and had tried to convince the latter that they were betrayed by the former. May-day 1929 once more had shown that this was not so and that the policy of the leaders more or less agreed with the views of the members. As a result a new theory was proclaimed, to the effect that every single member of the socialist parties and every single active member of the trade unions was 'a little Zoergiebel', i.e. an active enemy of the proletariat. Attempts were made to prove that this whole stratum, four-fifths of the politically and industrially active proletarians were directly bribed by the bourgeoisie. Open conflict with these elements was the first duty of every true revolutionary, if possible with the means of physical force. But this was not yet enough. Here and there the idea had been raised within the communist ranks that a Fascist policy could be carried through by a socialist party. The careers of Mussolini and Pilsudski went to show what element of truth there was in such a contention. The communists, moreover, were always inclined to regard every forceful stroke directed against them as a symptom of Fascism, and concluded that Zoergiebel and his like, who after all were quite minor personalities, were the arch-Fascists. At that time the Reich government was formed of all moderate parties to the exclusion of the extreme right and the extreme left, and the socialists participated; the chancellor,

Hermann Mueller, was one of their men. Now after the May-day disaster, the communists concluded that this was essentially a Fascist government under socialist leadership. The socialists were 'social-Fascists'. Democracy and Fascism were finally identified. He who fought democracy fought also Fascism. All through the years 1929 and 1930 the war-cry of 'social-Fascism' was raised and followed up by a series of physical conflicts between communists and socialists.

In July 1930 the German coalition government under socialist leadership was overthrown, the Catholic Brüning became chancellor and the Reichstag was dissolved. The new elections, to the surprise of everybody, brought 107 Nazis into the Reichstag. It was the beginning of the end. But the communists had no eye for the general situation. They were entirely filled with the hatred of their competititors the socialists, a hatred which, among the leading personnel of the party and the old members, originated in the sense of inability to break the very stable ranks of the unions and the Socialist Party; among the masses of the unemployed, the same hatred arose out of disappointment with the organizations which had not been able to help them. Nowhere was there an attempt to bring the working class into the forefront of politics again. The communists, powerless to influence events, sought consolation in taking their vengeance on the competititors within the labour movement which they had been unable to overcome. Vengeance had by now become the only driving idea behind communist tactics. It led the party to incredible lengths. In spring 1931 the Nazis, together with the conservative Nationalists, launched a campaign for a referendum to overthrow the Prussian provincial government, where the socialists still held a leading position. A referendum in Germany proceeded by two stages. First 10 per cent of the electorate had to sign their names in lists demanding a referendum; then the referendum itself took place. It was sure beforehand that the Nazis and nationalists would obtain the 10 per cent necessary to bring about the referendum. When they had obtained that, the communists joined the Nazi campaign. This was no longer simply the theory of 'social-Fascism', the belief that there was no difference between Fascism and democracy and that the social-democrats were just as bad as the Nazis. The communists were to have reason to contemplate, in the cellars of the Gestapo, the relation of this theory of social-Fascism to social reality; but their participation in the Nazi referendum implied more. It implied the view that to overthrow the last defence of German democracy, the Prussian government, in co-operation with the Nazis, meant progress, that a Nazi régime was preferable to a democratic régime. The view was voiced openly in public propaganda at the time; the situation, it was contended, was revolutionary. To overthrow democracy was therefore a step forward, because it meant actual revolution. And such a revolution must be communist in character. They had their revolution; it happened to be a Fascist one. But they did not get it yet. For their own electorate refused to follow them, and not more than from two and a half to three million communist votes were cast in favour of the Nazi referendum.

The phalanx of the socialist and trade-union movement was later to be broken by the Nazis; but to the last day it remained immune to communist attacks, or nearly so. The communists, in their blind frenzy, acted like people who for ten years, with various methods, have tried to break through the front of the enemy, and now, exasperated by repeated failure and by the new sufferings and strains of economic depression, suddenly start to leap about aimlessly and by doing so butt their heads against a wall. Looking back at that period to-day, it is obvious that the tactics applied by the communists during this phase, tactics which had no longer anything to do with the interests of labour, but were uniquely dictated by a desire for revenge on their most bitter enemies, the socialists, were the last stage before the approaching disintegration of the movement as a whole. The man who carried these tactics out was, again, Heinz Neumann, the man with the craving for ruthless and irresponsible action. He had been in disgrace after Canton, but with the left-wing policy unfolding itself the German party had obtained forgiveness for him and called him back. It was only after the defeat of the referendum campaign that the most extreme aspects of his policy were criticized in Moscow. Moscow insisted that a difference be drawn again between the simple socialist members and their leaders, that the 'united front from below' be applied. It made very little difference in practice; but Heinz Neumann opposed even that much and fell into disgrace a third time, never again to emerge.

There was, however, one aspect of the political situation which was really apt to make the German communists over-estimate their own forces: parliamentary elections. There was one in 1928, which had given the party three and a quarter million votes; then a new one in 1930, two campaigns for the presidency of the Reich in 1932, and general elections in July and November 1932 and in March 1933. At almost all these elections the communists were able to book considerable gains, and in November 1932 actually obtained six million votes, or between one-sixth and one-seventh of the total poll. The socialists, till the end, remained somewhat stronger than the communists, and the Nazis, at the elections of July 1932, had obtained fourteen million votes. But this fact, by far more significant than the relatively small communist increase, was overlooked. In deep self-satisfaction the communists decided that one communist vote equalled several Nazi votes in importance. Actually, the contrary was the case. When the electorate was called to the polls millions expressed their disgust with democracy and the economic misery by voting communist; but the same people were not to be brought to any more serious action.

This state of things revealed itself very clearly in the industrial field. Up to then, with a short break in 1924-5, the communists, in the elections of the shop-stewards in the factories (in the German republic the shop-stewards were an institution acknowledged and organized by law), had voted for the lists presented by the trade unions; they had attempted to throw their weight as a party into the scales not in the shop-steward elections themselves, but in the nomination of the trade-union candidates, trying to capture as many of those candidates as possible for the party. In 1929, however, the party decided that the unions, in their evolution from social-patriotism to social-Fascism, had ceased to be working-class organizations, in spite of their four million members, and that the party must in every factory oppose the trade-union list with its own list. Experts in trade-union matters forecast a tremendous defeat of the communists, but were deceived. On the whole, the communists did very well with their independent lists for the shop-steward elections. As in the political elections, so in the factories, the workers gave the communists their votes in great numbers when called to the polls. It did not imply any responsibility, and things were different when it came to action. After the shop-steward elections of 1929 the employers simply dismissed certain communist shop-stewards, and the workers who had voted for them now flatly refused to strike in order to obtain their reinstatement.

During these years the Communist Party carried on an almost continual agitation for both political and economic strikes. From 1929 to 1932 the party issued the slogan of a general strike no less than six times. The first time, in May 1929, one sweetmeat factory responded, but later on not a single factory. Used in such a way, the idea of a general strike was discredited. This had the most disastrous effects when German democracy was finally overthrown. On 20th July 1932 the new Chancellor of the Reich, Papen, simply threw out the Prussian government, which the Nazis and communists together had not been able to overthrow the year before. The socialists failed to launch a general strike, such as they had launched against Kapp in March 1920. We are not concerned here with the history of the social-democratic movement, but it must be said in order to put the defeat of the communists in its real context that, whatever the chances, the failure to fight in defence of their government, which had been ousted by a *coup d'état*, sealed the fate of German socialism. The communists had their full share of the disaster as well. When they called for a general strike in order to defend the government which they had attempted to overthrow the year before, not a soul moved. And the same situation reproduced itself, with much more disastrous effects, with the arrival of Hitler.

As to economic strikes, little need be said. The communists decided that they must break loose from trade-union discipline, as the unions were decided not to fight in the thick of the crisis. Manifestly unable to carry with them large numbers, the communists induced the individual factories where they were in the majority to strike. The effects were invariably disastrous. Strikes without the support of the bulk of the organized workers, undertaken in a crisis such as that raging in Germany, were simply hopeless, and the communists lost what authority they had. But that led only to a new move. The communists had been excluded all along the line from the unions for their manifold breaches of rules and discipline and now started to set up their own unions, called 'revolutionary trade-union opposition'. These unions never won more than a few thousand members. It is noteworthy, however, that the few branches where they won any allegiance at all were specifically aristocratic branches. Outstanding among them were certain groups of mechanics, who owing to their high-grade specialization, could never be replaced and were still able to fight while the mass of the proletariat was helpless. But even here the attempts to strike led invariably to defeat. On the whole, with all its splits, agitation, moves, and slogans, the Communist Party, during these four years, certainly did not persuade more than a hundred thousand workers to strike, and those only for a few days and with invariably disastrous results.

All this did not pass entirely without resistance from the ranks of the party. When the new policy was inaugurated the elements of the right wing which had joined Thaelmann in 1925 were thrown out of the leading group, submitting meekly and confessing their sins. But there were those who had never agreed or never been allowed to enter the middle group which had led the party since 1925. Among them were Brandler and Thalheimer, the leaders of the party in 1923, and a relatively numerous group of their friends. They did not compromise, did not confess their sins, and were accordingly excluded in 1929. They made an attempt to carry on with an organization of their own, called 'Communist Opposition', and a number of old communist trade-unionists joined them. They had a number of successes, but the first provincial elections showed that they would never be able to become a mass movement, and they slowly disintegrated. The reasons for their failure were the same as those which had brought down the left, Maslow, and Ruth Fischer, two years before: the masses did not understand the tactical differences between the various wings of the communist movement and voted for the one which represented Moscow and a mass movement.

In our description of the new tactics we have concentrated on Germany, because the new tactics in their most extreme form were evolved there and because they had their share in bringing about the success of Hitler; in other countries the action of the communists had no such historical importance. But the essential features of the new tactics were the same everywhere: the doctrine of 'social-Fascism', the complete break with the social-democratic parties, and occasional collaboration with the parties of the right, the split within the trade unions and the attempts to create communist unions, the playing about with general strikes, the pretence that a proletarian revolution was approaching, and finally the ruthless exclusion of all elements which opposed these tactics. But whereas in Germany the turn to the left happened to coincide with a political crisis of historical bearing, the sole effect, in most other countries, was nearly to annihilate the existing communist parties.

In Holland a split had already occurred in 1927 and the most outstanding leaders of the party, Wynkoop and van Ravesteyn, had been excluded. Part of the dissidents returned after the policy had again been changed to the right. But the Dutch Communist Party had no importance. The effects of the new policy in Sweden were much more disastrous. The Swedish Communist Party had not suffered, like other communist parties, from the repeated splits it had undergone; on the contrary, after the exclusion of Hoeglund and his group in 1924 it had flourished. From about eight thousand members it had increased to eighteen thousand under its new leaders, Kilbom, Samuelson, and Flyg. It was still a small party compared with the socialists, but a rising one. The Swedish party had done competent work within the trade unions. Therefore in the new era it must be regarded as right-wing. But it was not only right-wing, it was independent. It had managed, alone among about forty parties, to make itself financially independent of Moscow. When the new policy was inaugurated almost the whole of the leaders turned against it. It was a case of dangerous rebellion. Practically the whole of the Swedish Communist Party was immediately excluded. As the whole of the old leaders, most of the press and of the active members went with the dissidents, they were not in such a helpless position as was Brandler in Germany. Repeatedly, in general elections, they scored a considerably higher poll than the official Communist Party which had been formed out of the remnants of the old Communist Party.[1]

Few right-wingers remained to be excluded in France. In England the party bought off the menacing split by meekly submitting to the new policy *en bloc*. The Czechoslovakian split has already been mentioned. The right wing in Poland was now excluded. So was the right wing in Austria, in Finland, and elsewhere. The split in the Communist Party of the United States was particularly grave. Here the two factions of Foster on the one hand and Lovestone on the other had fought one another almost since the party existed. Neither of them could be regarded as specifically 'right' or 'left'. But Lovestone had made the mistake of allying himself with Bukharin. Stalin looked to it that he and his group were pushed back to the wall. In their defence they took up the fight against the new tactics. They were excluded, taking with them a very considerable part of the party.

In most countries the importance of these splits for general politics was near zero. But their importance for the character and evolution of the communist parties was very great, and indirectly these splits influenced political developments in many countries when, in 1934, the communist parties turned again to the right and emerged again as a political force. Between 1928 and 1934 the communist parties had largely changed their character. With all the preceding exclusions and the rigid discipline which had always been a hallmark of communism, the communist parties of the previous period had known a certain amount of intellectual liberty. Definite departures from communist doctrine had been anathema and had been rewarded with immediate exclusion. But it had been regarded as normal though as undesirable for a communist party to harbour in its ranks various opinions, some more to the right, others more to the left. The first interference of the Russian factional feuds in Comintern affairs had dealt a heavy blow to this relative liberty. Together with Sinovjev and Trotsky, the left leaders in the parties of the Comintern had been excluded. Now the fight between Stalin and Bukharin implied the same fate for the leaders of the right. Thus, during

[1] Until finally, in 1937, the majority of the dissident communists joined the socialist party of Sweden.

the early period of the Comintern all those who had not desired a full break with the socialists had been driven away, and during the later developments first the left and then the right wing had been broken. Those who remained had been obliged to deny at least once their political convictions, with all the effects inevitably implied by such an action.

We have repeatedly pointed out, however, that this evolution was not entirely due to the change of character of the Russian régime. The very idea that defeats are generally due to some sort of betrayal involved the search for scapegoats and repeated exclusions. And now, during the period of the turn to the left, this mentality had reached its highest pitch. Every socialist worker, every active trade-unionist, bribed, a social-Fascist, a traitor? Such conceptions had little political opinion behind them, they were an expression of impotent rage. But if all these descriptions applied to the socialist arch-enemies, what then of those who suggested a certain amount of co-operation, or at least a certain amount of consideration for the prejudices of such villains? What about a Brandler or Kilbom or—in Poland—Warski, or—in Czechoslovakia—Jilek or—in America—Lovestone, who were impudent enough to suggest that normally the communists must not break trade-union rules and must do their best to avoid exclusion? Allies of the social-Fascists, worse than those rascals themselves, arch-traitors among the traitors! Between the two there was, however, a difference. The high pitch of communist insults touched the socialists very little; it made it easier for them to keep their flock away from communist influence. But the small groups of communist right-wingers were not in the same boat. They were helpless against these attacks, and the left-wingers, while failing to break the power of the socialists, took their revenge in a ruthless hunt after right 'deviations' within the party. Thus the very fact of failure drove the communist parties to ever more extreme forms of left extremism.

But after a time an entirely new situation arose within the communist parties. Hitherto there had always been some overt criticism and opposition to party politics. After 1930 there was none, either in Russia or in the West, and this made the finding of scapegoats very difficult. In an attempt to understand the tens and probably hundreds of thousands of condemnations for 'wrecking' in Russia one must not forget that the series of sensational trials of that class started when the last overt opposition had disappeared. And immediately the practice was transferred to the International.

One day in 1931 a number of former Russian Mensheviks confessed that Abramovich, a leading Russian Menshevik and member of the executive bureau of the Second International, had been to Russia in order to form a conspiracy for the overthrow of the Soviet government. The defendants confessed that Abramovich had acted at the direct orders of the bureau of the Second International. It is doubtful whether, to-day, the communists like to remember that on that occasion they charged men such as Léon Blum with organizing conspiracies in Russia. Anyway, Blum has been kind in not again mentioning the story of late. As to Abramovich, it was easy for the socialist International to reprint an old photo in which he sat amidst his colleagues of the International bureau just the very day when he was supposed to have been conspiring with the Mensheviks in Moscow.

It was not long before 'wrecking' started within the Communist International itself. This happened in connection with the very slow, hesitant, and insignificant turn to the right which, as mentioned, the Comintern effected at the end of 1931. At the eleventh plenary session of the executive bureau Heinz Neumann, as explained, was ousted and at the same time the communist parties were ordered to take a less sectarian line. Practical effects in politics there were hardly any. But the effects were big inside the communist parties themselves. Confessions such as those deposed before Russian courts were not obtainable outside Russian territory, but at one moment, and as if an order had been given to all communist parties simultaneously, intentional wrecking activities were discovered within almost every communist party. We will quote a few examples, because neither the 'régime' nor the policy of communist parties in the present phase is intelligible without a somewhat closer investigation of these cases.

Let us start, at random, with the case of Esthonia. It is a case not very interesting in itself, but interesting for the truly staggering revelations produced from official communist sources.

'With the help of *agents provocateurs*', writes *Imprecorr* (No. 104, 1932), 'the secret police succeeded, during the last five or six years, not only in arresting many underground workers and killing them, but even in destroying whole organizations of the Esthonian communist party. But the most important thing is that the police succeeded in deviating for several years the policy of the left-wing trade unions and in pushing them along the way of opportunism. The agents of the secret police who had managed to enter the central committee of the left-wing trade unions transformed them during these last years into small, sectarian opportunist organizations, which stood outside the revolutionary struggle of the prole-tariat and hampered it. . . . In consequence, and as a result of the weakness of the Esthonian Communist Party, the secret police even succeeded in carrying two of its agents to parlia-ment upon the lists of the left-wing workers. Among the editors of the paper of the left-wing unions were agents of the police too. . . . At the beginning of 1932 the leaders of the Esthonian Communist Party declared ruthless war on the system of provocation. The parliamentary group of the left-wing workers decided to exclude the provocateurs Roman Laes and Tamson from the parliamentary group.'

Had the two deputies thus excluded from the parliamentary group of the left-wing unions (which stood under communist leadership) betrayed this or that communist into the hands of the police? A careful reading of the document goes to show that this is not even alleged in it. The charge of their being in the service of the police is based uniquely on their 'sectarian, opportunist' policy. The combination of the words 'sectarian' and 'opportunist' seems to be self-contradictory. 'Sectarian', in the ordinary use of the word, means a policy which avoids close contact with the masses, 'opportunist' a policy which takes too much account of the masses. To speak of 'sectarian opportunism' is equivalent to saying 'the leaders of the right left extremists'. As to the fact that others have betrayed com-munists to the police, it is only mentioned in order to create the general 'atmosphere' in which words such as 'police agents', 'provocation,' etc., seem credible. As to their 'sec-tarian opportunist policy', it had been carried out under orders from Moscow; during this period Stalin kept an iron control over all details of Comintern work, and both the policy and the lists of parliamentary candidates of the communist parties were rigidly controlled by Moscow. The Esthonian Communist Party started its campaign against 'provocation', in reality against the previous policy of the Comintern, immediately after, at the eleventh plenum, a change of policy had been ordered. In the light of all these circumstances the sensational disclosures about the connection of two Esthonian communist M.P.s with the police boil down to the following: the Esthonian communists have carried out, at the orders of Moscow, a policy which, at the eleventh plenum of the E.C.C.I., was regarded as sectarian and had annihilated the party's influence among the workers. Those who had stood for that policy were immediately excluded and their policy, in order to discredit it, was described as the work of *agents provocateurs*.

For how could it otherwise be explained that, as in Esthonia, the whole policy of the Communist Party in France had been determined by the political police? In No. 1, 1932, *Imprecorr* informs the surprised members of the Comintern that 'a closed, conspiratorial group has existed for several years within the French Communist Party and has concealed its existence from the Comintern'. To this group belonged, among others, the comrades Barbé, Celor, Loseray, Billoux, Guyot, Couteilhas, and Galopin. The discovery of this group in Paris coincides almost exactly in time with the discovery of the group in Esthonia and immediately follows the eleventh plenum. What a coincidence! The charge of collaboration with the police is not raised at once. To begin with, the existence of this conspiracy is made responsible, as in Esthonia, for the complete failure of the policy of the party. The party has failed, says the same article of *Imprecorr*, to weaken the social-democrats, the strongest social support of the dictatorship of the bourgeoisie, and that in spite of the increasingly cynical betrayal of the socialists and the reformist trade unions (C.G.T.). 'One of the chief reasons for this situation' is the conspiracy just mentioned. But if in January the conspiracy is simply a secret faction within the party, more has been discovered in later months. Or rather, some of those who have been discovered have submitted and recanted, whereas others have persisted in their views, have been excluded, and are now charged with connections with the political police. No. 84 of *Imprecorr* of the same year, in announcing the exclusion of Celor, adds the following comment:

'The decision of the central committee to exclude Celor will certainly be a surprise to many. Nothing is more intelligible. Celor left the party in ignorance of his dark past, hid his betrayal behind a model simplicity and modesty, always created the impression of being absorbed in the work of the party to the exclusion of every other interest, did not allow himself a holiday in spite of his illness, was always full of activity and zeal; this man was not a common traitor. No, he was a master of hypocrisy, which he used with quite exceptional cleverness. This explains how this agent of the bourgeoisie could abuse the confidence and the sympathies of many comrades and thus could become a leading figure of the party.' Vague accusations of police connections follow, without the slightest attempt at giving concrete evidence. In Esthonia it is impossible for a communist to go to the courts with an action for slander or libel without endangering the lifes of many of his comrades. In France that is not so. Any concrete charge would lead to immediate refutation.

Space does not allow the quotation of more instances, among them a similar discovery, at the same time, under the same circumstances, of how in reality the Polish secret police determined the policy which up to then Moscow had believed with good reason it had determined itself. It is noteworthy, however, that at that time the idea of an international conspiracy had not yet been hatched, which makes the coincidence only more miraculous. It appears that at the same time, under very different circumstances, the political police in Nanking, Reval, Warsaw, and Paris, not to mention other places, had used the same methods, with the same results, and that its agents had been found out at the same time; but it is not alleged that these police organizations had worked in co-operation, nor that a Russian faction had been behind the organization. We mentioned Nanking and must enlarge a little on the instance of China because, by pure chance, this example allows of closer investigation. Edgar Snow has told the public the story of the Li-li-sian rising in the Kiangsi Soviet territory, as Mao-tse-tung had told it to him, and as we have repeated it from Snow's account in the last chapter. The story, as told there, is very different from the mysterious stories about conspiracies within the communist parties in other countries. There is nothing to arouse suspicion. The fact that the Chinese communists tended to settle their differences arms in hand can be traced in other sources than the account of Mao-tse-tung. The rising at the end of December 1931 was reported not only in the communist press but also in the Kuomintang press. The political motives of the rising are completely intelligible. The rebels were left-wingers who protested against the relative moderation of Mao-tse-tung. Naturally, they did not look for support from the Kuomintang—their only aim was to fight it more ruthlessly than Mao-tse-tung—and Mao, in his account, does not charge them with co-operation with the enemy. All seems to be perfectly clear. But let us see now what Wan-min, Chinese representative at the Comintern in Moscow, has to tell us about the same event (in *Imprecorr*, No. 9, 1932):

'These elements were able to enter the ranks of the party and of the Soviets by simulating left-extremism and revolutionary activities. . . . Using their positions they carried out a policy full of phrases but totally impracticable, in order to discredit the Soviets in the eyes of the masses and to undermine the confidence of the poor peasants in the Soviets. Through the captured General Yo-wi-djun they established contact with Chiang Kai-Shek; but the vigilance of the nursing personnel of the hospital where the captured general lay undid the attempt.' A long account of the repression, arrests, executions follows. 'The correct line of the Communist Party', the report goes on to say, 'and the fight against two fronts within the party' was of the highest importance in overcoming the danger.

So far *Imprecorr*. In order to interpret its report one must keep in mind Snow's statement that Wan-min's reports are always 'fantastic' and that the Chinese Soviets had for years no contact whatsoever with *Imprecorr*. If nothing but a Kuomintang conspiracy within the Soviets had happened Mao would have told Snow so. But the report as given in *Imprecorr* implies that from the very beginning the extreme left wing within the Chinese Soviets had no aim but to discredit the Soviet régime in order to help the enemies of Chinese communism, and that they joined the party and the Soviets for that purpose. But if that was so there must have been contacts with the Kuomintang from the beginning, and not for only a few months before the revolt broke out. But it would be difficult for Wan-min to make a statement to that effect. The people expelled and executed are the very people who for years have led the Chinese communists, with the full consent of the Comintern and in accordance with its orders, orders which came from Stalin directly. In the end, as so often in Russian and Comintern history, the question arises whether Stalin has conspired against himself. If he did not do that the remaining interpretation, and the one carrying a considerable amount of probability, is that he changed his mind. As for China, this change occurred in the summer of 1931; as for the Comintern as a whole, the line was changed at the eleventh plenum, and it was here that the 'fight against two fronts', against both the right *and* the extreme left, was launched, whereas before only the right wing had been the object of condemnation and vilification. At the same time all over the world it was discovered that the leaders of the extreme left were *agents provocateurs*. Is the suggestion too far-fetched that the case of a *real* rising of the extreme left in Kiangsi was too good an opportunity not to be fitted into the general scheme by people in Moscow who knew nothing about the details of the event?

From the beginning the communist parties, naturally, had struggled against spies and *agents provocateurs*. Repeatedly it had been alleged by anti-communists that police spies held leading positions within various communist parties, but this time it was the communists themselves who stated that the most outstanding leaders of some of the most important parties had been *agents provocateurs* and that the whole of the policy of these parties had for years been the work of the political police. It was the same policy which, in every detail, had been ordered by Moscow. And the difficulties arising out of this fact would be insoluble were there not one more factor implicated. At the end of 1931 the Comintern attempted to change its policy somewhat to the right. This went together with a general reshuffling of the leading personnel. That a change of policy must bring a change of personnel with it was by this time already a matter of course, and—this is the decisive fact—those who submitted were not particularly roughly treated. Only those who resisted were immediately denounced as police spies, with or without proof. A novel element had entered into the Comintern: denunciations within the ranks of the Comintern itself as a normal means of minor political changes.

It is truly remarkable how little importance reality had for the communists at that stage. The decisions of the eleventh plenum, implying a turn to the right, were never carried out in practice. All remained the same for many years: the same hopeless lack of influence within the existing mass organizations, the same fratricidal feuds with the socialists, the same political insignificance of the communist parties. The one thing which had been changed was the leadership of the parties; it had been purged of the last elements likely to stick to a definite policy or reluctant to accept every order from above. And the members seemed quite content to have found scapegoats. International communism had reached its lowest ebb. But what was this membership which accepted, without murmuring, such a system? We must describe now the social and political character of the communist parties during this period.

CHAPTER XXI

THE STRUCTURE OF THE
COMMUNIST PARTIES

Statistics are the normal means of knowledge about the strength, the social structure, the age structure, and other essential facts of a modern organization. But one seeks in vain for regular and reliable statistics of the communist parties, such as those published regularly by many trade unions and socialist parties. The primary necessity for such statistical work, the need to work out a regular budget, is lacking. Almost all communist parties are largely dependent on money from Moscow, money which comes in rather irregularly, according to the good or bad position an individual party holds at Moscow, according to the political importance Moscow considers a given party to have at a given moment. Therefore, budgets on the basis of membership never existed within the communist parties. It is necessary, however, to point out that this financial dependency on Moscow, important as it is, does not account simply and directly for everything in the history of the Communist International, as is sometimes believed. With its money alone Moscow might have bought people ready for every sort of action except the sacrifice of their lives. But there are hundreds and thousands of communists who are prepared to sacrifice their lives. It is not money, to be sure, which has determined their attitude, and the reason for their unquestioning allegiance to Moscow is not money but the mythical authority of the Russian revolution. But we must return to the problem of communist statistics.

Besides the lack of a regular budget all communist parties have suffered from other great irregularities. Repeated prohibitions and persecutions of many parties have disorganized the ranks and made it impossible to get a clear picture of the character of the membership. The factional feuds, the frequent wholesale change of leadership, have worked in the same direction. More important, perhaps, is the desire of every party leader to look well in the eyes of Moscow. This has made for the publication of sometimes quite fantastic figures which deserve no confidence.

Control of facts concerning the structure of the communist parties was soon impossible, as far as the party members themselves might have wished to exert such a control, for policy and administration became concentrated in a few hands. At the beginning most parties had been under the leadership of fairly numerous 'central committees' which generally represented all shades of opinion existing within the individual parties, but since about 1925 these central committees had gradually lost their importance and been replaced, de facto, by so-called 'political bureaux', formed after the model of the Russian 'Polit-Bureau', which consists of seven members and leads the destinies of the Russian people. In these 'polit-bureaux', the critical tendencies within the parties had no longer a voice. They represented those few shades of opinion which were allowed to participate in the working out of party policy, and the general trend was to allow finally only one group, one leader with his obedient partisans, to form the political bureau. At the same time the federal autonomy of the individual regions and districts which made up a national party was seriously curtailed, to the point of annihilation. At the beginning, those districts had been more or less free to elect their own regional committees; in the process of time, those committees, and with them the editorial boards of the provincial as well as of the central press, were de facto named by the 'polit-bureau'. Finally, the active membership itself was deprived, as early as 1926, of any possibility of exerting in practice its formal right to participate in the laying down of party policy. This happened in connection with the formation of 'nuclei', soon to be discussed in another context. The essence of this reform, which was introduced after the model of an age-long Russian tradition, consisted in the grouping of all communists within a single factory, and sometimes within a small group of several streets, into one 'nucleus'. Most of these nuclei before

1935 were very small and few had more than fifty members. Previously, the active members of a big town had been called together for weekly or fortnightly conferences, where various opinions had been voiced and put to a vote. These conferences of the active membership, to which practically every party member was admitted, represented the really democratic element within the communist parties. These conferences, to give one instance, overthrew Brandler after the defeat of October 1923. But as soon as the nuclei were introduced little of this democracy remained. When a new problem arose, the nuclei were informed by speakers chosen from the party machinery, and the opposition had no chance to voice its opinion adequately in hundreds of nuclei meetings. Only when every opposition had disappeared were general meetings of the members again permitted.

But if every sort of control from below was rigorously suppressed, control from above became only more important and more rigid. The 'polit-bureau', which could largely ignore the opinion of a membership that was exclusively instructed by themselves, trembled before Moscow. And what knowledge we have about the structure and inner life of the various communist parties derives mostly from the attempts of the Comintern to investigate the doings of its subordinates. Soon after the Comintern had become a regularly working organization, an organizing bureau, shortly called Org-Bureau, was created, whose exclusive aim it was to control the practical everyday work of the communist parties. At the head of this bureau stood one Ossip Piatnitzki, a man who had acquired a very large experience in underground work as an early member of the Bolshevik Party. The leaders of the Comintern were changed: Sinovjev was followed by Bukharin, Bukharin was followed by Molotov. But through all these changes Piatnitzki remained at the head of the Org-Bureau. Piatnitzki had a chance of comparing, from day to day, the serious revolutionary work he had done in his own youth as a Bolshevik with the flippant inefficiency of most Comintern parties. He soon developed a strong contempt for his subordinates, and together with it a deep-seated conviction that the one possible remedy for their incompetence was to lash them publicly. This was in the old Bolshevik tradition. The time had not yet come when self-criticism meant criticism whose content, object, and result had been ordered from above. Thus, for many years, from time to time Piatnitzki on public occasions gave the real data concerning the structure of the most important communist parties and opposed them to the pretences made by those parties. His utterances constitute an invaluable source of Comintern history. Naturally, such frankness could not continue indefinitely. From the moment when, in 1934, Dimitrov was named president of the Comintern, Piatnitzki had to stop his criticisms. The result is that after 1934 we are almost as completely ignorant of the real state of the communist parties as we were before 1924, when Piatnitzki started his reports. This, on the whole, distorts the existing evidence to the damage of the Comintern. For there is no doubt that the year 1934 marks the lowest ebb of communist influence and that since this moment the influence of the communist parties, with a complete change of policy, has increased very considerably. But, considerable as the increase is, we cannot accept simply the official communist utterances concerning it. Where Piatnitzki more than once has attempted a serious analysis of the rough membership figures, the official utterances after his time limit themselves precisely to those rough figures which carry little conviction. What for instance is the value of knowing that the Spanish Communist Party in March 1937 had 250,000 members (provided the figure is exact) if we are not allowed to learn how many of these were foreigners, Catalans, Castilians, how many were town workers, agricultural labourers, peasants, intellectuals, officials, police agents, officers, etc.? We are forced to limit ourselves to those data which are sufficiently ample to allow of a real analysis.

The control work of Piatnitzki, as carried out between 1924 and 1934, is closely connected with the attempt to introduce the Russian system of nuclei into the factories. In problems of organization, as in all other problems, the Russians were somewhat naïvely convinced of their own superiority. They overlooked, as usual, the differences between Russia and the West. Their idea was that revolutionary actions of the proletariat must start from the factories and must fail unless the communist parties obtain a direct hold on the factories. Therefore the communist parties, instead of being grouped as the socialists according to the boundaries of parliamentary and municipal constituencies, must be grouped according to their work. In Russia it was an admirable system for many reasons. The enemy there was mainly the police and not the factory-owner, who, on the contrary, very often looked more than mildly upon the organizing work of the revolutionaries. With the passive and sometimes the active help of the liberal bourgeoisie the Bolsheviks hid themselves successfully in the factories. Moreover, industrial and political organization were not clearly differentiated any more than industrial and political conflict, and the nuclei in the factories assumed largely the functions of trade-union organizers. It was different in Europe, where the communist nucleus stood, primarily, against the majority of the socialist and trade-union workers, who did nothing to protect it, and, in the second place, against the owners. In these circumstances the nuclei usually had the choice between keeping silent or seeing all their members dismissed within a very short time. The members themselves regarded work in the nuclei as an almost unbearable threat to their economic existence. The danger was made worse by the rapid change of communist policy; if, for instance, the communists broke trade-union discipline in a given factory all those who were active in defending this policy were known automatically and treated accordingly by both unions and employers. The factual collaboration of union officials and employers in such cases provided arguments for the talk about 'social-Fascism'. But so long as the communists actually lived in a state of war with the majority of the workers, the nuclei were a hopeless failure.

The results were the same all over the world. The majority of the members of the party avoided entering the factory nuclei from the beginning; and in due course, in spite of all efforts, the number of nuclei diminished and their work became less and less active. Piatnitzki was hardly justified in complaining about it; he asked the communists outside Russia to achieve the impossible. Thus, to quote only one figure out of a voluminous series of endless complaints, the Communist Party of Czechoslovakia had 1,301 factory nuclei in 1926, 954 in 1928, and 399 in 1930. In this last year no more than 14 per cent of the total members of the party were organized in factory nuclei; which does not mean that an equally small percentage was working in factories. In the same year, 1930, the Communist Party of Great Britain, according to Piatnitzki, had 1,376 members, but only 218 members were organized in factory nuclei, of which there existed thirty-nine in the whole country (*Imprecorr*, No. 63, 1931). During the era of left extremism the various parties were asked to make up for these deficiencies by forced campaigns, after the model of the work of the Russian *oudarniki*, the shock workers in the factories, during the first Five-Year Plan. These campaigns brought new members, but they did nothing, or very little, to strengthen the factory nuclei. 'The Communist Party of Czechoslovakia', says Piatnitzki on another occasion (*Imprecorr*, No. 32, 1932), 'had the ambition to win 6,000 new members within three months, 50 per cent of them in factory nuclei. Instead of 6,000 new members the party won 15,020, but only 1,757 in factory nuclei.' And those who first joined the nuclei generally dispersed after a certain time or were dismissed by the factories. Thus Piatnitzki, in the same place, quotes the following figures concerning the English party:

	November 1930	February 1931	June 1931	November 1931
Members	2,555	2,711	2,724	6,279
In factory nuclei ..	218	190	141	266
Percentage of total membership ..	8·5	7·0	5·1	4·2

Within the very short period considered the membership of factory nuclei had substantially declined, whereas the membership of the party as a whole was on the upward trend. The spectacular rise between July and November 1931 was due to a big campaign, which brought results, but very small results to the factory nuclei. The gains of such campaigns were not lasting, moreover, as we shall soon see. Similar figures could be quoted for Germany, France, and the United States. For the underground parties, of course, no figures are available.

But the figures just quoted do not give any idea of the real numerical strength of the parties. Piatnitzki's statements abound in complaints about the difference between the figures of those who at one time or other have taken membership tickets and those who actually pay their fees. It must be noted that the unemployed pay only nominal fees and that unemployment accounts for little in the phenomenon. Piatnitzki's complaints, moreover, continue in years both of good and of bad business. Thus about France, in *Imprecorr*, No. 84, 1926: 'In January 1925 . . . our nominal membership was 76,000. At the end of 1925 we observed that about 60,000 members paid their fees. On 1st May 1926 the exact number of paid tickets was 55,213.' And years later, in *Imprecorr*, No. 32, 1932: 'The figure for the total registered membership of the German Communist Party at the beginning of 1932 was about 320,000, of which 260,000 paid their fees. In England there were 8,000 to 9,000 registered members, of which 2,500 paid their fees. In the American Communist Party the corresponding figures are 11,750 and 7,500.' This is very far indeed from the Bolshevik idea of a party whose members are the natural vanguard of their class.

But of which class? The communist parties are very weak indeed in the big factories and the majority of the members comes from small and medium-sized factories. Statistics about this fact speak most clearly in Germany, but the fact itself is universal at that period. It is revealed in numerous complaints that those factory nuclei which exist, do so mostly in small and not in large workshops. But occasionally statistics reveal the real situation directly. Thus one W. Kaasch, in No. 19 of *Communist International* (1928), gives figures for the party membership in the Ruhr, of all big industrial centres of the world the one where, at that time, communist influence was strongest.

Factories with communist nuclei

Number of workers employed	Number of workers to each communist
500–1,000	70
1,000–3,000	143
3,000–5,000	172
more than 5,000	235

The bigger the factory, the smaller the communist influence; in the industrial giants it is altogether insignificant. A few years later the situation has altogether deteriorated all over Germany. In No. 63 of *Imprecorr*, 1932, are contained

THE STRUCTURE OF THE COMMUNIST PARTIES

Piatnitzki's figures for the number of factory workers within the German Communist Party.

Percentage of Factory workers in the C.P.G.

1928	1929	1930	1931
62·3	51·6	32·2	20–22

These are not the figures of those working in factory nuclei, which, by 1929 were down to 14 per cent. Thus in 1929 only betweeen one-quarter and one-third of the communists working in factories had joined their nuclei; the rest were floating about, with no concrete influence over any definite group of people. But more decisive is the general trend of the figures quoted above. They tend somewhat to exaggerate the real state of things because during the years of the big slump the party as a whole considerably increased in membership. The decrease in the factories, expressed in percentages, need not imply loss in absolute figures. But one thing is certainly proved: the party is losing its character as a party of the working class, actually employed. Effects of the slump? Not at all! The decline was already very considerable between 1928 and 1929, at the height of the boom. Whatever followers the Communist Party had won in this year, they were not proletarians within the factories. Before the depression, at the height of the boom, the Communist Party had started to transform itself from a party of the workers into a party of the unemployed. By 1931 the process had taken on catastrophic dimensions. Those who knew things were inclined to regard Piatnitzki's figures as still too optimistic. And the unemployed the party won over were not occasionally unemployed. They had been unemployed for years, as many were at that time, and it was very doubtful how far, in psychology and interests, they were still part of the working class. Anyway, the same social stratum gave hundreds of thousands of recruits to the Nazis, whereas they were never able, before their final victory, seriously to force their way into the factories.

But there was another aspect, and one directly contrary to that just mentioned. In one sense the Communist Party, in spite of its theory, was a party of the workers' aristocracy. Germany is the one country where a serious attempt has been made to analyse the social composition of the Communist

Party. The figures obtained, relating to 1927, are contained in the article by Kaasch which we quoted above. According to the official figures given in that article the members of the C.P.G. could be grouped as follows:

			Percentage
Skilled workers	..	..	39·92
Unskilled	..	..	28·18
Agricultural	..	..	2·21
Independent Craftsmen	..	9·57
Commercial employees	..	1·73

The remainder fall in various categories, among which women with no employment are by far the most important. The figures quoted above need serious criticism. The very numerous bureaucracy of the party, and of various Russian institutions abroad, are not mentioned but hidden under the category to which they belonged before becoming employees of the party or of the Russian state. The same applies to the unemployed. They are hidden behind the figures of skilled and unskilled workers. But the fact remains that skilled workers and people who have been skilled workers make up two-fifths of the party membership; if their womenfolk were added they would probably make up nearly half. From trade-union polls it is easy to know that by far the majority of these communist skilled workers belonged to the metallic industries and the building trades, in Germany two of the best-paid branches of industry. If there is any such thing as a workers' aristocracy, here it is. It would be interesting to know how many of them have become unemployed in later years. But, from the general laws of unemployment it is obvious that its effects must have been stronger among the unskilled than among the skilled. Ultimately, in 1932, the German Communist Party (if we leave aside the party bureaucracy) must have consisted of about three-fifths unemployed, one-fifth or a little less workers' aristocracy, and very little in between. Those who knew the party will probably agree that this corresponds with their experience. It agrees perfectly with the fact that besides the unemployed those groups which were open to the new policy against the trade unions were precisely the very best-paid groups of workers in Germany, groups such as the pipe-layers, tool-makers, and turners. Neither is there anything surprising in that. Those highly paid workers are highly paid because they have a monopoly of their jobs, and even in times of bad business can fight and obtain advantages which are forbidden to the average worker. These same strata are less burdened with everyday misery and more apt to live for an ideal. The workers' aristocracy, far from being a reactionary group, has in fact always been the vanguard of the rest of the workers. But the co-operation of certain aristocratic groups, which have broken away from the bulk of their class, with elements no longer belonging to that class, because they have been for years deprived of work, is something strange indeed. Figures are lacking in other countries. But the fact itself, the forming of the communist membership out of the most miserable categories of unemployed on the one hand and workers' aristocracy on the other, though in various proportions, is international. The function of communism has been to produce a break between the bulk of the working classes and the two extremes of aristocracy and unemployment.

But this description needs a qualification. Communist membership has been mainly recruited out of these two groups, and these two groups have been most deeply influenced by communist ideas and policy. But never has a communist party in any country really controlled the bulk either of the unemployed or of the well-paid skilled workers. There are few aspects of communism about which there is such ample material as about its failure to keep those whom it had won. The membership of the communist parties was subject to an almost incredible amount of 'fluctuation', about which complaints abound. This phenomenon is the more remarkable because trade unions and socialist parties generally enjoy a considerable amount of stability. A fringe, going up to 50 per cent of their total membership, may come and go in times of big excitement. But the other 50 per cent at least have proved to be absolutely loyal in Britain and Germany, and relatively loyal in France. We must compare this with the state of things within the communist parties.

No. 74 of *Imprecorr*, 1929, reports Piatnitzki's complaints about this subject at the tenth plenum of the Communist International. We quote his figures and comment as they can be found in that document. The Communist Party of Czecho-slovakia showed the following development of its membership:

1924	..	138,996	(Our comment: the round
1925	..	93,220	figures for 1927 and 1928
1926	..	92,818	are perhaps not quite as
1927	..	138,000	reliable as the exact figures
1928	..	150,000	for the other years.)
1929	..	81,432	

'In 1926, for instance,' adds Piatnitzki, '26,801 members have joined the Czechoslovak Communist Party.' Therefore, these new members, together with the 93,220 members of 1925, must give, in 1926, a total of 120,021 members. But in reality the Czechoslovak Communist Party had only 92,818 members. That means that in 1926 27,203 members left the party, 402 more than had joined it in the same year. For the British party the figures are as follows:

1925	..	..	..	5,000
April 1926	..	..	..	6,000
October 1926	..	..	..	10,730
January 1927	..	..	..	9,000
March 1928	..	..	..	5,556
1929	..	..	..	3,500

For the French party:

1924	..	..	..	68,191
1925	..	..	..	83,326
1926	..	..	..	65,213
1927	..	..	..	56,010
1928	..	..	..	52,526
1929	..	..	..	46,000

'In 1926', adds Piatnitzki, 'the party has registered 5,000 new members, and in 1927 has made a campaign for new members in connection with the campaign against the new military laws, which brought the party 2,500 new members. And with all that the total declines every year.'

The figures for the Communist Party in the United States are:

1923	..	..	..	..	6,532
1924	..	..	..	..	8,456
1925	..	..	..	..	4,100
1926	..	..	..	..	2,371
1927	..	..	..	..	3,257

'In 1928', is Piatnitzki's comment, '2,452 new members were registered. Altogether, during the last five years the party registered 27,186 new members. To-day the Communist Party has only between 9,000 and 10,000 members.' In this case Piatnitzki's comment is very suspicious. 1929 was the year of the split between Foster and Lovestone; it is very unlikely that the Communist Party should have trebled in membership in that year. But even admitted that the figures are correct, about two-thirds of those who joined the party have left it again within five years. Next year brings similar complaints, as can be gathered from the now oft-quoted No. 63 of *Imprecorr*, 1932.

In Germany, according to Piatnitzki's data, things have evolved like this:

			Gains	*Losses*
1929	..	..	50,000	39,000
1930	..	..	143,056	95,399

An important point obtrudes itself. The beginning of the slump has brought a big increase of communist membership, but the party does not thereby simply become stronger. Almost a hundred thousand members, nearly a third of its total official membership, leave it in this one year, which is not on the whole a year of obvious defeat for the party. Piatnitzki passes to the Czechoslovak party, which, as a result of the overthrow of the old leaders has suffered considerable losses: the membership figures are as follows:

Oct. 1928	Feb. 1929	April 1929	July 1929	End of 1929
48,000	30,000	24,000	37,181	38,998

'And now the Czechoslovak comrades say they have about 40,000 members. How many members have joined during this year remains a puzzle: we do not know. But I am convinced that great fluctuation exists within the communist party of Czechoslovakia.'

As to England, in six party districts, 'during the period

between May and November 1930, 423 members have joined and 510 members have left the party'. In the United States, between December 1929 and July 1930, 7,178 members have joined and 5,210 members have left, about 3,200 of the latter having joined in the same year. More than one-third of the newly won members leave the party after a few months.

The fluctuation in France is as follows:

1929	1930	1931
45,000	38,240	35,000

'While the French party continually registers new members, the total membership figures are in continual decline.' A continuation of the same sort of figures would add nothing to the lesson they carry.

But we must return once more to the figures quoted by Kaasch in No. 19 of the *Communist International* (1928), because they throw light upon certain aspects of fluctuation not yet mentioned. There have been organized in the German Communist Party of 1927, according to Kaasch, since

				Percentage of present members
1920	..	..	..	27·79
1921	..	..	..	14·42
1922	..	..	..	6·80
1923	..	..	..	13·34
1924	..	..	..	6·61
1925	..	..	..	9·15
1926	..	..	..	14·73
1927	..	..	..	7·88

These figures reveal two things: first, that the range of fluctuation has considerably increased in later years. It is considerably smaller in 1927 than in 1931 and 1932. Secondly, even on the assumption of the slower momentum of fluctuation as revealed in these figures, they imply a complete exchange of membership within one decade. It must be remembered that between 1920 and 1928 the total membership of the German Communist Party decreased slightly. Therefore the percentages given in the figures above are not due to any increase in absolute numbers of membership. Mortality, moreover, played a very small part; the average members were between twenty-five and forty-five years of age, and those were not years of persecution. The simple fact is that within seven years three-quarters of the members who had taken part in the Spartakusbund or come over from the U.S.P. at the Halle congress had left the party. Kaasch himself has tested the result for one region, Thuringia. 'Of the 10,000 members', he says, 'who went over from the U.S.P. in this region only 2,771 remain in the party.'

In the *Neue Blaetter fuer den Sozialismus*, a periodical of the German Christian socialists, a former communist, Walther Rist, in 1931 (No. 9) has given an even more careful analysis based on official unpublished communist material. 'Fluctuation', he says, 'is estimated in Berlin at 40 per cent a year. . . . Out of 248 delegates to the congress of the most important district of Berlin (in 1932) . . . the following delegates had a duration of membership as follows:

		Percentage
Less than one year	109	44
1–3 years	55	22
3–5 ,,	38	15·4
5–7 ,,	11	4·4
7–10 ,,	20	8
More than 10 years	15	6 '

The congress of an urban district is not a political affair in the proper sense of the word. Only local affairs and the local application of the general policy of the party are discussed at such a meeting. It assembles, not the 'big ones', but the most influential of the rank and file. The figures, for all that, are only the more interesting. They show, what does not appear in the sum-totals, that there is a stratum of about 15 per cent—of the delegates, not of the members—which has kept its faith in the party through all vicissitudes. What percentage of the membership may correspond to this percentage among the delegates? Delegations to district conferences are usually made on the basis of one delegate for every five or ten members. The majority of the old members in a district can be supposed to be very active workers and have a good reputation—otherwise they would not have remained so long within the party—and a very considerable percentage of these old members will have been delegates. Taking these facts together, one is led to assume that a nucleus of about 5 per cent remains faithful whatever happens. The rest is shifting very rapidly, so that it is impossible to find sufficient people who have been members for at least one year for relatively important kinds of work. The Germans have a well-justified reputation for the stubbornness with which they stick to allegiances once established. There is little doubt that this stock of members who, after having joined, remained members for their lifetime was smaller in most other countries. 'The very highest estimate', Rist goes on to say, 'of the percentage of party members who have stayed in the party since the times of its formation is some 4–5 per cent. And, coming back to one of the social reasons for this instability, he says, 'In 1930, the percentage of unemployed among the members of the party . . . in the Ruhr was about 90, the average over the whole Reich almost 80.'

All that applies to 1932. Since then the percentage of unemployed has naturally declined in most countries, but the weeding out of old members has continued, with the incessant exclusions. It is important to note that those 4–5 per cent who in 1932 still remained from the early times did not belong, in most cases, to the leading group. There, on account of the innumerable reshufflings, the percentage of old members was very small indeed. The communist with the unshakable faith came and comes mostly from what one might call, by a simile, the 'lower middle classes' of the party, the stratum which gives the party the unpaid or only occasionally paid organizers of small nuclei in the factories, of small armed groups, etc. It is this group, rather than the leading group, which in humble devotion has given the parties their martyrs. Here is a decisive difference between the West and Russia. In Russia political leadership and the highest degree of devotion to the movement went invariably together. Those who were most intelligent and most important were most subject to persecution. In the communist parties of the West, this is not generally true. One need only look at the example of Germany. Three times outstanding leaders of the central committee have been called before the courts, Brandler in 1921, in a case already mentioned, Maslow in 1924 and Torgler in the Reichstag fire trial in 1933. Lack of space precludes any discussion in detail of the two latter cases and I will therefore limit my remarks to the statement that, in the case of Maslow as in that of Torgler, the party had reason to state publicly that the leaders had behaved in a way unworthy of the party. The fact is cast into stronger relief by the behaviour of the Bulgarian Dimitrov, a man who had grown up in a tradition close to that of the Russian revolutionary movement and behaved in court, in 1933, like a man imbued with such a tradition. But this stratum of professional revolutionaries, which has made the new Russia, though the new Russia has thrown them over, was conspicuously lacking in the West, and is more lacking there every day. While many of the party leaders behaved most unbecomingly, in the hour of trial, simple party members, in hundreds of cases since 1918, in many countries displayed that heroism which was foreign to many of the leaders of their parties.

The statistical data quoted above are scarce, but they are sufficient to allow a general analysis of the character of the communist parties. There is a small stratum of devoted servants; it could not be called the nucleus of the party, because its influence upon the parties is very small. Then there is an enormous mass of people who come and go, and of these shifting sands the communist parties are made up. The character of the change varies. In times of economic slump the joining of the communist party is usually the result of despair and excitement which burns out after a short time. As soon as the discovery is made that nothing can be changed by the party, the new members drop out again. In those periods the big majority of the party members join and leave again within at most three years. In times of relatively good business the trend is somewhat different. Fluctuation still is extremely strong, but not so strong as in years of slump. Only about one-fifth of the membership in times of good business changes within one or two years; the big changes occur when a party suffers some spectacular defeat. But within 5 to 7 years the effects have been the same; practically the whole of the party membership, with the exception of the stable 5 per cent, have disappeared and been replaced by new members. Biggest of all, naturally, was the change between 1930 and 1934. There are very few members, to-day, in any communist party who have seen anything of its history. An iron guard, unshakable, integrating the experience of a generation of revolutionary fighters, is the official ideal of a communist party. Shifting masses, imbued with a deep hatred of the old mass organizations and their humdrum activities, but without any stability or fixed conviction of their own, are the reality.

How far and in what sense are these parties 'proletarian'? It is a question which it is not very easy to answer. The ideology of international communism is that of the proletarian class struggle. But behind the words are hidden very different meanings. In the beginning, in 1919, the small communist groups were formed out of the most varied social elements. They were too small to have many workers among their members and those who came were mostly new-comers to the working-class movement. Intellectuals, bohemians, demobilized soldiers, *déclassés* of the war, abounded. The splits of 1920 and 1921 brought a change. Sections of the big proletarian mass movements joined the Communist International and made it a thoroughly working-class organization. But by far the greater part of those who then joined left within a few years. The result was to make the communist parties again gradually less proletarian. In some cases this evolution went to extremes. In China, for instance, in the end the workers refused so much as to listen to the communists, who had at the same time a considerable following among the peasants. It would be wrong, however, to define the Chinese Communist Party as a peasant party. The core of the Chinese Communist Party is the Red soldiers and the administrative personnel of the Chinese Soviets; most of them have once been peasants, but their social character has been transformed by a decade of life in a different milieu and with a different occupation. In Germany, which before 1933 was second in importance only to China as a basis for the Comintern, the party ceased altogether to be a working-class party during the slump and became a party leading the unemployed against the employed workers; this was not entirely a novelty. It had once occurred already in 1921. In Britain the party for a decade was mainly a party of the decaying mining areas, until of late it has become largely a party of certain sections of the lower middle-class intelligentsia. In the United States it had never any roots within the English-speaking working-classes and was exclusively a party of a small section of the foreign workers. Its social content defies analysis most successfully in France. We shall have something to say about that when discussing the contemporary history of French communism.

Whence this variety? Essentially it derives from the basic principle of communism. Communism, in Lenin's definition, is not the party of the proletariat; it is the party of revolutionaries linked with the proletariat. A link can become closer or looser. And in fact the link between the communist parties and the working classes was loosened continually until, in 1937, very little of a communist proletarian movement survived in most countries. The identity of interests between the Communist Party and the proletariat is an ideal removed from fact. In fact, there was a revolutionary staff at Moscow. This staff sought allies in Europe for its revolutionary aims and took them where it found them. It believed that the majority of the workers would come, but they did not. Then, the revolutionary staff was faced by a dilemma: submit to the non-revolutionary mass organizations of the modern proletariat, or fight them. It was thrown hither and thither between the two alternatives, unable to take a final decision. But its waverings led precisely to tremendous defeats. Had the Comintern submitted to the majority of the Western workers the adventure of communism in the West would soon have been over. Had Lenin listened to Gorter in 1920 a small sect of convinced communists would have been formed. The Comintern attempted a middle course, attempted to steer between sectarianism and opportunism, and in reality was merely destroyed by both at once. This, we hope to have shown, was not the result of any single mistake, not due to any wrong 'line'. The task itself was impossible.

The left extremism of 1929–34 marks only the last phase of this evolution. Every hope of real success was over. In fury the Comintern threw itself against the old mass organizations which it had failed to conquer. In doing so it lost only what little foothold it had kept among the working classes. Its furious attacks won it the allegiance, shifting and unreliable, of strata *déclassé* by the world economic crisis, strata which, to a much larger extent, joined the ranks of the Fascists. In countries such as France, Britain, and the United States, where no Fascist mass movement was afoot, where the number of *déclassé* elements was considerably smaller, left extremism simply led to the practical annihilation of the communist parties. We have quoted the many statements where the 'polit-bureaux' of various parties and their leading members are accused of having transformed their respective parties into insignificant sects. In other countries, Fascism or semi-Fascism put an end to a movement which had lost its footing long before.

By the end of 1932 all outside observers believed that the Comintern was visibly approaching its end. But in reality it was only about to change its skin. While the communist parties lost rapidly in strength, their character was transformed. Between 1929 and 1934 the communist parties finally and definitely transformed themselves into quasi-military organizations ready to obey anything. The structure did not change: at the top a bureaucracy from which every single man likely to oppose orders had been weeded out; in the middle a small stratum with an absolute unquestioning faith in every order; at the bottom a shifting mass unable to draw comparisons, because it had no past, and filled with absolute confidence, as the other groups, with the one difference that here confidence did not survive the first shock. In one word, the communist parties had definitely cut the tie which connected them with any sort of democratic mass movement. They had become an obedient army of crusaders, listening to the orders of their Führer only. In structure the communist parties had become very similar to those of their Fascist antagonists. Thus reborn, they entered the scene anew.

CHAPTER XXII

HITLER: THE TURNING-POINT

The turning-point in the history of the Comintern, as in so many other matters, was the victory of Hitler. As late as November 1932 the communists had joined a big strike against the Berlin transport board led by the Nazis. In February 1933 the whip of Fascism lashed them and taught them that there *was* a difference between Fascism and democracy. But they did not immediately change their minds. For one more year they stubbornly stuck to their convictions, which by now had become rather shibboleths of left extremism than attempts to analyse the situation. Throughout the rise of Fascism the communists had talked of the approaching proletarian revolution. When Fascism finally won, and, with the Reichstag fire, destroyed them, they did not launch the slogan of a general strike, which they had launched six times before with less reason. On those other occasions the call for a general strike had not been meant very seriously. This time it would have been. The communists submitted to Fascism without resistance, exactly as the socialists. It was amply proved that the existence of a communist party had not strengthened, but perhaps seriously impaired, the capacity of the German workers to resist. But though there was obviously no difference between socialists and communists at this decisive juncture, the communists continued to call the socialists 'social-Fascists'. And they did not believe, for many months, that Hitler's success had seriously changed the situation.

Imprecorr had been transferred to Bâle, where it reappeared under the name of *Rundschau*. 'The momentary calm after the victory of Fascism', says *Rundschau* of 1st April 1933, 'is only a

376

passing phenomenon. The rise of the revolutionary tide in Germany will inevitably continue. The resistance of the masses against Fascism will inevitably increase. The open dictatorship of Fascism destroys all democratic illusions, frees the masses from the influence of the Social-democratic Party and thus accelerates the speed of Germany's march towards the proletarian revolution.' Heckert, one of the responsible leaders of the party, added (*Rundschau*, No. 10, 1933) 'The talk about the German communists being defeated and politically dead is the gossip of philistines, of idiotic and ignorant people. . . . The jailing of a few thousand communists cannot kill a party with a following of about five millions. Instead of those who have been arrested the politically and culturally highly trained German proletariat develops new forces and will always develop them.' Starting from this conviction that there was no defeat, that those who had fallen in the fight would be automatically replaced, and that the revolutionary tide was rising, the communists continued to spread leaflets and pamphlets almost openly and went so far as to order the members to undertake public demonstrations. But, in fact, the millions of adherents of yesterday were rapidly drifting away and the party suffered frightful losses which led it to the brink of complete destruction, until, after two years of vain sacrifices, it had to admit that it had been defeated, that Fascism was more than an episode, and that very cautious methods of work under Fascism must be elaborated. It is noteworthy that the Italian Communist Party had gone through the same experience since 1927, when Italian Fascism became totalitarian and all other organizations were forbidden. It was the bad luck of the Italian communists that this development coincided with the period of left extremism in the Comintern. In the attempt to carry on semi-public methods of propaganda the Communist Party of Italy was actually destroyed. The Communist Party of Germany stopped these suicidal methods somewhat earlier, but not before a strange scene had been enacted.

After the defeat the party leaders had only one immediate care: to prove that it had been three times right in everything it had done. During the months of destruction of the German labour movement there was a general feeling among the socialist workers that a close co-operation between socialists and communists might have averted the catastrophe. This was exactly what Trotsky, in a number of pamphlets in 1931 and 1932, had written from exile, and what the right-wing communists around Brandler had said. It was easy for both to make use of the obvious objections against the policy of a party which, while claiming to be a working-class party, had repeatedly collaborated with the Fascists but continually refused, since 1929, to collaborate with the socialists. For all that the fury of the defeated communist leaders was only the stronger. 'The complete purging of the state apparatus from the social-Fascists', says an official communist resolution printed in *Rundschau*, No. 17, 1933, 'and the ruthless suppression of the social-democratic organizations and press does not change anything in the fact that now as ever they [the social-Fascists] are the chief social support of the dictatorship of capital.' Thus, while socialists and communists went together to the concentration camps and the Socialist Party was practically annihilated, the communists continued to talk of the socialists as 'social-Fascists' and to regard them as the chief supporters of the régime, and in consequence as the chief enemy, while real, as opposed to 'social' Fascism took second place in their thoughts. In face of this attitude something unexpected happened. Neumann and his friends had sat sulking since the beginning of 1932. They now saw their opportunity and started to accuse the leaders of the German communists, calling forth even more furious replies. 'Their chief theories', says the resolution quoted above, 'are that the Fascist dictatorship means a complete change of the political régime, that the *Lumpenproletariat*, to-day, is the leading class, subjecting the bourgeoisie to its interests, that the power of the bourgeoisie has been strengthened, that the proletariat has lost a battle and been defeated, that Comrade Thaelmann and the central committee of the party are responsible for the realization of a Fascist dictatorship.' Not everything in these views appears correct to-day, in the light of later experience. The *Lumpenproletariat* of the Storm Troopers has long since ceased to be a decisive factor in Germany. But it sounds almost incredible, to-day, that in the German Communist Party it was regarded as a crime to consider the advent of Fascism, the downfall of democracy, as a material change in the political régime, and to admit that the party had been defeated. The contention that the party had been responsible for the advent of Fascism was a gross exaggeration; but this exaggeration was only the logical consequence of the very exaggerated ideas the party had of its own importance. And there can hardly be any doubt that the party was partly responsible, together with all other groups of the left, for what had happened.

But this was not the view of communist official circles. The views of Neumann and his group, the resolution goes on to say, 'constitute an open attack not only upon Comrade Thaelmann and the leaders of the party, but upon the Comintern, Comrades Stalin and Manuilski, the decisions of the eleventh and twelfth plenums of the Comintern.' It is never advisable to doubt the infallibility of the gods. 'The views of this group', the resolution continues, 'are a crass mixture of naked opportunism, insidious Trotskyism, and downright Putschism.' It was not for nothing that three years later Neumann and his followers were shot in Moscow. They had, in fact, never had any contacts with Trotsky; it would have been quite beyond the scope of Heinz Neumann's character to co-operate with the powerless.

By now no political considerations of any sort whatsoever moved the machinery of the Comintern. Left extremism on an international scale was driven to incredible lengths. Thus, for instance, No. 13 of *Rundschau*, 1933, prints an article about the American New Deal, entitled 'Roosevelt the Saviour of the World? Feverish War Preparations', in which one finds sentences such as this: 'Every important law since submitted or accepted increased Roosevelt's powers on the grounds that an emergency similar to that of a war existed. The real aim of all this law-making is indeed the preparation for war.' Throughout 1933 in Austria the tension which, a few months later, was to issue in civil war between the socialists and the government was growing. No. 34 of *Rundschau* during this crisis prints an article entitled: 'Otto Bauer's Fight against Fascism'. 'Kill—whom? The revolutionary proletariat.' Otto Bauer was the leader of the Austrian socialists and the implication was that the Austrian socialists, while pretending to fight Fascism, were preparing a massacre of the workers. The Austrian socialists represented a tendency strongly to the left within the international socialist movement. About this left, primarily in Germany, but equally in Austria, *Rundschau* of 28th July 1933 has to say: 'The dissolution of the Social-democratic Party by the Fascist dictatorship changes the forms and methods of the betrayal of the workers by the social-Fascists [meaning by this word, as usual, the social-democrats] but does not bring it to an end. It makes the sphere of action of the Social-democratic Party as a bourgeois legal working-class party narrower, but increases at the same time the danger of new 'left' impostures, new knavish forms of co-operation with the bourgeoisie'. If the concentration camps of Hitler engulf the left-wing socialists, this is a new, knavish form of co-operation with the bourgeoisie.

It is useless to multiply quotations of the same sort; they would run to hundreds and thousands. In fact, at that time communist activity reduced itself more or less to this sort of raging invective. While the success of Hitler was followed by a number of Fascist and semi-Fascist coups throughout the European east, from Finland to Greece, the communists had to remain in helpless inactivity; they had lost all influence.

At the beginning of 1934 the scene changed once more. The Austrian socialists rose in February. Democracy had been abolished in Austria in March 1933, a few weeks after the advent of Hitler, and since then the legal existence of the Socialist Party, the strongest in the world, had been increasingly menaced. The socialist leaders, with Otto Bauer at their head, had waited and waited and tried to bring about a compromise. But when it became manifest that there was no hope of obtaining one and that the choice lay only between perishing with or without a fight, the military organization of the Austrian socialists, the 'Schutzbund', rose in Vienna and in some provincial towns, on 12th February. Fighting went on for four days. The number of those who took arms did not exceed a few hundred, and in spite of a strong wave of sympathy among the workers an attempt to proclaim a general strike failed miserably in the crisis-ridden country. In itself it was not a big affair, but the impression of the armed resistance offered by the workers was strong enough to forestall an immediate re-enactment of the German story in Austria. The

Social-democratic Party was officially dissolved, but continued to exist and to control large masses of workers.

But stronger and more important were the effects abroad. The attempt, however unsuccessful, of the Viennese workers contrasted strongly with the meek capitulation of both communists and socialists in Germany. It was after all possible to fight; the workers were not hopelessly delivered into the hands of the Fascists. The Vienna rising did more to restore the spirits of the labour movement than many a brilliant success could have done. And this feat, admired not without exaggeration against the background of so many capitulations without struggle, had been achieved by a socialist party. So after all it was not true that socialists could never fight, could only betray. What was the good of the whole international split if the communists did not fight and the socialists did? In Vienna a few individual communists had followed the socialist lead in the rising. The Austrian Communist Party as a whole was far too weak to do anything. The last *raison d' être* of communism had been clearly destroyed, but the reaction of the communists to the new situation was only a new outbreak of boundless rage. Gottwald, the leader of the Czechoslovak party, wrote in *Rundschau* (No. 19, 1934): 'The parties of the Second International try to make capital out of the blood of the Austrian proletariat, try to cover with its blood their interminable betrayals and crimes. But the facts convict these hyenas and traitors, the facts prove incontestably that the Austrian Socialist Party has brought the proletariat under the knife of Fascism.'

History gave an immediate answer to these views. Whereas in no Western country the communists counted as a force in 1934, in Bulgaria they still held a considerable amount of influence among what remained of the labour movement. The Bulgarian communists, as all other communist parties since 1929, had followed the methods of left extremism. Early in 1934 a military coup abolished Bulgarian democracy, which had never been fully abolished before and had been gradually restored after Zankow in 1926 had left the government. The new coup found no resistance, least of all among the communists. At the seventh world-congress, in 1935, Krumov, a Bulgarian delegate, discussed the reasons, speaking openly, for in the meantime Comintern had turned to the right. 'The reason for the defeat', says Krumov, 'was that the leading sectarian group within the party consistently refused to see the increasing Fascist danger and the preparations of the Fascists for a coup. They led the party in the fight against the peasants' union in the first place, as being the primary enemy of the toilers and the primary Fascist danger. The impotence and passivity of the party during the military Fascist coup and afterwards, during the attacks against the proletariat and the party, were due to the formal, wooden conception of the leaders about the general strike. The mass campaign of the party was not connected with the everyday interests of the masses ... and was limited to small meetings of the party and its youth organization, which were isolated from the masses.' Social-democracy, in Bulgaria, is very weak. Therefore the principles of left extremism in that country had been applied in action against the chief mass party of the left, the Peasants' Union, founded by Stambuliiski and already once destroyed by a semi-Fascist coup in 1923. Then the communists had not moved, because they regarded the peasants' union as the chief enemy and had a 'formal, wooden idea' of the general strike. In the meantime they had risen in isolation, in September 1923, and been defeated; they had undergone the tragedy of the attempt of the Sofia cathedral and the massacres which followed it; they had experienced and condemned all shades of left extremism. And, in the end, in 1934, they had acted exactly as if it were June 1923. There seems to be something in the roots of communism which makes it unfit to learn, in the long run. Its evolution is a process of going from one extreme to the other, in endless repetition.

Something very similar had happened in Finland. But that was a minor matter. The climax of left extremism had already been reached, on 6th February 1934 in Paris. There the enemies of democracy, strengthened by a big financial scandal concerning a certain Stavisky, had attempted a coup by calling a demonstration in front of the Chamber. The communists called a demonstration at the same place, for the same hour, with the same aim: overthrow of the government of the radical party. The two groups did not issue a joint manifesto. But by their actions they co-operated in overthrowing the democratic government. They reached their immediate goal. After heavy firing and a considerable number of casualties the government of M. Daladier had to resign. For a moment it looked as if even France would become Fascist. But then Moscow was frightened by its own success. Moscow had firmly believed that Hitler would be only an episode. When it was forced to realize that it had been mistaken, that Hitler stood firm and that Germany was rapidly becoming a first-class military power, it had to change front. Under those circumstances a success of Fascism in France would draw after it the destruction of the Soviet Union. Stalin veered round. It was immaterial that, on February 8th, the communists in Paris called a demonstration of their own against Fascism. But it was of high importance that when the reformist trade unions, the C.G.T., called a general one-day strike on February 12th the C.G.T.U., the communist unions, joined in. 'February 12th' was the first united action of communists and socialists which had occurred in any country since 1929. It proved to be a big success. It was the turning-point in French politics, which from that day started to move in the direction of what later became the *Front populaire*. And it initiated an all-round change in communist politics. During the next months, with amazing speed, all principles of left extremism were overthrown, slandering and vilification of socialist parties was stopped, and increasingly successful attempts were made to bring about united action with them. A new chapter of Comintern history was opened.

Next to no resistance occurred within the communist parties. Onlookers may stand amazed at seeing that men and women willingly accept a task which only a few months ago they had denounced with all their vocabulary as crime, betrayal, provocation, and Trotskyism. But those of intellectual independence had long been weeded out. Now the duty of the communist was no longer to discuss but to find suitable arguments for what had been ordered from above. The willingness with which the about-turn was accepted showed that the transformation of the Comintern had been accomplished in the previous era. One must add that it was not very difficult for the ordinary members to accept the change. Left extremism had been too obvious a failure and the desire to form a front of all democratic elements against Fascism was growing every day. After all, in spite of doctrines, there *was* a difference between Fascism and democracy. It is more remarkable that those who were pledged personally to the opposite policy came round without resistance.

Still, a change was necessary, or at least desirable. Those who had led the Comintern during these last years, Molotov, Manuilski, Kuusinen, were poor figures. More important, Molotov passed through a phase of disgrace in Russia. Gregorij Dimitrov had made a brilliant defence in the Reichstag fire trial. He was the right man. Being a Bulgarian, he was welcome because Stalin regarded a stronger separation of the Comintern from Russian politics as desirable. On the other hand, he was, as a Bulgarian, practically a Russian by tradition and mentality. His defence was the one thing which had won the communists' sympathies during this period. The power of Dimitrov's defence was due not so much to any superlative political gifts of his own as to the extraordinary amount of courage and devotion to his cause he displayed. As a political leader Dimitrov had been primarily responsible for the Bulgarian disaster of June 1923, and had not objected to the hopeless coup of September 1923; but he had objected to the adventure of the Sofia cathedral and since then had been hated by the Bulgarian left. He was sent away when the left, in 1929, again took over, and thus found himself in Berlin when the catastrophe occurred. There he displayed before the Western world a thing it could never witness closely under normal conditions: the devotion and courage of a revolutionary of the Russian school. The obvious and striking difference between Dimitrov and Torgler was an epitome of the difference between Russian communism and Western 'communism'. But at the time of the trial the world did not know Dimitrov's real ordeal. His own party, for reasons of factional feuds between left and right, hardly supported him! Such was the report of Krumov on the seventh world-congress, which we have already quoted: 'The adverse effects of the factional policy of the leading sectarian group of the Bulgarian party', he said, 'can be judged by the scandalous fact that the campaign about the Leipzig trial in Bulgaria was carried out very weakly indeed.' There are a number of other statements to the same effect. The man upon whom the whole world looked as a model of heroism was regarded as half a traitor by the Communist Party of his own country! But precisely on account of the enmity of the extreme left he was the right man for carrying through a more moderate policy. He was formally elected general secretary of the Comintern, after being *de facto* at its top for many months, by the seventh world-congress. This seventh world-congress, which ought, according to statute, to have been called in 1930, was called in 1935. It was the first world-congress without any disagreement. The debates of this congress are therefore of limited value for the understanding of the new turn to the right. But we must now study this new policy, which was inaugurated in 1934.

CHAPTER XXIII

CHAMPIONS OF DEMOCRACY

The events after 1934 belong to contemporary politics. In the history of the Comintern 1934 represents an entirely new phase. To-day that organization has little in common with what it was between 1919 and 1934. The old Comintern has been destroyed, irrevocably, in the extremes of 1929 and after, and in the catastrophic eruption of Fascism. Even now, four years after the change, it is not quite clear what the new Comintern is.

It is useless to describe in detail how the change proceeded. It started with the dropping of violent attacks against the democratic parties; continued in attempts to form close alliances with them, alliances no longer limited to the socialists, but extended to 'bourgeois' democrats and occasionally to conservative and even semi-Fascist groups. The climax of it all was reached in attempts to merge the communist with the socialist parties; in the course of these attempts the independent communist trade unions were actually dissolved. The final aim was not clear at the beginning. Only in the course of the new turn did its implications become clear. They can be summed up in two main items: the idea of a proletarian revolution receded far into the background, so as to become almost indistinguishable; the support of Russian foreign policy became the openly admitted paramount aim of world communism.

It was a change of policy deeper than any the Comintern had undergone before. It is true that the previous change, that which had led the Comintern into the wildest exaggerations of left extremism, had also been unprecedented. But the new change went even further to the right than the previous one had gone to the left. It implied a wholesale overthrow of the basic principles of communism. Instead of the class struggle, co-operation with the bourgeoisie. Instead of the Soviet system, eulogy of democracy. Instead of internationalism, nationalism. The revolutionary ideals had failed conspicuously. But if there were any people on earth who had believed in them and claimed still to believe in them, it was the communists. Hundreds of responsible communist leaders, a few months before, had denounced everybody as a Trotskyist traitor who spoke of co-operation with the socialists and the necessity of defending democracy; now not a single one of these leaders rose against the change. In France the reversal of policy was carried out with particular speed. At the end of 1933 J. Doriot, a leading communist, had left because he was no longer willing to follow the policy of the Comintern, and began wildly to denounce left extremism. Six months later the French communists did exactly the thing for which they had excluded Doriot, who, it is true, was about to become a Fascist in the meantime. This sort of thing was general. The fury of communist denunciations did not abate. But in 1933 it was the partisans of a cautious united-front policy and of the defence of democracy who were opportunists, Trotskyists, social-Fascists, traitors, mad dogs, hyenas; now all those who opposed merging with the socialists, opposed complete alliance with the democrats, etc., were pelted with the same kind epithets.

Hitherto, Russian foreign policy had interfered with the policy of the Comintern, had hampered it, had sometimes partly determined its aims. Since 1928 the fight against the danger of war against Russia, then entirely imaginary, had been one of the chief tasks of the Comintern. At that time Moscow pretended to feel itself menaced by Britain, France, and the United States. But precisely because the idea of such a menace was at that time preposterous, it could not be said that the policy of the Comintern was then in fact dictated by the necessities of Russian foreign policy. The war-scare belonged essentially to the atmosphere the Russian rulers thought fit for the execution of the first Five-Year Plan, for the destruction of every opposition, notably the opposition of the right wing, and for the establishment of a fully totalitarian régime. The Comintern, during these years as so often since 1923, had been made an instrument, not so much of Russian foreign policy, as of the dominating Russian faction in its struggle with other factions.

But this changed radically in 1934. As soon as Hitler became a real menace to Russia the latter realized its position and its reactions became entirely different from those of the time when the war-scare had been mere pretence. Now the factional dissensions receded into the background. It is not that a more tolerant régime was adopted. On the contrary, the fight against Trotskyism or what was described as 'Trotskyism' by the Comintern machinery soon became more furious than ever. But it was itself an element of Russian international policy, one of the many arguments by which Russia attempted to convince the Western powers that it had definitely dropped all revolutionary intentions and was worthy of an alliance. To the attempt to create an international alliance against German and Japanese Fascism everything was subordinated.

Let us sum up this decisive development once more in a few words: at first the Comintern had aimed at being an instrument of international revolution. With revolution receding into the dim future, first in the West and then in the East, it had increasingly become a card to be played in Russian factional fights, an instrument without any importance of its own. Now for the first time it became essentially an instrument of Russian foreign policy; and the first aim of this policy was: break Russia's isolation; the principal means: inspire confidence, wipe out Russia's past. The main conclusions from this premiss were obvious.

Russia sought a close alliance with the potential adversaries of Germany and Japan. First among these adversaries were France and Czechoslovakia; it was desirable to bring Britain and the United States into the same fold. In 1934 Russia concluded alliances with both France and Czechoslovakia; at the same time it joined the League of Nations. It would have been simplest to combine these actions with a straightforward dissolution of the Comintern, which had no *raison d' être* after Russia had dropped all revolutionary plans. It would have been an act likely to convince the democratic governments of the West, and at the same time an undeniable refutation of the

388

charge of the Nazis and the other Fascist powers that Russia still fostered revolution abroad. Without a Comintern there could not have been an anti-Comintern pact such as that concluded between Germany, Italy, and Japan. The alliance between these three countries would have been equally well effected, but it would have been deprived of its best pretext.

Institutions just as individuals cannot break completely with their past. In this our world, unfortunately, sympathies in the international field depend largely upon affinities in political doctrine. Russia had been the country of revolution. The parties of the right hated it all over the world and it was doubtful whether this attitude would change rapidly. Anyway, Russia laid store upon having in every country an organization at its orders, an organization ready to maintain that particular country on the path desired by Russian foreign policy. Russia decided to double its action in the international field by interference in the home politics of every country. It was to be an interference no longer hampered by that revolutionary Utopianism which had made every previous communist action ineffectual. The method was simple: Russia and the communist parties must be the champions of a democratic *ralliement* against German and Italian Fascism.

The new policy was inaugurated in France, where co-operation in the strike of February 12th was followed by repeated communist offers of common action. There is no need to recount the details of this development. At first the socialists were very reluctant, suspecting one of the usual manœuvres of the united-front tactics, intended to 'unmask' them. But when the communists pledged themselves not to attack the socialists during the period of co-operation the latter were convinced of communist sincerity and agreed to co-operate. The movement, from the very beginning, was enormously popular among all parties of the left in France. The coup of the right on 6th February 1934 had frightened all democratic elements and it was generally felt that only a united front could forestall the advent of Fascism. In October 1934 the movement for united action acquired tremendous momentum through the impact of the Spanish events to be described in the next chapter. The revolt of the Spanish socialists in Asturias in October 1934 was infinitely stronger than that of the Vienna socialists in

February of that year. Though it was defeated it gave the left a feeling of pride and strength. This time the small Communist Party of Spain had helped the socialists, and the Comintern had taken advantage of the opportunity to approach the Second International in order to bring about a united action on behalf of the Asturian insurgents. Though the Second International refused, the offer was not without consequences; for the French socialists accepted and common demonstrations for the Asturian miners took place in France.

In 1935 the movement of the united front increased rapidly. The communists offered to merge with the socialists and a commission was appointed to study the technicalities of the problem. The communist and socialist youth organizations were merged in France and so were the two trade-union centres, the C.G.T. and the C.G.T.U. With all that, the movement to the left won increased strength. The trade unions grew rapidly in membership, and by-elections went to show that the power of the right was on the decline.

The next step was the extension of the united front beyond the limits of the labour movement. The first man to launch this idea in France was Gaston Bergery, a left-wing democrat, not a socialist. He devoted his paper, *La Flêche*, to a campaign for such an extended united front. With the growing trend to the left, the 'united front' of communists and socialists was extended into the 'front populaire' of communists, socialists, and radicals. Already the pressure of the left had forced the resignation of the semi-Fascist cabinet of Doumergue and installed instead the moderate conservative governments of Laval and Flandin. Then even Flandin had to resign and Sarraut, a moderate radical, took over and carried through the impending general elections. To these elections the communists went in a close alliance with socialists and radicals. The Popular Front won a complete victory.

Then came a very unexpected event. The new government of the *Front populaire* did not simply take over. It received a welcome from the masses such as does not often occur in history. France, of all Western countries, was most backward as to wages, hours of work, and social legislation in general. This was partly due to the backwardness and weakness of its labour movement. Under the double impetus produced by the menace of Fascism and the hopes held out by the victory of the Popular Front the masses, with a single leap, attempted to obtain what they had neglected to obtain for decades. Suddenly a sort of general strike broke out all over France. During the years of deepest depression the normal forms of strikes had proved entirely unavailing for the defence of the workers' wages. In various countries strikes had occurred where the workers, driven by despair, had occupied the factories. This new method, hitherto applied in defensive action only, was now for the first time used by the French workers in a big offensive move. The stay-in strikes proved a complete success for the moment. The conservative grew as frightened as the workers had been two years before. In a single night the French right accepted an ample improvement of social legislation together with a substantial increase of wages. There was indeed, from the beginning a flaw in the success. The improvements were obtained by political pressure at a moment of economic depression. It was obvious enough that they would hamper French economic recovery. But it is not our intention to discuss here the details of the economic policy of the French *Front populaire*. It had given the working class the biggest success ever obtained in any country for many years. If the new communist tactics were a rupture with communist dogma they certainly were common sense, successful, and heartily welcomed by all democratic elements.

One of the reasons for such a swift success of the united-front tactics in France was the relative radicalism of the French socialists. Most socialist parties were much more to the right, and, suspecting the communists of still aiming at an advanced, though no longer at a revolutionary policy, refused to co-operate with them. During this first phase of the new tactics the communists found their road much more stony in most other countries than in France. In Austria, where the socialists had always been much to the left and were even more so after the struggle of February 1934, a united front was easily effected. It was no longer unimportant, because the communists had witnessed a considerable increase of strength after the defeat of democratic socialism through the dictatorship and were again, for the first time since 1919, a mass party. In Spain too the idea of a united front found little resistance, as we shall describe in the next chapter. A certain degree of co-operation was effected in Switzerland, and most of the socialist youth organizations of Europe merged with the communists. But in Norway Tranmael and his party consistently refused to accept unity of action with a party led from Moscow, because they regarded Russia as something very near a Fascist state. And the traditional right wing of the Socialist International, the social-democratic parties of Sweden, Denmark, Holland, Belgium, Czechoslovakia, Poland, and the British Labour Party flatly refused co-operation. In some of these countries some elements of the united-front policy were nevertheless put into effect. In Czechoslovakia the communist trade unions merged into those socialist unions which they had left in 1921. In Britain a united front was effected, not with the Labour Party, but with the Socialist League and the I.L.P., but this broke the Socialist League, which was forced to dissolve itself. Then, gradually, the scene, which had already changed rapidly in 1934, changed for a second time.

There are people who contend that the Saar plebiscite made a deep impression in Moscow. In the Saar, in spite of a well-functioning united front of socialists and communists, the Nazis in an incontestably genuine referendum had polled about 90 per cent of the votes. The superiority of nationalism over democracy and socialism had been proved, in this one case, at least. It is true that nationalism, in these times, has an enormous momentum. But the Saar plebiscite alone was hardly sufficient to reverse the whole policy of the Comintern. These were months of big successes for democracy. During 1936, in Spain, general elections gave the left a brilliant victory against tremendous odds. In Belgium the Fascist attempts of the Rexists were defeated. In France the *Front populaire* was master. And the whole move to the left was crowned by the brilliant re-election of President Franklin D. Roosevelt, an event which surprised most experts. If, nevertheless, Moscow started to think that a policy of simple defence of democracy was not enough it was hardly due to the situation abroad but to the change of atmosphere in Moscow.

In Russia the year 1934 had been one of relative calm. The first Five-Year Plan was over, the second plan was started with much more moderation than the first, the excesses of agrarian collectivization had been stopped, an economy on a money basis had been restored. All opposition to Stalin was finally and definitely squashed, and an era of tolerance was initiated. But then a half-crazy young man killed Kirov, the leader of the Leningrad administration and the chief advocate of moderation. Immediately the old ruthless régime of persecution and of continual extermination of real and imaginary oppositionists started again. First, more than one hundred hostages, admittedly free from the slightest suspicion of having collaborated in the murder of Kirov, were shot as a reprisal. Then the Sinovjev group was gradually exterminated. In Europe this was interpreted as a definite break with revolutionary traditions. But soon it became clear that the terrorism was not aimed only at the old Bolsheviks. It carried to their graves the leaders of the army, the G.P.U., the autonomous republics, just as much as the old leaders of Bolshevism. It is not our task here to investigate whether any of the victims of this wave of terrorism were guilty of those attempts upon the life of Stalin which they confessed. The question moved public opinion while only a limited number of victims were killed under definite charges to which they had themselves confessed. It has lost all interest; hundreds and thousands are killed all over Russia on accusations never specified. We are here only concerned with the effects upon the Comintern.

Of all the 'purges' of the Russian administration the only one which reflected directly upon the Comintern was the one aimed at the old Bolshevik guard. The immediate effect was that the ruthless persecution which raged against the old guard in Russia was transferred to the West, where the communists started a furious campaign against Trotskyism, accusing of this capital crime both many who were real Trotskyists and many who were not. This campaign against Trotskyism won importance in connection with a broader change of Comintern views. Stalin was aiming at replacing the out-of-date ideology of social revolution and the class-struggle by something more stable and was naturally driven to rely upon Russian nationalism and the worship of his own person as the *voshd*, the 'wise leader of peoples', the Fuhrer in one word, the superman, the saviour. History was rewritten for this double purpose. It was rewritten so as to give the idea that Stalin had been the first lieutenant of Lenin, which implied systematic oblivion of all his real lieutenants, who have been exiled by Stalin or are rotting in their graves. But history was rewritten equally with the aim of taking away the character of a class-war from the civil war of 1918–21, to interpret it as a national war against foreign intervention. And the glorious tradition of the Tsars was again held up to admiration.

How could this change have left the Comintern unaffected? The Comintern had been the primary expression of Russian revolutionism. It must therefore rigidly conform, now, to the new patterns. It was unthinkable that the Comintern could have an ideology divergent from that imposed by the infallible leader of Russia. Here foreign policy did not even take place of honour. The Comintern from beginning to end remained a church where unity of the credo was the paramount considera-tion. But considerations of foreign policy played their part too. If Russia had won France and Czechoslovakia for an alliance it had failed to win a firm foothold in Britain and in the United States; it wanted a close alliance with nationalist China. For these aims an even more spectacular departure from the old revolutionary creed was needed.

Thus the double credo of present Russia, nationalism and the worship of the leader-superman, was transferred to the Comintern. Thorez in France, Pollitt in Britain, Earl Browder in the United States, José Diaz in Spain, no one of them at all of outstanding ability, were given a sort of absolute power within their parties and their personalities were advertised in a manner hitherto unknown, but closely akin to the worship of Stalin, Hitler, and Mussolini. This worship was even extended to the German Thaelmann in prison. At the same time nationalism took the first place in communist propaganda, a communist nationalism in every country. In France, for instance, the communists speak of themselves as 'a true people's party, flesh of the flesh of the French people, the party of youth and future, the party of a free, powerful and happy France'. In Britain, they oppose the Mosley group with the slogan that it is 'un-British'. In Austria they advocated support of Schuschnigg with the argument that he aimed at the defence of the Austrian nation. In China the party renounced officially every other aim but national defence. In Spain every other slogan has receded before the propaganda for a national war against foreign intervention. And even in the United States the communists dress up as American nationalists. This last combines with Stalin's solemn declaration to Howard, an outstanding American journalist, that the idea of world revolution is a 'tragi-comical misunderstanding'.

There are drawbacks to these tactics. Nationalism and Führer-worship are not things as easily transferable as the communists seem to think. The successful Führers of our time either owe their success to their personal fascination, as Hitler and Mussolini, or to the conquest of the machinery of an established dictatorship, as Stalin. But neither condition applies to the other countries where the communists treat as supermen the leaders instituted by orders from above. Dimitrov, the chief of the Comintern, has at least the well-deserved prestige which he acquired during the Reichstag fire trial. But Thorez, Pollitt, and Browder, Diaz, Thaelmann, and all the others have neither a personal appeal to the masses nor the means of compulsion of Stalin. They can acquire absolute authority within the communist parties but not outside them. Moreover, Stalin would be the last man to see them acquire a personal prestige which would make them independent of his orders. The same applies to nationalism. Nationalism is the worship of one's own nation, the readiness to sacrifice everything to its interests. But it is public knowledge that the communists are only ready to sacrifice everything to the Russian nation. The interpretation they give to their nationalism must always coincide exactly with the interests of Russia. In Russia, both Führer-worship and nationalism are adequate, because there nationalism means devotion to one's own nation and the Führer who has arisen out of it. But international nationalism and Führers chosen from abroad are self-contradictory. The whole attempt only shows that the old revolutionary faith is dead. Again, as ever before, the Russians attempt to eat the cake and have it: to renounce revolutionism and still to keep alive the Comintern, the organization of international revolution.

In the meantime this last change of policy, gradually brought about since 1935, has had some important effects. The most immediate was a change of allies. At first the left-wing socialists had welcomed the united front. Now, with the new turn, the left-wing socialists, who believed in the class struggle, in revolution, and in internationalism, were thoroughly disappointed. A more or less complete break with the Austrian socialists, the left wing of the French socialists, and the British I.L.P. was the consequence. But the communists were not compensated for this loss by increased authority among the right-wing socialists. In Spain, as will be described in the next chapter, they effected a close collaboration with the right-wing socialists for a certain period, only soon to get into trouble with them. And they won strong sympathies among certain right-wing German and Italian socialists living in exile, which, after all, did not mean much. But generally speaking the right-wing socialists were those most strongly pledged to democracy. They might have appreciated the final renouncement of revolution, had it not coincided with the killing of all leading people in Russia. The English, Belgian, Dutch, Scandinavian, Czechoslovakian and Polish socialists maintained their initial reserve.

In this context the campaign against Trotskyism won a new meaning. The Trotskyists themselves are a group without importance. It is true that, in the beginning, immediately after he had been exiled, Trotsky won strong sympathies among all those who, while believing in revolution, hated the later development of Russia towards a totalitarian dictatorship. But these sympathies Trotsky had wasted long ago. In exile his conceptions had grown ever more rigid and he had carried the Bolshevist ideal of orthodoxy to lengths incompatible with the existence of any mass organization. One after another his friends had broken with him, or rather he had broken with them, until only an insignificant group of a few dozen remained in all the world. It is needless to say that this group has no influence whatsoever in Russia. But, in the new communist language, Trotskyism simply included all those who thought that Russia had 'betrayed' the revolution. It was extended so far as to include all those who reject Bolshevism as a whole. Finally, everybody who disagreed with Stalin was regarded as a Trotskyist. In denouncing people as Trotskyists at random, the communists are fighting against their own shadow: Trotskyism is showing them in live stature what they were in 1921.

All these moves have importance within the fold of the labour movement only. But since 1934 the Comintern no longer limited its actions to this movement. When, in 1936, it grew increasingly difficult to keep any hold on the socialists, the communists resolutely turned towards alliances with forces more to the right.

This was the case even in France, where it became obvious from the beginning of the government of the Popular Front. The communists refused to send some of their members into the Cabinet, a move which, at the time, seemed to imply that they were still to the left of both radicals and socialists. But soon it became clear that the liberty of action which the communists had thus won enabled them to play quite a different game. Occasionally they attacked the government for its hesitations, especially when it refused to interfere actively in Spain. But, at the same time, they consistently aimed at collaborating with the radicals against the socialists. Repeatedly they launched the idea of an extension of the government to the right, so as to include Flandin's *Action démocratique*. The government, instead of being one of the *Front populaire*, ought to be one of the *Front français*. But Flandin rejected these offers in a way which left no doubt. Still, during this period the communists won an ever stronger footing within the French labour movement. This was hardly due to their politics but to the fact that, at a moment when all labour organizations tended to increase rapidly, they were the only people who had organizers able to cope with the task. Thus the party won more than 200,000 members and its influence within the united C.G.T. grew to such an extent as to raise the talk of a 'colonization' of the C.G.T. by the Russians. But these successes were not without a flaw. Resistance within the C.G.T. grew with the increase of communist influence, and the Socialist Party broke up the unity negotiations at the first opportunity. Then, the communal elections brought outright defeat on the communists. It is difficult to say whither French communism is going. France is the only country in the world where to-day the Communist Party is still a working-class party in its social structure. This will force the communists, in the impending crisis of the Popular Front, either to break with their present policy or to lose part of their following.

In France, anyway, the communists have now achieved the task which had been put before them since 1920: to create a real working-class party. But in other countries such parties existed before any communist international. The simple fact that the communists have become as non-revolutionary as the socialists does not exert a particular attraction upon the English, the Scandinavian or the Dutch worker. In most countries, therefore, with the big turn to the right, the communists found a new footing not among the workers but among other, non-proletarian strata. Most outstanding in this respect is the case of Spain, which we will treat in another chapter. Let us just mention that both in Britain and in the United States the communist parties have exerted, with their new policy, a considerably stronger attraction upon university students and certain Bohemian groups than upon the workers. In Austria this was not the case in the beginning. But then, from 1935 onwards, the communists started to advocate an alliance with the Austrian government against Hitler, and that seriously impaired their following among the working classes. Those workers who were socialists resented the new policy as an alliance with their enemy. Those who were for the dictator-ship were already organized in the government camp and did not care for the communists. But if the latter lost a considerable amount of the influence among the workers which they had won after February 1934, they kept and increased their influence in certain sections of the intelligentsia. The new policy reaped similar successes among the refugee intellectuals of both Germany and Italy. But in many countries there was not even this success and the results of the new policy remained small. Most complete was the failure in Catholic circles. The communists attempted very seriously to form a close alliance with the democratic wing of international Catholicism. But the attempt had already been a wholesale failure in the Saar. In spite of many efforts, the Catholics generally refused to co-operate. Those who wanted to fight Hitler did not think that it was compatible with their ideals to ally themselves closely with Stalin.

In China the Communist Party had no longer a proletarian following to lose. It had long since ceased to be a working-class party. Difficulties were smaller therefore, and the Sino-

Japanese struggle provided a unique opportunity for applying the new methods. The transference of the Soviet centre from Kiangsi to Shensi had uprooted the Chinese Soviets. Stalin conceived an ingenious plan. The Chinese Soviets were to abandon their social programme and to attempt to win China for a struggle against Japan. This fight, as it finally came, was not exclusively due to the actions of the communists. It would probably have been inevitable anyway. Nevertheless the communists played a considerable part in the events. From 1934 onwards the fight against Japan was emphasized above everything else in communist agitation in China and it was openly proclaimed that the communists would no longer expropriate landowners or any other people, except those who had dealings with the Japanese. This policy was carried out and even missionaries were again admitted into Soviet territory. At the same time the communists now, in Shensi near the border of the Japanese zone, tried to win over those Kuomintang generals who were most directly menaced by Japanese aggression. Chief among them was General Chang Hsue-liang, son of Chan-tso-lin, who had been the worst enemy of the communists. But Marshal Chang had been driven out of Manchuria by the Japanese and hated them since. He had been ordered by Chiang Kai-shek, the head of the Kuomintang and of the Nanking government, to fight the Shensi Soviets. But he was brought to realize by the communists that they no longer followed a policy of social revolution and that they were ready to help him against Japan. He no longer opposed them and entered into a secret alliance with them. Chiang Kai-shek, in December 1936, went to Sianfu, Chang's headquarters, in order to make the anti-Soviet drive operative again. Instead, open conflict broke out between him and Chang; he was arrested by his subordinate and had to realize that, if he continued to fight the communists, he would find a number of his own generals at their side and would have to face a major civil war. He preferred to give in. Chang formally submitted, but, *de facto*, the anti-communist drive stopped and preparations for resistance against Japan were hastened.

A few months later, when war between China and Japan broke out, the Soviet government was formally abolished by the communists themselves. This did not mean that the communists evacuated the territory they held. Only, this territory ceased to be a 'Soviet' territory and became a 'special area' and the communists submitted to orders from Nanking in the war against Japan. By doing so they obtained one considerable advantage. They could work openly again in Kuomintang territory. From quite a minor they had become a major force in Chinese politics. It is quite impossible to know, at present, what secret agreements exist between Chiang and the Chinese communists. Chiang is not likely to have given them freedom of action in his territory without sure safeguards. But this is a matter of conjecture. As it is, the Chinese policy of the Comintern stands as the model of what is happening to-day with communism all over the world. The social content of communism has been given up, or, more precisely, deferred *usque ad kalendas Graecas*. But the Communist Party has not on that account dissolved. It has kept all its fortresses, a force uniquely pledged to serve, by all means, the interests of the holy country, Russia. This became even clearer in the case of Spain.

CHAPTER XXIV

SPAIN

Throughout our account we have had no occasion to mention Spain, for the simple reason that communism in Spain was practically non-existent. Since the end of the nineteenth century, and even since its beginning, Spain was one of the countries most deeply upset by revolutionary unrest, by the struggle between the forces of the old order and those of intruding modern Europe. It is impossible, in this context, to give detailed consideration to the problems implied. Be it sufficient to say that, for a long time, the Spanish labour movement had been thoroughly revolutionary but that this attitude, in Spain, had found its embodiment, not in Marxism, but in anarcho-syndicalism. The history of the Spanish labour movement, in consequence, had been full of violent strikes, revolts, assassinations. At the end of the nineteenth century the reformist socialists appeared, and with their peaceful methods created a certain counterpoise to anarchism. But anarchism remained always the stronger of the two and held the labour movement of Barcelona, the most important working-class centre of Spain, completely under its sway. In the general revolutionary atmosphere even the socialists were forced, more than once, to have recourse to violence.

The communists gained no ground in Spain with a working class thoroughly anarchist; there was no need for a new movement introducing revolutionary ideas and fighting reformism, and the authoritarian methods of Moscow were distasteful to the proud sense of independence of the Spanish anarchists. The anarcho-syndicalist organization, the C.N.T., had joined the Comintern in the early days, but left it after the second world-congress. The Communist Party arose mainly out of a small split within the ranks of the socialists. A few elements from Barcelona which had gone through the experience of anarchism and been converted to Marxism joined. But the only result was that the small Communist Party was repeatedly split and rent asunder by dissensions in its own ranks. Mass influence there was absolutely none. And at one time the whole central committee took sides for Trotsky against Stalin, which naturally provoked a number of exclusions. The party was so insignificant that Primo de Rivera, the military dictator who ruled Spain from 1923 to 1929, did not find it worth his while to prohibit it, and the communist press appeared during the whole period of the dictatorship.

Then Primo fell, and a year later, in April 1931, a democratic republic was proclaimed. These events coincided with the period of left extremism of the Comintern, which naturally thought the change from monarchy to democratic republic entirely worthless for the workers. When the democratic enthusiasm of the masses, shortly before the revolution, rose very high, the communists resolutely threw themselves into the battle against it. The socialists co-operated with the democratic republicans in the fight against the monarchy. 'Treason!' shouted the communists. Thus, according to *Imprecorr*, No. 25, 1930, the national conference of the Communist Party of Spain 'put special emphasis upon the fight against the illusions created by the liberal and republican bourgeoisie—naturally their social-Fascist allies support them to the best of their ability and try to create the impression that it is possible, in Spain, to create a bourgeois democratic régime. . . . The conference resolved to fight with the utmost energy the attempts of the right- and left-wing social-Fascists who, with the support of important sections of the anarchist movement (Pestaña), attempt to form a united front with the liberal and republican bourgeoisie.' The principal slogan of the party, the resolution continues, is and remains: 'A workers' and peasants' government of the federative socialist republic of the peninsula, . . . based upon workers', peasants' and soldiers' Soviets.' The immediate task of the communists is to reconstruct the C.N.T., the anarcho-syndicalist organization, which has been disorganized during the years of military dictatorship and has been betrayed by its leaders, notably Pestaña and Peirò, who want to lead it into an alliance with the bourgeoisie. This was too much for a number of party leaders, who thought that, as the Bolsheviks in Russia since the first day, so the communists in Spain must fight for a republic together with all other republican elements, not, of course, without safeguarding their political independence. Already Trotsky had given hints in that direction and a small group of Trotskyists, who, under the leadership of Andrès Nin, had broken away from the communists, had sought co-operation with the socialists in the fight against the military dictatorship. In 1930, when the problem of republic versus monarchy grew more acute, a second group which was not Trotskyist broke away, under the leadership of Joaquin Maurin. 'Maurin', says the sentence of exclusion from the Communist Party, 'does not imply that the proletariat . . . must play a leading role in the process of this revolution.' He launches the slogan of a revolutionary constituent assembly, 'a slogan likely rather to foment the illusion that bourgeoisie and petty bourgeoisie could be the leading forces of the Spanish revolution than to increase the leading role of the proletariat.' Maurin is reproached, moreover, with speaking of the rule of a constituent assembly instead of the rule of the Soviets. He collaborates with 'Trotsky, Nin, and other petty bourgeois'. Those who do not know the communist literature of earlier times will be surprised to learn that Trotsky's crime in 1930 is not support of a Spanish Soviet régime but opposition to it. The groups of Nin and Maurin united during the following events and together formed the P.O.U.M. (Marxist Party of Working-class Unity). In 1930 the Comintern attacks the P.O.U.M. for advocating a democratic republic and a united front instead of a Soviet régime and the destruction of all 'social-Fascists'.

Those were years when nothing satisfied the Spanish communists. In 1933 the swing to the left in the country was at an end; the impending general elections were to bring heavy defeat to the left and to hand power to the right. But the communists were unaware of it. 'The revolution of the workers and peasants', says a resolution printed in *Rundschau*, No. 12, 1933, 'has not yet unfolded all its forces. . . . Very likely . . . the next explosion will open the period of decisive struggles . . . and lead to the capture of power.' Thus, while the reaction is preparing to destroy forcibly all working-class organizations, the communists see their day approaching. The next number of *Rundschau* informs the public of the exclusion of a group which has advocated the 'Trotskyist view' that an unconditional united front of all working-class organizations is necessary. It is interesting to note that in 1930 Trotskyism was what communism is to-day and that communism then was what is to-day called Trotskyism. Things continue in the same tone into 1934, with Jesus Hernandez, later on Minister of Education and one of the bitterest enemies of the left-wing labour forces, leading the chorus of communist extremism. This time the Spanish party is purged of Mensheviks and Trotskyists, for divergences of opinion not on Spanish but on German problems. 'The social-democrats, Trotskyists, and all renegades of communism', says Hernandez in *Rundschau*, No. 10, 1934, 'declare that the accession of Hitler opens a new era of Fascist terrorism and that the labour movement has been heavily defeated. With the help of this fraud they attempted to create a wave of pessimism and distrust, to kill the confidence of the masses in their class party, and to make the Comintern and the German Communist Party responsible for the German events. In the plenum of our central committee, in April 1933, the delegate of Salamanca attempted to voice this view. He found no support whatsoever and was excluded from the party.' The same article goes on to say that the anarchist paper, *La Tierra*, is financed by Deterding, the oil-king.

But then there is a sudden change of tone. During the summer of 1934 the Comintern veered round. Democracy had become important again. Spain was one of the first countries where the swing to the right could be applied. In October 1934 the socialist organization of the important mining districts of Asturias, in the north of Spain, rose in insurrection against the reactionary government. This rising, in contrast to the socialist rising in Vienna in February of the same year, found real mass support. For a fortnight Asturias was ruled by a sort of Soviet government. But the essential aim of the rising was the defence of the Spanish republic. The anarchists, in childish sulking, abstained, and outside Asturias, the attempted revolution was a miserable failure. In Asturias, however, it developed tremendous strength, and here the communists for the first time joined hands with the socialists. They were infinitely weaker than the latter and were still regarded as a force to the left of the socialists; but, after all, they had freed themselves from the anarchists and fought together with the socialists for the democratic republic; the turn to the right was achieved. The impression on the Spanish workers was considerable. It did not bring the communists new members, for, precisely by the Asturias revolt, the socialists had proved that they were willing to defend the republic by any means, but their participation brought the communists a new sort of authority, embodied in the popularity of Dolores Ibarrurri, a Basque communist working-class woman who, during the fight, had emerged as a leader and as an orator of unusual gifts and unusual sincerity; she has since been called 'La Pasionaria'. Next to Dimitrov at Leipzig, La Pasionaria at Oviedo won back for the communists the prestige they had so conspicuously lost during the preceding years.

The Asturias revolt made the accomplishment of the new policy a relatively easy affair. The French *Front populaire* provided a suitable model for the new policy in Spain. Only a year after declaring every advocate of co-operation with the socialists a Trotskyist traitor the communists joined hands not only with the socialists but with the bourgeois republicans. All groups of the left united in a popular front, to which the anarchists and the insignificant P.O.U.M. gave underhand support. But still the communists, numerically, were not stronger but rather weaker than the P.O.U.M., and had only a few thousand members. In February 1936, at the new elections, the Popular Front was triumphant and the communists gained a number of seats on the common lists of the left. Yet they were still insignificant.

They automatically became one of the parties supporting the new government of the bourgeois republicans. The socialists had participated in the first government of the left, in 1931–3, but in the meantime their chief, Francisco Largo Caballero, disgusted with the defeat of his party in 1933, had gone much to the left, in spite of the opposition of a right wing within his party under Indalecio Prieto. The socialists in 1936 still supported the government of the republicans, but refused to participate in it. During the few months between the elections of February and the outbreak of civil war in July it became obvious that, on the whole, the Caballero wing of the socialists was more radical than the communists. The latter had inclined their heads, and, like Clovis, king of the Franks, had adored what they had despised and despised what they had adored. They now rejected every idea of a workers' revolution, insisted upon the strictly democratic character of the movement, and tried to the best of their ability to mediate between revolting peasants and the government, which wanted to use armed forces against them.

Then came July 19th, the Franco rising. The communists, very insignificant and, with their moderate tactics, deprived of any chance of winning the allegiance of the excited masses, had no opportunity to interfere. But a few weeks earlier they had prepared an important measure which was effected a few days after the beginning of the war. The Catalan socialists, under the leadership of Señor Comorera y Soler, were more to the right than any other section of the Spanish socialists. In Barcelona, where the labour movement was anarchist, they saw their chief task in fighting anarchism. Now, on 23 July 1936, the communists merged with the Catalan socialists and the P.S.U.C. (Catalan Unified Socialist Party) was founded. It was the first example of a socialist political party merging with the communists. It was a move extremely favourable to the communists. Before creating the P.S.U.C. they had had, in all Catalonia, not more than two hundred members. But immediately thousands of foreign communist volunteers, among them only a few Russians, but numerous Frenchmen, Germans, Italians, Englishmen, Americans flocked in. The foreign communists gave all the weight of their experience as organizers, and so valuable an asset did they prove to the Catalan socialists in their traditional fight against anarcho-syndicalism that soon the communists had complete command of the united party. The situation of the P.S.U.C. was difficult at the time, because the anarchists showed a strong tendency to terrorize all other groups and the P.S.U.C. was much too weak to resist. But they were not the only ones who had reason to dread the anarchists. All bourgeois republicans, the whole intelligentsia, the shopkeepers, the well-to-do peasants, and most of the state and private employees were equally frightened. From the beginning these elements started to unite around the newly created party.

But there was a big handicap. Moscow disliked the whole Spanish trouble. During the first months of the civil war it gave absolutely no support to the Spanish republic. It had only one aim at that time: to prove to the powers of the West that it had ceased to be revolutionary and was a desirable ally. Accordingly, the Spanish communists carried on a violent propaganda against all revolutionary measures. But the outbreak of civil war had created precisely an atmosphere of revolution. The communists opposed the rule of the committees, a Spanish counterpart to the Russian Soviets, which everywhere had been instituted by both anarchists and socialists. They opposed measures of expropriation, opposed the creation of a workers' militia, opposed terrorism against the forces of the right. In his presidential palace sat Manuel Azaña, the democratic president of the republic, helpless, his authority swept away by the mass movement. The communists came to his help, attempted to restore his authority, and together with it the authority of the officer corps, of the police and gendarmerie, of the old civil service. Non-revolutionary Moscow and its European staff had come into contact with revolution, and naturally the fight began at once. But with Moscow refusing to help, the communists' attitude was only to their discredit. The socialists were far from approving anything the anarchists had done, but Caballero felt that the communists' attitude was directed, not only against the anarchists, but against him as well.

This situation could not last. Moscow may have liked ever so much to remain neutral in the Spanish struggle. The issue did, in fact, concern it very directly. It is, in a certain sense, the tragedy of Russia that it cannot get away from its revolutionary past. This past obliges the Russians to seek alliances with the anti-Fascist forces because, for the Fascist countries, Russia is still the country of 1917. A defeat of the left in Spain would seriously jeopardize the Franco-Soviet pact. It would be a big defeat of the international left. It would wreck the Communist International and leave Russia even more exposed to Fascist aggression. Whether it liked it or not, Moscow had to realize that defeat in Spain would be its own defeat. And defeat approached quickly. The government of Caballero was as inefficient as that of the republicans, and Franco approached Madrid rapidly. At this moment Russia interfered, sending pilots, instructors, aeroplanes, guns, but most of all, the 'international brigades', a well-disciplined force not consisting of Russians but of foreign communists. On November 8th the international brigades saved Madrid. They could have entered the fight a week earlier and have saved Madrid the horrors of bombardment had not Moscow insisted that, before it sent help, a definite change to the right should take place in the politics of the government. Even so, its intervention was, for the moment, decisive. And then the communists started to introduce that element of organization without which the struggle was lost. Then, in the name of better organization of the army and the hinterland, they started to carry out their specific anti-revolutionary policy.

Through Russian help and through the international brigades the communists won definite military superiority over the anarchists. The 'international brigades' formed out of foreign communists and sympathizers, under rigid ideological control, ruthlessly exterminating many members who did not agree with communist policy, became for a time the paramount military force. In Catalonia all people who had been frightened by the anarchists flocked to the P.S.U.C., which now had arms, and gradually pushed the anarchists back. And at every suggestion of opposition the communists threatened to withdraw their help.

Strong as they had suddenly become, they started a drive against all the forces to the left of themselves. Forces to the right of the communists there were none within the republican camp; for they co-operated very closely with those sections of the republicans who were farthest from the socialists. For a time, though only for a time, the Basques, a conservative group, profoundly Catholic, and republican primarily because the republic had granted them regional autonomy, were their closest allies. Their drive against the left started with the P.O.U.M. The P.O.U.M. had joined the Catalan regional government but was forced to leave it again, because the communists threatened to withdraw all armed support. Then, by the same means, they obtained the dissolution of the committees, the reorganization of the army. They started a strong campaign against collectivization of the land.

But perhaps most important of all was the administrative aspect of the new phase of events. The Russians, while sending relatively few military people, mostly pilots and instructors, sent numerous administrative advisors and even more G.P.U. agents. Generally they managed to lay their hands upon a considerable part of the Spanish police work, and besides the regular police created independent G.P.U. agencies which arrested, investigated, and executed on their own account, backed by the military forces of the communists. Soon the ordinary administration was powerless against the independent actions of the communist police, and on this ground a serious rivalry between the two forces developed. The G.P.U. and the communist police groups formed at its advice acted in conformity with communist policy only and made it their business ruthlessly to persecute all those who disagreed with communist policy. Chief among their victims was, naturally, the P.O.U.M. Of its leaders Maurin, at the beginning of the civil war, had fallen into the hands of the insurgents and been shot. Nin had quarrelled with Trotsky or, more exactly, Trotsky had quarrelled with Nin because the latter, aware of the tremendous power of the united front, had made the P.O.U.M. participate first in the block of the left at the election and, later, in the Catalan regional government. Only a very small Trotskyist group remained within the P.O.U.M.; but, on the other hand, the P.O.U.M. as a whole hated Stalin and the Russian régime and stood for a policy of social revolution such as the communists had advocated in 1930. They behaved just like old-time communists: very weak, they regarded themselves as the only people able to save the revolution, and, while lacking in strength, attempted to lay down the law. Utterly naïve in all their doings, a helpless group of sincere and insolent sectarians, they were quite unable to counter the furious, well-organized onslaught of the G.P.U. But not only the P.O.U.M. people were subjected to serious persecution. The same applied to many anarchists, and even the left-wing socialists, under Caballero, after a time were made to feel the communist whip.

Then even the propaganda for democracy was pushed more

and more into the background and propaganda was concentrated on Spanish nationalism, on the fight against German and Italian aggression. It is perfectly true that in Spain the Germans and Italians are hated, even in the Franco camp. But the interference of the Russians and other foreign communist volunteers is just as much resented in the left camp by the old staff of civil servants and liberal republicans.

As it were, in Spain the communists decided that the one way to save democracy was to abolish it. Definite attempts were made to merge with the socialists and the republicans. In the end communist policy was aiming at a democracy controlled by only one party, defended by an army, a police, and a civil service under the control of Moscow. This led to clashes.

In Catalonia the anarchists had been pushed gradually back until, finally, on 4th May 1937 a minor incident evolved into an all-round fight between anarchists and communists. The communists had hoped to find many allies, but though the anarchists were hated by all the other parties, the communists were deceived in their expectations. The Catalan army stood by, inactive; the central government sent troops, but only in order to divide the fighting adversaries. The communists had to do the work themselves. Troops of the P.S.U.C. and the Catalan police fired into the anarchists of Barcelona. The rising was ended by a compromise, very unfavourable for the anarchists. Only a few weeks later the leading group of the P.O.U.M. and hundreds of its rank and file were arrested and charged with having conspired for Franco. No attempt was made to prove this in a public trial; but the corpse of Nin was found, a few weeks later, in a street of Madrid, where he had been brought from Barcelona. At the same time the left-wing socialists with Caballero were pushed out of the government. Totalitarianism seemed to have won for good.

But it had not. By fighting the forces of social revolution the communists had simply put into their old positions the old civil service and the old political groups. They thought they held them firmly. They had no hold over them at all. A totalitarian state is as little an article for export as nationalism. A totalitarian régime is dependent upon the existence of a national Führer, who can really and sincerely appeal to the national sentiment and count upon a following which is his own. In Spain all the elements of the army, the police, the civil service, the political parties, who had collaborated with the communists had only done so in an attempt to defeat the forces of social revolution. This done they reassumed their independence. Prieto, the leader of the right-wing socialists, whom the communists had regarded as their closest friend, started to check them as soon as he had become the leading figure of the reconstructed government. This was no longer a fight in the open. It was a fight for positions in army and administration, a fight where the clannish, closely connected Spaniards had all the advantages over the foreigner. The suggestion for a merging of the socialist and communist parties was rejected. The socialists managed seriously to impair communist influence in the army, first by enlisting national instincts against the communist commander, General Kleber, and enforcing his removal, then by abolishing the institution of political commissars for the army through which the communists had controlled the military. Essentially it is the same evolution as in France and elsewhere: the communists have easily defeated, with their new tactics, the forces of the socialist left. By doing so they have once more exposed the futility of those ideals of social revolution they themselves had held for two decades. While doing so they had enormously increased in numbers, an increase not deriving from the working classes but, in Spain more than anywhere else, from the intelligentsia, the army, the civil service, the police, the well-to-do peasants, the white-collar proletariat. Moreover, in Spain, they have managed to enrol many thousands who always drift to the party which has administrative power. But finally they have been checked, not by the forces of revolution, but by the forces of moderate liberalism. It would be rash to assume that the resistance of these forces will bring about full democracy, and it is very doubtful whether Spain would stand it. But they have already checked, to a considerable degree, the advance of totalitarianism by ways of communist influence and will probably continue to do so.

In the meantime Russia has definitely become less interested in Spanish affairs. No brilliant victory is likely to lie ahead. Russia is occupied to-day with the extermination of its own leading personnel. Since it has started to eliminate the heads of its army and its administration, its international position has become considerably worse, and Spain to-day is mostly a liability. What will be Moscow's next move, both in international and Spanish home politics, remains a query. The Popular Front in Spain is not so directly menaced by disruption from within as in France, because the iron force of war holds it together. But there will not be war for ever and when it has ended, every surprise is possible.

CHAPTER XXV

CONCLUSIONS

The history of the Communist International, as it has unfolded itself between 1919 and the present day, is certainly a puzzling phenomenon. It is difficult to find a central point in the story around which to group the whole. There is no climax. The events seem to pass one after another, without any very close link between them. The history of the Comintern can be summed up as a series of hopes and disappointments. Ever and again Russia and the communist parties abroad imagined that in this or that country revolution was approaching, victory near. The front of the bourgeoisie would be broken, and through the gap world revolution would make its way. Then, instead of success, there was always failure. Progress made by the various communist parties during difficult years of struggle, won at the price of heavy sacrifices, vanished into nothing within a few days, as in Germany in 1923, in England in 1926, in China in 1927. The communists hunted a phantom which deceived them continually: the vain phantom of social revolution such as Marx had seen it. The history of the Comintern contains many ups and downs. It contains no steady progress, not a single lasting success.

But against this disappointing reality there stand the firm hopes of the communists. They are convinced, every single time they enter on a new policy, an attack on a new country, that this time it will be different from what it was before, that now they have found the true method, that this time advance will not end in a complete rout. The basic conviction of communism is that it needs only a truly 'Bolshevist' party, applying the appropriate tactics, in order to win. Therefore every defeat

—and the history of the Comintern consists of defeats—brings about a change both of leadership and of policy. One day the Comintern tries a policy to the 'right'; then the importance of democracy is emphasized, collaboration is sought with the other sections of the labour movement, care is taken to participate in the day-to-day struggles of the workers and of the lower classes in general, the communist parties grow, both in membership and in influence. Everything seems to be smooth going till the decisive moment when an attempt is made to leap out of the preparatory stage into revolutionary action. Then, suddenly, the parties feel somehow unable to make the jump and break down. The communists are convinced that the failure was only due to wrong ideology. In taking account of the pacifist and constitutional 'prejudices' of the masses the communists have imbued themselves with them, have themselves become 'opportunists'; that is the view of the orthodox. A turn to the left is effected. Often armed insurrection, which was not undertaken at the height of communist mass influence, is launched when the decisive moment is over and the party has lost all influence or at least every chance of victory: thus in Bulgaria in 1923, and in China in 1927, to mention only two outstanding examples. But even when no sudden rising takes place the turn to the left implies a wholesale change of policy. Suddenly the communists refuse to acknowledge any difference between democracy on the one hand and autocracy and Fascism on the other. All contacts with the democratic mass parties are broken off. Attempts are made to split the trade unions. Bona fide participation in the day-to-day struggles of the masses is decried as 'opportunism'. Propaganda of revolution takes the place of every other sort of propaganda. And the parties are rigidly purged of all 'opportunist' elements. But if the policy of the 'right' wing has led to defeat at the decisive moment that of the 'left' wing reduces the party to the exiguity and the lack of influence of a sect, until the decline is patent and the policy of the 'right' is given a new trial. And so forth in endless rotation.

The movements of communism proceed with an increasing momentum. At first the 'right' and the 'left' wing policies are not clearly distinguishable. Only after the end of the revolutionary period is this distinction established. And then every turn to the left or to the right exceeds the previous one in vehemence. The communist parties seem to be driven to avoid the repetition of the failures of the preceding period by trying something still more extreme. On the whole six phases of Comintern policy, three of a 'left' and three of a 'right' character, can be distinguished. Taking the 'left' turns first it is interesting to note that, in 1920 and 1921, the social-democrats are simply 'social-patriots', 'social-traitors', and the like. During the left period of 1924–5 they are already regarded as a bourgeois party, the 'third party of the bourgeoisie'. But during the extreme rages of the left tack of 1929–34 they have been promoted to the rank of 'social-Fascists', and both the German and French communists unite in practice with the real Fascists of their respective countries in order to defeat 'social-Fascism'. Taking the swings to the right, the first one, that of 1922–3, limits itself to a thorough use of the tactics of the united front, with a tendency to assimilate the language of the party to that of the democratic working-class parties. The next swing to the right, that of 1925–6, however, implies already a partial liquidation of the basic notion of the task of a communist party. Sinovjev himself states that in Britain revolution may come, not through the door of the Communist Party but through that of the trade unions. Similar hopes are cherished as to the American farmer-labour movement and to the Croat peasants, and, in China, the Communist Party is ordered not to oppose, in any respect, the Kuomintang of Chiang Kai-Shek. We need not enlarge upon the extension of these tendencies during the present, third swing to the right, which implies attempts at merging with the socialists, denial of all revolutionary intentions, opposition to all sections of the labour movement in Spain as too advanced, etc. Only one thing the communists seem unable to acquire through all the shiftings of their policy: a sense of the adequacy of means and ends. During the rapid swings from right to left and from left to right there is generally one short moment when communist policy moves along a middle line: as when, lately, in 1934, the communists veered round to defend democracy together with all other democratic forces. But those are only points of transition between opposite extremes.

From a description of this basic law of the evolution of the

Comintern evolves at once one important result: it would be a grave mistake to overestimate the role of Russia, or, more correctly, to regard the basic character of the communist parties simply as a result of 'orders from Moscow'. Moscow's influence upon world communism, rooted both in its prestige and its financial power, of late even in the control the Russian G.P.U. exerts over all communist parties, is strong indeed. But this domination of Moscow over the Comintern is much more the result than the cause of the evolution of communism outside Russia. As long as there were relatively strong revolutionary movements outside Russia, these movements, in spite of all the prestige of the Russian revolution, did not accept orders from Moscow. Kun in 1919 flatly refused to sever the organic links with the social-democrats during the Hungarian dictatorship, in spite of Lenin's advice. Rosa Luxemburg and Levi, while leading the Spartakusbund, saw to it that the Russians were treated as allies but not as masters. No other section of the Comintern has ever had so much independence as the Chinese Soviets, and only when their vigour was broken by Chiang Kai-shek's 'annihilation drives' did they become simple instruments of Russian foreign policy, which during the last year decided to dissolve them altogether. When the Comintern was founded, during the year 1919, at the height of the post-war revolutionary crisis, it ought to have had tremendous authority. In reality, precisely during that year 1919, it was quite an insignificant force because the revolutionary movements of other countries did not care to take orders from Moscow.

The Comintern as an organization under the sway of Moscow is itself a product of defeat. When in 1920 it became clear that the post-war revolutionary wave was ebbing away, the star of Moscow rose. The ideas of Bolshevism, the dogma that the labour movement must be purged thoroughly of all unorthodox elements before being able to win, was only now accepted by the defeated left wing of the Continental socialist parties, and the split inaugurated by the second world-congress of the Comintern started from that assumption. Only this split led to the formation of communist mass parties. The new communist parties, believing that with the creation of a communist party the chief condition of success was fulfilled, threw themselves into battle, only to learn in the German disaster of March 1921 that they had been entirely mistaken and that the existence of a communist mass party could not make up for the lack of revolutionary impetus in the masses. When the Comintern was born the revolution in the West was already at an end.

The coincidence of these two events was not a matter of chance. Before the war, no revolutionary socialist had conceived the idea that the proletariat could win in a state of disunion. Yet already the outbreak of the war had brought about precisely such a state. The majority of the labour parties all over the world had buried the ideals of the class-struggle precisely at the moment when these ideals, for the first time for many decades, would have had practical revolutionary implications. The revolutionary minority, which stood firm to its convictions, cried treason. But this is a moral point of view and its acceptance depends on the conviction that it is the duty of a decent man to be a revolutionary. The majority of the workers and their leaders, however, had thought at that moment that it was their duty to defend home and country. The national allegiance had proved to be much stronger than the social one. It was a long time before the revolutionaries accepted this verdict of history. Even in 1919 Lenin and Sinovjev imagined that it was sufficient to raise the banner of the new, revolutionary International for the workers to gather swiftly round it. But this was not the case and so the split, with its twenty-one points, grew from an incident to a lasting reality. The twenty-one points, with their stipulations about repeated purges, started from the implicit assumption that a large section of the labour movement, not to mention the other sections of the lower classes, would always remain reformist, as long as the capitalist régime existed. But if this was so, how was a proletarian revolution to succeed? By the very act of its creation as a mass organization, by the perpetuation of the split which it implied, the Comintern signed the death warrant for the proletarian revolution to which it was pledged and which had never had many chances.

What followed was again natural enough. In matters of organization and finance the communist parties, who had only a relatively small following of their own, had to rely on help from Moscow, on which they became thus dependent. But more important still was the ideological dependence on Russia. The further real chances of revolution recede into the background the more the adoration of the accomplished revolution in Russia takes their place. Every defeat of revolution in the West and in the East is accompanied by an increase of admiration for Russia. During the first years of the Comintern there is still a very serious concern for the possible chances of revolution abroad. There are constant attempts to square these interests with the interests of Russia as a state, but these attempts gradually change in character. On the one hand, Russia leaves its own revolution ever further behind. Precisely because revolution in Russia is an established fact, the revolutionary impetus of Russia abroad fades out. At the same time, revolution recedes further into the background everywhere, at least that sort of revolution which the Russians regard as desirable.

The defeat of the Chinese revolution is the turning-point in this respect. During the year 1925 the dissensions in Russia had begun to influence the Comintern considerably. Now the chances of the left wing of the Chinese revolutionaries are really spoilt by Moscow. In all other cases the revolutionary chances existed only in the heads of the communists. In Germany in 1921 and 1923, in Britain in 1926, there could not have been a revolution. But the Chinese revolution was in fact ruined by the interference of Moscow, which tried to square its interests with the interests of the revolutionaries, which proved to be impossible. The defeat of the Chinese revolution destroys the last serious chance of the Comintern in all the world. Henceforth the Comintern, which has no longer a serious task of its own, becomes a plaything in the hands of the ruling group at Moscow. The left extremism of 1929–34 is largely a manœuvre of Stalin in his factional fight against the right of Bukharin and Rykov in Russia.

The situation changes once more with the advent of Hitler. Moscow for the first time since 1921 feels itself seriously menaced and feels its revolutionary past as a handicap in its defence. The Comintern must stop its extremist talk, which might hamper Russia's attempts at finding suitable alliances, and by doing so becomes automatically an instrument of Russian foreign policy, which it had not before primarily been.

CONCLUSIONS

Thus, three periods can be clearly distinguished. During the first period the Comintern is mainly an instrument to bring about revolution. During the second period it is mainly an instrument in the Russian factional struggles. During the third period it is mainly an instrument of Russian foreign policy. The boundary lines between these three periods are naturally not rigid. But one thing remains clear: for the true communist this whole evolution can only be the result of an immense betrayal. Leon Trotsky fills the world with his accusations that the German, the French, the Spanish, the Belgian, and what not revolution had been possible, had only Stalin not betrayed. In reality it is the other way round. The evolution of the Comintern and partly even that of Russia are due to the fact that that international proletarian revolution after which the Bolsheviks originally hunted was a phantom. After many disappointments they had indirectly to acknowledge it by their deeds, and take things as they were. This change of the function of the Comintern is the real trend of its evolution behind the welter of shifts to the right and to the left which constitute its surface.

This change could not possibly remain without effect on the structure of the communist parties themselves. This structure did not from the beginning correspond at all to the ideas which the communists held about their own party. In Russia the Bolshevik party had really been, to a great extent, what Lenin wanted it to be: a select community, a sort of religious order of professional revolutionaries, crusaders of a materialistic faith, a selection of the most self-sacrificing, the most decided and active among the revolutionary intelligentsia. But the structure of the communist parties of the West and the East never corresponded to this idea. They consisted essentially of shifting elements, which came and went. This character of the membership explains to a great extent the rapid changes of policy. Such contradictory policies as those followed by the various communist parties could not have been carried out one after another by the same men. The complete lack of tradition has the same source. Russian Bolshevism was conscious of having its roots in the deeds of the revolutionaries of a century before, and the membership kept a close memory of the history of the party, until Stalin ordered the reading of a revolutionary history entirely of his own invention. The membership in the Western and Eastern parties, however, is a new one every five years and ready to believe anything the newest version of official communism tells it about the past of the party. Serious studies of party history are not encouraged. But this lack of consistency and of tradition has one still more important consequence: with the shifting of the membership the social character of the communist parties shifts too. There was a moment, after the second world-congress, in 1921, when the more important communist parties were really working-class parties. But this has changed long since. With the shifting of the membership the communist parties tended to attract, more and more, *déclassé* elements: young intellectuals with Bohemian leanings on the one hand, unemployed on the other. During the period of left extremism between 1929 and 1934 most communist parties consisted primarily of these elements. To-day an even more radical change announces itself. In China the Communist Party is a party of the peasants and the Red army, in Spain it is a party of all classes except the urban proletariat, in Britain and U.S.A. it is mostly a party of young intellectuals; among the refugees of many countries communism is enormously popular, but the majority of these refugees have also been bourgeois intellectuals. Only in France and, to a certain extent, in Czechoslovakia, can the communists still be regarded as a real working-class party with real influence on the proletarian masses.

In this slow transformation of the social structure of the Communist International we strike again one of the roots of its history. The proletarian revolution, in which Marx and Lenin believed, seems to be incompatible with the real labour movement as it is. Certain elements of Marx's and Lenin's revolutionary predictions have proved only too true. It is true that the 'capitalist' society of private ownership and private initiative is unable to cope with the problems of our period. It is true, as Marx has predicted, that at a certain stage of its development it enters on a cycle of gigantic economic crises for which, as most experts are agreed to-day, there is no remedy but state control, state interference, and planning. It is true, moreover, that economic crises bring with them tremendous social dislocations and political convulsions. Only one thing is certainly not true: the idea that, at the height of such a crisis, the proletariat will rise and, throwing all the propertied classes into the dust, will take the lead of society, abolish private property in the means of production, and create a régime where there are no more classes. This leading role of the proletariat in the upheavals of our time has proved to be the Utopian element of Marxism. In Russia, not the proletariat, but a quasi-religious order of professional revolutionaries of the intelligentsia took the lead, with the help of the peasants, the peasant soldiers, and the workers. In the West, where there was neither such an order nor masses willing to follow it, the idea of a proletarian revolution proved to be a complete illusion.

There are many reasons for this, reasons which have little or nothing to do with a betrayal. Had all the socialist leaders sided with the revolutionaries the majority of the proletariat would simply have left them for some more moderate party. For the idea of the proletariat opposing, victoriously, all other classes of a complex modern society is a fantastic one. In the West there are no revolutionary peasants such as in Russia. Moreover, in Russia there existed that absolute cleavage between the people and the ruling classes which is completely absent in the West. The old civilization of the West has given its seal, not only to an alleged workers' aristocracy, but to all strata of the working classes, who all have something to lose, who all share with the upper classes their chief loyalties and beliefs. If somebody wants to express this in Marxist terms he may say that in the most developed modern countries all classes and groups are much too 'bourgeois' to make a proletarian revolution a practical proposition.

Therefore, in the West only two solutions for the crisis of the existing social régime remained: in some countries a revolutionary party coming from all classes and taking a stand above them all has curbed the class struggle with iron hand and subordinated all group antagonisms within the nation to the violent struggle for domination of their own nation over all others. Such is Fascism. In other countries, and this is the second possibility, all classes, by a tradition of co-operation and compromise, have hitherto managed to hold the inevitable social antagonisms within bounds and co-operate in the gradual bringing about of a new type of society: this is typical of a progressive and evolutionary democracy. There is no third solution in the conditions of highly developed modern industrial countries. Industrially backward countries such as Russia, Spain, South America, China, are a different matter.

The labour movement of the West, moreover, knows very well why, by instinct and conviction, it holds to democracy. The achievements of the dictatorships may be ever so brilliant; but not from the end of the crisis in Germany, nor from the colonial expansion of Italy, nor from the Five-Year Plan of Russia, have the masses had more than the slightest advantages. Liberty of movement for the working-class organizations, notably the trade unions, is the primary condition for the workers to share in the fruits of the economic and political successes of their nation. But the liberty of the trade unions depends on liberty as a basic principle of the political régime. To this liberal and constitutional spirit of the Western labour movement the communists could only either submit, and then the Comintern would have dissolved itself, or they could fight the bulk of the labour movement, which they did. But in doing so they gradually severed their ties with the real proletariat. The possibility of such a severance was contained in Lenin's basic assumption when he formed the Bolshevik Party: the revolutionary party must not be an agent of the proletariat, but a separate group, only knitted with it by its convictions. The Western labour parties are the labour movement itself, are identical with it. The communist parties were only linked with it. But what is linked can be severed.

The communists wanted to lead the proletariat along their road. But their own rule, the dictatorship of the Communist Party, was their primary aim from the beginning. When the Western proletariat proved not to be responsive it was only natural for the communists to seek support elsewhere. The fight for the power of the party and the International was and remained the central point. It was not a result of any betrayal, therefore, but the most logical result of their basic assumptions that, in due course of time, the communists became a classless party, held together by the worship of their totalitarian state— Russia—and their *voshd*, their Führer, the leader-superman, Stalin. In this transformation the communist parties had only followed the evolution of other mass movements in those

CONCLUSIONS

countries which were ridden by revolution. Everywhere, in eastern and central Europe in 1919, parties of proletarian revolution had been in the forefront, had failed, and then the revolutionary trends had been taken up, in a different manner, by classless, Führer-worshipping parties, in one word by Fascist parties. In this development, inevitable unless countries are successfully managed by way of democratic compromise, the Comintern simply participated.

But it did so in a paradoxical way. Much of what the Comintern does to-day is conscious and intentional imitation of Fascism: the Führer-worship of the leader of every communist party, the nationalism, the appeal to youth, the military atmosphere. But: 'Si duo idem faciunt non est idem.' The Germans worship Hitler, who is a German. The French workers cannot worship Stalin, who is a Russian. German Fascism is sincerely nationalist and aggressive for its own nation. But a Fascism aggressive on behalf of a foreign nation is a preposterous idea. With all their beliefs in Russia, the French, British, and other workers cannot be Russian nationalists. The idea of a nationalist international is perhaps not contradictory in itself if movements rooted in their respective countries join in it. But a movement whose loyalty is split between its home country and a foreign country can never have the convincing force which the genuine Fascist movements have had in their respective countries. It was impossible for Russia to transfer its revolution abroad. It will prove equally impossible for it to spread its totalitarian régime.

Besides, it is very doubtful whether Moscow at present really wants the communist parties to win power in any country. The imposition of a nationalist dictatorship implies no less a revolution than the social upheaval wrought in Russia in 1917. Russia, in its obvious desire to remain allied with Czechoslovakia, France, and China and to become allied to Britain and to the United States, cannot at present wish any deep upheaval in those countries, not even one which might conceivably bring the communists into power. Communist policy is therefore self-contradictory. To launch a policy full of Fascist or semi-Fascist elements, and not even to want to win with it, is a strange attempt, indeed. Yet this is what is actually taking place.

CONCLUSIONS

It is the more surprising, in view of this basic wish of Russia for the political stability of her allies, that the new moderate policy was originally initiated under the lure of very sanguine hopes. But then the Russian communists have never been very subtle in their appreciation of the effects and implications of communist policy abroad. Their aim doubtless was to unite with the democratic socialists all over the world, to permeate the whole labour movement, to link it closely in 'popular front' movements with the other parties of the left, to create a very strong international left-wing current, and thus finally to control the policy of all non-Fascist European countries for the benefit of Russia. But this plan failed. With the exception of those in France and Spain, the democratic labour movements refused to be permeated, and no 'popular front' movement of any appreciable strength was formed outside these two countries. In France the Popular Front has broken down and left deep estrangement between its partners behind. In Spain nothing is further away than a victory of the Popular Front, and even there, where communist support is most needed, the forces of genuine democracy, socialists and republicans, have, in the end, disengaged themselves more or less from the communists, distrusting their co-operation. In Austria an attempt to form a popular front of all forces from the Heimwehren to the socialists has been crushed by Hitler's arms. In China, Chiang Kai-shek, while accepting communist support, is anxious not to grant the communists too much influence. Finally, in May 1938, the congress of the International Federation of Trade Unions in Oslo rejected the application of the Russian unions for affiliation, against the votes of France, Spain, and Mexico, with Norway in an intermediate position. The great mass organizations of Britain, of the United States, of Scandinavia, Belgium, Holland, Switzerland, and Czechoslovakia, and many other smaller groups, took the view that the totalitarian 'trade unions' of Russia had as little business in a democratic mass organization as the German labour front and the Italian corporations. The high hopes cherished in Moscow in 1936 have been thoroughly disappointed, and there are already symptoms which suggest that the moderate policy of recent years may be followed, in due time, by a new turn to the left.

CONCLUSIONS

But the time is obviously not yet ripe for such a swing in the opposite direction. If there is nowhere a chance of decisive success the policy of the Comintern can still have certain minor, but not unimportant results. The latest elections in France have gone against the communists, yet the moderate line followed during the last few years has given the French communists considerable strength both within the unions and at the polls. The elections of May and June in Czechoslovakia have shown that the communists in that country are strong among the Czech part of the population, though they have lost all hold over the German-speaking workers. In China the communists, by pressing in the direction of a forward policy, keep Japan busy and win breathing-space for Russia. And a similar, though less thorough, result is obtained in Spain with regard to Germany and Italy. In one word, communist policy, though quite hopeless in its wider aims, is a very serviceable instrument of Russian foreign policy and no deep change is to be expected as long as this state of things continues.

From the point of view of the countries in which communism is active all this presents a factor not to be neglected. Russian policy and communist aims have become much more modest than before. It is nonsense for the anti-Comintern powers to denounce present-day communism as an attempt to destroy property, family, and religion, as if we were still in the year 1917; with these contentions those powers only cover their own unavowable aims. But communism has not become less dangerous for that; on the contrary. The revolutionary menace for which communism seemed to stand in 1917 was never much more than a phantom in which visionary revolutionaries and frightened employers believed in common. In the West communism hardly ever was more than a big nuisance for the police. And Trotskyism, which still keeps to the principles of 1917, is not even that and could hardly ever be. But if communism as a revolutionary force was something infinitely more futile than its fervent adversaries would be ready to admit, the same thing need not apply to present-day non-revolutionary communism with its narrower aims. The fact is that in many countries to-day Moscow disposes of forces strong enough to influence national policy, forces loyal and moderate as long as the policy of their respective countries suits Russia, but threatening wrecking and rebellion as soon as this is no longer the case. This may not matter very much in peaceful times but must matter enormously in moments of tension, when relatively small forces may upset the balance. Numerous mass movements completely at the orders of a foreign power, and bound by no other interests and considerations, are a symptom of disintegration of the political system of those countries in which such movements exist. But the movements are there and the task of dealing with them ought not to be underrated.

It is true that the appeal of present-day non-revolutionary communism is a strange psychological phenomenon. It is not due to a revolutionary programme, because the communists are no longer revolutionary; it is not due to a moderate programme, because there is no lack of moderate parties of old standing. It is due, however, to the strange merging of an utterly unrevolutionary and anti-revolutionary policy with the belief in the myth that paradise on earth has already been achieved over 'one-sixth of the earth's inhabited surface'. At home the masses which vote communist would never fight against democracy, for revolution. It is only the more gratifying, therefore, to adore the dictatorship in Russia and to indulge, in its service, in all those impulses of violence, of vilification and extermination of one's adversaries, which cannot be satisfied at home. Present-day communism is essentially the belief in a saviour abroad; for this very reason it is a serious symptom of the decay of liberalism and democracy. For the essence of both is a belief in the capacity to manage politics without a saviour, by the forces of the politically emancipated people themselves. The communists may perorate about the defence of democracy and liberty; in fact, the basic impulses upon which their appeal relies are diametrically opposed to both. Nor can this strange combination of moderation at home and worship of violence and horror abroad continue indefinitely. At present, in most countries, the real 'toilers' are hardly touched by communist propaganda. If these real 'toilers' at any time should lose their faith in liberty and democracy under some very severe stress and look out for a saviour, the happy smile on the photos of Stalin would give them no consolation. They would then turn to a saviour, not abroad but at home, as they did in Germany. And, again as in

Germany, many thousands who have been communists would then become Fascists. In those countries where Fascism has not yet had any opportunity, communism, in its present form, supplies that belief in a saviour which is essential to Fascism; but its saviour is more remote, as is suitable, in a situation less tense, for social groups far away from practical possibilities of action. Yet the effect, the slow sapping of the democratic and liberal spirit, is there. As the constant interference of communist forces in the foreign policy of their respective countries sometimes constitutes a serious nuisance in matters of international policy, so communist ideals represent a constant menace to the basic forces of the European polity. It is not that the communists want to overthrow this polity at present; on the contrary, few men are so intensely interested in the strength and fighting power of the democratic countries as is Stalin, though this interest will change to the contrary the very day that Russia finds it suitable to change her foreign policy. Whether Stalin wants an alliance with the democratic countries or not is immaterial, however. The effect of communist ideals is to menace liberty and democracy; and in the end, in all likelihood, the effect of communist propaganda will have been to strengthen Fascism.

From the point of view of the democratic powers the question naturally arises whether there exist means to check these effects of communist activities. Is it unavoidable that, while France and Czechoslovakia are scrupulously abstaining from interference in Russian affairs, Russia, by money and orders, directs big communist parties in France and Czechoslovakia which would doubtless threaten rebellion the very day Stalin and Hitler came to an understanding? Democratic powers cannot use the means of repression which are customary in Italy, Germany, and Russia, and it would obviously be very bad policy to evolve a system of pin-pricks, which would only be apt to create exasperation without being efficient. But the question remains, whether, from the point of view of Moscow, the Comintern is so valuable an asset as appears at first sight.

There can be little doubt, in fact, that the superficial advantages derived from the existence of communist parties abroad are balanced by very heavy liabilities for Russian foreign policy. With all its efforts to be a great military power, and with all the pains taken to drown its revolutionary past in a sea of blood, Russia, up to now, has not won a single reliable ally; not even Chiang Kai-shek, in his desperate straits, can be regarded as such. At one time France seemed likely to become a very close ally of Russia, but on second thoughts drew much nearer to Britain than to her eastern partner. One of the chief reasons for this reluctance on the part of all powers to combine with Russia is the existence of the Comintern. At the same time, the Comintern provides the Fascist powers with their best pretext of aggression, and it is the existence of the Comintern which is invoked by those parties of the right which, in democratic countries, favour co-operation with Germany in preference to co-operation with Russia. The dubious and limited influence Russia exerts in the political game of various democratic countries through its communist parties is certainly not worth the price paid for it. There is every chance that, in case of a large-scale international conflict, the Comintern will prove almost powerless, but will contribute to the isolation of Russia and to the grouping against it of many forces which might have remained neutral. To allay these consequences it will not be sufficient to cut off as many heads of ancient communists as are available. The very existence of the Comintern, in public opinion at large, rouses anxieties deriving from the aims it originally pursued. And there is no saying that, in a final emergency, the Comintern may not return in fact to its original methods. As long as the Comintern exists the average citizen and even the average politician in the West will judge Russia more after the revolution of 1917 than after the execution of Sinovjev and Bukharin. It would therefore be in the interest of Russia itself to dissolve the Comintern and to prove, by scrupulous abstention from interference abroad, that it can be treated on an equal footing with those democratic powers whose ideals it professes to share. Closer co-operation between the great democratic powers and Russia would become a practical proposition as the result, and the mere possibility of such closer co-operation would be a powerful contribution to the maintenance of peace and the prevention of aggression.

Whether such a solution will come about will mainly depend on the psychology of the leaders at Moscow. Unfortunately, precisely the attitude of Stalin and his staff is one of the sorest spots of international politics. Comprehension of the West, its views, impulses, and driving forces has never been the strong point of Russian Bolshevism, and this has led already to more than one miserable failure. Moreover, a naïve sort of Machiavellism has been adopted in Russia, with metaphysical thoroughness. Lenin and the original Bolsheviks were already actuated by the conviction that all capitalist promises are deceptions and all ideals cheats. Under Stalin this view has evolved into a real all-round belief in human wickedness. Both in Russian home politics and in the activities of the Comintern double-dealing has been carried to such a degree as to defeat, very often, its own ends. Stalin, the man who could not allow a single one of his old companions to live, is the last man to believe in the possibility of sincere collaboration in the international field. A man such as Stalin cannot be brought to reason by argument. There is, however, just a small chance that events will teach him, and that when finally given the choice of complete isolation or a genuine dissolution of the Comintern, he will choose the latter. It would be highly desirable from the angle of those ideals to which he and his Comintern are paying continual lip-service: to the causes of liberty, democracy, peace, and to the integrity and greatness of the Russian people.

BIBLIOGRAPHICAL NOTES

An official history of the Communist International by Christo
Kabakchiev, the theoretician of the Bulgarian Communist
Party, appeared in German in 1929, but is both out of date
and out of commerce. The one available general history of
the Comintern is L. R. C. James's *World Revolution*, a study
which reflects throughout the Trotskyist point of view. The
earlier history of the Comintern is dealt with very summarily,
and the later period is envisaged entirely to prove Stalin's
'betrayal' and the correctness of Trotsky's views. The history
of the Comintern is dealt with, occasionally, in a number of
books devoted to the history of the Russian revolution. Victor
Serge, *From Lenin to Stalin*, gives again the Trotskyist point
of view. Boris Souvarine's *Stalin* is undoubtedly one of
the best existing studies and contains very interesting occasional remarks about the history of the Communist International. Professor Arthur Rosenberg, in his *History of Bolshevism*, interprets the events in the light of orthodox Marxism.
Of all these works only that of Souvarine relies on independent
research. Most material concerning the history of the Communist International can be found in two periodicals: the
Communist International, which has appeared in four languages
from the foundation of the Comintern to this day, and *Imprecorr*
(*International Press Correspondence*), which, again in various
languages, has appeared since 1922 and is by far the richest
source of Comintern history. In our account we always quote
from the German edition, which is generally fuller than those
of other languages, and all quotations are therefore translated
from German. In 1933 *Imprecorr*, which had hitherto appeared

in Berlin, moved to Bâle, under the name of *Rundschau*. It is difficult to find adequate compensation for the lack of *Imprecorr* as a source in the early period. A perusal of *Kommunismus*, a German periodical which appeared in Vienna from 1920 till 1922, is useful. Next to these two organs of the Communist International itself the periodical press of the various parties ought to be consulted if necessity arises.

CHAPTER I

Suffice it to note that there exists a bulky literature about the pre-war labour movement, but that adequate comprehensive works are almost entirely lacking. A rich field of research remains for the student. The British trade-union movement has been exhaustively studied in the standard work of the Webbs, but a study of the political labour movement in Britain is lacking. For Germany Franz Mehring's *Geschichte der deutschen Sozialdemokratie* ends with 1890 and is not altogether free from bias. For the later period Paul Froehlich's introductions to the three volumes of Rosa Luxemburg's works give valuable material, especially for the history of the German left. The protocols of the various national and international congresses of the socialist parties and of the Second International are invaluable. A comprehensive and convincing summary of the divergences of views in pre-war socialism is contained in A. Rosenberg's *History of Bolshevism*.

CHAPTERS II AND III

The literature about the Russian revolutionary movement is bulky. Perhaps the best idea of the connection of Bolshevism with pre-Marxist Russian revolutionism is to be got from Souvarine's *Stalin*. By far the best history of the Marxist labour movement in Russia is Martov-Dan's *Geschichte der russischen Sozialdemokratie*. The account is reliable and fairly impartial, though both authors have been leading Mensheviks. All official histories of Bolshevism, and notably those by Sinovjev and by Yaroslavsky, must be treated rather as propaganda than as history. W. H. Chamberlin's *Russian Revolution* will always have to be consulted. Trotsky's brilliant account contains little which is valuable in our context.

CHAPTERS IV AND V

For the position of Bolshevism during the war: Lenin and Sinovjev, *Gegen den Strom*. For the German left: Paul Froehlich, 10 *Jahre Krieg und Buergerkrieg*. For the history of the Spartakusbund: *Spartakus-Briefe* and *Spartakus im Kriege*, both published by the German Communist Party and containing the underground literature of the Spartakusbund during the war; very rare to-day. Rosa Luxemburg, *Kritik der russischen Revolution*, with an introduction by Paul Levi, 1921. Karl Liebknecht, *Reden und Aufsaetze*. For the Revolutionary Shop-stewards, Richard Mueller, *Vom Kaiserreich zur Republik*, 3 vols. For the revolutionary movements in Austria and Hungary, Otto Bauer, *Geschichte der österreichischen Revolution*. For the movement in the Allied and neutral countries it is best to consult the protocols of the national party congresses, especially revealing in the case of Norway. For Bulgaria consult *Kommunismus*, Vienna, 1920. The best description of the revolutionary movement in Spain is contained in Salvador de Madariaga's *Spain*.

CHAPTER VI

By far the best account of the Hungarian dictatorship, with a quite exceptional wealth of documentary material, is contained in Wilhelm Boehm, *Im Kreuzfeuer zweier Revolutionen*. Compared with this account of the chief commander of the Red army all other accounts are insignificant. The book aims at justifying the policy of the social-democrats during the dictatorship. Oskar Jaszi, *Revolution and Counter-revolution in Hungary*, contains valuable material about the economic policy of the Soviets and about the problem of the middle classes. For the Communist view compare Bela Szanto, *Klassenkaempfe und Diktatur des Proletariats in Ungarn*, 1920, not very revealing. For the economic policy of the Soviets Pawlowski (Eugene Varga) *Die ökonomischen Probleme der proleterischen Diktatur* is very useful; the author was People's Commissar for Socialization. The amount of knowledge to be gained from the publications of the Whites after their success is scanty.

BIBLIOGRAPHICAL NOTES

CHAPTER VII

For the general history of the German revolution English readers will best consult R. T. Clark, *The Fall of the German Republic*. A brilliant study of the fall of the German monarchy, based upon documentary research, is contained in Arthur Rosenberg, *The Origins of the German Republic*. A useful account of the years 1919 and 1920 is given in the same author's *History of the German Republic*. For the history of the Spartakus-bund and of the U.S.P. the protocols of the party congresses of those years are the chief source. For the U.S.P. compare, moreover, Eugen Prager, *Geschichte der U.S.P.* For the history of the Munich Soviets it is useful to consult the *Internationale*, the theoretical periodical of the German Communist Party, 1919.

CHAPTER VIII

Protocol of the First Congress of the Communist International. Commemorative number of *Imprecorr*, March 1924. *Communist International*, 1919. Angelica Balabanoff, *My Life as a Rebel* (very subjective). *Manifeste, Richtlinien, Beschluesse des I. Kongresses, Aufrufe und Offene Schreiben des Exekutiv-Kommittees bis zum II. Kongress*, Hamburg, 1920.

CHAPTER IX

For Lukacz's views compare Georg Lukacz, *Geschichte und Klassenbewusstsein*, which contains his doctrine of the Communist Party. For the secret doctrine of amorality, cf. Ilona Duczynska, 'Zum Zerfall der K.P.U.', in *Unser Weg*, Berlin, 1922. For the factional fights in other parties the protocols of all world-congresses from the second to the sixth should be consulted.

CHAPTER X

The protocols of all international conferences concerned, notably those of the Second International in Berne, Lucerne, and Geneva. For the reconstructionist movement very valuable material is contained in the collected essays of the Russian Menshevik, P. Axelrod, which have recently appeared in German. Chief source for the split and its motives is the

Protokoll des II. Weltkongresses der kommunistischen Internationale (no English translation exists). For the split itself the protocols of the congresses of the U.S.P. at Halle and of the French socialists at Tours must be consulted. Sinovjev, *10 Tage in Deutschland*, is a well-written personal account of the president of the Comintern. For the fight with the ultra-left, Lenin, *Left-wing Communism, an Infantile Disease*, Hermann Gorter, *Offener Brief an Genossen Lenin* (from the viewpoint of the left-wing opposition).

CHAPTER XI

For the Italian crisis a perusal of the congress protocols and of *Avanti*, the central organ of the Italian Socialist Party, is indispensable. For the insurrection of March 1921 in Germany, *Taktik und Organization der revolutionaeren Offensive*, anonymous, very rare, because scrapped immediately after publication, renders the official view of those who undertook the rising. Paul Levi, *Unser Weg*, gives the view of the right-wing opposition. *Die Enthuellungen zu den Maerzkaempfen, Enthuelltes und Verschwiegenes*, contains the incriminating material against the German Communist Party, published by the party itself.

CHAPTER XII

Protocol of the Third World-Congress. Soon after this congress *Imprecorr* becomes the chief source, containing practically all the official and semi-official documents of the Comintern. We do not quote every single time it has been used. Besides *Imprecorr*: *Protokoll des Leipziger Parteitages der Kommunistischen Partei Deutschlands*; *Protocol of the Fourth World-Congress*.

CHAPTER XIII

This chapter is based exclusively on the rich material contained in *Imprecorr*.

CHAPTER XIV

Die Lehren der deutschen Ereignisse, containing a number of documents relating to the discussions in Moscow after the October defeat. The pamphlet was originally only accessible to party members but could be bought easily in second-hand bookshops in the later years of the German republic. The numbers of *Die Internationale* from November 1923 till April 1924 contain valuable material.

CHAPTER XV

Protocol of the Fifth World-Congress. Report of the delegation of the British T.U.C. to Soviet Russia. *Der Neue Kurs*, containing the open letter to the German party.

CHAPTER XVI

Two recent publications deal with the history of the British Communist Party and its role during the general strike: T. G. Bell, *A History of the Communist Party of Great Britain*, and A. Hutt, *A Post-war History of the British Working Class*. The recent discussion about Bell's book in the British Communist Press has not brought forward any facts hitherto unknown.

CHAPTER XVII

Protocol of the Second World-Congress and theses of this congress about the colonial question. *Protocol of the Baku Congress*. For the Negro question: *Protocol of the Sixth World-Congress*. For the rising in Dutch East India: *Imprecorr* and *Communist International*.

CHAPTER XVIII

Perhaps the best picture of the communists' situation during the decisive months of the Chinese revolution is given in a novel, André Malraux's *La Condition humaine*, translated into English under the title *Storm over Shanghai*. Malraux was an eye-witness, and though some of his characters are invented all the political material is authentic. Of the delegates of the Comintern Manabendra N. Roy has written a voluminous study of the Chinese revolution, in German, *Revolution und Gegenrevolution in China*, a very valuable and impartial, though critical account. The Trotskyists have got into their hands and published a confidential report of three observers of the Comintern on the spot, which contains valuable material: *Wie die chinesische Revolution zu Grunde gerichtet wurde*. Berlin 1928. We do not quote here the ample literature about the Chinese revolution in general.

CHAPTER XIX

Protocol of the Sixth World-Congress. Imprecorr. The one comprehensive account, and a very valuable one, is Edgar Snow's *Red Star over China.* It is regrettable that Snow has not studied either the details of the agrarian problem or the way the communist dictatorship is put into effect through the G.P.U. in the Soviet territory. We remain in the dark on these two essential points.

CHAPTER XX

Protocol of the Sixth World-Congress. Imprecorr.

CHAPTER XXI

All reports of Piatnitzki are contained in *Imprecorr.* Together they constitute a rich material for the study of the structure of the communist parties. Additional material can be found in various articles of *Communist International* which have been quoted in the text.

CHAPTERS XXII AND XXIII

Protocol of the Seventh World-Congress. Imprecorr.

CHAPTER XXIV

A rich collection of works about the Spanish civil war from the communist point of view have appeared in all languages. But this literature is of little value for the understanding of the social and political evolution of the Spanish republican camp, which it tends rather to obscure than to elucidate. The best communist material there is about the subject is again contained in *Imprecorr*, notably in the articles of Kolzov, the correspondent of the Moscow *Pravda* in Spain. The viewpoint of the P.O.U.M. is defended, not very strongly, in *Red Spanish Notebook*, by Juan Brea and Mary Low. Cf. too George Orwell, *Homage to Catalonia.* The communist point of view is amply stated in George Jellinck's, *The Civil War in Spain.* Neither anarchists nor socialists have given their distinctive views in any comprehensive publication. I must mention, in this context, my own study, *The Spanish Cockpit.*

INDEX

A

Abd-el-Krim, 290–1
Abramovich, 350
Adler, Friedrich (Fritz), 79, 93, 127, 189
Adler, Victor, 79
Amanullah, 290, 295
American Federation of Labour, 168, 189
Anarchism (Spanish), 64, 167, 401–10
Austrian Communist Party, 92, 128, 145, 175, 205, 333–4, 381, 391, 395–6, 398
Austrian 'left-radicals', see Austrian Communist Party
Austrian Socialist Party, 93, 233, 333, 380–1, 396
Axelrod, Paul, 61, 433
Azaña, 407

B

Bakunin, 25, 28, 34, 168
Balabanoff, Angelica, 90, 433
Barbé, 352
Bauer, Otto, 93, 95, 127, 379–80, 432
Belgian Communist Party, 205
Belgian Labour Party, 59, 70–1, 185
Bell, T. C., 435
Beneš, 93
Bergery, G., 390
Bernstein, Eduard, 61, 85, 90
Bettelheim, E., 128–9
Billoux, 352
Bismarck, 19
Blagoyev, 63, 96–7, 240
Bluecher, see Galen-Bluecher

Blum, Léon, 200, 350
Boehm, Wilhelm, 115, 123, 125–6, 132, 432
Bolen, 336
Bordiga, 209, 211, 223, 239, 271
Borodin, 304–5, 309–10, 312, 314–15, 317, 320, 333
Brandler, H., 154, 159, 220, 225, 235–7, 241–56, 258, 261–2, 266, 271, 346–7, 349, 359, 371, 378
Branting, Hj., 69
Brea, 436
Briand, A., 60
British Communist Party, 145, 180–1, 187, 190, 193, 205–6, 274–83, 334, 348, 362–3, 367–9
British India, Communist Party, 288–9, 395, 398
British Labour Party, 17–19, 60, 72–3, 89, 205–6, 275–83, 334, 392
British Trade Union Council (T.U.C.), 17–19, 187, 264, 275–83, 334
Brouckère, de, 71
Browder, Earl, 394–5
Brüning, 342
Bulgarian Communist Party (Tesnyaki), 62–3, 89, 95–98, 103, 162, 166–7, 197, 227, 238–42, 381–2
Bukharin, 45, 69, 163–4, 227, 270–1, 278–9, 312, 319, 332–7, 339, 359, 418, 426

C

Caballero, F. Largo, 405–10
Cachin, M., 64, 200–1, 203, 228
Celor, 352–3

INDEX

H

Haenisch, K., 61
Haubrich, J., 125, 130
Heckert, F., 377
Henderson, A., 72
Hernandez, J., 404
Hicks, G., 281
Hilferding, R., 189, 195, 197, 199
Hillquith, 197
Hitler, 148, 151, 234, 240, 247–8, 331, 334, 340, 345–6, 376, 380, 394–5, 398, 418, 423–4
Hodges, F., 275–6
Hoeglund, Z., 69, 262–3, 347
Hoelz, Max, 215
Hoersing, 215, 217
Ho-lung, 320
Horner, A., 276
Howard, N., 395
Hungarian Communist Party, 108–33, 145, 162, 171–6, 205
Hungarian Socialist Party, 91–2, 108–33, 185
Hutt, A., 435
Hyndman, 61

I

Ibarrurri, Dolores (La Pasionaria), 405
Independent Labour Party (I.L.P.), 62, 185, 188, 199, 205, 233, 265, 392, 396
Irish Communist Party, 285
Italian Communist Party, 145, 211–3, 223, 227, 271, 377
Italian Socialist Party, 64, 90, 169–70, 208–13
I.W.W. (Industrial Workers of the World), 65, 168, 190

J

James, C. L. R., 430
Japanese Communist Party, 62, 295
Jaszi, O., 432
Jaurès, 19, 61, 68
Jekov, 242
Jellinck, G., 436
Jilek, 336, 349
Joffe, 304, 306
Jogiches, L., 78, 148, 151, 161

Jouhaux, L., 201–2
Julier, 131

K

Kaasch, W., 363, 365, 369
Kabakchiev, 212
Kameniev, 45, 54, 165, 321
Kapp, 153, 239–40, 249, 345
Karolyi (Count), 111–2, 117, 120, 126
Karski, 78
Katayama, 295
Kautsky, K., 50, 52, 58, 61–3, 80, 85, 138, 189, 195, 197
Kemal Pasha, 123, 289–90, 292–4, 309
Kilbom, 263, 347, 349
Kirov, 393
Kleber, 411
Koeth, 137
Kolarov, 240, 242
Kolzov, 436
Korean Communist Party, 295
Krassin, 28, 165
Krishanovski, 28
Kropotkin, 28
Krumov, 381–2, 384
Krupskaya, N. K., 25
Kun, Bela, 114–33, 174–5, 180–1, 213, 219, 223, 254, 267, 415
Kuusinen, 105, 339, 384

L

Laes, R., 351
La Follette, 265
Landauer, G., 149, 151
Landler, E., 124–5, 172
Lansbury, G., 274
Latvian Communist Party, 106
Laval, 390
Lazzari, C., 209
Legien, 153–8
Lenin, 18, 25–7, 42–57, 61–2, 65, 73, 80–91, 94–7, 101, 103, 105, 109–10, 113, 115, 117, 122, 138–40, 159, 161–2, 164–6, 168–9, 172, 174, 181, 188–94, 205–6, 221, 223, 225–7, 231, 234, 236, 254, 258, 262, 274, 284–5, 291–2, 298, 316–18, 337, 374, 415, 420, 422, 430, 432, 434

INDEX

61090